Barbara London

VIDEO/ ART

The First Fifty Years

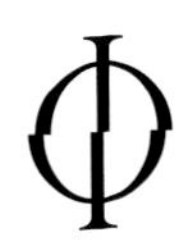

Phaidon Press Limited
2 Cooperage Yard
London E15 2QR

Phaidon Press Inc.
111 Broadway
New York, NY 10006

phaidon.com

First published 2020
Reprinted in paperback 2021, 2024
© 2020 Phaidon Press Limited

ISBN 978 1 83866 358 2

A CIP catalog record for this book is available from
the British Library and the Library of Congress.

Commissioning Editor: Rebecca Morrill
Project Editor: Bridget McCarthy
Production Controller: Jane Harman
Design: Hyperkit

Printed in China

Introduction

In the fall of 2018, while in London for a conference, I crossed the city to see *UUmwelt*, the new installation by Pierre Huyghe (b. 1962) at the Serpentine Galleries, anticipating an eye-opening prod from this singular artist. For several decades, I have appreciated how he challenges viewers with well-researched, timely subjects that he transposes into a finely tuned composition—and *UUmwelt* did not disappoint. It brought me face-to-face with enigmatic, vaguely figurative images shown on imposing LED screens. My movement through the galleries caused slight shifts in the forms; I imagined one shape to be an odd prehistoric animal, another an abandoned car. Each was situated in a desolate, desert-like landscape. Reading about the project, I learned that Huyghe had created the images using the brain waves of someone who had been asked to imagine a situation, in an informatics lab in Japan. In other words, Huyghe had managed to capture the entities straight from the inner machinations of the human brain. What would have seemed far-fetched and unfeasible forty years ago has now entered the realm of possibility.

Huyghe's installation is evidence that the urge to experiment is as strong as ever, and that the field originally defined as video art has slowly, radically transformed to encompass a far wider range of technological explorations in art—moving from fringe to mainstream during the period that began when I landed my first position, a research post, at the Museum of Modern Art, in late 1970. The innovations of trailblazing artists like Huyghe are what have kept my mind nimble throughout a long and rewarding career as a curator, writer, and professor.

The story of video art begins as video gear first reached the consumer market in the mid-1960s, when much of the world seemed to be in radical transition. The time was right. We thrived in the "now," adapting Polaroid's instant photograph, the xerographic photocopy, and the telephone answering machine to art and everyday life. We busily recorded and exchanged cheap audiocassettes with favorite playlists of the latest music. David Bowie's song "Space Oddity" moved up the pop charts in 1969, the same year that two US astronauts drifted out of Apollo 11 and walked on the moon. With the aid of technology, humans seemed capable of anything. At the same time, 1960s counterculture instigated alternatives to social norms, with its free love and free speech and the increasing prevalence of meditation and mind-bending drugs that torqued the individual's perceptions and imagination. Out of this environment, video art burgeoned from the grass roots.

It began with the portable camera, the monitor, and black-and-white videotape—the long, narrow strip of plastic with a thin, magnetizable coating that contains the image and/or sound. During recording and editing, video was visible on a monitor screen and audible through a sound system or headphones. It was easily replayed, copied, broadcast live or later from a tape, and today is streamed. I fell in love with the newly accessible medium and worked hard to learn whatever I could.

This book describes the madcap trajectory of a pliable medium, as video opened up and became a multifaceted art form that grew to encompass a range of formats, including not only single-channel videos but also multi-screen installations and projections; immersive audiovisual environments (sometimes incorporating interactive components); and moving-image works that are streamable as digital files. The field has moved in from the periphery of the art world and has morphed into the more expansive category of media art, defined by the quality of being dependent on technological components to function. This account of how *video* became simply *art* follows my own journey as a proponent of its progress.

Discovering Downtown

I grew up in New York in a household of tinkerers, ham radio operators, scientists, and engineer-inventors who circumnavigated the globe. Normal was the wireless hum of otherworldly static and the wafting scent of molten plastic. Fascinated by anything new, my family raced over to the Guggenheim Museum in 1959 for the inaugural exhibition. We proceeded up the ramp and scratched our heads, baffled even more by Jackson Pollock (1912–1956) and Abstract Expressionism than by Frank Lloyd Wright's unconventional spiral building. As a thirteen-year-old raised on road trips across the forty-eight contiguous states, breathtaking sunsets at the Grand Canyon had planted conventional notions of beauty in my head. At the Guggenheim, Pollock's immersive paintings ousted a predilection for Claude Monet (1840–1926) and primed me for contemporary aesthetics.

As a baby boomer comfortable with technology and eager to ferret out uncharted terrain apart from family where I could stake a claim, I set off at a young age on a lifelong, itinerant search for a patch with some elbow room. In 1967 I joined the first summer internship program for budding undergraduate art historians at the Metropolitan Museum of Art. Our uniforms consisted of special Anne Klein–designed dresses and Brooks Brothers suits. Treated like royalty, sixteen of us spent weekdays at a majestic desk in the lobby helping visitors plan their tours and in storerooms researching departmental collections. Evenings we had cocktails at the homes of Park Avenue trustees before we headed downtown to catch throbbing sound and light shows at nightclubs and music venues such as the Electric Circus and the Fillmore East. (The latter was known as the "church of rock and roll," where the electronic visuals of the Joshua Light Show saturated the stage behind musicians such as Janis Joplin and Jimi Hendrix.)

In 1968 I began graduate studies in Islamic art at New York University's Institute of Fine Arts and also studied Persian so I could read the *Shahnameh* by the tenth-century poet Ferdowsi in the original. Fascinated by the way textile motifs had moved back and forth across ancient trade routes between China and the Near East, I rejected well-bred connoisseurship—which tends to privilege an art object's formal characteristics over its usage—and opted to tackle cross-cultural exchange. I was interested in communication: how information traveled, whether slowly on the backs of camels or surging rapidly over airwaves. That year news reached me instantly about the deaths of Martin Luther King Jr. and Robert F. Kennedy, as I sat horrified listening to a little transistor radio in my tiny fifth-floor walk-up. Our twentieth-century life moved at a scarily fast pace.

During the 1960s, I gravitated toward the work of counterculture activists who were blurring the lines between music, art, and literature. While working on my MA uptown, I spent my free time downtown, side-stepping overdosed bodies to hear music and art crossovers carried out by riled-up bands, including the Velvet Underground and the Fugs, a bawdy, subversive group known for its staunch anti–Vietnam War stance. I socialized with graduate school peers studying modern art, a subject that, at the time, stopped abruptly at the Second World War. Aroused by everything current, we stayed abreast of avant-garde actions and pondered interconnections.

We were aware of Merce Cunningham (1919–2009), the long-limbed choreographer who valued process over product and who regularly collaborated with like-minded innovators. One evening in 1970, we managed to catch a cerebral performance by Cunningham at the Brooklyn Academy of Music. Taken out of his intimate, open studio workplace, this public Cunningham event for a large audience occurred well before BAM became the "it" place for unconventional performance and before Cunningham became recognized as one of the most important artists of the twentieth century. Onstage Cunningham barely moved at first. Suddenly, he stretched out on a park bench to read, his face hidden as his graceful arms turned pages of the *New York Times*. I realized then that art could consist of everyday actions carried out live, rather than static images locked down in concrete forms. My obsession with time-based art began here.

Cunningham and his partner, the composer and theorist John Cage (1912–1992), together radicalized my concept of time and space, which I started to see as elastic, composable materials. I read that Cage had processed the anarchic ideas of innovative Austrian composer Arnold Schoenberg (1874–1951) and pioneering conceptual artist Marcel Duchamp

(1887–1968), as he meanwhile took inspiration from East and South Asian cultures and Zen Buddhist philosophies. Cage broke down the divisions between the temporal and the tangible realms of art production, and liberated younger artists to take risks and to engage with the unpredictability of chance. He took the gravity out of art, making it weightless and idea oriented, and played with levels of time, questioning what is past and what is the ever-unfolding present.

The curious, bright-eyed Cage expressed pleasure in his connection to Fluxus, the avant-garde movement spearheaded by George Maciunas (1931–1978) and characterized by the playful subversion of previous art. This loosely affiliated group of young international artists, composers, designers, and poets, including several video pioneers, devised intermedia happenings and were more committed to ideas than to the art object. Some lived in the downtown lofts that Maciunas took over in derelict cast-iron edifices built by nineteenth-century manufacturers.

Cage witnessed the original performance of *Fluxus Sonata II* by Korean-born video pioneer Nam June Paik (1932–2006) in Düsseldorf in 1962; I saw the 1974 performance in New York. In it, Paik moved slowly and deliberately onstage. After an hour of rather mundane actions, he picked up a sledgehammer and smashed an upright piano to smithereens, instantly severing a connection between the piano and bourgeois culture. (As a child, Paik had practiced music on the family piano, the symbol of an educated household.)

I realized that every aspect of culture and life had become fair game, as artists looked beyond traditional vocabularies. As a result, what to some might have appeared barren, to others could be the very essence of the heroic.[1] One evening in the early 1970s, I saw the austere choreographer Lucinda Childs (b. 1940) move across the floor of the decrepit gym at the 14th Street Y. Slowly and deliberately, she walked up and down each floor-board in silence for at least sixty minutes. As time seemed to stretch on for an eternity, I struggled to fathom the uncompromising Minimalist stance of Childs's measured movements. She had studied with Cunningham and once noted that he "elucidated a kind of particularity and clarity in dance that felt distinctly separate from anything [she] had experienced up to that point."[2] In Cunningham's studio, Childs met the artist Yvonne Rainer (b. 1934), who encouraged her to become part of the Judson Dance Theater, where she was emboldened by performance-oriented artists[3] and structuralist filmmakers engaged in demystifying the film process. I realized I was now consumed by the present and not the past. I abandoned all thoughts of a PhD in Islamic art.

After I left graduate school in 1970, I immersed myself even further in the milieu of downtown Manhattan, a crossroads for artists, composers,

writers, filmmakers, designers, architects, dancers, and even chefs. It was
an international community, a small one at that, which shared an anticom-
mercial and antiestablishment sensibility. Many members of it created
events, long before the term *performance* was used to define an area of art
practice. Once word would go out, artists caught each other's events. Paik
once wrote: "To my surprise, Mr. Joan Miró (famous Spanish painter) came
to my film-concert in cinemathek, and stayed until the end, and liked 'quite
much' my show. It was a funny feeling."[4]

High on my list of where to be in the early 1970s was Max's Kansas City
in Lower Manhattan. Part social club and part screening-and-performance
space, here I would buy a cheap beer and stand at the bar and catch wind
of fringe exhibitions and edgy performances as I eavesdropped on artists'
heated exchanges about plans for new work. Other leads came from the
fliers artists pasted onto building walls or stacked by Max's front door.

At a table near the entrance sat a fluctuating stream of up-and-coming
artists. I remember a soon-to-be-famous trio—Chuck Close (b. 1940),
Richard Serra (b. 1938), and Robert Smithson (1938–1973)—suddenly emptying
a saltshaker on their tabletop. When an unsuspecting soul walked by, they'd
insist that he or she make a stylistic guess as to who had just drawn the
lines through the white mound. The three of them would soon ride a tsunami
of talent and bravura, creating paintings, sculptures, and earthworks
while also plunging into film, video, photography, or any other preferably
intangible and uncollectable format that functioned as an alternative to
the commercial art system.

I remained ensconced inside Max's until I gained access to the famed
back room. There I stood quietly on the side as Andy Warhol (1928–1987) held
court with singer-songwriters Patti Smith (b. 1946) and Lou Reed (1942–2013),
and a select few of other glamorous artists, writers, actors, and musicians.
Later I'd head upstairs for the weekly screenings of episodic Super 8 films
by underground filmmakers Beth and Scott B. (b. 1955 and 1952). As scenester
intermedia mavericks without federal or state funding, the pair managed
to make each new chapter of their film by taking the admission fee of the
previous week's screening. Underground artists had to be enterprising.

The tactic of extended duration had begun to permeate everything I saw
downtown. Was this development, I wondered, the result of the contrarian
temperaments of the artists or radical politics? Was it related to an attempt
to reach a fourth dimension by smoking pot or dropping acid? Some of the
people I knew were traveling to India to sit for weeks with a spiritual guru or
raga musician. I simply hopped on a subway to little-known venues in grungy
lofts to listen for hours to the intricacies of the drone sounds in the works of
filmmaker-musician Tony Conrad (1940–2016). Years later I understood that

my early viewing experiences served as a prologue to what lay ahead and how I would navigate through the colorfully evolving field of media art.

Video was shaped by its DNA—new technology, real-world politics, and the persistent mutability of contemporary art. As a space-age medium, video arrived in the 1950s, initially developed for commercial television and definitely off-limits to artists. Two-hundred-pound (90.7 kg) cameras sat locked into position in TV studios and were handled only by card-carrying union engineers. The Cold War space race was fueled by advances in technology that slowly trickled down and led to the introduction of audiovisual hardware on the consumer market, including the cordless telephone, satellite television, and the videocassette. The cassette contributed to consumer video's taking off, which was also a by-product of both the Vietnam War and the burgeoning porn industry. From then onward, each technological advance would give users tantalizing new prospects: Radio and television networks that had sent Vietnam War coverage directly into living rooms were shifting away from broadcast and toward cable delivery, which opened up public access to alternative programming. In the late 1970s, the boombox expanded the transportability of sound, and subsequently the Discman and the mobile phone did too. Video games shifted from arcade console to cartridge and eventually onto the personal computer, bringing the freedom to play games at all hours in the comfort of one's home.

In the 1960s and early 1970s, my generation—sickened by the Vietnam War—accepted pundits' avowal of an easily networked global village proffered by the affordable analog audiovisual electronics that were starting to permeate the consumer market. We were poor, but revolution seemed possible, inspired by prophets of the electronic age, especially the media theorist Marshall McLuhan. Best known of the new technologies was the portapak, a battery-powered, self-contained analog camera and videotape recording system that could be carried by one person. It offered an immediately accessible, instantly replayable image with sound, which made it possible to capture the elusive present as recordable "real time," a phrase that seemed to be on everyone's lips.

Without an established lineage, video attracted artists from different disciplines, with divergent viewpoints. Keeping one foot in music or dance or sculpture and the other in video, they forged brand-new strategies for art making. These young strivers were spurred on by the work of earlier interdisciplinary innovators, from contemporary choreographers like Cunningham, who experimented with duration, to the Dadaists, who, in the early twentieth century, had attempted to destroy traditional values in art and create a new art to replace the old. Because video also offered inexpensive distribution possibilities, artists saw it as a means to buck the rigid art system, with its ingrained pecking order and its pigeonholing of makers by medium. Contrarian painters, sculptors, and other artists, including many women, turned toward the brand-new field, eager to leave a mark and make history.

At the beginning, a vast chasm separated commercial television from independent video. Video makers were adapting video to bold pronouncements to be shown on monitors. They typically disparaged all forms of power and considered television the despicable enemy that padlocked its airwaves against anything experimental (i.e., below broadcasting's stringent technical standards). Commercial broadcasters deemed artists' grainy black-and-white videos, made with portable consumer cameras, junk that was unfit for the airwaves. (An exception was nonprofit public television, which garnered funding in 1972 to produce and air, late at night, the work of a few carefully selected artists.) Video makers put the television industry in the same category as museums—a high-handed adversary that, for the most part, treated them like outcasts. With considerable vengeance, a number of artists appropriated TV programs and made work that critiqued the closed system and the rigid formats imposed on content, addressing the split that divided popular culture from high art, as Warhol had done a few years before.

It was all about taking control of their work, making and showing it with little regard for the marketplace. They looked at forms of persuasion in contemporary popular culture and optimistically believed that their small-format consumer videos would gain an enthusiastic audience as something more authentic than imperious broadcast fare could ever be. Passing a camera around as easily as a joint, the early video artists made difficult-to-collect art best suited to artist-run, rough-and-ready venues that started to sprout up in New York and other run-down cities.

Video makers overlapped with experimental filmmakers in their resistance to the commercial side of their respective mediums (filmmakers making work that aimed to challenge Hollywood's influence). But in general, video makers shared a different set of technical and often conceptual interests than their filmmaker counterparts. As a material, film is light readable, which means that when you hold up a section of processed film, you will see individual images (called frames). If you take a length of videotape, you won't be able to see anything except a brown strip of plastic; the visual information is an electronic signal that is recorded magnetically onto a section of videotape and requires a machine to view it. Film had to be sent out to a lab to be developed before it could be projected, whereas video imagery could be seen on a monitor as soon as the camera was turned on. Consumer video editing was crude and often left glitches, but the benefit was that recorded tape could be rewound and replayed or rerecorded immediately. Video was also more practical than film in terms of copying over and recycling a used tape, and in terms of distribution—a videocassette was lightweight and could easily be carried in hand or dropped in the mail.

The critical discourse around video began with heated conversations among artists themselves, who for the most part had emerged from the visual arts. I kept up with what was being said and read the infrequent texts that appeared in *Studio International*, *Arts Magazine*, and *Interfunktionen*, roundups by critics who skimmed the field's surface. Critics would sometimes write, "Video has come of age," forgetting they had written the same thing a year before. Experimental film largely belonged to cinema studies, an academic discipline that deals with theoretical, historical, and critical approaches to film. *Expanded cinema* became the term used to describe radical experimentation with the moving image, be it film, video, multimedia performance, or even an immersive environment. Expanded cinema practitioners rejected the conventional one-way relationship between the audience and the image, and most opposed commercial film's two-dimensionality. Many directed their attention toward the installation and experimented with what they considered the physicality of time and space. Despite the ongoing differences between video and film, American theorist Gene Youngblood identified parallels in their disparate worlds in his eloquent 1970 book *Expanded Cinema*, which sat prominently on my shelf. I admired his voracious curiosity and lucid descriptions of difficult-to-categorize art made with new technology.

Some artists took the newly available consumer gear into their studios, where they worked quietly alone (something painters have always been able to do). Placing their camera on a tripod and tracking their live image on a monitor, artists single-handedly recorded performative actions that investigated the limits of their body and their perception of space. Some took their gear out onto the street to make guerrilla videos, using alternative journalistic techniques and on-the-spot invented tactics that confronted entrenched commercial television and radio formats.

Artists living in penury in borderline neighborhoods pooled equipment and contributed to each other's work by serving as performer, camera-person, or editor. Some combined resources to purchase and share a portable camera and deck, which cost around $1,000 and together weighed a good forty pounds (18.1 kg). In New York, artists Warhol, Paik, Les Levine (b. 1935), Juan Downey (1940–1993), Frank Gillette (b. 1941), and Joan Jonas (b. 1936) had gotten hold of portable video cameras, along with Bruce Nauman (b. 1941), a Californian briefly based near Manhattan, on Long Island. In Los Angeles, Paul McCarthy (b. 1945) brought gear home from the hospital where he worked. In San Francisco, Paul Kos (b. 1942), Tom Marioni (b. 1937), and Terry Fox (1943–2008) borrowed a camera from the de Saisset Art Gallery and Museum in nearby Santa Clara. To economize, most video makers reused tapes by recording over what they had just shot or stashed work in hot attics or damp basements, where forgotten tapes turned to gunk. Few thought about preserving their early exploratory work.

Collectives published how-to journals and shared technical information and philosophies about the new video tools. *Radical Software*, a theory and grassroots how-to magazine founded by artists Beryl Korot (b. 1945), Phyllis Gershuny Segura (b. 1945), and Ira Schneider (b. 1939), included Paik's futurist views of a global information highway open to all, decades before Al Gore made his well-publicized pronouncements. Government studies on soon-to-arrive public access television (which debuted with cable TV and took off in the early 1970s) gave artists hope, and for years Paik dreamed of an artists' video cable channel. In general, for these early video artists, process took precedence over saleable product.

At the start, video had an aspect ratio of 4:3, proportions similar to an analog boxy television set. The early consumer video image was crude and grainy, the opposite of its smooth, broadcast-quality counterpart. When video progressed from analog, picked up color, and moved on to digital and more recently to high definition, its aspect ratio switched to 16:9 (that of Hollywood film and flat-screens) and it gained a polished, commercial look. Image and sound became intangible bits of software information tucked into a digital storage system.

As video installation evolved, new projects were often made according to artists' radical politics that influenced their approaches to the technology or the specific exhibition site, perhaps an alternative space in a repurposed industrial area, or occasionally a museum. In the early 1970s affordable video projectors were still a decade away, so artists experimented with cubelike monitors—stacking them to make substantial video sculpture or using them in other unconventional ways. Korot ingeniously got around the boxy monitor's brawny physicality. For her four-channel installation *Dachau 1974* (1974), she embedded the four monitors in the gallery wall, their screens flush and lined up in a row, thereby attaining a cinematic kind of look.

Mary Lucier (b. 1944) incorporated the monitor into her radical performance *Fire Writing* (1975), in which she directed lasers at herself, something

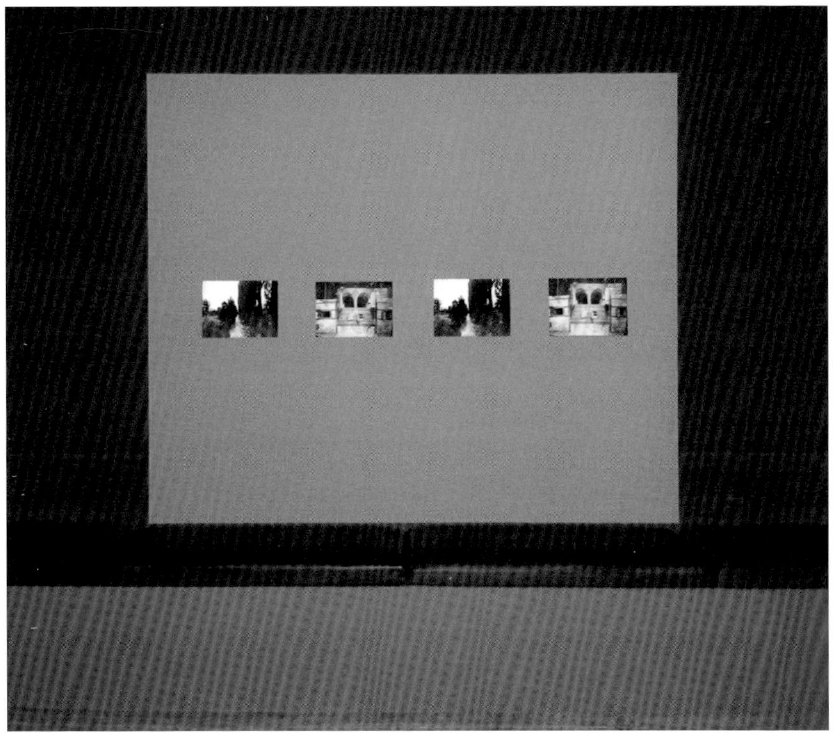

Beryl Korot, *Dachau 1974*, 1974
Four-channel video, four screens, black and white, sound, 24 min.

potentially damaging to her eyes. At the Kitchen, I sat on the edge of my
seat and watched as she stood on a pedestal and towered over the audience.
She covered one eye with a protective patch and used the other to look
through her video camera lens. She choreographed her turning body, moving
in concert with two crisscrossing lasers suspended high overhead from the
ceiling. Peering with her one eye through the lens toward the lasers, she
proceeded to burn her camera's vidicon tube. (It was considered bad practice
to point a camera toward the sun, let alone a laser, because the burned lines
would make the tube unusable for anything else.) I followed the Pollock-like
swirling lines of Lucier's movements as the lasers burned the selfsame onto
the tube; simultaneously they appeared live on adjacent monitors, connected
via cables to her camera.

The quality of being *live* is characteristic of video (an important distinction from film). Once a video camera is turned on, an image of an action

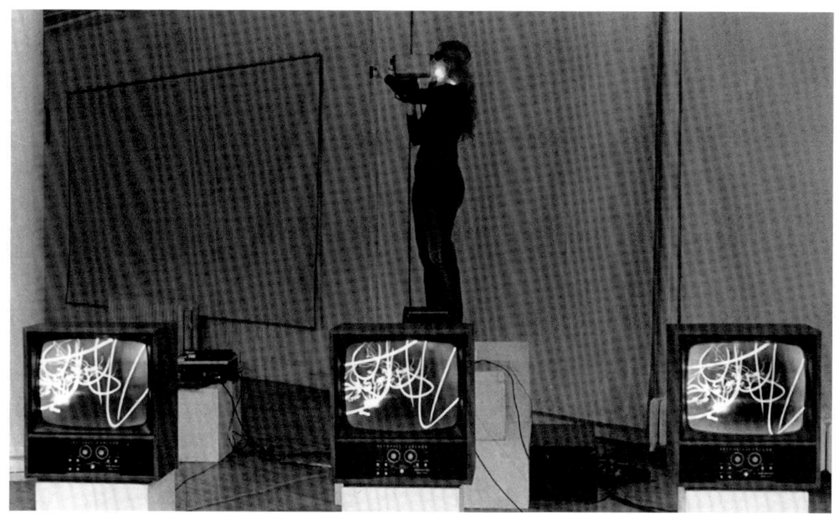

Mary Lucier, *Fire Writing*, 1975
Performance at the Kitchen, New York, October 25, 1975

unfolding in real time can be displayed indefinitely on the monitor to which the camera is connected. This live, or "open circuit," image—an impossibility in film—to most eyes appears identical to a prerecorded version. Artists adapted this verisimilitude to installations that boggled viewers' minds. Nauman's *Live-Taped Video Corridor* (1970) confounded and defied the narcissist in everyone. A camera was set above the entry to the work. Those who walked down the corridor saw only the backs of their heads as a live image on a monitor at the far end of the corridor. Stacked on top of this monitor was another that displayed a recording of the empty corridor where the confused participants should have seen themselves standing but didn't.

Dan Graham (b. 1942) had a different approach. Shown in MoMA's video gallery, his *Two Viewing Rooms* (1974) baffled visitors as they encountered their live image captured by an unseen camera behind a two-way mirror and presented on a monitor right next to them. The same live images also figured in myriad reflections, like in a fun house chamber of mirrors.

Art writers who already covered certain video makers' work in sculpture and other traditional mediums had context and a bridge into these artists' videos, which might otherwise seem difficult to describe. Some critics with little patience shied away from long, drawn-out work. Critic Rosalind Krauss readily adapted the early videos of Vito Acconci (1940–2017), Nancy Holt (1938–2014), Nauman, and Jonas to her theoretical interests of the moment

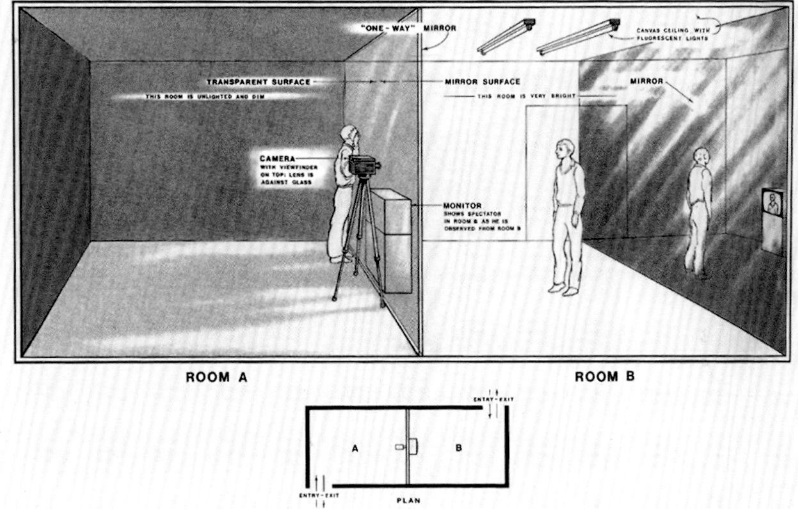

Dan Graham, diagram of *Two Viewing Rooms*, 1975
Two-way mirror, fluorescent lights, video camera, and monitor,
98 ⅜ x 98 ⅜ x 236 ¼ in. (249.9 x 249.9 x 599.9 cm)

in her article "Video: The Aesthetics of Narcissism" in a 1976 issue of the journal *October*.[5] Krauss built her theory around videos with interminably long actions performed by artists who were their own subject and/or physical material. That same year, Paik astutely wrote: "Much confusion about today's video art comes from the lack of categories to distinguish 'good and boring art' from 'bad and boring art.' Boredom itself is far from being a negative quality. It is rather a sign of aristocracy in Asia. And again, this confusion stems from the confusion about INPUT-time and OUTPUT-time."[6]

During these early years, in the late 1960s and early 1970s, experimental art in North America was bolstered by newly established federal, state, and foundation funding, which contributed to video's advance but sometimes caused contention between those who did or did not receive grants. Independent video artists and experimental filmmakers were divided into two distinct camps, the latter worried that the new medium would grab most of the funding.

In Great Britain, France, Holland, Germany, Austria, and Australia, video also reaped federal support, especially during the 1980s. In Japan, the land of electronic manufacturing giants, however, video artists were on their own, with funding from neither government nor corporations. In Latin America, where conditions were even more adverse, video evolved on the periphery.

Dictatorships branded consumer video cameras illegal and kept a tight lid
on counterculture experimentation. Juan Downey of Chile and David Lamelas
(b. 1946) of Argentina went to Europe to connect with avant-garde artists,
before settling in the United States, where they excelled with video. Jaime
Davidovich (1936–2016) went from Buenos Aires straight to New York and
linked up with other conceptualists and video enthusiasts. In Brazil, Sonia
Andrade (b. 1935) and Anna Bella Geiger (b. 1933) stealthily worked on their
performance videos, as did Lotty Rosenfeld (b. 1943) in Santiago, Chile. It
took another decade or so for portable consumer video technology to reach
India, where activist artists Nalini Malani (b. 1946) and Vivan Sundaram
(b. 1943) picked up gear and made forceful statements.

With enthusiasm and perseverance, video artists formed informal networks with young curator-programmers like me; up-and-coming theorists
writing for *Afterimage: The Journal of Media Arts and Cultural Criticism*,
published by Visual Studies Workshop in Rochester, New York; and budding
producers and distributors who attained nonprofit credentials. The post
office functioned as the principal means of distribution. In general, the small
group of early video artists shared technical expertise and came together
for screenings but in the late 1970s eventually split into different camps
that were motivated by intention (in other words, by the then-evolving fields
of conceptual and performance art) or by technology—in particular, special
effects and feedback techniques.

The Museum of Modern Art

As the field of video art was beginning to take shape, I began my career
at MoMA. At the time, professionals—curatorial, conservation, and publication staff—were 75 percent women and were all instructed to wear
dresses or blouses and skirts; the administration—directors and department heads—was 75 percent men, all in suits. Curatorial departments
operated as medium-specific strongholds of the twentieth century, the
historical development of their respective art forms segregated and their
budgets skewed in markedly descending order, according to trustee interests: painting and sculpture, architecture and design, prints and illustrated
books, and drawings, with photography on the rise. The Film Department,
with its isolated four-hundred-seat theater built in 1935, had its own art
history and discrete audience. Senior curators engaged in territorial scuffles
rather than cordial cross-medium explorations of contemporary art. Spar-
ring erudite chiefs ruled the Byzantine environment.

Back then, museums were small enclaves run by elite connoisseurs, who
for the most part turned their backs on anything temporal. MoMA was an

exception; in 1935 it had acquired the archives of several Hollywood studios and launched its film collection. This gave D. W. Griffith and Alfred Hitchcock —and, therefore, the moving image—the kind of ranking associated with the likes of Pablo Picasso.

From within this entrenched hierarchy, I pursued what the museum considered experimental. I attended in-house programs where film veterans Michael Snow (b. 1929) and Shirley Clarke (1919–1997) discussed their latest moving-image experiments. I took the elevator down to the film theater, where I sat entranced by Conrad's film *The Flicker* (1966) and Snow's *Wavelength* (1967). I remember a member of the audience once yelled out during a screening of *Wavelength*, with its loud sound that felt like an amplification of the artist's buzzing nervous system, "Projectionist, something is wrong with the equipment!"

I also studied the disfigured self-portraits made with an "instant" self-developing Polaroid camera, by the artist Lucas Samaras (b. 1936), recently acquired and installed in the Photography Department's collection galleries. He had smeared the wet emulsion of each tiny photograph as soon as it slid out of the camera's base, before it had a chance to dry. MoMA appeared to position photography as tangential to painting and sculpture, but Samaras's visceral and carnal-seeming performative approach to what is "now" fascinated me more than the elegantly cerebral Minimalist sculptures of Donald Judd (1928–1994), which distinguished the museum's aesthetic.

After spending months clambering up grungy staircases to catch the articulate new artwork of Martha Wilson (b. 1947), Antoni Muntadas (b. 1942), Rhys Chatham (b. 1952), and so many others, once at MoMA I sought to support the yet-to-be-defined (and eventually to be acquired) works my colleagues then considered too emergent and crude to consider. I turned toward those who were working with video and performance and far-out music. I regularly visited artists' studios and worked one-on-one with these cutting-edge video makers, which was the only way to gather information. I paid attention to what they were thinking and to how they were reacting to political issues carried over from the sixties.

Museums and contemporary collectors initially were skittish about acquiring or even exhibiting video, mainly because preservation is a complex issue. Ownership requires an understanding of what an artist's intention and aesthetics are, and a commitment to future responsibilities to upgrade a work's obsolete and malfunctioning hardware and software. It wasn't until the 1990s, when easier-to-use digital gear came on the market, that technophobia and institutional resistance to video started to disappear. Museums now were routinely integrating video into contemporary programming. Fortunately, the field of fine art conservation has expanded to embrace video, media, and software-driven art, with trained conservators prepared to share their expertise. This has made video installations more marketable in the hands of dealers. Once it began to enter private and public collections, video as art stood a strong chance of surviving.

As the field of video art developed along with advances in technology, categories and definitions also took shape and shifted. Today the label *time-based* is used for a broad category of contemporary art that works with the element of duration. Video, sound, independent film, software art, and internet art unfold over time. Artists engaged with these temporal forms have had to navigate the never-ending evolution of consumer technologies, which they have fused with interdisciplinary practices.

Performance, of which duration is also an integral part, is generally defined as a live event, with or without props or media. The action may or may not be carried out before an audience or in front of a live camera; it may be accompanied by prerecorded moving images and sounds and props. Performance is a form all its own, as well as a genre of video, one of many that have also included conceptual, body, identity, narrative, documentary, and image processing, among others. Definitions are helpful handles but are inadequate, laborious to pin down and revise. In terms of format, the simplest terms remain: *single channel*, *multichannel*, and *installation*.

Today's young artists consider *moving imagery* one category, which they view in miniature on smartphones or laptops and occasionally experience projected. Media artists now work with the latest technologies on a routine basis; their tools are comparatively more affordable and accessible than in video's earliest years. The status of television, newspapers, and magazines has diminished and the internet, video games, and virtual and augmented realities have gained in importance, and the content now combines contemporary ideas surrounding social utility, gender, art, and our relationship to technology. Meanwhile, audiences have become more knowledgeable and are enthusiastically responsive to the most up-to-date iterations of the experiments I first discovered as a young curator in underground art venues.

During my long career, I have worked with thousands of artists, and each one generously contributed to my understanding of what art could be. The chapters that follow explore these developments.

Defining a Medium, Defining a Field

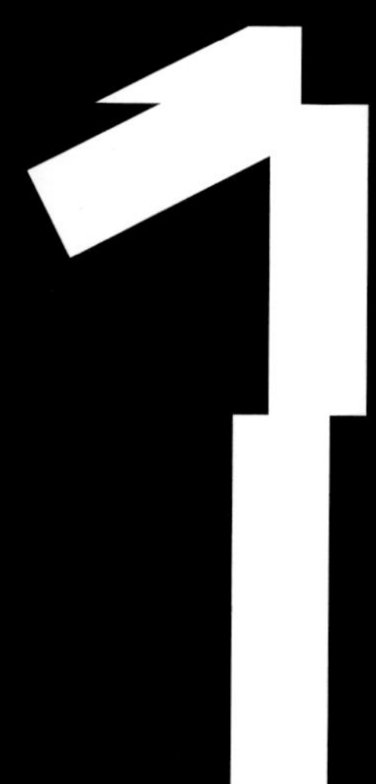

During the late 1960s, art and technology were engaged in a tentative dialogue, both operating as separate, specialized areas that were intersecting with increasing frequency. As a few artists began experimenting with video, the art-world establishment remained largely lukewarm about the rough results and, at the same time, paid little attention to most engineering advances. Meanwhile, engineer-technologists longed to have art curators appreciate their audiovisual innovations, which were often dismissed as *computer art*, a vague term used to describe any art in which computers played a role in the production or display. In the broad category of computer graphics, practitioners participated in specialized exhibitions that tended to be identified more with commercial design, in which technical expertise and elegant software code took precedence.

Back then, computers were room sized, and artists eager to enter the high-end technological domain could only gain limited access to such tools by working in partnership with specialist technicians. This collaborative process surged in 1966, when the engineers Billy Klüver and Fred Waldhauer at Bell Labs, the research arm of telephone conglomerate AT&T, joined with the intrepid visual artists Robert Rauschenberg (1925–2008) and Robert Whitman (b. 1935) to found the nonprofit organization Experiments in Art and Technology (E.A.T.). Eager to humanize technology tainted by Cold War applications, the organization fostered non-medium-specific investigations by artist-and-engineer teams that adapted computers coupled with telephonic prototypes to stage live cultural events.

In what became E.A.T.'s first large-scale event, ten artists—John Cage, Lucinda Childs, Öyvind Fahlström (1928–1976), Alex Hay (b. 1930), Deborah Hay (b. 1941), Steve Paxton (b. 1939), Yvonne Rainer, Rauschenberg, David Tudor (1926–1996), and Whitman—spent ten months collaborating with some thirty Bell Labs engineers to create *9 Evenings: Theatre & Engineering*, a series of live avant-garde theater and dance performances held October 13–23, 1966, at the 69th Regiment Armory in New York. Each of the nine evenings brought the creators and audience toward a new definition of what art could be. As part of the process, Klüver encouraged the collaborating engineers to consider themselves as artists too. For curators like me, this project was to become a touchstone—a prototype for integrating new technologies into current artistic practices.

Incorporating advanced electronics into sound, movement, and space, a group of engineers worked with seven of the artists—Childs, Fahlström, Alex Hay, Rainer, Rauschenberg, Tudor, and Whitman—to bring closed-circuit live video and video projection onstage for the first time. Performed

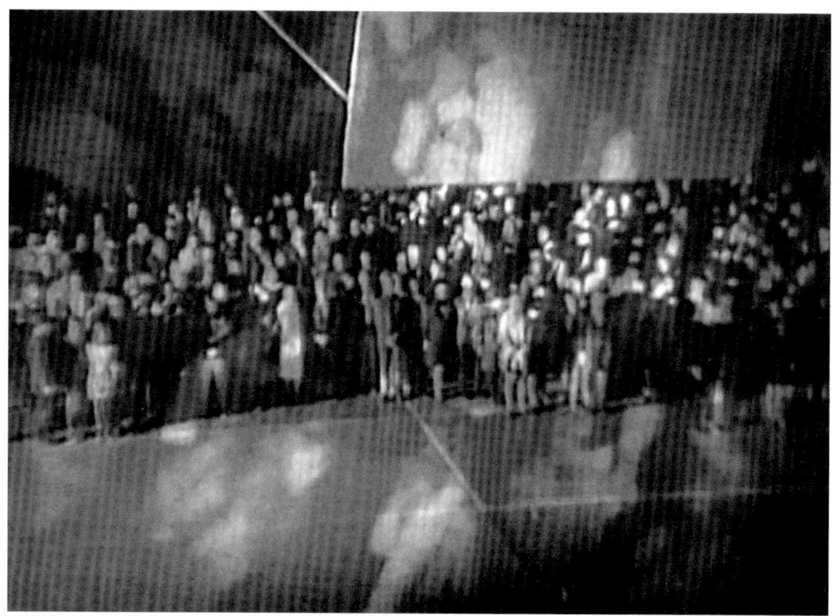

Robert Rauschenberg, *Open Score*, 1966
Performance for *9 Evenings: Theatre & Engineering*, 69th Regiment
Armory, New York, October 1966

on October 14, Rauschenberg's *Open Score* revolved around a tennis match
played by painter Frank Stella (b. 1936) and his pro teacher. With each volley,
special transistor microphones inserted into the players' tennis rackets
directed the pinging sounds to enormous speakers encircling the space and
caused spotlights to dim progressively. Plunged into darkness, audience
members suddenly saw ghostly, live video images of themselves projected
onto a large screen attached to the ceiling.

Looking back, I realize that Rauschenberg, like Nam June Paik (only
seven years his junior), had started out as a risk-taker. Each had a mischievous streak, as well as an insolent style that enabled him to tread a
fine line between rebellion and propriety. They enjoyed the freedom of
technology-derived art as a wide-open, undefined field as much as I did.

The work of both Rauschenberg and Paik was featured in MoMA's *The
Machine as Seen at the End of the Mechanical Age*, one of several early landmark exhibitions that tracked the interactions among science, technology,
and art. The expansive historical survey, which opened in late 1968, began
with a drawing of Leonardo da Vinci's flying machine and went on to feature

one of Rauschenberg's so-called combine sculptures, *Oracle* (1962–65),
a found-metal assemblage made in collaboration with Klüver that included
five sculptural pieces, each of which housed radio receivers and speakers.
Viewers could interact with *Oracle* and change the volume and the rate of
scanning across the AM dial for each radio. The exhibition concluded with
Paik's *Lindsay Tape* (1967), a work based on a clip (purloined off broadcast
television) from a press conference of John Lindsay, New York's mayor at
the time. Lindsay's gestures are repeated over and over, trapped in Paik's
dancing "wave pattern"; Paik had discovered a year prior that he could
produce a looping image on a color TV screen by combining three audio input
signals. This portrayal of the very familiar Mayor Lindsay bears connection
to Warhol's silk-screened paintings with serialized portraits of Marilyn
Monroe appropriated from print media. Shown in a MoMA gallery as a loop
of half-inch (1.3 cm) video Scotch-taped together and run between two open
reel decks set on the floor, Paik's video played for two days before it broke
and had to be removed.

It was important to me that Paik's video work became a part of
a historical continuum when seen in the context of Leonardo. Yet when
I asked my art critic friends why they weren't reviewing the *Machine*
show, they responded that technology was largely outside the central
discourse on art, especially since Minimal and Conceptual art were in the
air. Although *Machine* was a popular success, my friends thought that
neither the premise of the show nor any of the contemporary pieces in
it constituted a significant breakthrough.

Another 1968 exhibition also helped sketch an early definition of the
interplay between art and technology: *Cybernetic Serendipity*, organized
by art historian Jasia Reichardt at London's Institute of Contemporary
Arts. In the catalog Reichardt identified the show's optimistic outlook: "one
cannot deny that the computer demonstrates a radical extension in art and
media techniques. The possibilities inherent in the computer as a creative
tool will . . . increase the scope of art and contribute to its diversity."[1] The
show featured the work of forty-three composers, artists, and poets, and
eighty-seven engineers, doctors, computer scientists, and philosophers
from around the world. Machines and sculptures with different sensing and
sonic mechanisms were a significant part of the exhibition. The eccentric
British filmmaker Bruce Lacey (1927–2016) contributed his radio-controlled
robots and a light-sensitive owl. Paik was represented by his *Robot K-456*
(1964) and his *Magnet TV* (1965), a television set with manipulable abstract
images. Swiss artist Jean Tinguely (1925–1991) provided two of his painting
machines. The American Wen-Ying Tsai (1928–2013) presented his interactive
cybernetic sculptures of vibrating stainless-steel rods, stroboscopic light,

and audio feedback control. Computer-generated movies were represented by *permutations*, a piece by one of the fathers of computer animation, John Whitney (1917–1995), and a Bell Labs film on its technology for producing movies. The eclectic presentation demonstrated the multitude of directions that art might take and the two-way street that can join artists and scientists.

In a *Sunday Telegraph* review on August 11, 1968, the critic Michael Shepherd bluntly noted, "This exhibition . . . serves to show up . . . desolation to be seen in art generally—that we haven't the faintest idea these days what art is for or about."[2] At about this time, Rauschenberg offered a different sentiment: "If you don't accept technology you better go to another place, because no place here is safe. . . . Nobody wants to paint rotten oranges anymore."[3] While Rauschenberg saw a great future, the elite contemporary art cognoscenti deemed most of the new work the mere by-product of experimentation, as did critics, who remained nonplussed for years. I allied myself with future-thinking artists engaged with technology, mindful that the initial work marked a first step. Bold undertakings, the *Machine* and *Cybernetic Serendipity* shows attracted sizable crowds and business-oriented press eager to predict future applications of the tools.

In New York, Howard Wise had a gallery that he ran for a decade on West 57th Street, where he started out with a focus on Abstract Expressionism. He became an advocate of kinetic art, believing that the future of art would be an alliance between artistic and technological concerns. Word-of-mouth recommendations meant that even MoMA's director, René d'Harnoncourt, would occasionally stop by. Considered Wise's most influential and provocative show, *TV as a Creative Medium*, held in 1969, connected the kinetic art and art-and-technology movements with the up-and-coming field of video art. Wise's show presented closed-circuit video installations, performances, and sculptures by twelve artists. Each of the works was as spectacular as what many considered the centerpiece of the show, Frank Gillette and Ira Schneider's nine-monitor *Wipe Cycle* (1969), an installation that incorporated live video of viewers, snippets of prerecorded videos, and clips appropriated from television. Also shown were Thomas Tadlock's *Archetron* (1969), with mirrors and fluctuating, kaleidoscopic imagery pulled directly from broadcast television; and *Everyman's Mobius Strip* (1969), by Paul Ryan (1943–2013), in which the viewer sat on a stool in a curtained booth facing a camera and monitor and responded to provocative questions, their answers recorded, replayed, and then erased. Ryan was exploring video as a psychological mirror, a social tool, and a communications device.[4]

The well-known critic Barbara Rose wrote in her review in *Vogue* that the show was "an apt finale to the 1969 art season, in that it represented the pinnacle of pretension and the nadir of achievement, the exhibition managed to illustrate every current art-world cliché from 'process art'. . . to the spurious concept of 'spectator involvement.' . . . Generally the level of imagination in these works was so low that the tube was merely treated as a kind of animated easel picture."[5] In retrospect, I think *TV as a Creative Medium* did signal the end of the 1960s and the burgeoning of video art, and, as such, the show holds an important position in the early history of video as art.

Eager to understand video's context as a form of new technology, in 1970 I saw my first computer art shows at Automation House, an elegant business conference center that hosted electronic art on East 68th Street in Manhattan. The physical manifestation of the American Foundation on Automation and Employment, Automation House was founded by labor mediator Theodore Kheel, who used flashy, protechnology art exhibitions to encourage the press to give a positive spin on machines that were eliminating jobs, in an attempt to placate union leaders and their rank and file. The computer programming was outstanding, but as visual art, it was often not that inspiring, and I came away wondering why computer graphics usually seemed so visually simplistic and dull. In talking with artist friends, I grew to realize that trailblazing software inspired brilliant engineers who were blessed with expansive technical skills but tended to have limited visual imagination.

As part of my student membership to MoMA, in 1970 I received a copy of the catalog for *Information*, an exhibition that explored the new field of Conceptual art. In keeping with the show's radical point of view, the catalog was unusually designed in crude photocopier style on newsprintlike paper— and I was intrigued. In his introduction, curator Kynaston McShine remarked that the featured artists were "part of a culture that has been considerably altered by communications systems such as television and film, and by increased mobility. Therefore, photographs, documents, films and ideas, which are rapidly transmitted, have become an important part of this new work. This has led to an intellectual exchange and an international community of artists."[6] As Brazilian artist Hélio Oiticica (1937–1980) noted in the catalog, "I am not here representing Brazil; or representing anything else: the ideas of representing-representation-etc. are over."[7]

I was keen to find out more about this newly identified terrain of Conceptual art. Defined as art in which the idea presented by the artist is considered more noteworthy than the finished product, Conceptual art embraced the temporal and incorporeal medium of video, in tandem with its older cousin, experimental film. I stood on the precipice ready to jump into the fray, receptive to the idea proposed by the exhibition that new technologies had globalizing and democratizing power. Like other members of MoMA's young audience, I sensed that *Information* would change the course of art.

When I went to see the show, what excited me most was the Italian manufacturer Olivetti's elegantly designed, colossal "information machine," a "visual jukebox" installed right at the entrance to the exhibition. I stood under the large umbrellalike structure and poked my head into different cubbyholes to watch experimental work by Bruce Conner (1933–2008), Hollis Frampton (1936–1984), Les Levine, and others. A total of forty films were available for individual viewing. Seen on a small Olivetti screen in the gallery, it was practically impossible to distinguish the difference between a work shot in video or in film. I knew that at such a small scale, a prerecorded artwork made in either time-based medium appeared nearly identical. Production was what differentiated the two mediums.

Ideas were central to a series of early media art exhibitions (often overlooked today) at the Finch College Museum of Art, located in Manhattan on East 78th Street and operational from 1952 until the small women's college folded in 1976. The museum showcased video and film in the context of Conceptual and Minimalist art. Elayne Varian, the well-to-do Upper East Side matron, initiated the school's contemporary exhibition program while teaching art appreciation there. (Her students included Grace Slick, who later became well-known as a singer with Jefferson Airplane, and Tricia Nixon Cox, daughter of President Nixon.) Guided by the conceptual artist Mel Bochner (b. 1940), who was a friend of hers, Varian turned from an interest in conventional landscape painting to cerebral art by the downtown avant-garde. The shows she organized included slides, film, and video by Vito Acconci, Robert Smithson, and Dan Graham, and are among the important early examples of how video art slowly grew to be taken seriously.

At about this time, a series of landmark exhibitions was also taking place in Germany. In Düsseldorf between 1968 and 1970, the German curator and TV producer Gerry Schum invited artists to conceive new artworks specifically for viewers to watch in the comfort of home on their own TV sets. This was a novel concept, to use German government-operated television to disseminate artwork into the domestic space. Through his Fernsehgalerie (TV Gallery), Schum produced and broadcast films and videos by many of the same artists featured in McShine's show. (Schum had hoped to be able to broadcast the work on a regular basis, but his hopes were not to be fulfilled.) The idea was radical: Schum single-mindedly challenged convention by eschewing both the brick-and-mortar gallery and the standard television broadcast, believing that the airwaves should carry art and that he could operate as a gallerist-curator in this way. Schum explained: "We no longer perceive the work of art as a painting or sculpture not connected with the artist. On television, the artist can reduce his work to an attitude, a simple gesture, referring to his concept. The work of art is conveyed as a unity of concept, visualization, and the artist who provides the idea."[8]

Exhibition and Distribution of Video

By the early 1970s, video had squared off into distinct formats: single channel and installation. At the time, practitioners often explored both. The format that was most straightforward and easiest for museums to use (especially in-house education staff, often before curators, who initially were a little more cautious) was the single-channel video presented on a TV screen. Released in 1971, the three-quarter-inch (1.9 cm) U-matic cassette is what turned video into an easily distributable and exhibitable medium. Unlike half-inch open-reel video, which necessitated manually handling the tape, the three-quarter-inch tape sat within a closed cassette, which, when inserted into a playback deck, operated on its own. Artists with a utopian spirit, eager for a wide audience, rented or sold their tapes to educational institutions in unlimited editions at modest prices. (Unlimited editions were licensed to the buyer only and meant that artists would make as many copies of the work as there was demand for, rather than limiting the work to a fixed number of editions, which is often done in the interest of increasing a work's value.) Playback decks with automatic-rewind buttons assuaged the fears of technophobic programmers. A blank tape cost under ten dollars, and an artist's unlimited-edition video was relatively inexpensive to rent.

Video was more practical than traditional art forms in terms of distribution. Video artists could tuck a brand-new tape under their arm for an open-call screening, or mail it in a padded envelope to distant colleagues and festivals. (By contrast, large-scale paintings and sculptures are unique and, when shipped, require costly crates for packing and large vehicles—trucks and ships—for transportation.)

The second of the two formats to emerge early on—three-dimensional media sculpture and installation—dealt with space. The term *multichannel sculpture*, sometimes used to describe this type of work, meant there were multiple monitors displaying video images, from either prerecorded or live sources. The term implied that a work was usually more environmental or spatial than a single-channel piece and often incorporated supplementary materials. In 1969 Les Levine, a New York–based artist originally from Ireland, presented his finely honed, formative sculpture *Iris* (1968), which contained six monitors, color gels, and a surveillance system that captured images of viewers in the gallery, at the immaculate New York Cultural Center,

2 Columbus Circle—a building that much later became the Museum of Arts and Design. Another one of the first multichannel video installations was *60 TV Sets* (1972) by London-based David Hall (1937–2014). Exhibited in *A Survey of the Avant-Garde in Britain* at Gallery House, London, in 1972, Hall's installation comprised sixty old TV receivers. Placed on industrial scaffolding that lined the periphery of a room, the TVs were tuned to different channels, each with its sound on very loud. Some TVs operated normally, a few had flashing distortions, some displayed an image intermittently, and others emitted sound only. Amid the atmosphere of media overdose, TV repairmen in white lab coats tended to the sets in fruitless efforts to correct the faults.[9]

Unlimited-edition video received a boost in 1971 when Howard Wise, encouraged by Paik, closed his New York gallery and formed the nonprofit Electronic Arts Intermix (EAI), a postproduction and distribution facility where hundreds of important early video art pieces were eventually edited. Soon I regularly immersed myself there, previewing work that explored image processing or had documentary leanings, as I sat at an EAI office desk wearing big earmuff headphones. With its nonprofit status, EAI was eligible for federal and state grants, which made it viable financially. (EAI became one of the most important video resources for artists and art-world professionals and continues to thrive today.)

For most people in North America and for many beyond, the center of the art universe was New York. In 1971 European-born Leo Castelli and Ileana Sonnabend—astute uptown art dealers who had remained good friends after a divorce—opened their big box galleries on two floors of a building at 420 West Broadway in SoHo, contributing to the development of the area as an international art mecca. On Saturdays hordes walked up and down four flights of stairs and traipsed through their gallery building to look and be seen. On a Saturday afternoon that September, I joined hundreds of others eager to see the over-the-top event that launched Sonnabend's gallery. Gilbert & George (b. 1943 and 1942), the young duo just in from London, performed *The Singing Sculpture*. Dressed in identical tight tweed suits, their faces and hands painted bronze, they stood on a small table in the middle of the gallery and, with stylized gestures and blank expressions, sang the words to an endlessly repeating audiotape of a 1930s British music-hall ditty, "Underneath the Arches." I was fascinated by the duo's flamboyant challenge to New York's regional chauvinism about what was considered "new" in contemporary art and by Sonnabend's bold prophetic stance as a dealer.

Each in their seventies at the time, Castelli and Sonnabend stood at the pinnacle of the contemporary art gallery pyramid. They joined professional forces to form the moving image distribution arm of their galleries, Castelli-Sonnabend Tapes and Films, in 1974. Both had sharp eyes

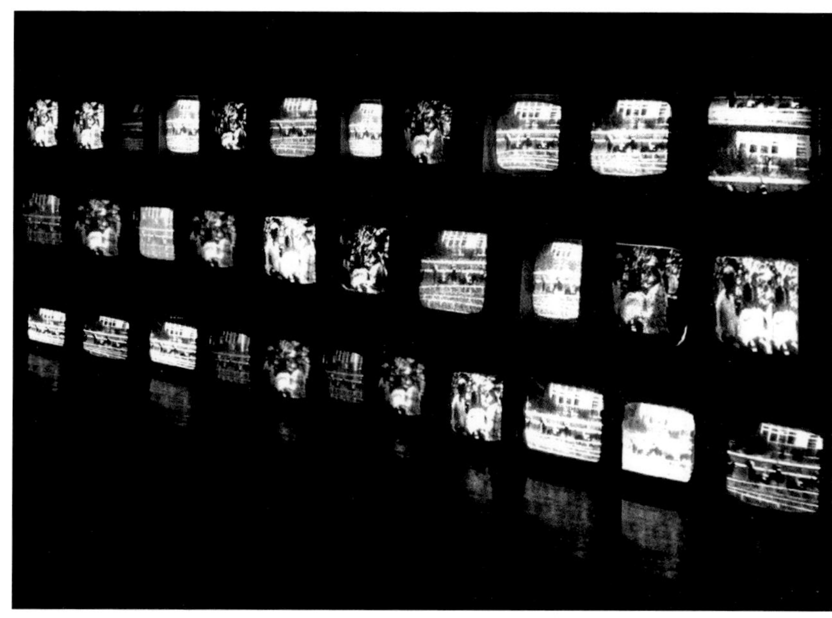

David Hall, *60 TV Sets*, 1972
Multiscreen video installation

for art and good ears for listening to artists when they talked about the developing art scene. Both wanted to be remembered for perspicacity and foresight. What better way to be remembered as progressive than by supporting their stable of eminent young artists, including Bruce Nauman and Joan Jonas, in their experimental use of moving-image mediums. The dealers made time-based art a little more acceptable to the handful of contemporary curators and collectors receptive to art without resale value. At the time, Los Angeles–based Stanley and Elyse Grinstein were about the only contemporary art collectors who acquired unlimited-edition videotapes, all by artists relevant to their collection and all from Castelli-Sonnabend.

Well-read and exceedingly gracious, Sonnabend, sometimes identified as a cross between Buddha and Machiavelli, never divulged her views on anything, including video.[10] Castelli, on the other hand, toward the end of his life admitted that video never did much for him. If "a great genius" such as Nauman couldn't persuade him about video, he doubted that anyone could.[11]

I often chatted with Castelli's accommodating staff, who sat poised at the entrance to his gallery behind a tall counter lined with press releases and catalogs. Then I would walk behind the scenes into the offices and private

showroom. Seated at his commander-in-chief desk, the urbane Castelli
would courteously say hello before I disappeared into a tiny, airless closet
of a viewing room, where I spent long afternoons previewing unlimited-
edition independent videos, overseen initially by the dealers' daughter,
Nina Sundell, and then by Joyce Nereaux, who continued to run the
archive tucked away in a back room. One day in 1974, Nereaux handed me
a document she'd devised—the new Castelli-Sonnabend Tapes and Films
catalog with insightful texts written by art and film theorists. Prices ranged
from $30 for rental to $300 for purchase of work by even such prominent
artists as Claes Oldenburg (b. 1929). The Castelli-Sonnabend distribution
enterprise lasted fifteen years. As pioneers, they were ahead of their time
in committing to work released as an unlimited edition at low rental fees to
museums and art schools; ultimately, the revenue did not prove sufficient
for the gallerists to maintain a staff and preservation materials.

Castelli-Sonnabend Tapes and Films and EAI were eventually joined by
other distribution facilities, including Ingrid Oppenheim in Cologne, Germany,
and then Video Data Bank (VDB), founded by Kate Horsfield (b. 1941) and
Lyn Blumenthal (1949–1988) in Chicago; V/Tape, founded by Lisa Steele
(b. 1947) and Kim Tomczak (b. 1952) in Toronto; and LUX, which had started
out as the London Film-Makers' Co-operative. Each was committed to
making artists' videos accessible to museums, art schools, universities,
festivals, and public libraries in cassette format at relatively low cost
through rentals and sales in unlimited editions for the life of the tape.

Another important resource was the indefatigable Vancouver-based
International Video Exchange Directory, launched in 1971 by the Canadian
artist Michael Goldberg (b. 1945). The organization kept its ear to the ground
and sussed out isolated mavericks making experimental videos out on the
margins. Goldberg worked with local artists, writers, and cultural producers
involved in intermedia art, and through the directory he provided an overview
of video artists in North and South America, Japan, Australia, and Europe.
The assiduous Vancouver team followed the example of Fluxus, whose artists
had made the postal service the distributor of their "mail art." The directory
team solicited information through the grapevine about faraway video activity and sent out questions on postcards to one thousand artists; answers
arrived in the form of single-channel videotapes. The works were then cata-
loged and the information collated. The annual *International Video Exchange
Directory* evolved to become the *Video Guide*, a periodical that focused on
matters concerning video production at the local, national, and global levels.
The small group of dedicated early subscribers, who paid a modest fee,
included festival programmers, art school and museum libraries, educators,
and curators like me.

As a budding curator of a new medium, I sponged up information wherever I could. I was officially brought on staff at MoMA in 1971. At first through exhibition and then acquisition, I sought to position video as art, as it was taking off in many directions. My colleagues at MoMA often teased and called me "catholic," as I sorted through everything deemed independent video.

It was Jennifer Licht, the contemporary curator in the Painting and Sculpture Department, who had taken me under her wing and encouraged me to pick up the mantle of video. Licht and I selected a small video art component for a 1973 MoMA exhibition that the International Program was sending to Australia. *Some Recent American Art* featured sculpture by prominent young artists who made their names by challenging the definition of sculpture, opting to work with CorTen steel, fiberglass, felt, and polyurethane, instead of the conventional carved stone and wood, or cast metal and plaster. A number of them had also briefly experimented with video. We included tapes by Vito Acconci, Lynda Benglis (b. 1941), Robert Morris (1931–2018), Richard Serra, Keith Sonnier (b. 1941), and William Wegman (b. 1943). Years later I learned that *Some Recent American Art* had considerable impact on artists in Sydney and Melbourne, who for the most part only had access to secondhand information in *Artforum* and other magazines.

Once word seeped out that a young MoMA curator was tackling video art, unsolicited tapes started to pour in. Previewing the work required effort and some mechanical ability on my part. Sitting in a former utility closet in the museum, I would carefully thread an artist's half-inch tape through a secondhand open-reel deck's pinch rollers and around the helical heads, which would scan, or read, the electromagnetic signal carried on the tape's magnetic particles once I pushed the "play" lever. Unlike a painting, whose entirety can be seen in a glance, video required considerable time, watching a work unfold on a monitor. An artist's video usually continued for twenty, thirty, or sixty minutes before the tape came to an end. I had to resist the fast-forward button, because I never knew when a magical or clarifying moment might occur.

With my art history background, I had limited technical experience, so I enrolled in two production classes to study video's technical structure. I took the first one at Downtown Community Television (DCTV), a grassroots nonprofit cofounded in 1972 by activist documentarians Jon Alpert (b. 1948) and Keiko Tsuno (b. 1944). With a camera slung over my shoulder, I set out to interview Chinatown residents about a rent strike and create a tape of my own. I attempted to ask questions in a relaxed way so that interviewees would open up and give interesting responses. My camerawork and editing were crude at best, but I was learning something about the process, which my Print Department peers did by making etchings.

For my second class I met with a crew of high-end postproduction wizards in a town house on East 80th Street, the headquarters of Dolphin Computer Animation, a prosperous company catering to big-budget television advertisers. My small class scripted and created a promo for the tall ships en route to Manhattan for the United States' Bicentennial, which later ran as a public service announcement on newly formed public access cable during the Bicentennial. As video production transitioned from pricey into smaller, more affordable and flexible systems that made the upper tier superfluous, Dolphin would later go out of business.

Given the general lack of video coverage in newspapers and magazines, I gathered much of my information by attending screenings like the Saturday-afternoon programs that the indomitable artist and video curator Shigeko Kubota (1937–2015) organized at Anthology Film Archives, then located in SoHo. Occasionally, I went with the receptive *New York Times* art writer Grace Glueck, who had been drawn to the avant-garde by happenings in the 1960s. I admired her ability to effortlessly boil down complex ideas and concepts for her articles, which is what I aspired to achieve in my exhibition wall texts. After the screenings, Glueck occasionally joined me and a small group to continue the conversation at a nearby Tex-Mex restaurant, where we talked for hours.

I regularly stopped by René Block's upstairs gallery at the corner of West Broadway and Prince Street in SoHo. Block had strong ties to Fluxus and retained a home base in Berlin. Block's gallery assistant, Marcel Odenbach (b. 1953) (Paik's former student, who went on to become an accomplished artist), kept me up-to-date about future activities at the gallery as well as far-flung events, especially shows and performances happening in Germany. In May 1974, I checked in on the weeklong cohabitation by Joseph Beuys (1921–1986) with a coyote. Entitled *I Like America and America Likes Me* (1974), the performance began when Beuys landed at John F. Kennedy International Airport from Düsseldorf. He reached Block's gallery in an ambulance and departed the same way, never setting foot on US soil. I observed Beuys with his customary shepherd's staff and felt cloak covering his face, living together with a coyote fenced into a temporary cage. For a week they both paced and ignored each other. Daily issues of the *New York Times* piled up as a measure of the passing days.

Documentary footage of the action was quickly edited by Sandra Devlin at her midtown postproduction studio, and straightaway I featured the twenty-five-minute video in a MoMA exhibition and managed to acquire this example of work that posed a never-ending conundrum: What is art and what is artifact, and when does one become the other? Through my working method, which is to be both prudent and as comprehensive as possible, aware that culling and redefining can be carried out later, MoMA's collection garnered what are now considered early gems, like the Beuys video. The tape effectively perpetuated the inscrutable artist's legend. What no one knew is that when the gallery closed at six p.m., Beuys left the cage and retreated to a nightly dinner party in Block's apartment upstairs.

In 1974 I got my hands on back issues of *Avalanche*, the interview magazine cofounded in 1970 by writer-artists Liza Béar (b. 1942) and Willoughby Sharp (1936–2008), who emphasized the perspective of the artist rather than critics. They focused particularly on Conceptual art and new forms, incluuding video, and captured the grit and criteria of video art and performance coming out of what were vital art centers—Manhattan, Los Angeles, London, and Cologne. Those at a distance from the scene followed *Avalanche* to discover what otherwise could only be gleaned by talking with a difficult-to-reach artist over a beer at a local bar.

Sharp's winter 1971 interview with Nauman was one of the first to shed light on the withdrawn maverick's mind-set. Nauman had picked up Super 8 film and video in the late 1960s, when he was investigating perceptions of the physical body (his or his viewer's) in space. Nauman sketched out his ideas on paper and explored them alone. In the interview he went into the evolution of his work *Performance Corridor* (1969), which became *Live-Taped Video Corridor* (1970), the work for which he had placed a pair of movable walls parallel with barely enough room for him or a viewer to walk through. Above the entrance he set a camera, and at the far end he stacked two monitors, both depicting the empty corridor. One monitor showed a prerecorded video; the other was live and would briefly reveal the back of someone as he or she approached the monitor screens.

In the interview he told Sharp: "I have tried to make the situation sufficiently limiting so that spectators can't display themselves easily. . . . It has . . . to do with my not allowing people to make their own performance out of my art. . . . [A spectator] can do only what I want him to do. I mistrust audience participation."[12] I understood the rationale, because I saw museum-goers play with anything and everything, especially when challenged by the new.

In 1970, Los Angeles gallerist Nicholas Wilder had debuted Nauman's *Live-Taped Video Corridor*. It not only galvanized local California artists; dealers Castelli and Sonnabend, as well as Bruno Bischofberger from Switzerland, all dispatched emissaries or traveled themselves to see the work. In 1971, when Count Giuseppe Panza di Biumo shrewdly acquired a group of Nauman drawings, the Italian collector obtained a sketch of the masterpiece and rights to it. In 2016, while a scholar at the Getty Research Institute in Los Angeles, I read Count Panza's papers and learned that misunderstandings arose when word seeped out that a second copy of *Video Corridor* might be sold by Castelli and Sonnabend. After an exchange of conciliatory correspondence, *Video Corridor* remained a unique artwork owned by the resolute count. It would take another three decades for the video installation to be sold in editions—a development that arose in tandem with the increased use of laptops, hard drives, and other digital storage devices.

Public Debates

By 1974 a group of prominent art critics, museum directors, and public TV producers were hopping onto video's bandwagon. For three days in January of that year, over one hundred of these early supporters and curious souls had convened for MoMA's "Open Circuits: An International Conference on the Future of Television," instigated by a zealous troika: Boston Public Television arts producer Fred Barzyk, *Newsweek* critic/artist Douglas Davis (1933–2014), and Buffalo State College, State University of New York media studies professor/philosopher Gerald O'Grady. They worked with MoMA's film curator, Willard Van Dyke. The organizers of the conference believed in a future for art on television, as did many of the invited artists and theorists.

I sat with invitees who included people involved with expanded cinema from around the world—artists, scholars, television producers, writers, museum directors, and curator Evelyn Weiss from Aachen, Germany, who had founded the first museum collection of single-channel video at the Neue Galerie, now called Ludwig Forum. The fifty conference speakers included Gregory Battcock, Vilém Flusser, Frank Gillette, Allan Kaprow (1927–2006), Bruce Kurtz, Jane Livingston, David Loxton, and Stan VanDerBeek (1927–1984), among other notables, and ranged from the sanguine to the dubious. As a neophyte, I listened and thought about why some attendees spoke with enthusiasm and some with indifference.

In a lucid talk, the avant-garde pioneer Hollis Frampton avowed that video emerged from the Jovian backside of television.[13] He noted that although film and video share paleontologies, film yields racehorses and video yields wrestlers who lack a history.[14] I was surprised by his words, because I regarded experimental film and video makers in a similar light; both had to be feisty and determined to create their often down-and-dirty new work, which they exhibited at alternative venues like the Kitchen and Global Village.[15] Art critic Robert Pincus-Witten, a conference speaker who expressed a view held by several other attendees, complained that video artists' belief in the utopian myth of the future was no longer sufficient to justify the uncritical acceptance of the art of their generation.[16]

Film was represented by the experimental stalwarts Shirley Clarke and Jonas Mekas (1922–2019), who addressed relevant social issues in their work as they strove for the kind of realism that had challenged the Hollywood system in the 1950s. Clarke had established the Filmmakers Cooperative, with Mekas, in 1962, with VanDerBeek, Robert Breer (1926–2011), Michael Snow, and other filmmakers soon coming on board. In 1970, on the Chelsea Hotel's roof, Clarke had launched the Tee Pee Video Space Troupe workshop and collective, which produced experimental video and theater. The same year, Mekas founded the Anthology Film Archives as a permanent home for avant-garde cinema. From the start he championed video makers Kubota and Jonas.

In his talk, Acconci straddled the divide between the two moving-image formats by revealing why he alternated between film and video. For him, film is a medium for landscape, albeit one like a drug that washes over the viewer confined to a theater seat. He concluded that as a companion at home, video is a medium for close-up. The talking torso—the newscaster— has a face-to-face encounter with the viewer seated in front of a TV screen.[17]

When it was her turn to speak, the Japanese-born feminist Kubota showed an excerpt from her autobiographical *Broken Diary* video series (1970–86), which merged her signature electronic processing with art historical and cultural references and a strong sense of female identity. Always straightforward, she baldly proclaimed: "Men think: 'I think, there-fore I am.' I, a woman, feel: 'I bleed, therefore I am.' Recently I've bled ten thousand feet of half-inch tape, every month. . . . Video is Vengeance and Victory of Vagina."[18] Kubota concluded her frank statement with a hearty belly laugh and sat down. (Just a year prior, Kubota and I connected at the New York Women's Video Festival at the Kitchen with the artist Susan Milano [b. 1945], another early feminist who picked up the mantle of video as a clean slate.)

We also heard pronouncements by other technology upstarts—Paik, the unwavering Steina and Woody Vasulka (b. 1940 and 1937), Stephen Beck (b. 1950), and Tom DeWitt (b. 1944)—artists who probed the nitty-gritty of the electronic audiovisual signal and used jerry-rigged special effects processors to colorize their black-and-white work. The great Tokyo-based experimental film and video maker Toshio Matsumoto (1932–2017) showed his sardonic *Mona Lisa* (1973), in which the inscrutable figure sits before a changing global landscape. Matsumoto explained that in making *Mona Lisa* he experimented with the idiom of the personal "trip," a journey into self, through a device called Scanimate that had just been introduced in Japan.[19]

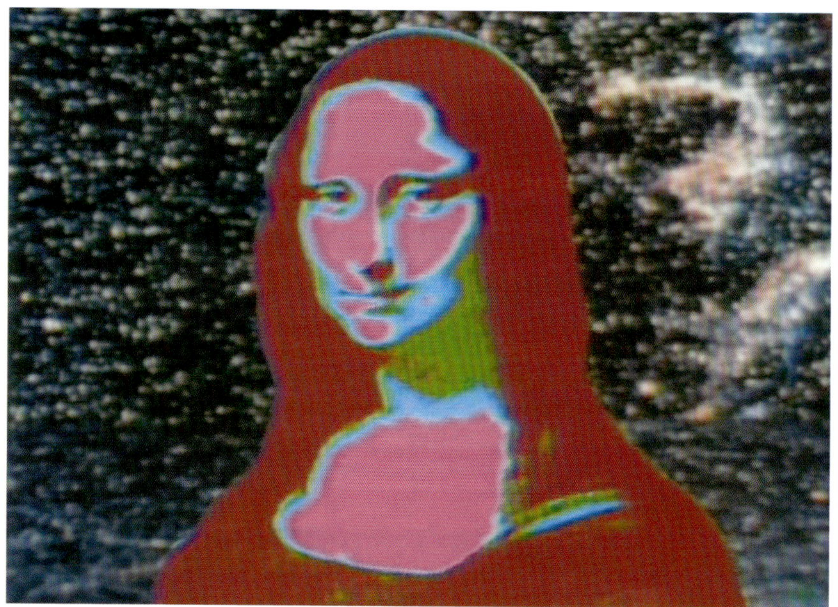

Toshio Matsumoto, *Mona Lisa*, 1973
Video, color, sound, 3 min. 30 sec.

The Buenos Aires businessman-collector-theorist Jorge Gluesberg cannily positioned Argentine artists in the mix. The director of the Museum of Contemporary Art of the University of São Paulo, Walter Zanini, did the same for Brazilians.

Exasperated by the different camps' grandiose proclamations and seemingly superficial infatuation, Los Angeles artist and founding California Institute of the Arts (CalArts) professor John Baldessari (b. 1931) commented that he felt like an outsider at a religious convention. "To have a three-day conference on video is akin to having a conference on The Pencil. That is, I think that for there to be progress in TV, the medium must be as neutral as a pencil. Just one more tool in the artists' toolbox. . . . To have a conference on any device implies that it has too much importance, too much power, and that we are serving it. The case should not be, 'I'm going to make a video piece,' but, 'What I want to do can best be done with video.'"[20]

Baldessari made everyone chuckle when he screened an excerpt of his thirty-minute video *I Will Not Make Any More Boring Art* (1971), which shows his hands writing the title over and over on a sheet of copybook paper as he enunciates the promise again and again.

The conference had a big impact on me. It heightened my awareness of politics, especially about how individuals make chesslike power moves, and how a new field gets carved up and how players interact. Large traditional institutions have the biggest budgets and staff, and the most clout, the opposite of the generally underfunded, often distrustful small alternative venues where video art began. I was eager to see this dark horse of video fit into MoMA, the grand arbiter of taste. To make this happen, I would have to pay attention and try to make the right moves myself.

It turned out that a young film colleague of mine, Laurence Kardish, and I were the only in-house curatorial staff who persistently mingled with the presenters at this wide-open forum. Everyone else at MoMA revealed an inherent indifference, which proved I had the new territory to myself. A few years later the conference proceedings were anthologized, along with an essay by me, in *The New Television: A Public/Private Art*.[21] The publication is an important document of video's early era.

In April 1974, I joined a lively group of artists, museum curators and educators, arts programmers, and writers for another conference, this one titled "Video and the Museum," funded by the New York State Council on the Arts. Held at the Everson Museum of Art in Syracuse, New York, it had been organized by the young curator David Ross, encouraged by the museum's director, James Harithas, who championed emerging artists throughout a long career. Harithas had started the video program in 1971, having worked with Paik and Juan Downey in Washington, DC, a few years prior.

At the Everson conference, attendees spent two days hammering out the dynamics of the relationship between production and exhibition and the particulars of the new art form, agreeing that production, distribution, and exhibition go hand in hand. The disparate members of this fanatical tribe understood the synergy inherent to video. In order for the field to advance, more video artwork first needed to be created. As a next step, work required a network for delivery and platforms for exhibition. A few hardworking souls had set up alternative production centers upstate, such as the Experimental Television Center in Owego and Woodstock Community Video, where invited artists made work. Some of the conference participants organized annual video festivals with the newly made tapes, including Ithaca Video Festival and the Women's Video Festival at the Kitchen; others arranged installations with stacked-up monitors in nonprofit spaces for offbeat audiences.

A shrewd politician, Paik, in his presentation, stressed that technology's nonstop advances had a positive impact on art making. With a mischievous twinkle in his eyes, he spoke confidently in his heavy Korean accent, with the resolved cadence of a charismatic guru, as he expounded philosophically about change and the new possibilities he saw in the fruitful overlap of art and mass communications. Unlike his disgruntled cohorts who railed against the generally parsimonious electronics companies and rigid commercial broadcast stations, Paik was an ardent advocate for both.

The American artist Bill Viola (b. 1951) discussed his recent video *Information* (1973), a purely abstract work composed of bright squiggly scan lines with colorful squares superimposed on top. *Information* had been the result of a technical slipup; as Viola had devised the work, a videotape recorder had tried to record itself. *Information* is a study of electronic anarchy—a disintegrating and self-interrupting signal that perpetually reiterates itself.

Viola was the exhibition assistant for Paik's retrospective *Videa 'n' Videology* at Everson, which coincided with the conference. Both artists garnered the attention of attendees. Many boarded a bus and went across town to Syracuse University's Synapse TV studio, where Viola and several other fledgling media art students demonstrated how they were using the broadcast-quality equipment to make their work. The purchase of broadcast equipment was unusual for an art department back then, when few art schools possessed even one rudimentary video camera. With the exception of public television's short-lived Television Laboratory (TV Lab) at PBS stations in San Francisco, Boston, and New York, the brainchild of Howard Klein at the Rockefeller Foundation, broadcast-quality gear would remain the inaccessible domain of television industry professionals for years.

At the Everson conference, Viola explained that he paid as much attention to sound as he did to image, the two fundamental components of analog video's electronic signal. He recently had come to identify sound as a physical, sculptural material, after performing in the improvisational installation *Rainforest IV* (1973) by the experimental music composer David Tudor. During the four-hour event, a group of musicians each created particular sounds with a collection of suspended metal objects, including a set of bedsprings and an oil drum. The public wandered around and under the amplified objects, listening to the subtleties of the spatial electronic composition performed by the musicians. Tudor pointed out to Viola that his inspiration for *Rainforest* traced back to 1966, when he performed in John Cage's *Variations VII*, the sound installation developed for E.A.T.'s *9 Evenings*. The conversation made me think about artistic lineage—links that went from Cage to Tudor and to Viola. Lineage became an important factor of my curatorial practice. For years I have studied the work of artists using new tools and explored how their practice impacts other disciplines and other art forms.

Working with MoMA's administration, in August 1974 I launched the first ongoing video exhibition program anywhere. The National Endowment for the Arts awarded the museum a modest grant to buy the initial equipment: two monitors, a sound system, and a three-quarter-inch playback deck. MoMA allocated a small gallery that split its daily programming between video and *Lumia Suite, Opus 158* (1963), a mesmerizing abstract rear projection and a visitor favorite by Thomas Wilfred (1889–1968);[22] *Lumia Suite* showed in the morning, video in the afternoon. I had become a one-woman operation, an interpreter of an unruly domain that I introduced uptown by making a coherent selection of tapes that played in carefully scheduled programs with such no-nonsense titles as Video and Performance, which included tapes by Florentine conceptual artist Giuseppe Chiari (1926–2007), choreographer Viola Farber (1931–1998), electronic composer Robert Ashley (1930–2014), and musician–performance artist Charlemagne Palestine (b. 1947[23]); Video and the Computer, with early videos by Barbara Buckner (b. 1950), Dan Sandin (b. 1942), and Ed Emshwiller (1925–1990); and Broadcasting, with videos by Muntadas, Tava (a.k.a. Jane Hudson, b. 1940), Tina Girouard (b. 1946), Jon Alpert, and Keiko Tsuno.

The program was an important step into contemporary art for MoMA, which, at the time, was negotiating its relationship to modern versus contemporary art. William Rubin, the renowned art historian, Picasso scholar, and director of the Painting and Sculpture Department, kept MoMA on a solid modern course. He often said when lecturing, "Thank goodness Barbara London is handling video art, so my department's curatorial staff remains focused on painting and sculpture." Mindful of the status quo, I kept my head down and adhered to a small budget and institutional protocol, as I talked to every video artist I could find and read every flier sent.

I had the support of MoMA trustee and art collector William S. Paley, the founder of the CBS broadcast empire. He instructed his television engineers to train me and MoMA's two film projectionists. One afternoon in 1974 the three of us walked across 53rd Street to Paley's Black Rock headquarters. We learned how to take apart our new three-quarter-inch cassette deck, crucial because the exhibition videotapes that played continuously all afternoon gave us headaches by sometimes bunching up and jamming the playback machine. Meanwhile, as the videotapes passed over the rotating heads that read the electronic signal, gunky particles would build up and cause dreadful audiovisual distortions. From then on, rather than put up "out of order" signs, we were able to make simple repairs ourselves and keep the program going. I regularly stopped by to check that the machines were functioning properly and often found young lovers seated on the bench making out or children's toys on the floor. Visitors felt more relaxed in this informal, somewhat out-of-the-way lower-level space than in the white-cube galleries upstairs.

Video's interloper status meant that initially, I operated under the umbrella of Projects, a cross-curatorial exhibition series devoted to up-and-coming installations that was introduced following prolonged efforts by two contemporary curators in the Painting and Sculpture Department, Licht and McShine. With the support of Licht, McShine, and the Projects liaison, curator Riva Castleman, I furthered the ongoing series of exhibitions that surveyed the evolution of single-channel video, with an occasional video installation inserted into the program. I had started out naively thinking that as video art developed, it would quickly grow to be widely appreciated and subsume everything related to installation. This took decades to happen, as it turned out.

In 1974 I featured Gilbert & George's parodic videos *Gordon's Makes Us Drunk* (1972), *Portrait of the Artists as Young Men* (1972), and *In the Bush* (1972) in an early video show I organized at MoMA. The artists' mundane and mild-seeming actions performed alone for the camera were aggressive in their slowness. The London dealer Nigel Greenwood had recently released Gilbert & George's videos in a limited edition (an anathema then) of twenty-five for $10,000 each. Rare-books collectors understood editioning, but contemporary collectors were technophobic, skittish about high price.

I figured out procedures as I went along. Greenwood readily provided a submaster of the tapes. I then had to bargain with a New Jersey–based production facility to transfer from the European standard of 625 lines to the American 525. Several years later, the artists generously donated the videos to MoMA.

After seriously considering what video preservation would involve, in 1975 MoMA officially began acquiring artists' videos—making video the first new medium to enter the museum's collection program since film was added in 1935. MoMA's first purchases, now considered part of video art's canon, included Paik's *Global Groove* (1973), Jonas's *Vertical Roll* (1972), Nauman's *Lip Sync* (1969), Peter Campus's *Three Transitions* (1973), Martha Rosler's *Semiotics of the Kitchen* (1975), Emshwiller's *Scape-mates* (1972), and William Wegman's *Selected Works: Reel 3* (1972–73), which he performed with his Weimaraner Man Ray. In the mid-1970s, the going rate for the acquisition of videotapes was $250 per title. As we gradually added more videos to the collection, by the late 1970s I was able to organize Recent Acquisitions shows, as other curatorial departments had been doing for years. Video gained the status of the other art mediums at MoMA.

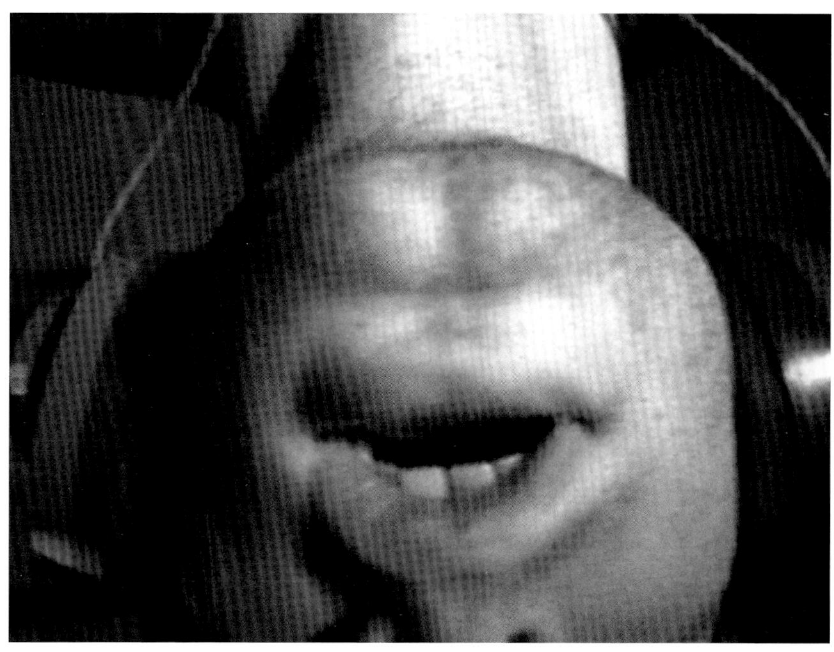

Bruce Nauman, *Lip Sync*, 1969
Video, black and white, sound, 57 min.

When the museum formed a video advisory acquisitions committee, an important one of its founding members was the soft-spoken, innately inquisitive and supportive trustee Mrs. John D. Rockefeller III. I saw her as a genuinely open-minded art collector who enjoyed talking directly with the video makers whose work we were acquiring. I once observed her take a seat next to Viola at a special event opening and candidly ask him to please explain what video art was. She was transfixed by his eloquent answer, which I remember overhearing him say. It went something like this:

> Video in the late twentieth century realized the dream of painters from the Renaissance to the late nineteenth century: to embody motion. Not only could artists now capture the cresting wave of the moment, but also they could observe themselves in the midst of it from a point of view outside their bodies.[24]

I was grateful that the exceedingly courteous Paik quietly operated as an ambassador and lobbied the Rockefeller Foundation on my program's

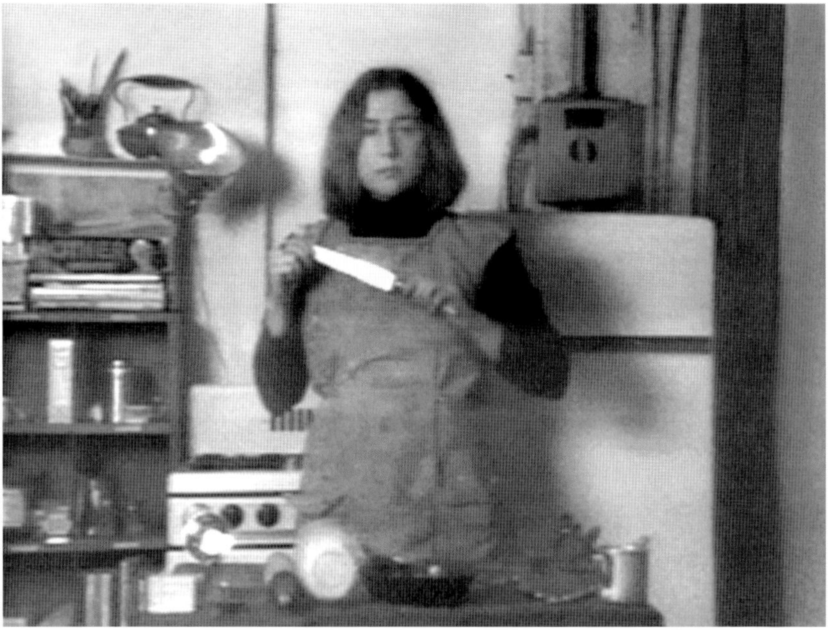

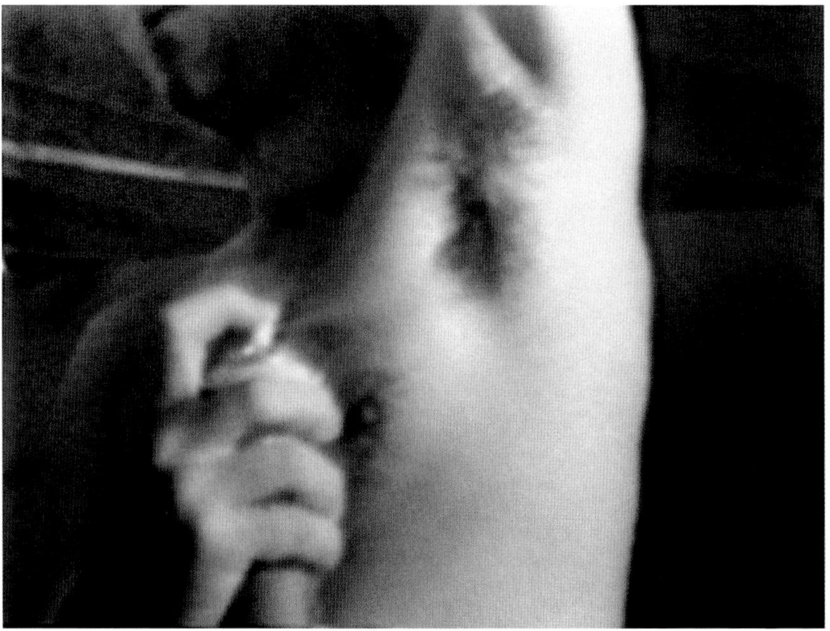

behalf, so that in 1976 MoMA was awarded a substantial grant to expand the video programs. The grant allowed us to continue our efforts to document the medium's early steps, and for that, we needed the direct participation of artists. In 1978 we launched Video Viewpoints, a series in which independent video makers were invited to present and discuss their latest work. I immediately understood the art historical importance, so from the get-go, we made audio recordings and transcribed each artist's words. Video Viewpoints quickly became a regular Monday-evening event with an interested audience of about fifty, including writers, artists, MoMA members, and others.

Video Viewpoints started out in MoMA's private Founders Room, the trustees' meeting room on the sixth floor. We would unplug our unwieldy three-quarter-inch cassette playback deck and two monitors in the video gallery and with the help of a burly porter would haul the equipment upstairs, where we would set up simple metal chairs. We worked hard to accommodate each artist's own way of arranging the room, from a theaterlike setup for the straightforward display of videotapes and slides to the careful re-creation of an installation. We were aware that by establishing a new tradition at MoMA we would be making history, and because of that, we tried hard to be broad-minded and inclusive in our selection of artists. For their part, artists were conscious of now being inside a major institution, and they were thorough in planning their presentations.

Gradually, the museum made a decision based on administrative and housekeeping reasons not to keep video in limbo under the Projects exhibition program any longer. Around 1979 the Film Department's old-guard staff grudgingly took me in. Slowly some of my Film Department colleagues started to see that, despite divergent technical characteristics and different temperature-humidity climate control storage needs, as durational art video shared certain countercultural motivations with experimental film. To MoMA the connection made sense; at the time, independent video and film both were considered peripheral mediums within the institution, identified by the catchall term *experimental*. Film Department curators and I became allies, despite the fact that moving-image practitioners remained divided into two distrustful camps—old guard cineastes versus analog gatecrashers, many of the latter with roots in performance art.

Opposite, top: Martha Rosler, *Semiotics of the Kitchen*, 1975
Video, black and white, sound, 6 min. 33 sec.

Opposite, bottom: William Wegman, *Selected Works: Reel 3*, 1972–73
Video, black and white, sound, 21 min. 41 sec.

Early Practitioners

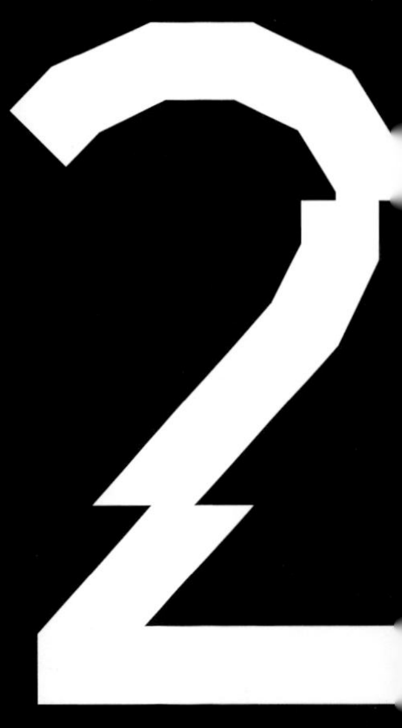

In the beginning, video as art was shaped by a congenial hard core that consisted of overlapping groups of early adopters, who were joined by others who simply passed through. Decisive strides were made by artists engaged with the medium in different parts of the world. Simply put, video functioned as a vehicle for ideas, and practitioners embracing video and the new naturally intersected with experimentation in performance and sound art, as well as more conventional disciplines. Each of these trailblazing artists contributed a distinctive approach that was proof of video's versatility as an artistic medium.

Nam June Paik

A bright-eyed, astute, and generous artist, Nam June Paik is celebrated as an interdisciplinary mastermind behind video art's rise. I was charmed when he greeted me with a cheery hello upon our first encounter in 1974, when we both happened to be riding the same bus. Paik early on had settled into a studio in Lower Manhattan on Canal Street, an ideal spot for an artist fascinated by the detritus of modern living. During the day, the shops along Canal would empty secondhand electronic and machinery wares onto the sidewalks. The helter-skelter piles of rusted motors and TV carcasses were the palimpsests of the Fluxus energy in Paik's assemblage installations. The corner deli was the only outpost of civilization in the handful of downtown artist neighborhoods of the late 1960s. The desolate streets were not a place to linger, but Paik often ran into fellow locals, such as musician Steve Reich (b. 1936) and Michael Snow. Snow once told me that their polite and enthusiastic sidewalk conversations resembled far-out performances. Paikspeak was rich and expansive and heavily accented, whether he spoke in Japanese, German, or English. Some listeners perceived abstract sounds rather than comprehensible language.

In the mid-1970s, whenever Paik was in town and not traveling, he would stop by my minuscule office in a former utility closet at the end of a long hallway. Surrounded by an overflowing bookshelf and an overstuffed filing cabinet, we would sit and chat about his new projects and the state of video and the world. He usually arrived with an armful of treasures: his out-of-print early catalogs; old, yellowed newspaper clippings with reviews that he would sign; posters and other rare printed matter. In his inimitable sagacity, he knew that my collection of ephemera document-ing video's history would one day become an important research archive. He understood I would save and organize everything, which I did, and eventually I transferred it to the MoMA Library. The reference materials Paik donated became important resources.

After these informal meetings at MoMA, Paik and I would head out for lunch at the nearby Hilton Hotel café, where the animated but disheveled artist attracted stares, waiters wondering whether this curious figure was an indigent. He usually wore multiple shirts and pairs of pants, three pairs of socks, and his habitual wool sweater tied around his waist to keep his insides warm. He suffered from acute diabetes that contributed to his slowly failing health.

Starting in the mid-1970s, I made a point of regularly dropping by Paik's studio. I followed in the footsteps of a long procession of interested visitors, including the ever-curious seeker of the new Andy Warhol. I would crawl over and through a maze of electrical wires, tubes, and old circuitry to find Paik often standing in rubber boots, so as not to be electrocuted. At the center of his labyrinth, he deftly applied magnets and degaussing coils—devices used to correct normally occurring magnetic color distortion—to get his own chance distortions on television screens. Pointing his video camera at the screen, he experimented with the repetitive patterning of live feedback. Many of his early discoveries occurred spontaneously, the unexpected results of everyday materials such as Scotch tape that he used to bundle cables or make edits of joined splices of videotape, back when editing was next to impossible.

In a six-page proposal from 1966 to Porter McCray (the JDR 3rd Fund director from whom Paik had received a grant to buy his first video camera a year prior) the artist had sought support to build a seven-channel video signal mixer whose "electro-magnetic vibration of head might lead way to electronic Zen."[1] Subsequently, in 1969, he was invited to join an artists' production program at Boston public television station WGBH led by arts producer Fred Barzyk. Through WGBH, Paik and engineer Shuya Abe improved upon their existing video synthesizer, a device that enabled them to generate a variety of visual effects without camera input through the use of internal video pattern generators. Paik delighted in adding bright color to black-and-white material. The result of Paik's experiments at WGBH was included in the 1969 broadcast *The Medium Is the Medium*, a program of commissioned works by artists for television.[2]

In 1971 Paik and Abe did workshops together at CalArts in Los Angeles. From there Paik wrote McCray:

Experimental Video Projects by Shuya Abe (distinguished Japanese engineer-artist) and me is quite popular. Students like our Video Synthesizer very much. Sony Video Tape recorder (as you remember you brought the first import of this kind to me six years ago) is so much in demand among students and faculty that there is one-

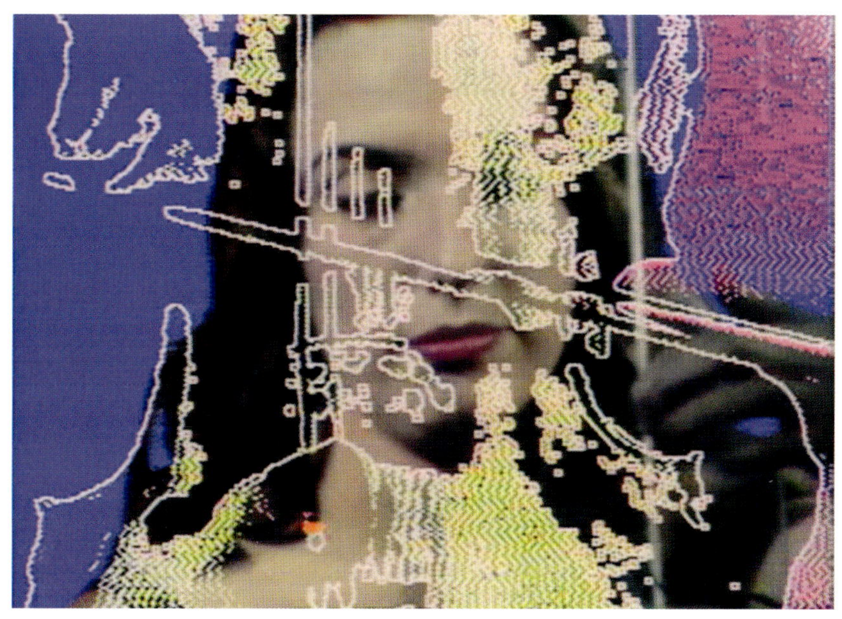

Nam June Paik and John Godfrey, *Global Groove*, 1973
Video, color, sound, 28 min. 30 sec.

week waiting line for the machines. Video is not one more chic fad in Manhattan but is here to stay. . . . Like pen and paper and canvas. . . . The camera makes everyone an artist.[3]

Returning to New York, Paik was one of a handful of artists—along with Ed Emshwiller, Shirley Clarke, Douglas Davis, and Dimitri Devyatkin (b. 1949)—invited to join the artist-in-residence program at the Television Laboratory (TV Lab) at New York's PBS member station WNET/Thirteen. (The TV Lab had grown out of a Rockefeller-funded initiative, spearheaded by Director of Arts and Humanities Howard Klein, and was introduced at PBS stations KQED in San Francisco and WGBH in Boston, in addition to WNET.) Funding for the WNET TV Lab came from a $150,000 grant from the Rockefeller Foundation, augmented by funds from the National Endowment for the Arts and New York State Council on the Arts. The productions that resulted from residencies highlighted the distinctions between video art made with crude consumer tools versus broadcast-quality devices.

In Paik's single-channel video *Global Groove* (1973), produced at the TV Lab, he interwove serious thoughts with his upbeat editing style that became standard television vernacular. He drew on a range of entertaining content. A young couple tap-dances to Mitch Ryder & the Detroit Wheels' "Devil with a Blue Dress On"; John Cage and Allen Ginsberg (1926–1997) recite; a traditional Korean musician drums while a Navajo singer chants; smiling children play on the beach and drink Pepsi-Cola to a Japanese advertising ditty. Paik concludes on a sensual note as he instructs viewers to close their eyes, then half-open them as a campy topless fan dancer gyrates. *Global Groove* exemplified Paik's rapid-fire editing style, which he had developed knowing he had one split second to grab channel-changing viewers' attention once they landed on PBS's transmission. His quick cuts and collage methods captured viewers and radicalized the old-timer union engineers he pushed to loosen up and stray from their standard broadcast production methods.

Between 1975 and 1977, the TV Lab organized and broadcast the *Video Tape Review* miniseries, hosted by curator and arts commentator Russell Connor. The program put video art in viewers' homes on Sunday evenings through WNET/Thirteen and several of its PBS affiliates. One evening in 1975 I walked over to one of Connor's monthly art salons at his apartment, several blocks from WNET/Thirteen's studios. I joined a lively group of artists, curators, art writers, and TV producers, as we celebrated *Suite 212* (1975), Paik's series of shorts made as a tribute to New York and designed to be aired as part of WNET/Thirteen's late-night schedule. My favorite section features a master Chinese chef smiling as he dumps just-made perfect noodles onto his head.

Paik used to say that Koreans are wild people and that he loved the messy "Siberian-Mongolian" element in his veins. He would plow through a variety of open-ended situations, cheerfully taking advantage of unexpected and unruly consequences. Paik was proud to be working with CMX, a computer-controlled video-editing system at the station. There were times when Paik invited me over to WNET/Thirteen when he was editing. Once he asked whether he should leave the time code running at the bottom of the screen. I gave a vague answer: "It looks good." Then he asked for aesthetic advice about a few other scenes. Sometimes he went along with my suggestions; at other times he didn't. In a way, I became a cog in the wheel of chance that steered Paik's work.

I relished the occasional invitations to join Paik and his partner Kubota for dinner in their loft, where I joined a spirited group of their interdisciplinary artist friends. I remember one visit on a particularly cold late autumn day in 1976, at a time when the cobblestone streets of SoHo were empty, years before chic stores outnumbered edgy galleries. Once inside the loft, I felt like I was swimming in an aquarium: dozens of monitors displaying images of fish cavorting through their watery domain hung from the ceiling, part of Paik's installation *Fish Flies on Sky* (1975/82), which had just come back from an exhibition at the Martha Jackson Gallery's warehouse space.

Another time I stopped by on New Year's Day and encountered lounging around the apartment a group of artists and composers, Japanese as well as American, who over the years worked with Paik, Kubota, and Cage to create the street actions and other events that Fluxus was known for in the 1960s. This gathering included Takehisa Kosugi (1938–2018), Richard Teitelbaum (b. 1939), Yoshi Wada (b. 1943), Joan Logue (b. 1942), Ay-O (b. 1931), and their elder neighbor, Francis Whitney (d. 2005), who like Paik was experimenting with lasers. On the long dining table in the middle of the loft there was an enormous hunk of tuna, torn out of a leviathan that the friends had jointly purchased at the Fulton Street market and hacked into shares. I was delighted that the tuna was real, not an image on a monitor, and I greedily joined the others devouring fresh sashimi until the tuna disappeared.

I followed Paik around the world to experience his shows not only in New York but also in Seoul, Tokyo, Paris, Düsseldorf, and Kassel, among many other cities. A nomadic genius, he was the definitive media artist/ thinker/teacher. I smile when I look back on something Paik wrote in 1969: he wanted "to shape the TV screen canvas as precisely as Leonardo, as freely as Picasso, as colorfully as Renoir, as profoundly as Mondrian, as violently as Pollock and as lyrically as Jasper Johns."[4] What this determined yet playful visionary philosopher-artist managed to achieve in his lifetime is breathtaking. We are fortunate that he made video an appealing and accessible art form, of the here and now, and part of posterity.

Vito Acconci

As part of my strategy of keeping my ear to the ground, I tracked the work of pioneers who understood the power of video, especially its fusion with sound and language. I frequently caught up with Vito Acconci, an artist often difficult to classify, due to his ability to move between mediums. He started out as a poet whose distinctive throaty voice got under your skin as he transitioned from readings to performances. Working with a small Super 8 film camera, he would record actions he carried out in his studio and would then drop off his ten-minute film at a nearby drugstore to be developed. Once he received the Super 8 film cassette back by mail, he would show the work with an unobtrusive projector that required minimal maintenance.

Acconci consistently picked up on trends; as a voracious consumer of pop music, he paid attention to its connections to visual art. (The film critic Amy Taubin would often say to me that Acconci stayed a step ahead of his peers, who eagerly followed his next moves.) Whether in New York or on

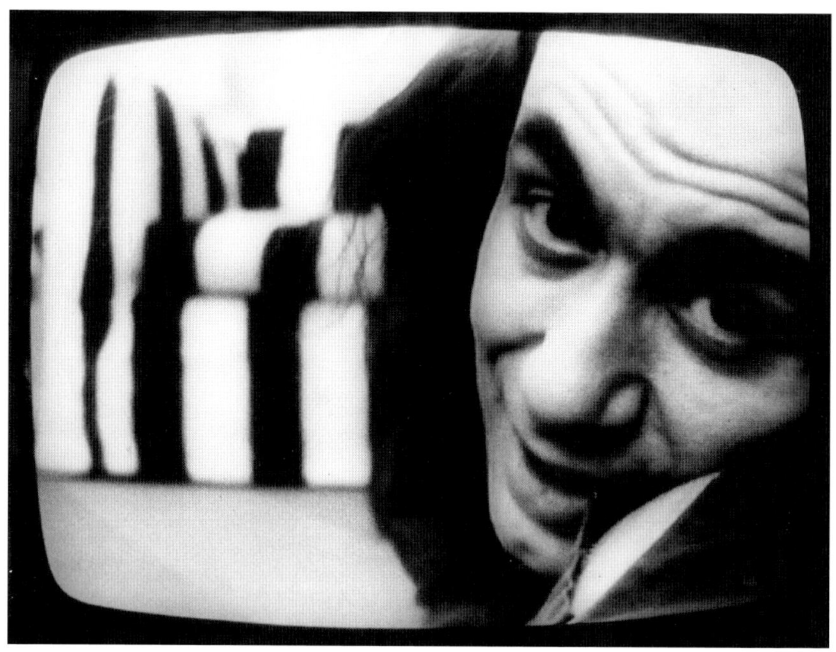

Vito Acconci, *Theme Song*, 1973
Video, black and white, sound, 33 min. 15 sec.

far-flung travels, he could be found in music stores buying records and CDs, which then fed into his visual art. As he later explained:

> At the end of the 1960s, at the beginning of my career in "art,"
> my medium was my own body; art was a presentation of self,
> a face-to-face encounter between artist and viewer. The music
> I loved then was Van Morrison, Neil Young; the tone was rural, the
> voice was solo, the songs were long, twenty-minute songs; there
> was room enough to drift through the country and find where you
> were, find out who you were—there was all the time in the world
> to build a cocoon for yourself and the person you sang to. (There
> was another music at the time, that came out of left field: the
> Velvet Underground. This was urban music, crowded music that left
> no place to be safe in—this voice, too, was solo, but it was drowned
> out by instrumentation, driven to destruction—a song was long
> because time was relentless.)[5]

Acconci's long, cajoling monologues, like pop songs, concern unrequited love. In his single-channel video *Theme Song* (1973), he lies cozily on the floor of a well-appointed living room at night. He attempts to turn the anonymous viewer into a partner. It is quiet, the perfect setting for a come-on. Gazing with anticipation at the camera, he looms large, entreating the viewer to come close and join him. A small tape recorder, filled with up-to-date music, sits on the floor within reach. He punches a button and Jim Morrison moans, "I can't see your face in my mind." Acconci brings up another song, and Bob Dylan croons, "I'll be your baby tonight." Acconci sweet-talks with "We'll have a dream love, an ideal love—but I won't control things; you'll have your say."

Whenever I met with Acconci—at an exhibition, at a bookstore, at my office, or after a film screening—we would talk about what we had seen or the music we had just heard. His sharp mind and bold ideas were always a welcome pleasure. Few were able to match his command of time and space or his verbal prowess as expressed in a videotape, an installation, a lecture, or simply words on a page. His voice still reverberates in my head.

Steina and Woody Vasulka

One afternoon in 1971 I went to the seedy old Broadway Central Hotel in Greenwich Village, its former ballroom and catering spaces recently renamed the Mercer Arts Center, where the New York Dolls and other music and performance groups appeared. It was known for being culturally and artistically a lively, polluted place that featured high art as well as trash. Down in the basement, I entered the kitchen, which had been transformed into a multiuse media theater by the artist partners Steina and Woody Vasulka. Having grown tired of hosting crowded, impromptu screenings of friends' work in their apartment, they founded the space to cultivate media art in an inclusive context. It was run on an ad hoc basis by a group that included artists Andreas Mannik (a.k.a. Andy Mann, 1947–2001), Rhys Chatham, Shridhar Bapat (1948–1993), Dimitri Devyatkin, Michael Tschudin (b. 1944), and subsequently administrators Robert Stearns and Jim Burton.

One evening I watched Steina, a classically trained orchestra-caliber violinist, play a tricked-out instrument that Woody, an engineer-filmmaker, had connected to specially designed devices. This included scan processors, which reorganize images by acting on the systems that control the scanning motion of the electron beam as it travels two times a second across a monitor screen; video sequencers, programmable electronic apparatuses that store sequences of images and sounds, to be used as needed during production; and multikeyers, image-making devices used to alter specific properties of the video signal. That evening Steina sang to the Beatles'

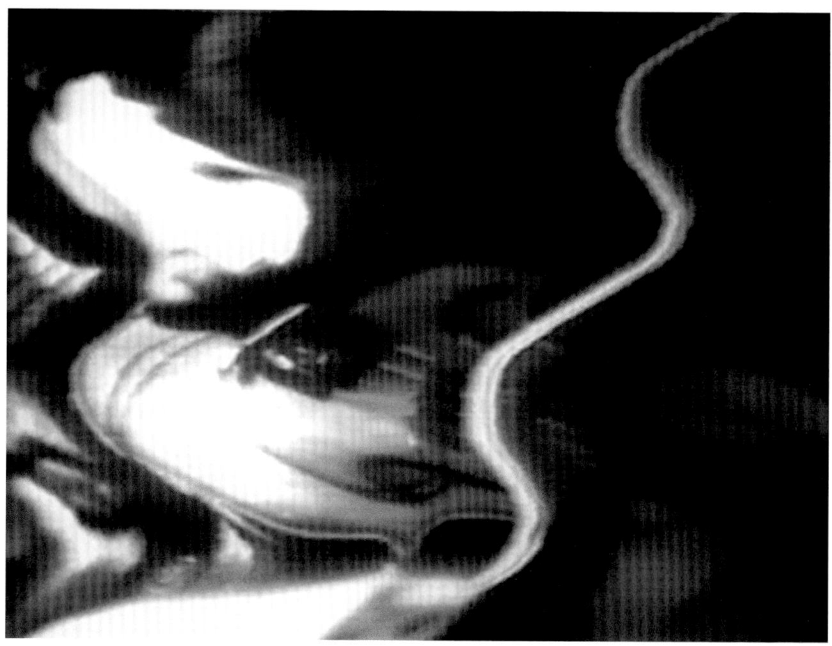

Steina Vasulka, *Violin Power*, 1970–78
Video, black and white, sound, 10 min. 04 sec.

"Let It Be" and played her customized violin, simultaneously generating abstract transpositions of sound and vibrations into live video. After that night, she often repeated the performance and eventually fashioned a multilayered, self-assured video likeness of herself that traces the chronological progression of her live action, *Violin Power* (1970–78). The videotape is a study of the relationship of music to the electronic image and comes close to capturing what I remember it felt like when she carried out the strange performance for the first time.

Steina's video career had begun when she used her first consumer video camera to capture the action downtown, including performances at the Fillmore East. The energy around the real-time light shows in the East Village—done low-tech with slides and mirrors—resembled the early days of video. She once noted:

We were interested in certain decadent aspects of America, the phenomena of the time—underground rock and roll, gay theater and the rest of that "illegitimate" culture. In the same way, we were

curious about more puritanical concepts of art inspired by [Marshall]
McLuhan and Buckminster Fuller. It seemed a strange and unified
front—against the establishment.[6]

Several years later, in 1973, the Broadway Central Hotel would collapse
and burn down. Fortunately, the Vasulkas had just turned their focus to their
own artwork, and their space, which everyone had come to call the Kitchen,
under Stearns's guidance moved a few blocks south to Wooster Street. The
enterprise grew to become a major nonprofit center presenting video,
music, dance, performance, film, and literature.[7]

In 1974 the Vasulkas moved to Buffalo, New York, invited by the media
scholar Gerald O'Grady, as faculty in the Department of Media Studies at
Buffalo State College, State University of New York. Woody turned his focus
more toward digital image manipulation, while Steina's practice centered
around environmental, mechanical, and physical relationships between body,
video, and camera. After they moved to Santa Fe, New Mexico, in 1980, both
of their work incorporated the sensual beauty of the surrounding desert
landscape. Artists from all over the world still make pilgrimages to meet
and learn from these dedicated video pioneers, who continue to work in
their studio filled with electronics to produce innovative installations and
videotapes that are collected and shown widely.

Peter Campus

Within the entrenched hierarchy of MoMA, I had learned straightaway that
the museum separated works strictly by medium—for example, separating
Richard Serra's sculpture, drawing, and film into distinct curatorial departments, with little dialogue about the entirety of his practice or his complex
personal networks, which included dancers, musicians, and experimental
filmmakers. I had seen enough by then to understand that it was more than
simply medium that connected artworks to one another. In the formidable ominous force of Serra's imposing metal sculpture, I saw a parallel
to the darkly foreboding early videotapes and closed-circuit interactive
installations of the pioneering video artist Peter Campus (b. 1937). *Double
Vision* (1971), a videotape Campus made with a pair of video cameras, by
superimposing two brooding images of himself, one over the other, had the
same dark severity as Serra's menacing steel sculpture *Equal (Corner Prop
Piece)* (1969–70), often on view in MoMA's collection galleries. Both of these
artists communicated the feeling of despair that permeated anti–Vietnam
War politics. Living downtown near one another, the two men had even
shared a black-and-white video camera with Joan Jonas in the late 1960s.

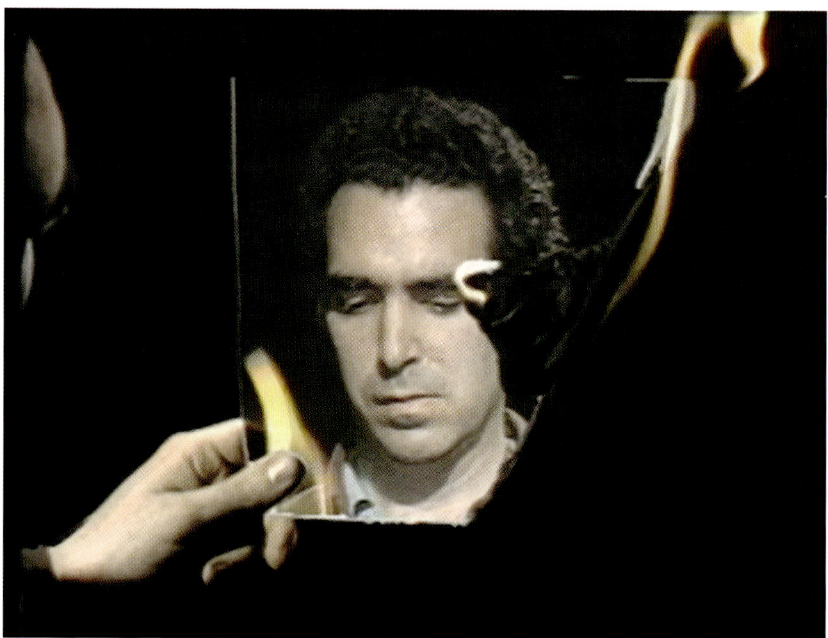

Peter Campus, *Three Transitions*, 1973
Video, color, sound, 4 min. 53 sec.

Each had used video to push his way clear of hidebound definitions of
what art is.

Campus was on my radar from the start, as a respected creator of
video and installations that revealed his conceptual and technical skills.
In time-based work produced up until around 1977—when for more than
a decade he abandoned video for photography—he explored issues of
spatial awareness and viewers' perception of their bodies in the construction
of identity. He was able to achieve this by using a consumer camera, early
video projectors, and live images. His installations offered individuals
peculiar and unsettling experiences—for example, a confrontation with
their double, which was separated from them in time and space and
challenged notions of the self.

Campus, who had a background in commercial film editing, would
become an artist in residence at the New Television Workshop at WGBH
in Boston, which supported the creation and broadcast of experimental
works by artists between 1974 and 1993. There he gained the respect of
studio engineers, who willingly contributed their expertise as he worked

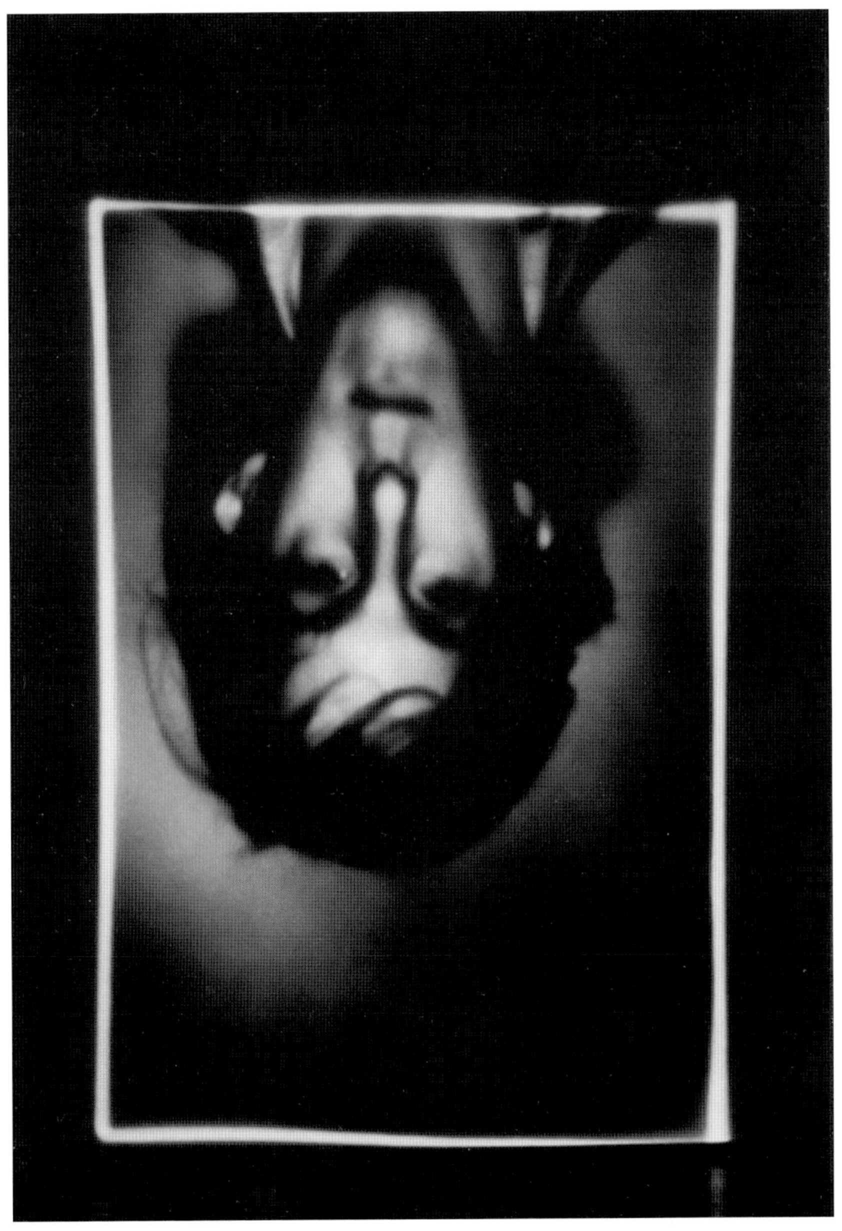

Peter Campus, *num*, 1976
Closed-circuit video installation, with surveillance video camera, video projector, and red light bulb

on *Three Transitions* (1973), a classic videotape that MoMA acquired. In the short piece, Campus repeatedly wipes out or annihilates an image of himself and replaces it with another, as if in a never-ending cycle of life, death, and rebirth. To create the work, Campus had experimented with chroma-key technology, which allowed him to superimpose images of himself, one image dissolving into the other. The result was that he appeared to be climbing through his own body—breaking through his own image.

One afternoon in 1975, I visited the Bykert Gallery on Manhattan's Upper East Side to see Campus's installation *aen* (1975), which consisted of an inconspicuously placed camera, a tiny light, and a then-hard-to-come-by video projector. Entering the space, I was startled to discover a somber upside-down live image of my own face cast directly on the gallery wall. The chiaroscuro appeared as stark, and the mood as brooding, as a Rembrandt portrait, but updated to a contemporary context.

I quickly brought *aen* into MoMA as a Projects exhibition. Its acquisition was delayed, due to a mandate that curators wait at least five years before proposing the acquisition of work by an emerging artist. The "wait and see" approach had been set by the founding director, Alfred H. Barr Jr., in order to keep a distance between the museum and the marketplace. By the time of our Campus acquisition in 1980, *aen* had been sold, so we purchased the comparable *num* (1976) from the same series.

We were working out many of the issues of equipment-dependent art. We acquired the rights to exhibit the unique installation, along with a floor plan and a detailed description of what the artist's concept and aesthetics for the installation were. It was understood, through an interview done at the time of the acquisition, that each time *num* would be exhibited, the gear most appropriate to the work would be chosen. Not being tied to a particular set of retro video equipment means that Campus's early tour de force is bound to a concept rather than to technology. This is a tactic similarly taken by other pioneering artists, such as Mary Lucier and Beryl Korot. There are exceptions who insist that original equipment be maintained, which means that in extreme cases conservators must work with TV repair specialists to handcraft obsolete parts. If equipment proves impossible to locate, a work's survival could be threatened.

Projekt '74, Cologne

Awarded travel monies from MoMA to make my first trip abroad to do field research, in July 1974 I flew to Cologne to see *Projekt '74*, an exhibition at the Kölnischer Kunstverein organized by director Wulf Herzogenrath, a leading expert on video art.[8] The night before the opening, I watched VALIE EXPORT[9]

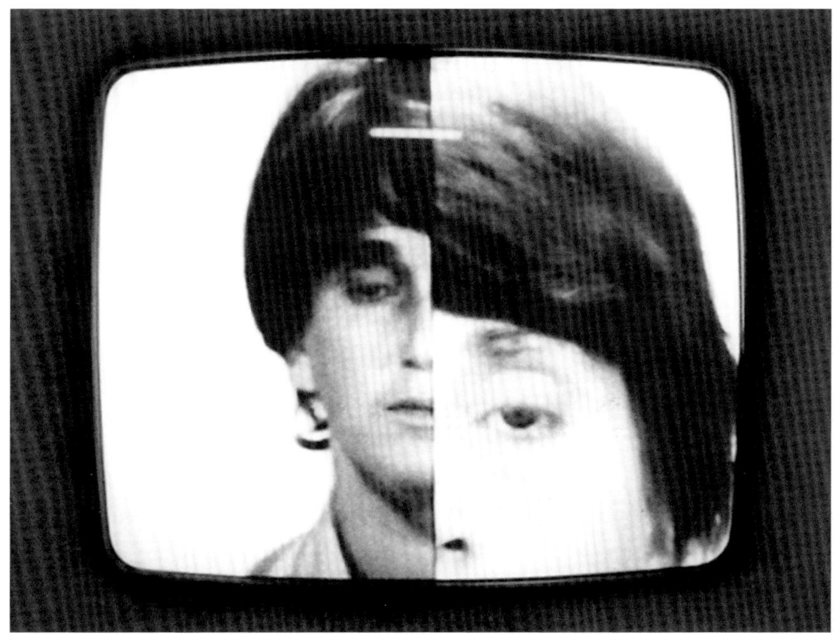

VALIE EXPORT, *Raumsehen und Raumhören* (Space Seeing–Space Hearing),
1973–74. Video, black and white, sound, 6 min. 19 sec.

(b. 1940)—the only woman among the early members of a subversive group
of artists known as the Vienna Actionists in the 1960s—create a cerebral
new work, *Raumsehen und Raumhören* (Space Seeing–Space Hearing) (1973–
74). She worked in a make-it-on-the-spot approach that was common then:
she had been invited to create her technically complex new project with
a three-person technical crew specially brought in with their equipment
from the video studio at the Lijnbaancentrum Rotterdam.[10] Given access to
a professional crew for a limited period, she meticulously planned the project
in advance and executed the production with extreme precision, standing
motionless in an empty gallery, determinedly facing four video cameras
arranged at different distances. I watched from the sidelines as live images
cycled onto a nearby monitor. The images followed a carefully scripted
sequence created through special switching and split-screen effects that
were synchronized with sound composed from four synthesizer tones.

VALIE EXPORT's impassive physical body offered a notable contrast
to her aggressively in-motion on-screen self. As she explained, the concept
and the intention behind her early experimental work—in both film and

video—was to decode how reality was manipulated in the moving-image reproduction processes.[11] Encountering her there in Cologne, I realized that she had well-defined theories and was tenacious about challenging ingrained ideas about perception and representation, and the limited standardized views of the natural and the artificial, especially technically derived images and uses of space.

At *Projekt '74*, I met a formidable group of local artists engaged with video and performance, including Ulrike Rosenbach (b. 1943), who carried out a performance, and Rebecca Horn (b. 1944), who showed me her video *Pencil Mask* (1973), in which she wore a mask made up of crisscrossing fabric straps. Where the straps intersected, a sharp pencil had been attached, so when she moved her face back and forth, the pencils marked the adjacent wall. Not being a purist, it did not matter to me that she recorded *Pencil Mask* in film, which she transferred to video, which I presented on a video monitor shortly afterward at MoMA.

Vito Acconci had flown over and created two works for the show: a sound installation, *Memory Box III (Vanishing Point)*, and a video called *Turn-On* in which he is seen in close-up confronting the viewer and is heard saying about his art, "I've been too abstract, now I can be concrete, no more galleries, no more museums." (He would later comment that his was the generation of artists who didn't travel packed with art to sell: "We were the ones who made things up on the spot, we did so-called performances and installations that were thrown away—out with the garbage—once we were through with them."[12])

Paik premiered his *TV Buddha* (1974) installation at the same exhibition. A sculpture of the Buddha sits in front of a video camera, which transmits the live image of the sculpture to what at the time was a futuristic-looking monitor. The sculpture of the Buddha gazes knowingly at his serene image on the screen, evoking an obvious question: What is the difference between the Buddha staring at a live (present time) image of himself and the Buddha confronted with a prerecorded representation? For a viewer studying the Buddha on the monitor, clearly there is no perceptible difference. As Buddhist philosophy teaches, time is an illusion; Western philosophers (from William James to Albert Einstein) express a similar idea when they say time is a human construct. The monitor is ordinary, while the sculpture of the Buddha is quite fine. Asia, in its timeless wisdom, appears adequate to the challenge of modern technology.

I showcased *TV Buddha* two years later in a Projects exhibition at MoMA. Paik's wife, Kubota, calibrated the ideal scale and perfect position of the pedestal, as she always did for installations of this work. When the show closed, I was sad to see the Stedelijk Museum in Amsterdam rather than

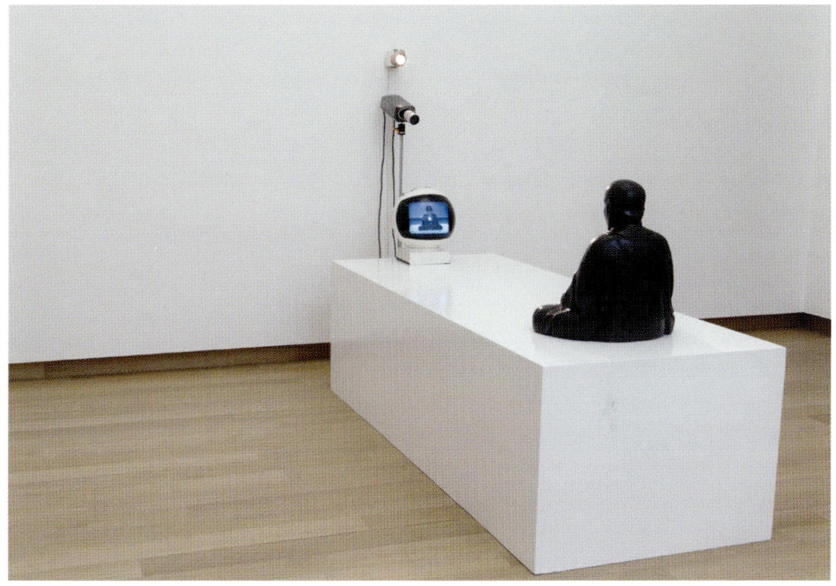

Nam June Paik, *TV Buddha*, 1974
Closed-circuit video installation, with eighteenth-century
Buddha statue

MoMA acquire the tour de force. MoMA would later deem video installation sculpture, but the Department of Painting and Sculpture was not quite ready to bend its hierarchical canon to the new temporal form's challenge to traditional definitions of static art.[13]

Video Art, ICA Philadelphia

Later that same year, a formal white-cube survey exhibition with the straightforward title *Video Art*, organized by Suzanne Delehanty, the superb scholar and director of Philadelphia's Institute of Contemporary Art, gave a serious overview of video activity and caught the attention of curators in the contemporary museum world. Herculean effort had gone into assembling six precisely conceived installations and seventy-six videotapes by artists from North and South America, Japan, and Europe. Delehanty's well-researched exhibition catalog became a programmer's guide. Until then, most video art exhibitions had been local in scope and modest in scale.

 Video Art marked the premiere of Paik's *TV Garden* (1974). I strolled along boardwalk-like pathways and gazed out over a bevy of belly-up monitors

nestled among sumptuously arranged potted plants. On one level, Paik's
monumental landscape reflected his Asian sensibility, which considers
natural and man-made materials as equal. Paik's cunning genius led him
to combine domesticated plants and ordinary television sets depicting
quickly edited, jazzy images and sounds he appropriated from his own
1973 tape *Global Groove*. He understood that a colorful spectacle with
upbeat sound would captivate viewers and hold them in his work. Paik's
art differs from fast-paced commercial programming, made with similar
tools and the same speedy rhythm, by the fact that his provocative insights
are waiting for you behind the entertaining facade.

In their installations, Peter Campus and Dan Graham each incorporated
a live camera, which came alive only when viewers entered and interacted
with their own images. Other works in the exhibition had a solemn tone.
The installation *Mar Mar March* (1972–73) by San Francisco–based Paul Kos
occupied a long room illuminated by one red light with two-by-four-inch
(5.1 x 10.2 cm) planks positioned horizontally across the floor. Like a military
corps, viewers stepped over the deliberately placed planks in a cadenced
pace. Advancing toward a monitor set on a pedestal at the far end of the
gallery, their footfalls mirrored the drumlike beat of typewriter keys that
over and over spelled out the words of Kos's title, shown on the lower half
of the monitor screen. The upper half depicted a woman walking back and
forth to the same beat.

The comprehensive videotape section of the show benefited from
the plugged-in video art community, which suggested titles to Delehanty.
This community was quickly becoming a catalyst for sharing information
and for broadening international exchange. One member was the Argentinian
Jorge Gluesberg, who had founded CAyC (Center for Art and Communication)
in his hometown, Buenos Aires, where he supported young local artists.
He proselytized about their work, some of which made it into *Video Art*.
Another was Walter Zanini, who traveled abroad and represented his
Museum of Contemporary Art at the University of São Paulo at international
meetings of museum directors even during Brazil's ruthless dictatorship.
After returning from Europe one time, he had portable video gear sent
to him via diplomatic pouch from Germany. He lent the gear to Anna Bella
Geiger, Sonia Andrade, and a few other artists, who were encouraged to
continue working with video.[14] The field operated seat-of-the-pants style
for a while.

In late 1975, *Video Art* traveled to the 1975 São Paulo Biennial, where
it boosted the resolve of local artists who felt hemmed in by an oppressive
government that considered the private ownership of a video camera
illegal. The few artists who managed to experiment were cut off from peers

facing similar political repression in nearby countries, which meant that video art evolved in Latin America with discrete national histories. Geiger and Andrade, for example, were unaware that Lotty Rosenfeld was making equally strong work in Santiago, Chile. Trying to understand, I learned that analysis of twentieth-century Latin American art had been bogged down by Latin American critics who were committed to a nationalist stance in the 1970s, rejecting what they saw as international trends that were preferred by Latin American elites who valued European art too much. The Argentinian critic Marta Traba was a central figure in these debates. A few believed that because electronic devices were imported from abroad, they were therefore suspect as art tools. Today a new generation of scholars is studying early video activity in Latin America and other parts of the world, while, fortunately, many of the overlooked pioneering artists are still alive.[15]

California

Interested in finding out more about what was going on in California, an area alien to me as a native New Yorker, in 1975 I stopped by Los Angeles–based Chris Burden's (1946–2015) *White Light/White Heat* show at Ronald Feldman's gallery on the Upper East Side. Burden was known for performance-based work in which the idea of personal danger was central to his artistic expression, such as *Shoot* (1971), in which he was shot in his left arm by an assistant from a distance of about sixteen feet (4.9 m) with a .22-caliber rifle. In the Feldman space, the artist lived for an entire week prone, high up on a ledge wedged into a corner of the gallery. Mystified by how he endured the ordeal, I understood that with his uncollectable action he was not only confronting real time but challenging the marketplace.

Burden kept tight control of his public image. Even as a student, he retained all rights to photographs and happenstance videos of his performances, which he regarded as part of his legacy. (In Burden's mind, a video document lamely divorced the viewer from the actual experience.) In 1973 he had paid for one week of a prime-time TV advertising slot and broadcast a ten-second clip of his performance *Through the Night Softly* (1973). Startled viewers saw him crawl bare-chested over fifty feet (15.2 m) of broken glass strewn across a busy Los Angeles street at night. Burden strategically used television to up his ante; 250,000 people a night saw Burden's disturbing and shocking video.

In 1975 Feldman's gallery released Burden's short "commercial" with several of the artist's other videos as a limited-edition videotape. This made Burden's video a multiple in the tradition of etchings and lithographs. But few museums or collectors were prepared to pay the high price.

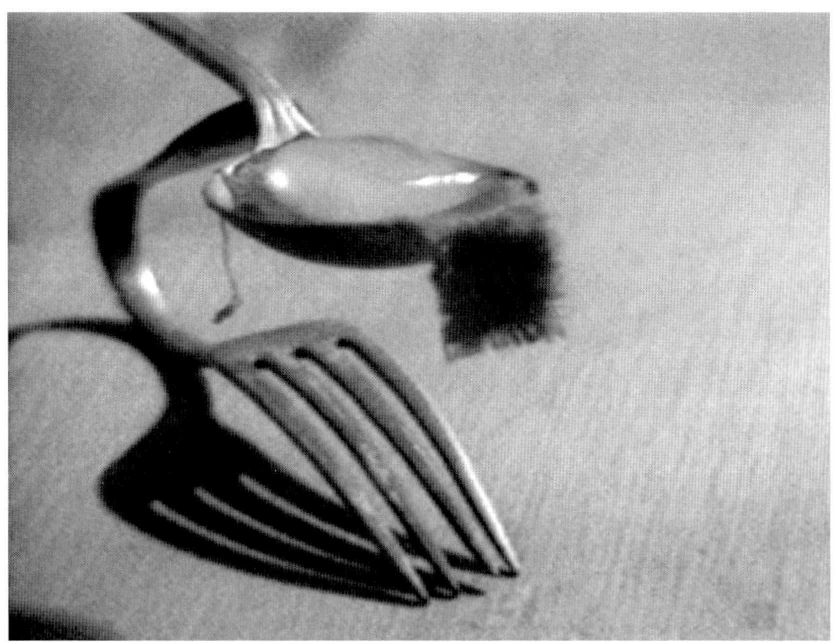

Terry Fox, *Children's Tapes*, 1974
Video, black and white, sound, 30 min.

Pushing the limits of the physical body cast Burden, Acconci, their New York–based colleague Dennis Oppenheim (1938–2011), and the Bay Area's Terry Fox into a grab-bag category that critics labeled *body art*. Developing their own singular aesthetics with distinct objectives, they were part of the vanguard of body artists using film and video in relation to performance and often were lumped together in biennial exhibitions. When I exhibited Fox's meditative *Children's Tapes* (1974) the year before, I'd smiled at how his actions reminded me of simple games played by resourceful children. Fox set in motion a series of chain-reaction home science experiments, which he slowly carried out with spoons and other ordinary household objects balanced on his kitchen table before a simple video camera.

Fox's work fit my clichéd view of East Coast–West Coast dichotomies. East Coast art was oriented toward European intellectualism, especially Paris-based Jacques Derrida and theories of structuralism. Helped by airfares' becoming cheaper and favorable exchange rates, artists who managed to cross the Atlantic for a gig could wander for months, connecting with Continental and British artists and absorbing European influences.

Greater Los Angeles artists had the vast desert nearby, Asia on the other side of the Pacific Rim, and feature-length Hollywood narratives. The University of California in Irvine and in San Diego had full-on video art and performance programs, which fostered collaboration and intermedia experimentation, but no access to broadcast-level equipment. To the north, the San Francisco Art Institute faculty and students included recalcitrant loners, like Fox, many with a Wild West pioneer spirit.

In March 1977, I flew out to the Bay Area and stopped by Fox's studio in a small, dilapidated artist-loft building in the Haight-Ashbury part of town. He showed me his sound installation *The Labyrinth Scored for the Purrs of Eleven Different Cats* (1977), derived from the maze on the floor of France's Chartres Cathedral. Rather than crawling devoutly on my knees as pilgrims once did, I moved among the speakers Fox had arranged on the floor to mirror the eleven rings of the Chartres design. A syncopated chorus of cat purrs filled the air. Our conversation turned to how sound and video have an intersecting lineage that entwines music and performance and installation. Fox's ideas complemented what Viola often said when we'd meet in New York, that at least 50 percent of video's impact comes from sound.

Walking down one flight in the same building, I met the reclusive artist Howard Fried (b. 1946). He showed me his *Fuck You Purdue* (1971) video, which was difficult to fathom. The long, grainy black-and-white tape managed to evoke the feel of a shouting match between two army sergeants (himself in both roles) barking out commands, which he patterned on his brother's military experience. I managed to deduce that the artist was giving me a peek into the dark depths of his troubled soul. When I exhibited Fried's video a few months later, journalists rushed over to MoMA. Reading his title in the press release, they assumed something salacious would be on view.

In her studio on the same floor, Fried's neighbor Judith Barry (b. 1954) showed me her performance-slide installation *Cup/Couch* (1977). Barry belonged to the uncompromising second generation of important California feminists that included video and performance artists Nancy Buchanan (b. 1946), Suzanne Lacy (b. 1945), Barbara T. Smith (b. 1931), Martha Rosler, Linda Montano (b. 1942), and Lynn Hershman (b. 1941), whose work I soon incorporated into MoMA's ongoing video exhibition series.[16] From a vantage point on the East Coast, I saw how these Californians were often overlooked by the male curators of documenta and other European surveys. The women were cogent innovators, and it took a good decade before their practices were seen as being central to the canon of video and performance art, the equal of Paul McCarthy, an artist who has always supported the work of women.

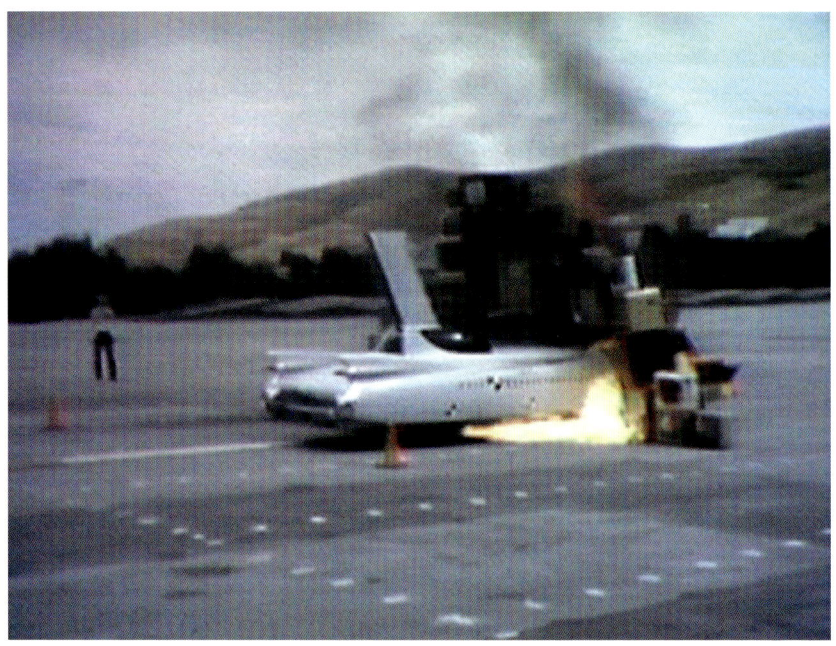

Ant Farm, *Media Burn*, 1975
Video, color, sound, 23 min. 02 sec.

On a scruffy pier out on the Embarcadero, I visited the Ant Farm
group's studio. The Ant Farm "commune" of three counterculture architects
straight out of school had crisscrossed North America in a van. Wherever
they stopped, they'd pitched a Buckminster Fuller geodesic dome tent and
proselytized about their ecology-minded design work. Unlike artists who
disdained television, Ant Farm cheekily engaged in corporate and mass-
media criticism. Their project *Media Burn* (1975) integrated performance,
spectacle, and media critique. Planning began with a well-written and crazily
designed press release that stirred up considerable interest, especially
among news media. Ant Farm's carefully staged event revolved around
an explosive collision of two of America's powerful cultural symbols—the
automobile and television—on July 4, 1975, at San Francisco's Cow Palace.
Ant Farm defined their action as the "ultimate media event."[17] A John F.
Kennedy look-alike delivered a short speech that set the project in motion.
In this alternative Bicentennial celebration, Ant Farm's "Phantom Dream
Car"—a reconstructed 1959 El Dorado Cadillac convertible—was driven
through a wall of burning TV sets. Afterward the group deftly incorporated

the "conned" television evening news coverage of the event with their own footage into what is now considered a classic tape.[18]

Returning home to New York, I acknowledged that my viewpoint was Manhattan, upstate New York, and further along the East Coast. California, with its deserts and earthquakes and Hollywood, would always seem to be a world apart. To jump over this hurdle of provincialism, I maintained an open-door policy, committed to grabbing a coffee with artists and colleagues, eager to know about video goings-on beyond my doorstep.

documenta 6

In June 1977, I flew to Kassel, Germany, for the opening of documenta, an expansive international contemporary art survey that happens more or less every five years, curated this time by Manfred Schneckenburger. The art world eagerly anticipates each documenta. Since the launch in 1955, the shows have redefined what art is considered to be, traced art's political, social, cultural, and aesthetic functions, and more recently examined migration, urbanization, and the postcolonial experience.

documenta 6 took a bold step by presenting each medium separately in extensive sections. Painting and sculpture had their own buildings, and photography covered half a floor. Film had its own large theater, while video and performance art occupied separate sprawling spaces. Rarely, if ever, had an overarching international exhibition given so much attention to alternative art forms before.[19]

The film section included a historical survey that went all the way from Sergei Eisenstein (1898–1948) up to recent work by Jean-Luc Godard (b. 1930) and Agnès Varda (1928–2019). The experimental program featured many short films by Lodz-based Polish artist Jozef Robakowski (b. 1939) and other Communist-bloc, state-sponsored artists working in 35 mm film. No artist in North America could afford this expensive Hollywood format. Unlike the videos and Super 8 films I had been seeing in New York, which often had rough edges, the films from the Lodz Film School, one of the oldest film schools in the world, exuded a professional quality. Still, they addressed issues that paralleled the concerns of other cutting-edge experimental filmmakers in the show, such as Anthony McCall (b. 1946), Ken Jacobs (b. 1933), and Michael Snow, structuralists who pursued a simpli-fied, sometimes even predetermined work. For them the structure of the film was crucial, the content peripheral.

documenta 6 treated video as a full-fledged art form. Wulf Herzogenrath organized the video section and showcased the installations of Acconci, Campus, Graham, Viola, and Muntadas. Nearby, the on-demand video library was a perpetual madhouse. People milled around, queued, and pushed their way into booths, eager to see the fifty international works that could be selected from the on-demand archive. documenta 6 took another major step by featuring a live satellite telecast of artists' work: performances by Paik with Charlotte Moorman (1933–1991), Joseph Beuys, and Douglas Davis were transmitted to over twenty-five countries. The exhibition helped put video art on the global map.

Post–documenta 6, video art began cropping up in other museum survey and biennial shows. Video had mostly been given a bad rap before then. Contemporary curators and critics often complained bitterly that a video installation's sound seeped into adjacent spaces and destroyed their experience of seeing a painting or sculpture. They hardly ever set foot in a dark, little-black-box video screening room with its poorly installed and crude-seeming display equipment.

Critics gradually acknowledged that my fellow media curators—Christine Van Assche at the Centre Pompidou's Musée National d'Art Moderne, Dorine Mignot at the Stedelijk Museum Amsterdam, John Hanhardt at the Whitney Museum of American Art, David Ross followed by Kathy Rae Huffman at the Long Beach Museum of Art—and I by now had considerable experience and solutions to some of their practical concerns. We learned how to instruct exhibition designers to build entrances that zigzagged to function as sound and light traps. We insisted on galleries built with a sandwich of double walls so that sound-absorbing materials could be packed inside. Video projectors were dropping in price and provided more luminous and sharper images cast onto gallery walls. We were on the verge of a big boom in video as art.

Multimedia:
Video, Performance, and Music

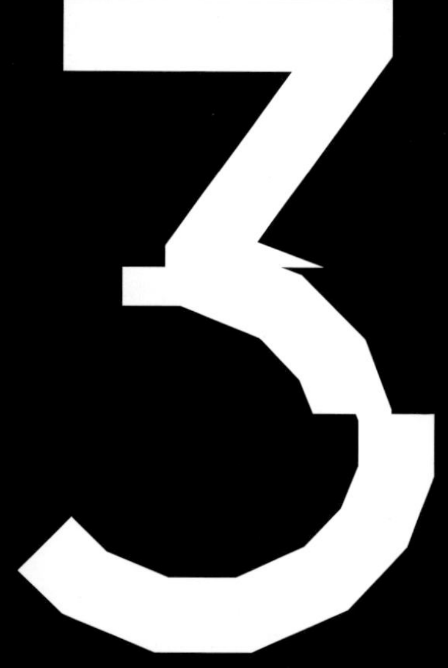

Artists' ambitions and their interconnectedness had far-reaching consequences throughout the 1970s. Adapting the now friendlier consumer tools
to single-channel tapes, performances, and installations, artists collaborated,
and crossovers multiplied exponentially. The dynamic cross-fertilization that
occurred between video, performance, and music was labeled *multimedia*.
I appreciated the diversity, especially the growing alliance between the areas
of video and music. Given that a video artwork is based equally on image and
sound, I followed how visual artists were engaging with music. Some found
the experimental-music scene more conducive to their iconoclastic ideas
than the handful of contemporary art galleries. After studying painting in art
school, Ana da Silva (b. 1948) and Gina Birch (b. 1955) in London and James
Nares (b. 1953) and Kim Gordon (b. 1953) in New York all formed noise bands,
initially performing in clubs where nonconformists gravitated, or in alternative spaces that were becoming professionalized and run by administrators.
The artist-musicians Laurie Anderson (b. 1947) and the Bay Area group the
Residents were among the first to make innovative music videos, before tran-
sitioning to interactive CD-ROMs.

Around 1976 I caught up with the American composer and visual artist
Arnold Dreyblatt (b. 1953), then the young assistant of Shigeko Kubota and
Nam June Paik. An impoverished multimedia artist and good friend of Bill
Viola and other interdisciplinary artists, Dreyblatt lived rent-free in the
attic of a big abandoned house (later torn down to make room for the South
Street Seaport complex), poaching electricity from a nearby streetlamp.
He was combining time-based installation art and music. At Buffalo State
College, State University of New York, his unconventional composition and
media studies professors had included experimental film and video makers
Woody and Steina Vasulka, Hollis Frampton, and Paul Sharits (1943–1993),
and electronic composers Pauline Oliveros (1932–2016), Morton Feldman
(1926–1987), and La Monte Young (b. 1935); at Wesleyan, he later studied
with experimental-music composer Alvin Lucier (b. 1931).

I kept my eyes on Glenn O'Brien, an adroit cultural insider whom Andy
Warhol had plucked out of Columbia University in the early 1970s to become
editor of *Interview* magazine, the crystal ball of pop culture, which featured
intimate conversations between celebrities, artists, musicians, and creative
thinkers. When he became *Interview*'s music critic, I would read his column
"Glenn O'Brien's Beat" and be sure to see the punk band performances,
graffiti artist shows, and work of other denizens rocking the underground
that he suggested. Making it past Tina L'Hotsky, the downtown "it girl"
and doyenne guarding the entrance to the Mudd Club, I'd dance under the
flashing lights until dawn like a sweaty maniac to the music of early DJ
turntablists Johnny Dynell and graffiti artist Fred Brathwaite (b. 1959, a.k.a.

Fab 5 Freddy). While there I would catch news flashes from Diego Cortez, a former guard at MoMA and an omniscient artist-curator who went on to organize the *New York/New Wave* show at MoMA PS1 in 1981.

O'Brien hosted his *Glenn O'Brien's TV Party* program on public access cable between 1978 and 1982, with filmmaker Amos Poe (b. 1949) as director. Guests on the show included musicians Mick Jones (b. 1955); David Byrne (b. 1952); Debbie Harry (b. 1945) and other members of the band Blondie; James Chance (b. 1953); performance artist Klaus Nomi (1944–1983); and the up-and-coming painter Jean-Michel Basquiat (1960–1988). Public access—a free-speech forum open to all on a first-come, first-served basis—was created in the 1970s as a means to derive public benefit from the laying of cables by private television companies on public land. It became a claimable venue for media experiments and cultural debates in the United States.

In London, correspondingly vociferous debates raged around the topic of access within the community video movement that had begun in the 1970s. Around this time, David Attenborough, director of programming for the British Broadcasting Corporation, summed it up when he wrote the following to the BBC's board of management:

> "Access" or "community" programmes, which are spoken of so frequently in the current debates about broadcasting, are taken to be programmes which are made by viewers who have applied for airtime, and for which professional broadcasters supply the technical facilities necessary for production and transmission, but play only a minimal part in editorial decisions. Two of the elements that such programmes can bring to a network are believed to be—(i) voices, attitudes and opinions, that, for one reason or another have been unheard or seriously neglected by mainstream programmes;—(ii) stylistic innovations, new ways of handling film or videotape which professional broadcasters have either ignored or rejected; new editorial attitudes that do not derive from the assumptions of the university educated elite who are commonly believed to dominate television production.[1]

With the rising tide of video, artists pursued all sorts of outlets. In 1978 artists were opening their own nightclubs; by 1982 they were launching galleries. New York, London, Berlin, and Tokyo, among other cities, proved to be incubators and facilitators of a few multimedia artists' successful trajectories.

At MoMA I found support in Riva Castleman, the curator of prints and illustrated books. She had backed my launching MoMA's artists' books collection—my first major endeavor as a curator there, prior to video— and recognized that the makers of inexpensive offset artists' books had motivations similar to those of video artists; both wanted their idea-driven work to reach interested audiences, outside of the art market. Castleman knew that a fledgling contemporary medium needed administrative support in order to thrive. Around 1976 she helped convince Director Richard Oldenburg to increase the small operating budget and give the video exhibition program a boost with additional funding for shows.

I worked to cultivate a reputable position for myself within the organization. I spent my lunch hours following in the footsteps of the more established curators by frequenting the same powerful 57th Street galleries they went to—Sidney Janis, Tibor de Nagy, Pace, Light Gallery, Blum Helman, and Marian Goodman—as well as visiting Holly Solomon in SoHo, hoping to make contacts upon whom I could eventually draw for professional advice as I contextualized video and navigated my complex organizational system.

My network was also expanding beyond Manhattan, as I connected with artists coming through town from abroad and across the country. My mornings at MoMA began to feel like Christmas, as growing stacks of incoming mail landed on my desk. Tearing open envelopes, I'd pull out artist-designed posters, fliers, and postcards exuding the same energy as the unruly events they announced. Then I'd cross-reference the fliers' mishmash of information with the growing coverage in alternative periodicals—the *Village Voice*, *SoHo Weekly News*, and *East Village Eye*. But even all the listings and reviews that I read highlighted only a fraction of what was going on. After the formation of PASTA-MoMA, the museum's white-collar union, and its first contract in 1974, the museum granted junior curators one afternoon a week to see gallery and museum shows or make studio visits. I was spending even more time than before tracking screenings, exhibitions, and performances.

I had started to save every shred of paper sent by artists, believing that these disparate documents would be essential for later research, since at that time there were so few catalogs. Friends teaching in the art departments at Berlin's Free University and New York's Bard College, Hunter College, and Columbia University recommended their best students for internships, and each semester I invited one of them to work with me. Their main task was to file the accumulating documentary material in a system arranged either by artist or by organization. After several years, by about 1981, the file drawers in my office—which by then had moved from a temporary space that had been the old paper conservation lab to the Film Department—had expanded from four to over forty, and presto, we had a small Video Study Center that was modeled upon the one for film study. Now as part of the Film Department, I made the ephemera available by appointment to graduate students and scholars who were researching video art. By the time we moved our files over to MoMA's library in 1998, their contents were considered primary reference materials.

During that first decade after the introduction of the video exhibition program, every year I organized roughly five shows based on themes derived from research and travel. California was one subject, as I investigated the differences between the work of Los Angeles and San Francisco video makers and their counterparts on the East Coast. For another show, I looked at video produced in Vancouver at Western Front, the artist-run center founded in 1973 that has consistently promoted critical investigations into interdisciplinary, media-based, antiobject, and ephemeral practices. Meanwhile, I was paying attention to documentary video, and I programmed the 1977 low-budget feature-length video *The Police Tapes*, by Alan and Susan Raymond (b. 1943 and 1945), about a New York police precinct in the South Bronx. Produced for and aired on public television, the startlingly graphic work is a survey of urban crime, violence, brutality, and cynical despair. The Raymonds' video vérité methodology is based on intimacy, accuracy, and complexity, which had an impact on the mainstream—in particular, the 1981 feature film *Fort Apache, The Bronx*, directed by Daniel Petrie (1920–2004).

Each show I organized was a spartan operation, based on compilation three-quarter-inch (1.9 cm) cassettes. Selected video works were carefully assembled one after the other in a certain order, copied from the artists' submasters at a postproduction house. (For *The Police Tapes*, we used the newly available ninety-minute cassette.) This meant that the MoMA film projectionists were able to run the program nonstop each day, by simply turning on and off the playback deck, which conveniently had an automatic rewind button. During the day, if a deck jammed and destroyed a cassette, the exhibition drew to a halt, and the public complained until the projectionist arrived with a backup cassette.

One morning in the mid-1970s, the tech-savvy, Chicago-based artist Dan Sandin (b. 1942) stopped by to show me his analog computer graphics. He appeared in my office wearing his beanie cap with a propeller on top. Before his show-and-tell, we sat on the floor of the video gallery—then just off the main lobby—as he very kindly took apart our workhorse cassette deck and solved a technical problem that had been plaguing me.

From the beginning my role as video curator included educating the public about the video art on view. Program notes were placed by the gallery entrance. Even if 95 percent of the notes ended up in the trash, I believed the other 5 percent would be taken home and read. I also felt that if viewers stayed in the video gallery even for a nanosecond, that experience would provide a context for the next video art they saw. The process of developing an audience moved slowly. Children who grew up with *Sesame Street* and weekend cartoon programs would enter the video gallery and comfortably hunker down in front of the screens, while adults often stood perplexed by art made with television technology.

Joan Jonas

During the 1970s, video and performance frequently melded together, with experimentation the norm. One of the most important female artists to emerge from this early phase in the late 1960s and early 1970s is Joan Jonas, who pursued performance and rehearsed short actions at home in front of her then partner, Richard Serra. She became engaged with a loosely connected, small but increasingly influential downtown underground art scene that included artists Robert Smithson and Nancy Holt, and the writer Spalding Gray (1941–2004) and his colleagues in the experimental theater collective the Wooster Group, which often gave Jonas a role in their plays.

Over the course of a long and productive career with video and performance, Jonas has often collaborated with poets, experimental theater directors, musicians, and fellow visual artists, their innovative practices influencing each other. Jonas, like me, was born under the zodiac sign of Cancer. Once we met, I identified with her tenaciousness, imagination, and loyalty as a sympathetic friend. I learned that over the years she found inspiration in many areas—film history, visual art, literature, and dance. She honed her technical skills by watching the work of film innovators, from Warhol to pioneers Dziga Vertov (1896–1954), Jean Vigo (1905–1934), Georges Franju (1912–1987), Sergei Eisenstein (1898–1948), and Yasujirō Ozu (1903–1963). With a BA in art history from Mount Holyoke College, she received an MFA from Columbia University in sculpture, with studies in modern poetry. One of her close friends from that time is the noted American poet Susan Howe.

I often saw Jonas, a shy, aloof figure, in Washington Square Park wearing chic thrift store finds as she walked her equally self-contained dog, Sappho. Occasionally, we met over a bowl of soup in SoHo at the laid-back restaurant, simply called Food, cofounded by her friend Gordon Matta-Clark (1943–1978), an American artist whose site-specific work critiqued architecture's role vis-à-vis the capitalist system. We would also run into each other at the same visual art, dance, and experimental theater events.

While I was trying to better understand cross-disciplinary collaborations and define video's impact on other art forms, Jonas, who was very loyal to her peers, was keeping an eye on what they were up to. She explained to me that in the early 1970s, the downtown dance community consisted largely of supportive female artists, while the painting, sculpture, and writing scenes were dominated by male practitioners. She was slowly developing her own intuitive technique, emboldened by the performances of the dancers at the Judson Church, who explored everyday movement in a John Cagean way. Although I had often found the Judson work too starkly minimal and dryly cerebral for my taste, Jonas's poetic work, in which she entwined movement with enigmatic props, enchanted me and drew me in.

For years Jonas and her peers found inspiration in Asian art and philosophy. She and Serra made a trip together to Japan in 1970, when his work was part of *Between Man and Matter*, the tenth Tokyo Biennale.[2] Jonas and Serra were both inspired by Noh theater. With its protracted movement, Noh unfolds in chapters that stretch from morning to night. Time becomes a malleable material punctuated by the spare sounds of guttural cries, plucked strings, and nasal-sounding wind instruments, and the clack of wood blocks smacked together. To their Western eyes, this must-see classical form of drama seemed the embodiment of a pure Japan, a sharp contrast to the garish advertising signs plastered all around them in Tokyo.

Jonas responded to Noh, interested in the elongated sense of time and its use of masks with frozen facial gestures identifying the iconic characters. At this point she knew that Serra's assertive Minimalism was not her cup of tea. Mythic tales with strong female characters and expressive masks held more appeal. Her experience in Japan of drawn-out time reinforced her affinity back home with the midnight events of underground cinema and performance pioneer Jack Smith (1932–1989). In his downtown loft, viewers watched Smith mill around, hand out joints, and assemble a costume from clothes piled up on the floor, assuming different flamboyant personas. No one could quite distinguish between his life and his art during those pro-tracted evenings. The time-based works by Smith, and similarly by others, were excruciatingly long; it was not uncommon for attendees to doze off during them or for just one or two people to be left by the end.

One evening around 1970, I climbed a splintery set of stairs and emerged to find Jonas and a group of collaborators holding full-length mirrors, moving slowly as if in partnership with their images on the luminous surfaces. When torqued, the mirrors became deep volumetric spaces with reflections of the audience captured inside. Jonas was honing her looking-glass tactics, her examination of the process, politics, and psychology of spectatorship. She was playing with the feeling that we, as women, have of not wanting others to catch us looking at ourselves. This is the taboo of the mirror.

> I brought to performance my experience of looking at the illusionistic space of painting and of walking around sculptures and architectural spaces. I was barely in my early performance pieces; I was in them like a piece of material or an object that moved very stiffly, like a puppet or a figure in a medieval painting. I didn't exist as Joan Jonas, as an individual "I," only as a presence, part of the picture. I moved rather mechanically. In the mirror costumes in *Wind* [her first film, of 1968] and *Oad Lau* [her first "action"], we walked very softly with our arms at our sides as in a ritual. We moved across the space, in the background, from side to side. When I was in other "Mirror Pieces" a little later, I just lay on the floor and I was carried around like a piece of glass.[3]

I learned Jonas was inspired by Jorge Luis Borges, an Argentinian writer who mentions mirrors in his book *Labyrinths*. She adopted the mirror as her first prop, and that would lead to the video monitor, an ongoing mirror. Jonas began adapting her interests in drawing and the sculptural object from graduate school studies to the possibilities of mixing sound, movement, and image, combining the different elements to make a complex statement.[4] She called these early works "events" or "actions," ten years before the label *performance* emerged.

During the 1970s, Jonas forged a unique path for herself by melding live video with performance—both of which are mutable, intangible (non-object-based) art forms that occur fleetingly in the present moment. Back then she was quietly experimenting with a black-and-white portable video camera. Alone in her loft, Jonas closely studied her actions as live images framed by the monitor. But her results went deeper than Narcissus. In confronting her identity, she appeared to burrow down into her soul, in search of the ineffable.

Video gave her the means to observe her live self on-screen, as she composed an action. If satisfied, she would hit the record button. Rewinding the just-recorded tape, she might replay it over and over to study, or she could straightaway redo or revise the composition she had set within video's shallow depth of field. Her pleasure in repetition had to do with refining a movement to the point where it became internalized, even automatic, much like a musician, dancer, or actor.

A good example of how she developed her work is the performance series *Organic Honey*, a magnum opus in which she dislocates space and fractures the image. In 1972 she established the video part of the performance at 112 Greene Street, where her friend, the artist Sol LeWitt (1928–2009), brought his students from the School of Visual Arts to be her audience. Shortly after, she carried out a fully developed performance of the work at LoGiudice Gallery in SoHo, where she presented the set and props, before taking the performance to Ace Gallery in Los Angeles.

In 1973 Leo Castelli invited her to perform *Organic Honey's Vertical Roll* at his SoHo gallery, which is where I first encountered the piece. I sat on the floor with Carlotta Schoolman, a mutual friend and early producer of Jonas's inspired 1971 videotape *Anxious Automation*, which Jonas based on an action made with Serra, recorded with two quickly alternating cameras at Automation House. We were surrounded by Jonas's downtown community of painters, sculptors, dancers, actors, musicians, and conceptualists.

Jonas had loosely carved out a performance space within the gallery, indicated by the family treasures she'd lugged over from her loft. In the center, she placed a small table on which she arranged a series of simple objects, including a big glass jar filled with water, a small shot glass, mirrors, a silver spoon, an old doll, a silver purse, and pebbles. She made two large mirror-image drawings of her dog, Sappho, and tacked them on a wall. The rather spare assemblage resembled a film set rather than a carefully realized installation.

Consumer video equipment was still crude at the time, with negligible editing and no razzle-dazzle special effects. The most Jonas could do that night was work with a second black-and-white camera and a switcher, which allowed her to alternate between live images of two adjacent spaces, as well as prerecorded video. This created a sense of ambiguity around the space within and around the monitor. Through switching she exploited what I call the "unedited present" by depicting different views of the same action as it unfolded.

Although diffident and ill at ease, Jonas, who had never had formal theater training, appeared cool and collected during the performance. Wearing the mask of a doll's face frozen in an enigmatic smile, inspired by the Noh theater she had seen in Tokyo, she transformed herself into an electronic seductress, identifying this new self as Organic Honey, a name taken from a jar on her breakfast table. As Organic Honey, Jonas put on a satin kimono and sashayed before changing into a shiny, revealing outfit and pivoting sensually like a belly dancer.

I watched her move ceremoniously and deliberately within the delineated area. Working in the round, she pursued several points of view

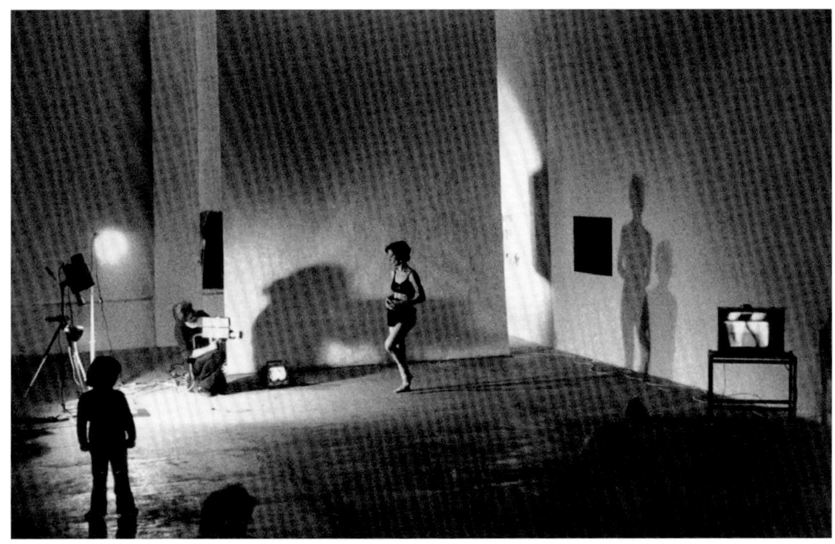

Joan Jonas, *Organic Honey's Vertical Roll*, 1972
Performance at Galleria Toselli, Milan, 1973

by incorporating live video with her actions. Her camerawoman was Babette
Mangolte (b. 1941), a French-American cinematographer and director who
made films of and collaborated with dancers and performance artists, such
as Jonas. Mangolte meticulously followed Jonas's rehearsed movements in
close-up. This meant that in addition to being physically present as she moved
before my eyes, Jonas simultaneously appeared on a monitor and in a large
projection on an adjacent wall. Meanwhile, she was able to track her actions
by keeping an eye on a tiny monitor placed inconspicuously within the set.

Fearless, Jonas was up to any task required to carry out her concept.
She had devised a beguiling soundtrack based on snippets of her hummed
words, taped music, and smacked-together blocks of wood. She excelled
as set designer, director, actor, and composer rolled into one. She had caught
the attention of a renowned Swiss art historian and curator of ground-
breaking exhibitions, Harald Szeemann, who had invited her to perform at
documenta 5, in 1972. This was the heyday of young American artists exhibiting abroad, when European compatriots thought they were primitives.
Jonas noted, "That was the advantage of being American; we were fresh,
and the language was fresh."[5]

Jonas and her artist friends were recognized in Europe before gaining
recognition at home. Some of the first public events she did were in Rome,

where she had both an audience and support. Unlike New York, where she and her peers often put on their own events, in Europe they had fiscal sponsorship, largely through civic arts festivals and exhibitions that offered production fees and honoraria.

It was impossible to grasp the myriad details of Jonas's carefully orchestrated compositions. I associated her simultaneous portrayals of time and space with Picasso's Cubist paintings, in which objects are so fragmented that their three-dimensionality is rendered as facets splayed all at once over the surface of the canvas.

Alternating between videotape and video performance, Jonas translated ideas from performance into tapes and back again. *Vertical Roll* (1972) is one of two single-channel videos that grew out of her performance as Organic Honey. The structure of the well-choreographed work is based on an irritating flaw common to early black-and-white TV sets, where the television image would scroll nonstop from the bottom to the top of the screen, stabilized only by a turn of the vertical hold knob until the dreaded roll would edge upward again. This early distortion—the vertical roll—was lost with the advent of digital television technology.

Vertical Roll was scaled to the boxy, terrarium-like monitor common at the time, which established a one-on-one, intimate relationship with its viewers. Jonas had positioned parts of her body close to the camera, the viewer's vantage point. The video opens with her outstretched hand. As the upwardly rolling image reaches the top of the screen, her hand gives a flip, and there is the illusion of a percussive smack, with sound and image perfectly in sync. Her hand quickly lands back at the bottom of the frame, and the process repeats over and over for several minutes.

In the video, with her torso gyrating as the tape rolls, Jonas becomes a fascinating and mysterious seductress circumscribed within a shallow space. Never revealing her full figure, she moves away and into a separate space as her legs are shown jumping up and down. Enticingly, she then gazes out from behind her mask, moving within and out of the restricted space.

Never stymied by the limitations of early consumer video and its imprecise editing capabilities, she made the nineteen-minute video in one nonstop take, a complex feat of orchestration with two cameras, carried out through teamwork with her assistant-friends. Even more surprising, she recorded the entire video with one camera directed at the monitor. This fact only becomes clear in the tape's concluding few seconds, when, mysteriously appearing in front of the rolling screen, she looks out and confronts us, her viewers. This enigmatic and complex tour de force reveals her mastery of her primary tools, the portable video camera and the monitor, her living mirror.

I was eager to see what Jonas would do next. I knew that Jonas Mekas had offered her the theater at Anthology Film Archives, just a block from her home, during off-hours so she would have ample time and space and feel unconstrained in developing a new performance. One June evening in 1975, I caught Jonas's new work at Anthology. Grabbing my seat as *Twilight* was starting, I noticed that she had redefined the familiar space by arranging monitors along the theater's periphery. The monitor screens became light sources in the bare-bones theater. I watched her move about in physical form, while appearing in live video and prerecordings of herself on the monitors. This time she was working with assistants who used cameras to expose concealed areas, such as the usually hidden spaces behind the film projection screen and behind her monitors. By doing so, she created the illusion of transparency.

Moving slowly, with resolve, Jonas "played" the large projection screen as if it were a musical instrument. She worked the mechanism to make the white projection screen very tall or very wide, expanding and contracting her big creaking prop and changing the screen's orientation from horizontal to vertical. When she disappeared behind it, the screen became a scrim cast with her movement in silhouette. At other times, she stood in front of the now opaque screen, bathed in the spotlight of projected white light.

That night she shattered my sense of propriety, when she suddenly emerged from behind the screen without any clothes on. Holding a small mirror, she impassively proceeded to meticulously scrutinize every inch of her naked body; bending down and around, she coolly studied the tiny image of a breast or pudendum in the mirror. This was the boldly transgressive act she had first carried out in her 1970 performance *Mirror Check*. But in 1975, it was still a shockingly brazen act for a woman to examine herself naked in public, especially with a mirror, even though the Living Theatre had been challenging the boundaries of public decorum since the 1960s, as had artists Barbara T. Smith, Carolee Schneemann (1939–2019), and VALIE EXPORT. Feminism, however, did not appear to be Jonas's motivation. Her performance was rather a consequence of the attitudes of the time and her own contemplation of what it means to be female.

I considered Jonas an enigmatic performer, an elusive guide through her Gesamtkunstwerk, her total synthesis of visual art and the performing arts in the tradition of nineteenth-century opera composer Richard Wagner and early twentieth-century Bauhaus school founder Walter Gropius. The latter believed that artists (and architects) should have experience working with different materials and mediums, including theater and music. This defines Jonas's approach perfectly.

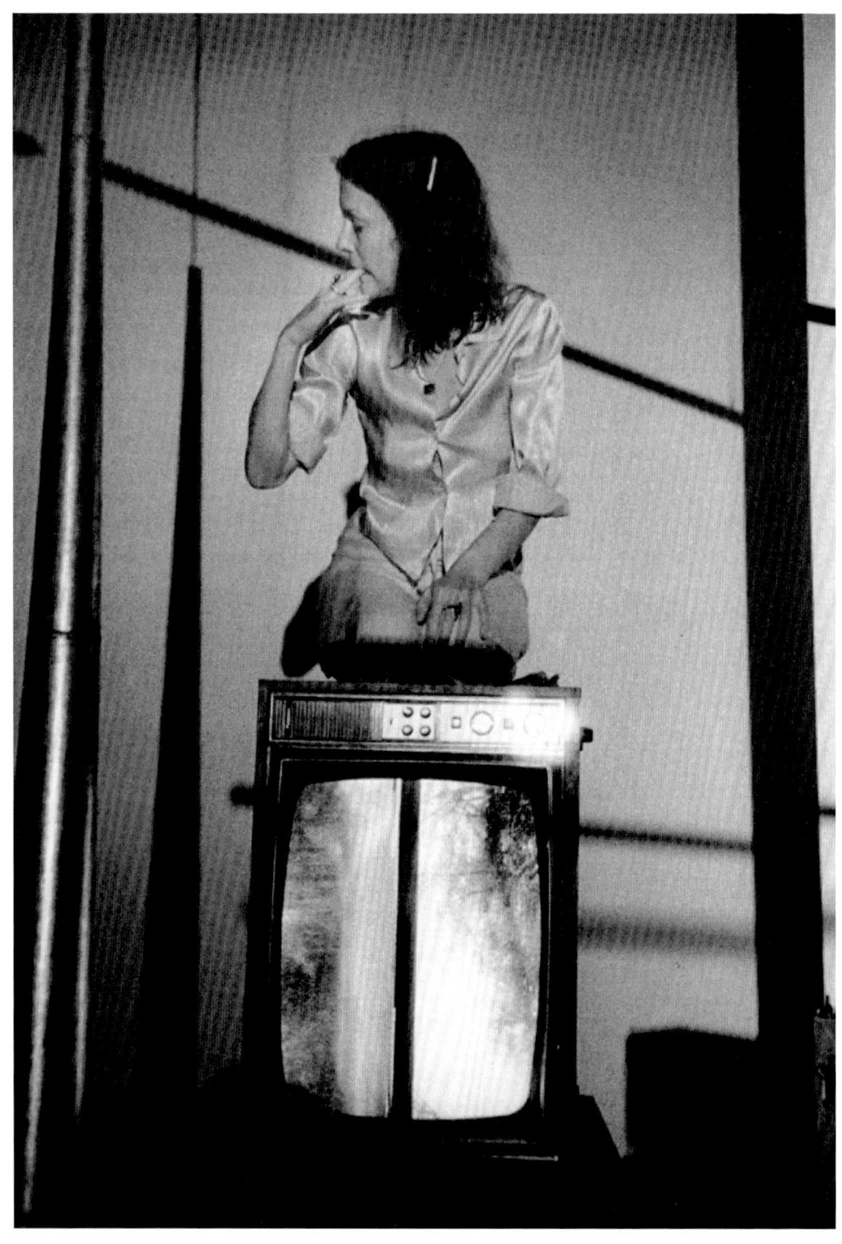

Joan Jonas, *Mirage*, 1976
Performance at the Institute of Contemporary Art, Philadelphia, 1976

In 1976 *Twilight* progressed and became *Mirage*, which Jonas again presented at Anthology. The work turned out to be Jonas's last performance that dealt with simultaneity. Again, there was her real, physical self in action, and videotaped versions shown on monitors and projected large on the film screen. One monitor set vertically, portraitlike on a pedestal, featured a prerecorded video Jonas had made as a kind of intimate diary. Whatever city she'd happened to be in during the previous year, she would stare into her camera (turned ninety degrees to one side) and sleepily say "good night" and, upon waking up, "good morning." The views of a disheveled Jonas exposed her private self and came close to the realm of dreams. In black and white, the tape was firmly detached from the colorful real world.

Each element of *Mirage* added a layer to her contemplation of what distinguishes illusion from reality. She worked with a treasure trove of materials. Among her props was a Mexican mask of a woman's beatific, inscrutable face. She also used tall, fabricated aluminum cones, which she looked through in the manner of someone using a telescope to search for ships on the horizon; sometimes she'd sing into one as if it were the megaphone of an ancient Siren.

Her level of energy was high, and she moved with determination and conviction. At times, she would draw and sketch on a blackboard with white chalk; then she would quickly erase the sun and moon outlines she'd just made, as day morphed into night and back into day. On a big sketchpad clipped to an easel, she drew a heart with stubby arteries that poked out like ears. Flipping the page over, she drew a similar form, her dog Sappho's face. Readily repeatable images like these constituted her lexicon, which she had culled from a film by the early experimental pioneer Maya Deren (1917–1961), *Meshes of the Afternoon* (1943), in which shapes are drawn over and over in the sand, and from the sculpture of Alberto Giacometti (1901–1966). After graduate school, Jonas had taught herself to draw by making copies over and over again of Giacometti's attenuated figures, until the process became rote.

Picking up a stick of chalk, she drew a tic-tac-toe grid on the stage floor and added the numbers one through nine. Next she used the grid as she performed the game of hopscotch—punctuating each jump with the determined thump of a long baton on the floor—and deliberately smudged the crisp chalk lines with her foot.

On the horizontal film screen, Jonas projected archival footage of nature's devastating cycles, including fiery volcanic eruptions and palm trees convulsing in hurricane winds. In tandem with nature's violence and its cycle of life, death, and rebirth in the films, she added large projections of TV footage of hurly-burly politics, with its own repeated motifs, such as ceremonial visits of heads of state. I related to her quest for meaning in the aftermath of Watergate and Nixon's impeachment process.

Although after a while Jonas stopped performing *Mirage*, its status as a major work endured. I was delighted when in 2005 she reconfigured her performance as an installation. This changed the perspective of viewers from seated to active as they moved through Jonas's piece. After tenacious fund-raising, I located eight donors who in 2009 supported the acquisition of the installation. My colleagues in the conservation, registrar, and audiovisual departments and I assessed *Mirage*'s configuration of monitors, props, projections, and photographs and their relationships, and determined the aesthetics of the installation. We conducted an artist interview, learning firsthand what Jonas considered essential to her vision of *Mirage*.

Jonas would move away from using herself as the focus of a scenario and turn to the prose sagas of medieval Iceland and the German folktales assembled by the Brothers Grimm. She continued to develop her acting skills by performing with good friends, especially the Wooster Group, a theater ensemble that mixed humor with political critique and incorporated video into their process. Remembering the group's performances, I can still see Spalding Gray's bright naughty-boy smile and hear the deep droll voice of Ron Vawter (1948–1994), and recall how much I relished the contrast between Jonas's taut manner and the energetic sauciness of Kate Valk (b. 1957).

Experimental theater, video, performance, and music continued to overlap and evolve together. Jonas introduced me to Richard Foreman (b. 1937) and his tiny Ontological-Hysteric Theater, located a block from her loft in SoHo, where in 1976 I saw *Rhoda in Potatoland* (1976). With a sword of Damocles suspended over his head and using his audience as judges, Foreman sat front and center as the vulnerable narrator speaking in a stentorian voice. He multitasked as the omnipotent author and director, turning knobs to adjust lighting and recorded music, as panels moved in and out from the walls, reshaping viewers' perceptions, shuffling image and sound as if it were a video edit.

A few months later, I exhibited and acquired Foreman's video *Out of the Body Travel* (1976). The tape opens as he intones in his commanding voice: "I'm going to teach you everything I know. Are you ready?" A woman's foot hovers over a tableau of voluminous tomes opened and piled up over each other. Foreman goes on to narrate the story of a young woman who finds herself surrounded by the relics of Western culture. He asks, is it in dreaming or reading that we understand our relationship to language and to history?

I saw Foreman and Jonas as stellar storytellers. Jonas's use of video was at the center of her practice. She was pragmatic in using video's shallow depth of field as a formal stage on which to weave her formalized gestures and body movements. As video went through a sea change over the next decade, Jonas slowly rolled with the changes, continuing to combine, take apart, and rework her innovations.

I was always eager to see Jonas. In the late 1970s, we once met for dinner at one of Manhattan's three Japanese restaurants, where we discussed our fascination with Japan and Noh theater. Both of us connected Noh's stately movement to *Rashomon* (1950), a period classic by the master director Akira Kurosawa (1910–1998), which had recently screened at MoMA. The film's plot device involves various characters providing alternative, contradictory versions of the same incident. We compared this to how perceptions of experimental art depend upon how open the viewer is to the new. And here I was with an insatiable curiosity about the world beyond my doorstep.

Japan

I was eager to learn more about the country that produced the best video equipment. The consumer cameras and the production gear that artists favored, as well as the monitors and sound systems exhibitors used, all were imported from Japan. I wanted to find out what Japanese artists were doing with the same video equipment.

My interest in Japan accelerated when I became friends with Porter McCray, then the executive director of the JDR 3rd Fund, a nonprofit founded by John D. Rockefeller III to promote cultural exchange between the United States and Asia. I regularly had lunch with Paik and the elegant McCray, often in the latter's apartment with every table stacked three feet (0.9 m) high with catalogs from Asian art exhibitions he had instigated. McCray was also an early supporter of Robert Wilson (b. 1941), Merce Cunningham, and Paik, among many others.

The gods smiled when in 1978 Rand Castile, founding director of Japan Society in New York, invited me to travel and conduct research for a Japanese video exhibition as part of the Matsushita Electric Corporation of America–funded Japan Now, a monthlong expansive program that would scatter special arts events across Manhattan. Such international cultural events had begun to crop up regularly by then, bankrolled by industries eager to promote and place their well-designed products in department stores and convention centers, and their cinema and graphic arts in museums.

Having already seen experimental activity from Japan in alternative venues in New York, I was ready to jump on board. Shigeko Kubota introduced me to the Tokyo-based video makers featured in the New York

Women's Video Festival, which she had cocurated with Susan Milano at the Kitchen. Bill Viola, who had recently returned from Japan, waxed poetic about the artists he'd met in 1976 while participating in the Tokyo meeting of Jorge Glusberg's CAyC. I further prepared for my visit by eating sushi, reading *The Tale of Genji*, and catching every possible Japanese film screening and every exhibition of traditional crafts at Japan Society.

Matsushita had awarded MoMA $5,000. With an exchange rate of four hundred yen to a dollar, I had enough to cover a two-week research trip, organize an exhibition, and even produce a catalog. Right before my departure, Paik asked that I carry with me an exhibition announcement card bearing the portrait of Fluxus art founder George Maciunas, who had recently passed away. Paik explained that even though Maciunas had never visited Japan, his connections to artists there dated back more than a decade—particularly to Kubota, whom Maciunas had designated vice chairperson of the Fluxus organization in 1964. I put the card in my notebook, thinking about how both Paik and Maciunas were artist-ambassadors and how their actions advanced dialogue between East and West. Always cagey, Paik loved playing with the duality in his cultural background. He would advance one or the other whenever it suited an immediate goal or when he wanted to hide behind inscrutability.

It was Paik who contextualized Japanese video for me, describing the multicultural and interdisciplinary bonds that had been cemented in the 1960s through activities at Tokyo's Sogetsu Kaikan, the clued-in art center where French New Wave cinema first reached Japan. Founded by the family of filmmaker Hiroshi Teshigahara (1927–2001), this was where the best and brightest of Japan, and quite a few from the rest of the world, met. Sogetsu had sponsored many new music events, such as John Cage's and David Tudor's first performances in Japan, where Paik had met Yoko Ono (b. 1933) and had become connected to members of Group Ongaku, along with Cage and Kubota. Group Ongaku was founded in 1958 as a collective improvisation group by Takehisa Kosugi and Shukou Mizuno (b. 1934), two students at Tokyo National University of Fine Arts and Music, soon joined by others, including Yasunao Tone from the Department of Literature at Chiba University.[6] The group had become essential to the fabric of the postwar Japanese music and interdisciplinary art scene. Tone later moved to New York, and Kosugi went on to compose for the Merce Cunningham Dance Company.

In 1978 long-distance phone calls were still hideously expensive. I spent months leading up to my trip writing letters to artists, who slowly (or never) wrote back. When I asked well-traveled MoMA colleagues for advice, William Lieberman, then curator of drawings, suggested I bring stretch pants because I would be sitting cross-legged on tatami mats for many meals. I boarded a plane in October 1978, prepared to spend the next two weeks visiting artists, temple gardens, and teahouses. I brought with me my carefully compiled annotated address book, which I promptly left at Narita Airport on top of a pay phone. To my astonishment, the notebook was turned in and delivered to my hotel the next morning. I realized that I was in a different world.

The day after I arrived, I set off for a dinner graciously hosted by Viola's good friend—the only person who quickly answered my initial letter—the artist Fujiko Nakaya (b. 1933) and her mother in their home. That evening, I sat comfortably on the tatami mat and judiciously ate with a pair of slippery lacquer chopsticks, while I became acquainted with a loosely connected group of fifteen artists who shared video equipment or expertise, who had all begun their careers in other mediums—experimental film, music, kinetic art, literature, printmaking, and computer graphics. They were finding their way in a rapidly changing society.

Mako Idemitsu (b. 1940) experimented with narrative and examined the relationship between mothers and children in a society where family comes first. Most of my other dining companions were the founders of the eclectic thirteen-member group Video Hiroba.[7] Several members of the group had collaborated with Nakaya on her first video, *Friends of Minamata Victims—Video Diary* (1972), which recorded a protest and lengthy sit-in at the headquarters of Chisso Corporation, located in the Mitsubishi Heavy Industries building in Tokyo's financial district. Demonstrators camped out 24/7 to speak out loudly against the chemical company's mercury pollution of the water supply in the city of Minamata, which led to thousands of deaths and disastrous health consequences. Nakaya placed a video monitor at the sit-in site, allowing the demonstrators on different shifts to follow recordings of the group's daily actions on closed circuit, which made the work a successful experiment with video feedback and an effective activist tool.[8]

I spent the next few days in Tokyo screening work both at the experimental film center Image Forum and in Nakaya's office, which in 1979 opened as Processart and in 1980 became Video Gallery Scan, devoted to the distribution of video art. The two organizations promoted international exchange and forged a future for media art in Japan. I visited the Video Information Center, a storefront equipment rental service cofounded by the art student Ichiro Tezuka (b. 1947), who with three friends painstakingly went about recording the ephemeral actions of avant-garde performers, including the great Butoh artist Tatsumi Hijikata (1928–1986) and dancer Min Tanaka (b. 1945). The two works made by Tezuka and his three friends made it into my exhibition.

As I moved around Tokyo, I remember feeling like the tallest person around. I towered over everyone in the crowded subway, and I stuck out with my Caucasian face, blond hair, and bright clothes. I quickly learned that Japanese culture deems it an honor to courteously assist foreigners. Since I was an outsider, people considered me their responsibility. Whenever I was lost and stopped to read a map, a rescuer would suddenly appear. Once a woman even tied up her dog and walked me to my destination ten blocks away. I slowly learned my way around Japan's complex society.

I came to understand that groups were everything. I found that even young artists kowtowed to a mentor, a *sensei* (professor) or a *senpai* (older graduate of the same university). An individual was expected to assist members of his or her own group first and foremost. Over and over I would ask who else was making video. Despite my persistence, insiders always identified their close associates.

I had purposely made the trip on my own, rather than travel under any local entity's umbrella. My independence allowed me to move quietly and discreetly between disparate groups. It was late in my stay when I finally discovered Ko Nakajima (b. 1941), an artist-activist pushing to keep public access community TV alive in Japan, by teaching classes in his small apartment and lending whatever equipment he had. Wearing inch-thick (2.5 cm) glasses due to poor eyesight, Nakajima described Video Earth Tokyo, a video-art collective he'd established. He showed me a video of the group's audacious 1975 performance *Shokutaku ressha* (Video Picnic), when they startled commuters by cooking and eating a meal on the platform of a subway station.

Although Tokyo is the cultural center of Japan, I heard there was a cluster of video artists in the Kansai area, which includes the cities of Osaka, Kobe, Nara, and Kyoto, and decided to visit. I discovered that art students in Kansai tended to have an unconventional streak and marched firmly to their own drum, as they refuted most forms of tradition. Away from the seriousness of the capital, they had an inherently wry sense of humor I found to be lacking in Tokyo natives. One rainy afternoon at a tiny café in Kyoto, I caught up with several artists. Concluding the meeting and rushing for my next appointment, I politely backed my way out of the small place. As a clumsy Westerner, I knocked over every umbrella standing at the entrance. I could only laugh about my uncouthness and set everything back upright.

Through Shinji Kohmoto, the respected curator of contemporary art at the National Museum of Modern Art, Kyoto, I met Hitoshi Nomura (b. 1945), who distrusted reverence for the art object. He considered natural and man-made materials equal and believed chaos to be the equivalent of order. He showed me an installation made of TV tubes arranged face down on his

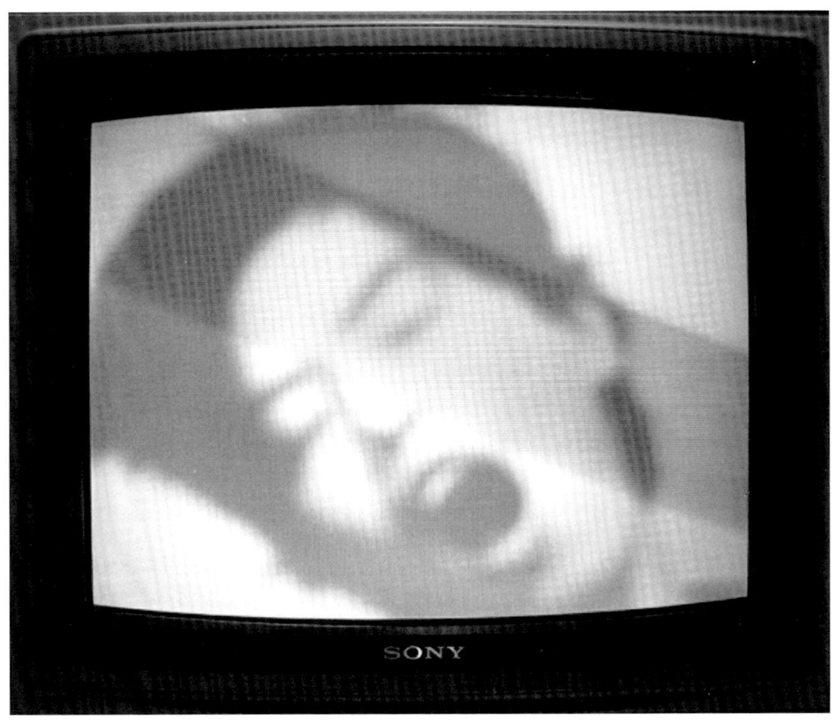

Hitoshi Nomura, *age: M→F*, 1978
Video, color and black and white, sound, 31 min. Color recording
of black-and-white photographs from 1975

studio floor with a natural sponge set on top of each. For my exhibition,
I selected his video *age: M→F* (1978), in which he contorted his face with
exaggerated grimaces, responding to electronic bleeps on the soundtrack
he'd composed.

Through the image-processed videos of the filmmaker Toshio
Matsumoto, an art and technology genius, I discovered that some Japanese
artists approached the two-dimensional subtleties of the TV screen in
a special way, namely as a flat plane, treating each frame as a separate
composition. Did this organizational method correspond, I wondered, to
traditional Japanese artists' handling of brush and ink, adapting their
technique to the season or a poem and the confines of the page? After
an informal meeting in Kyoto with Matsumoto, I posed this question to
Donald Richie, an American-born, Tokyo-based author who had written
extensively about the Japanese people and Japanese cinema. He confirmed

my hypothesis by explaining how the venerated directors Kurosawa and Mikio Naruse (1905–1969) composed a single frame of film in the same way.

On that first trip, I noted that in Japan the first comment about a work is often "Oh, how well it is made," emphasizing craft. In the West, our first words more frequently are "How interesting," highlighting content. I also found that Japanese artists would wait to execute their ideas until they could get their hands on (or afford) the authentic technical gizmo they needed, which I realized was out of respect for the original product. In North America, artists had a more pioneering spirit; when they were unable to afford or gain access to a specific piece of equipment, they'd immediately jerry-rig it, often tinkering in the garage or studio.

As a result of my research on this trip, I organized *Video from Tokyo to Fukui and Kyoto*, the first survey exhibition ever of Japanese video, presented at MoMA in 1979 as part of Japan Now. A steady stream of viewers came to the video gallery where the works were programmed sequentially one after the other on monitors, with enthusiasts returning to see everything. I was also able to acquire all thirteen works. The entire project was a mom-and-pop kind of operation, carried out by me and an intern, Viola's then girlfriend Kira Perov (b. 1951), who would soon become his wife and later his collaborator. Perov did all the necessary typing—catalog texts, artists' bios and statements, and the accompanying essays by me and Nakaya. I made stills of each work with my old high school camera. All of it—the research, exhibition, catalog, and acquisition of videos—was realized through the initial $5,000 grant, something impossible today.

I reached out to my network of curatorial colleagues and put the show on the road to fifteen other museums across the United States, Canada, and Europe; it was even sent to Japan, under the auspices of MoMA's International Program.[9] The timing was right. Institutions were curious about contemporary art that was coming out of Tokyo and elsewhere in Japan. I was delighted when the veteran New York dealer Ronald Feldman told me how the exhibition and catalog had shed new light on elusive Japan.

Over the next few years, my interest in Japanese art and technology grew, especially about interdisciplinary connections. The staff at Image Forum had introduced me to the poet Shuntaro Tanikawa (b. 1931) and the experimental theater director Shuji Terayama (1935–1983). On a subsequent trip, I was impressed by the pair's *Video Letter* (1982–83). In it, they updated the traditional collaborative poetry form called *renga* (linked poem), in which authors send a poem back and forth, each adding a stanza to what the other just wrote. For their video, made in the months before Terayama's untimely death, they exchanged a VHS cassette, in which each responded to the other by inserting a short recording that revealed intimate thoughts. The friends

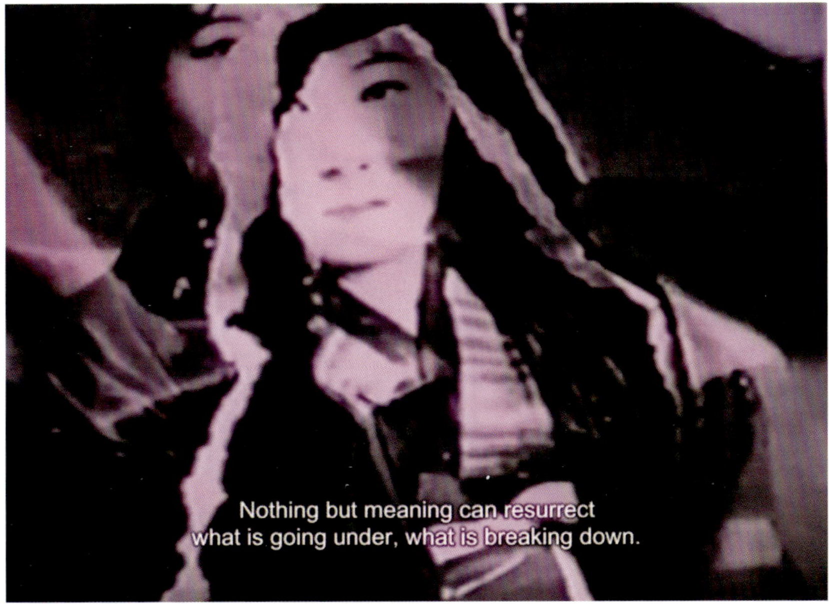

Shuntaro Tanikawa and Shuji Terayama, *Video Letter*, 1982–83
Video, color, sound, 75 min.

created a consummate video with the elegiac subtlety that is common in poetry, here with slightly aberrant behavior and sometimes flamboyant visuals. I was able to exhibit and acquire this unique collaboration.

Music and Sound

In the late 1970s, as electronic technologies for amplification, recording, and other functions improved and proliferated, and as opportunities expanded, I paid more attention to artists who used music as the main medium in which to express their criticism of the myopic society they saw all around them. They formed bands, moved between video, film, and sound, and honed new music and performance skills, as they took to the road. They showed their videos in new clubs. The audiocassette became a versatile distribution format: Uptown, groups danced in playgrounds to the latest music on audiocassettes played on boom boxes. Downtown in underground spaces, artists exchanged mix tapes with favorite playlists after performances. Once a taxi driver pulled a cassette right out of his cab's player and handed it to me, after we both waxed poetic about a David Bowie song.

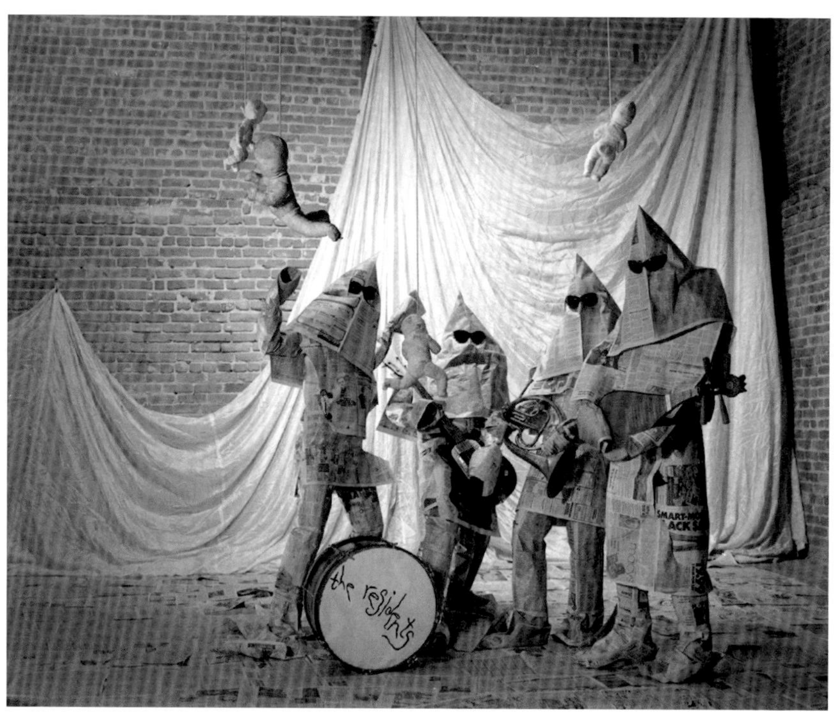

The Residents, *The Third Reich 'n' Roll*, 1976
16 mm film transferred to video, black and white, sound, 4 min. 16 sec.

Despite the broad cultural changes going on and the emergence of hybrid art forms, museums failed to take in punk or graffiti art, and rarely allowed music in any form—live, vinyl, or cassette tape—to cross their thresholds. Heaven forbid that sound would permeate hallowed galleries. Meanwhile, many with art school backgrounds took to video in the pursuit of performance and sound. This included David Bowie, the multi-instrumentalist painter Don Van Vliet (a.k.a. Captain Beefheart, 1941–2010), the art band Devo (founded in 1973), Suicide (a band founded by Alan Vega [1938–2016] and Martin Rev [b. 1947] in 1970), the Raincoats (a post-punk band formed in 1977 by Ana da Silva and Gina Birch), the Residents (founded in 1972), and singers Lydia Lunch (b. 1959), Cosey Fanni Tutti (b. 1951), and Laurie Anderson, who all made pre-MTV music videos and Super 8 films. Their approach was summed up by Devo band member Mark Mothersbaugh (b. 1950): "We thought sound and vision was going to bury rock & roll and that we were a part of something brand new that was much bigger than rock & roll."[10]

I followed the obscure groups' wit and rarefied electronic inventiveness. The Residents fused the dark storytelling tradition of the South with the eccentric, nonconformist spirit of the Bay Area in their video *The Third Reich 'n' Roll* (1976), which parodied pop music and 1960s commercials, as well as German Expressionist cinema of the 1920s. I began scooping up the Residents' early music videos and storyboards (preparatory drawings), which entered MoMA's Department of Film's well-maintained research and study collection.

Laurie Anderson

One of the most important boundary-crossing artists, Laurie Anderson is an unassuming, classically trained violinist and a charismatic radical who back then was developing an inventive form of electronic storytelling with a disarmingly straightforward style. After graduating from Barnard College with a BA in art history, she had taken classes with the conceptual-Minimalist artists Sol LeWitt and Carl Andre (b. 1935) at the School of Visual Arts and absorbed their emphasis on idea over material product.

In the 1970s, during my research missions, I occasionally visited Anderson, who was living in a loft on Canal Street, in a building then next door to a methadone clinic. Anderson and I had met around 1974 as I was assembling MoMA's artists' books collection (which led to the *Bookworks* exhibition in 1977). Here was someone who was literate, affable, and a real technology maven. She was using sixty-nine-cent speakers and other affordable gear that she picked up in nearby electronics shops. Her closest friends included local artists Joel Fisher (b. 1947), Jene Highstein (1942–2013), Dickie Landry (b. 1938), Tina Girouard, Gordon Matta-Clark, and sound engineer Bob Bielecki. These downtown artists with abundant energy but minimal means shared a DIY aesthetic and a strongly community-minded spirit. Anderson saw the area that eventually became Tribeca and SoHo as a raw frontier, "an alternate side of New York where everyone was hiding. . . . It was unbelievably exciting. We had taken a very dark part of the city and made it into something where ideas were everywhere. We really had a sense that we were making something new in a lot of different art forms."[11]

To support herself, Anderson taught art history at several local universities. Ever the storyteller, when she showed her students slides of ancient Egyptian architecture, she would improvise if she happened to forget details from her early studies. At exam time, she would ask her students to describe their own versions of the subject. For a while she wrote for *Artforum* and *ARTNews* to understand what was sitting in other artists' refrigerators. Because she twisted facts to suit her imagination, this part of her writing career ended abruptly.[12]

Anderson developed her persona by combining her skills as an accomplished wordsmith and beguiling raconteur. Her recollections morphed from simple written or spoken descriptions to actions that incorporated filmic elements. I saw her first exhibition, *O-Range*, in 1973 at the alternative gallery Artists Space. It had been chosen by Vito Acconci for the Artists Selected series. *O-Range* was composed of photographs and handwritten text panels referring to Maurice Merleau-Ponty, the twentieth-century French philosopher of phenomenology. A graduate philosophy course taught by art critic–philosopher Arthur Danto had introduced her to his work. In one photo, she held up two protruding orange halves, resembling wizened breasts, and masked her eyes with them. As part of the exhibition, on the gallery wall she projected a five-minute Super 8 film loop of herself in close-up playing the violin, her eyes hidden by her bowing arm. For the duration of the exhibition, she left her contact lenses on the windowsill of the gallery and spent three weeks with 20/800 vision. Blindness was her way of testing how the eyes and the brain see.[13]

In 1974, also at Artists Space, Anderson performed *As:If*, her first full-fledged audiovisual project. Wrapping her lips around a tiny pillow speaker inserted into her mouth, she molded the sound of her prerecorded voice, bizarrely distorting (and eating) her words, as meanwhile, a slide projector cast pairs of her hand-drawn words onto the gallery wall.

Anderson's work was picked up by the plucky dealer Holly Solomon, who indomitably offered alternatives to Post-Minimalism and Conceptualism. At Solomon's gallery, I saw Anderson's twenty-seven-minute silent Super 8 film *DEARREADER: How to Turn a Book into a Movie* (1974), which she codirected with her friend Bob George (b. 1949), an avid record collector and founder of the ARChive of Contemporary Music. The film is about sex in the 1940s. The opening shot is of a bedroom and two bathrobes, which are shown from the waist down. The robes come together, then a foot comes up and a slipper drops down to the carpet. Nothing prurient happens; instead it's all wit and good taste. *DEARREADER* had been inspired by literature, the innovative approaches to storytelling of American writer Herman Melville, who often addressed his reader directly, and by the English writer Laurence Sterne, whose *Tristram Shandy* (1767) was a forerunner of the modern novel. Anderson called her work a "performance film," because she played the violin at the beginning and end of each screening.[14]

By the mid-1970s, Anderson's practice had gone from simple vignettes to her primary art form: the media-enhanced performance of an illustrated story, which became more polished as she smoothly segued between slides, film, violin playing, and prerecorded and live stories. For Anderson, readily available and modifiable electronics merely facilitated the process of storytelling. She became the ultimate perfectionist in control of her craft. She was often so absorbed in making her work that she was late to her performances. "I'd barely finish editing the film, so I never got to the sound track. At the last minute, I'd grab my violin and run to the festival. I'd stand in front of the film, play the violin live and do the dialogue live."[15] She would soon turn to video as another electronic means of developing and disseminating spare visual stories that revolved around her identity.

Physically becoming part of the film was an integral element of her practice. In *For Instants: Part 3, Refried Beans* (1976), which she did in a very early performance series at MoMA in 1976, she planted herself in front of a grainy black-and-white Super 8 film projected on a wall and delivered an extemporaneous narration, bowing her violin to film images of floating curtains. Standing waiflike beside the projection, she charmed the small avant-garde audience.

The violin has been both Anderson's partner and a natural extension of her body, the perfect alter ego. She can hold it and walk around with it. It's the instrument closest to the voice, the human female voice. Over the years, her violin and bow have undergone many incarnations, including a bow outfitted with audiotape that she slides over a "head" planted in the violin's strut.

Anderson once noted that the software she used activates a different level of creativity: "It doesn't go through the hands the way an instrument does. I love the violin because it's a hand-held instrument, it's a very nineteenth-century instrument, something that you hold, as opposed to a keyboard, which reminds me of driving a car. But electronics is very connected, of course, in terms of speed, to your brain. It's very, very fast. So, there's a kind of immediate freedom you have."[16]

Everyone at the time was getting a fix on no wave, a short-lived avant-garde crossover art scene that emerged in Lower Manhattan in the late 1970s. The term *no wave* was a pun based on the rejection of the commercial "new wave" genre of rock music. The no wave art scene revolved around noise, dissonance, and atonality, reflecting an abrasive, confrontational, and nihilistic worldview. In 1978 Anderson and another media monologuist, Julia Heyward (b. 1949), staged a two-person opening act for the Nova Convention, a who's who of the American avant-garde in music, film, literature, and performance held at the Entermedia Theater on Second Avenue and 12th Street in New York. The three-day event featured no wave films, concerts, and talks by Anderson, Patti Smith, Frank Zappa, Allen Ginsberg, Timothy Leary, and William S. Burroughs. Music writer

Robert Palmer noted in a *New York Times* December 4 review of the event, "Laurie Anderson, one of a number of younger performance artists whose work owes a great deal to Mr. [Brion] Gysin's innovations, gave a delightful presentation on the future, using weird electronic distortion on her voice."[17]

At Nova, Anderson played her violin and sang using a harmonizer to alter her voice for the first time. As she did her part of the repartee with Heyward, the device would raise or drop her pitch so that she sounded like an authoritarian male or a gargantuan baby, among the other characters who appeared in her stories. "The machismo surrounding Burroughs was thick, and this filter was my weapon, my defense," she later explained. "It was the first time I used an audio mask, and being in drag was thrilling."[18]

In all of her performances, Anderson transgressed the laws of gender and genre, fluctuating between male and female, verbal and visual.[19] "In my work I strive for a sort of stereo effect, a pairing of things up against each other, and see myself as a sort of moderator between things. Sexuality is one of those things that I'm between," she once said.[20]

In the late 1970s, Anderson found invisibility a counterbalance to the exposure of performing live. We worked together to premiere her *Handphone Table* (1978) as an installation in MoMA's Projects series. The work consisted of an ordinary-looking plywood table with a pair of stools, accompanied by a blurred photograph of two people seated with their heads in their hands. Most visitors who saw the table sat right down and immediately put their hands to their heads. To their astonishment, Anderson's voice came through their hands, as if the artist were entering their consciousness. She had concealed within the table a special kind of speaker that transmitted sound vibrations through solid material rather than through air; the listeners' bones conducted her voice. Electronically distorting her voice, she spoke a line from George Herbert, a seventeenth-century metaphysical love poet who wrote, "Now I in you without a body move."[21] Anderson was present, but invisibly so, heard only in the viewer's head.

Walking into a museum and coming upon the disembodied Anderson in *Handphone Table* is bizarre, even surreal in the way sound enters the viewer's mind. In thinking about how new technology changes the way that ideas are transmitted, she sometimes talked about the jump cut, which in the twentieth century became taken for granted as a function of mind and cinema. Sharp and witty, Anderson admires the deliberate, up-front type of American humor found in the early American films of Buster Keaton, Harold Lloyd, and the Marx Brothers. In a way, like them, she works with humor as a disguise for banality, a method that tends to be more oblique and often disconcerting for the viewer.

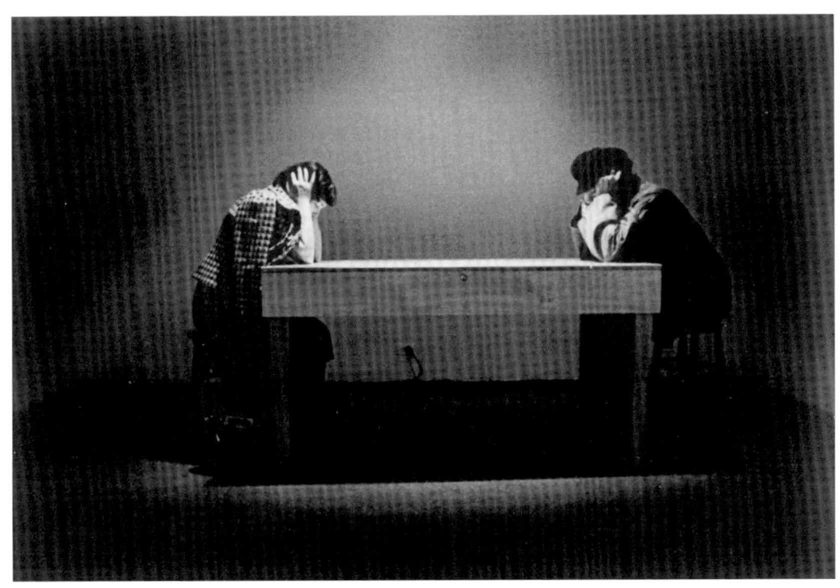

Laurie Anderson, *Handphone Table*, 1978
Wood and electronics

Anderson was starting to use video projection in her now more technically complex performances, initially with *Americans on the Move* (1979). It was in 1979 at the Kitchen that I saw this multidimensional work in which Anderson moved nimbly through a technological labyrinth and created a mythopoeic and personal roundup of American history.[22] In conjunction with the performance, she created "O Superman," a 45-rpm single produced by the independent New York label 110 Records. Anderson was surprised when the single reached the top of the pop charts in England in 1980, after which music scouts from the global conglomerate Warner Records signed Anderson on. Bob Regehr, then a Warner vice president in charge of artist development, described her music as one of the most exciting things he had heard since he discovered the Sex Pistols years before.[23]

The "O Superman" lyrics were inspired by a recording Anderson heard of the aria "O souverain, ô juge, ô père" (Oh Sovereign, Oh Judge, Oh Father) from Jules Massenet's opera *Le Cid* (1885). The singer was Charles Holland, an African-American opera singer during the 1940s, a time when racism was rampant in the classical music field. While Anderson's first line ("O Superman, O Judge, O Mom and Dad, Mom and Dad,") echoes the original aria, she digresses into an ode about pop culture and concludes

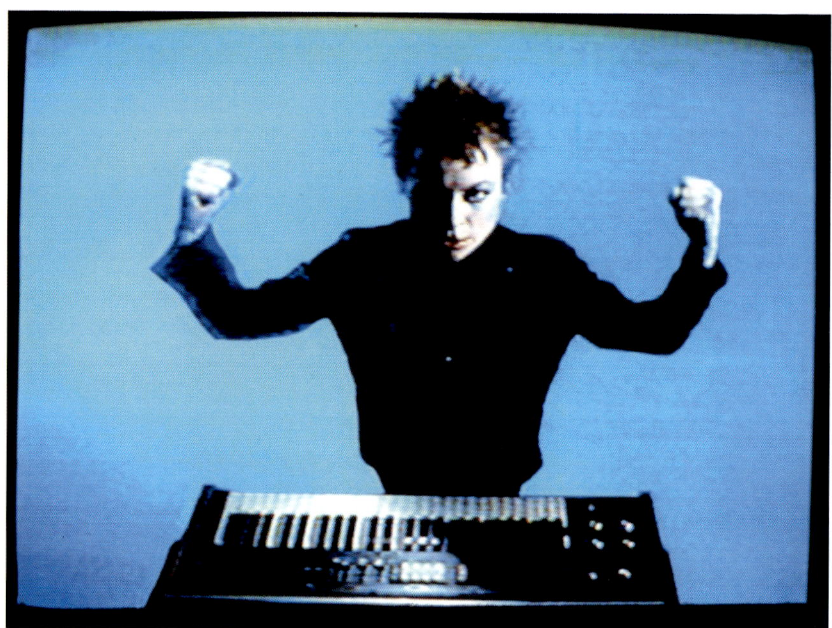

Laurie Anderson, *O Superman*, 1981
Video, color, sound, 8 min.

with "So hold me, Mom, in your long arms. / Your petrochemical arms. Your military arms. / In your electronic arms."

On one level, in "O Superman" Anderson addresses war and what she saw as the failure of technology in the US military activity around the Iran-Iraq War. At the same time, the song confronts what it means to be a working superwoman in the uphill struggle for career and equality. What all striving professionals need are assistants or clones—and her "I'm not here right now" refrain exemplifies the then new, inexpensive, and ubiquitous answering machine. That liberating sonic appliance placed an electronic surrogate between its users and the world.

As Anderson was raising the production level of her live performances, in 1981 she was able to achieve the same with videos when Warner Records produced her first music video, *O Superman*, with then state-of-the-art production values just in time for the birth of MTV. Hungry for strong content to fill its airtime, the station then was pro-artist and presented her video as one of the short art breaks they were commissioning. Multimedia artist and animator Perry Hoberman (b. 1954)—who had been turning obsolete technologies, such as 3-D slide systems, into droll animated narrative installations—joined Anderson as the video's artistic director.

Accommodating the still boxy, small scale of the consumer television set, they concentrated on close-up shots of Anderson, exaggerated versions of her in action onstage; she stands before a waferlike luminous moon up in the corner. When her face suddenly is in the dark, blood-red light emanates from her mouth, as she moves her lips with a tiny pillow speaker glowing inside her mouth, and emits a prerecorded violin solo that she modulates with her lips. She gestures with her arm and hand, which appear in silhouette against the moon. Extending her arm with her fist clenched, her hand then becomes a gun, and then points in a come-hither gesture. Her wit softened the underlying political edge of the video.

A few months later, Anderson and I traveled together to the Locarno Video Festival, in Switzerland. There I saw a lot of new videos that were becoming smoother and more polished, and caught up with fellow curators, including Chris Dercon before his first museum directorship at the Witte de With Center for Contemporary Art, Rotterdam; Dorine Mignot from the Stedelijk; and Biljana Tomić, curator of the Studentski Kulturni center in Belgrade. But the high point of the trip was driving with Anderson and Munich-based curator Helmut Friedel over the mountains to Lugano and the grave of Hermann Hesse. At the grave, we left a note that read: "Dear Hermann. We really don't like your work but were in the area and stopped by to say hello. And we don't like the way your wife's small tombstone marker is placed on the ground at your feet and reads, Ninon Aüslander" (foreigner).

The trip marked the start of a new decade, right before audiovisual equipment started to be controlled by computers. Anderson was abandoning the old seat-of-the-pants dynamics and moving on to larger and larger productions in which she performed on the concert stage surrounded by a plethora of audiovisual gear. At about this time, installation was morphing into more staged audiovisual environments. Before long, artists would turn to the global networks forming on the emergent internet and would stretch their wings in the dawn of a new digital era.

Video Takes Center Stage

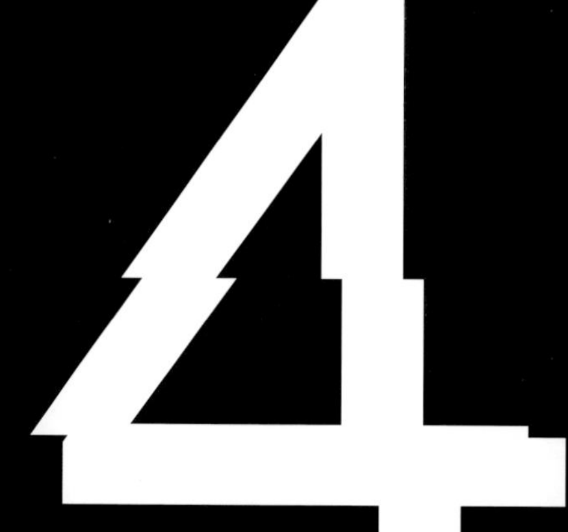

In the early 1980s, as technology grew in versatility, video blossomed as a dynamic, diversified field. With more activity to follow, I found myself busier than ever and kept in close touch with artists and involved critics, such as the *Village Voice* writer Amy Taubin, along with other media art travelers open to discovery. Three artists in particular—Bill Viola, Gary Hill (b. 1951), and Dara Birnbaum (b. 1946)—contributed to video art's acceptance as a serious contemporary form during this period. They dealt directly with video—the nitty-gritty of the electronic signal—as equipment morphed from analog to digital, experimented with unconventional methods, and found ways to gain access to more professional production tools. Around this time, the art biennials that started to proliferate took on the appearance of Olympic races, as these three artists and a number of others tried to slow down and develop ideas rather than vie for the lucrative rewards of instant fame.

Viola, Hill, and Birnbaum began their practices at a time when rents in cities like New York were still cheap, and they worked in supportive environments that could be found away from the mainstream. Each had a distinctive trajectory: Viola created "tuned environments," Hill interlaced image with spoken word, and Birnbaum challenged television's gendered bias. Viola and Hill were among the first artists to master analog audiovisual information systems that delivered live and prerecorded moving images with stereophonic sound. They experimented to understand how and why video's various components worked. Birnbaum's first videos, made in 1975, explored a woman's psychological states through physical gestures, which seem raw, direct, and unmediated. The young Birnbaum appears alone, as solo performer. There is a strong feminist subtext, which she further developed as she went on to examine sexism in the mass media. Her strong ideologies and approach gained critical respect. During the late 1970s and early 1980s, each of these artists' work was featured in group and solo exhibitions that helped to elevate the status of video.

Bill Viola

Viola and I first met in 1974 at the "Video and the Museum" conference hosted by the Everson, where the young, affable undergrad presented several impressive videos he had just made. Over a year later, I was pleased when he phoned and made an appointment to stop by my office shortly after he returned to New York from Florence.[1] The artist described his single-channel videotapes, at one point explaining that he made them both as "songs" and as "visual poems"—allegories in the language of subjective perception. He effused about the spiritual dimensions he perceived in the religious frescoes of the late Middle Ages Florentine painter Giotto, which he'd seen for the first time in Padua, and about the mystical poetry of the thirteenth-century Persian Sufi Jalal al-Din Rumi, which he had just started to read.

As I got to know him, I was amused that Viola likes to clown around and tell funny stories, especially jokes about himself. His playful demeanor often becomes serious, as it did early in our friendship when he told me about a powerful childhood memory of nearly drowning after falling out of a rowboat. The nightmarish experience may be what led to death's becoming a predominant theme in his art, coupled with the influence of his family's Catholicism. Of equal significance is the fact that he played drums in his high school band. Later he would pace his video edits to the rhythm of a heartbeat and elicit an unwitting response from his audience.

Viola once explained that his fascination with the artistic possibilities of electronics began at home in Flushing, Queens. In 1964 he discovered a back door into the nearby World's Fair and began sneaking in on the way home from school. For him, the majestic Italian Renaissance sculpture the *Pietà* by the great artist Michelangelo, loaned by the Vatican, played second fiddle to the pavilions in which high-tech corporations touted trailblazing hardware. In the pavilion of the Bell System (of telephone conglomerate AT&T), he experienced the Picturephone, which, prearranged, allowed him to talk to a friend at a special booth in Chicago, while seeing each other on a small video screen. For the first time, the public came face-to-face with room-sized mainframe computers that chugged away, attended by keyboard operators at adjacent workstations. Previously, these mysterious space-age machines resided out of sight in corporate back areas, described in prophetic articles published by *Newsweek* and *Time* magazine. Viola believed the proclamations made by manufacturers through their upbeat promotional displays that a dazzling, technology-enhanced future was in store for everyone. His dream that consumer electronics would become available as art-making tools soon became a reality.

When Viola entered Syracuse University in 1969 as an art student, he quickly discovered that painting and sculpture were not for him. Too impatient with Super 8 film, which had to be sent to a lab to be developed, he began using the art department's one portable black-and-white video camera to explore the parameters of a live video image—visible on a monitor in real time—versus its just-recorded-and-replayed video image, each with its concomitant crude sound. Viola's media prowess advanced rapidly. Motivated by the unusually open, interdisciplinary environment of the school's new Experimental Studios, he took advantage of the plethora of audiovisual gadgetry and studied electronic music and worked with the Moog, one of the earliest analog music synthesizers. The activity of experimental electronic musicians paralleled that of early video artists. Both recorded compositions captured as electronic signals onto oxide-coated mylar tape and found ways to process their sounds and images using synthesizers. It was natural that Viola would explore the school's Moog synthesizer, which offered seemingly infinite combinations of processed tones. He mastered reel-to-reel audiotape recorders and microphones and delved deep into control systems, circuitry, and electronic theory.

Eager to use electronics to express the images forming in his head, at school Viola studied 1960s experimental films by innovators Stan Brakhage (1933–2003), Hollis Frampton, Ken Jacobs (b. 1933), and Michael Snow. He analyzed how they handled the camera and structured recorded images, and how they anatomized ordinary actions in everyday settings. Through the filmmakers' simple yet hallucinatory effects, Viola found the tactics to develop his own audiovisual compositions.

For Viola, the electronic signal was a raw material that an artist could shape. He painstakingly did linear, tape-to-tape editing of his image and sound recordings, using the most basic, open-reel equipment to assemble his desired sequences—much like the cutting and pasting of a collage. But he soon felt frustrated by the lack of precision afforded by consumer equipment. Given how inexpensive blank consumer-format videotape was and thus how easy it was to overshoot—record video nonstop—emerging video art was often so long that critics would gripe that it was boring. Early video festivals generally lumped genres together, and Viola sometimes disparaged the rambling, guerrilla-style documentary videos that were presented in conjunction with his more meticulous work. Still, he agreed with John Cage, who stressed that it is much more important to promote curiosity and awareness than to make value judgments.

After Viola and several classmates set up Syracuse University's Synapse Video Center, a professional television studio created using tuition fees and reserved for art students' sole use, he became an adept editor. With a three-camera, broadcast-quality setup, he gained firsthand experience as a studio engineer, learning how to use a video switcher to do live editing independent of but simultaneous to recording, in the manner of television's low-budget soap-opera productions.

Meanwhile, the Everson's savvy video curator, David Ross, hired Viola to work on exhibitions with him. Viola gained valuable expertise as he assisted video pioneers with their solo shows at the museum. In 1972 he assisted Ross on a performance by Juan Downey. Downey had studied architecture in Santiago before joining the print atelier of Stanley William Hayter (1901–1988) in Paris, where he befriended the experimental artists Julio Le Parc (b. 1928) and Takis (1925–2019) and caught up with the new field of cybernetics.

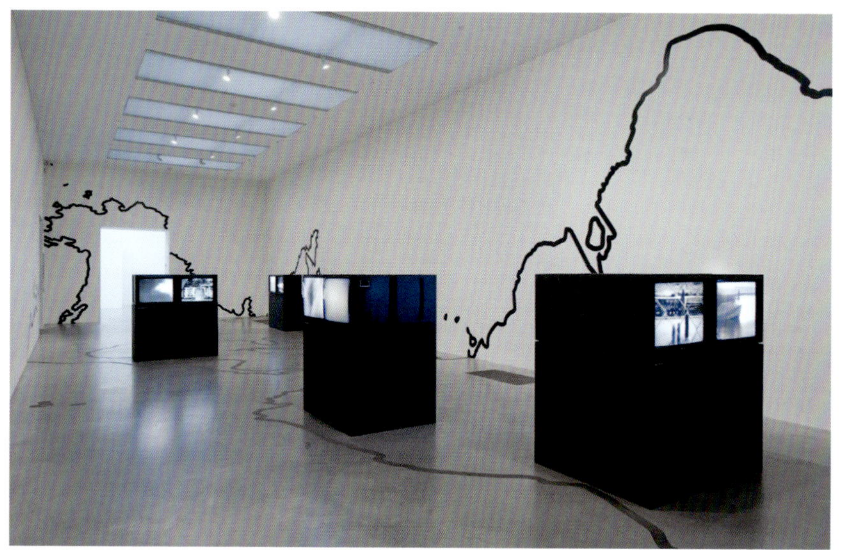

Juan Downey, *Video Trans Americas*, 1976
Video installation, with fourteen monitors, color and black
and white, sound; duration variable: 10 min. to 28 min. 9 sec.
Installation view: Tate Modern, London, 2010

At the Everson, Viola, Ross, Ross's brother, Downey's son, Everson director Jim Harithas, and Harithas's wife all performed in Downey's *Plato Now* (1972), a complex investigative performance that became a single-channel video. In *Plato Now*, the performers used voice-transmission laser beams and superimposed one another's faces onto their own by means of Super 8 film projections. The live event resulted in an installation, a collage of moving images that furthered Downey's interest in issues of illusion and perception of reality, which had a strong impact on the young Viola.

It's worth noting that Downey was about to set off on a journey that would become a precisely arranged, multiple-monitor installation, *Video Trans Americas* (1976), tracing Downey's journey by car, long before transnational highways. Armed with a portable camera, he went from New York and through Central and South America, following dirt roads into remote hamlets in which he would share his just-recorded videos with villagers who had never experienced television nor had ever heard music made by dwellers of an equally isolated area not that far away. MoMA acquired the work in 2013.

Viola continued serving as an exhibition assistant at the Everson, and while preparing for Paik's 1974 show *Videa 'n' Videology*, Viola heard the artist press "for a broader understanding of time as experience within the notions of randomness and indeterminacy."[2] Viola would go on to take delight in chance, which he always tapered with an overarching formal structure.

In 1974 Viola met Peter Campus, when Campus's video survey was shown at the Everson. Campus had abandoned the physicality of the boxy monitor and used the then rare and expensive video projector to create an image that consisted of light alone. Campus had found a link between the infinite expanse of time that surrounds the viewer and the loneliness of the inner self. By immersing the viewer in room-scaled projected video environments, he forced a consideration of the physiology of perception as well as the psychological dimension of observation. Viola saw that video technology gave Campus the ability to experience himself from outside himself, to objectify his subjectivity. Viola would later write that Campus's early live video projection installations "blazed a path into the depths of the living moment that few have followed."[3]

Viola graduated with a BFA in 1975 and moved to Florence, where he connected with his Italian roots. He spent eighteen months as technical director of Art/Tapes/22, the short-lived video production studio for artists within a gallery founded by arts patron Maria Gloria Bicocchi. (She modeled Art/Tapes/22 on Gerry Schum's Fernsehgalerie in Düsseldorf.) In Florence Viola worked closely with Greek-born Arte Povera artist Jannis Kounellis (1936–2017), among others invited to produce videos grounded in their performance and installation practices.

When Viola moved back to New York toward the end of 1976 we began meeting regularly to share information, often near Columbus Circle at the Cosmic Coffee Shop, its name well suited to Viola's interests in the metaphysical implications of consciousness. Over a slice of apple pie, he would describe how he began each video with a vivid mental image, a kind of diagram he would hold in his mind as he then spent weeks or months assiduously matching the image to the perfect setting and precise time of day. Outdoors, observing nature's seasonal change, he found the paradigm of timelessness, what he aspired to represent in the manner of his hero, the artist William Blake (1757–1827). This was the case with *A Million Other Things* (1975), his short video in which he used time lapse to capture the shifts in light and sound during an eight-hour period, from day to night at the edge of a pond. When the sun sets toward the end of the four-minute work, an individual standing in the distance remains the only visible object, illuminated by a single electric lamp suspended overhead.

Meanwhile, Viola had joined a new wave of practitioners invited into PBS's TV Lab at WNET/Thirteen in New York, which professionalized their work. WNET/Thirteen gave Viola access to broadcast-quality computer editing through CMX and to a sympathetic, highly skilled broadcast engineer, John Godfrey. Armed with new knowledge and high-end equipment, Viola was able to manipulate time more precisely, and his level of technical skill now matched the conceptual complexity of his videos. He told me that he wanted his new work to have the same polish as a beer commercial.

In the short works collected in his first WNET/Thirteen production, *Four Songs* (1976), Viola carefully recorded true-to-life images and made a synthesis of real time and edited time.[4] Assembled in much the same way that a musician arranges individual songs for a record album, each brief section was centered on a specific location. In the section entitled *The Space Between the Teeth*, the setting is the end of a long, dark corridor, where a man sits in an easy chair. He stares at the camera and after a while lets out a bloodcurdling scream, as the camera quickly hurtles backward down the corridor. *The Space Between the Teeth* concludes with a photograph of the man—a still image taken from the video. The photograph is thrown off a bridge, floats briefly, and disappears when the wake of a boat drags it away. Viola himself was the performer, and the video revolved around him as the initiator of feelings and ideas. It spun my perceptions around: Viola's careful editing caused me to experience a new metaphor for time—its elastic forward movement reminded me of a sock being turned inside out.

Dropped into the evening programming flow, Viola's new work aired nationally on PBS's *Video Tape Review* series, which ran briefly on Sunday nights. The network insisted on adding what I like to call a "talking torso" host, someone who would introduce and explain the unconventional work about to be broadcast. Viola found this unnecessary. He argued that viewers tuning into PBS, like visitors entering a contemporary art museum, were inquisitive and anticipated the challenge of encountering something new. Believing that context shapes interpretation, Viola felt that the public television audience was astute enough to decipher his video art on their own.

In this early phase of his career, Viola would develop each of his themes both as a videotape and as an installation, one linear with a narrative flow and the other spatial with an immersive dimension. His videotape *Migration* (1976) begins with a close-up shot of a drop of water that functions as a lens, which magnifies details of a man's face. A slow pan reveals that the face belongs to the artist seated behind the drop. In this work, Viola was contemplating how an eagle sees a field mouse from five hundred feet (152.4 m) up in the air. The eagle's comprehensive worldview had inspired him to make a tape that would focus viewers' attention, so they could perceive greater detail in what they see. "Reality," he wrote, "unlike the image on the retina or on the television tube, is infinitely resolvable— 'resolution' and 'acuity' are properties only of images."[5]

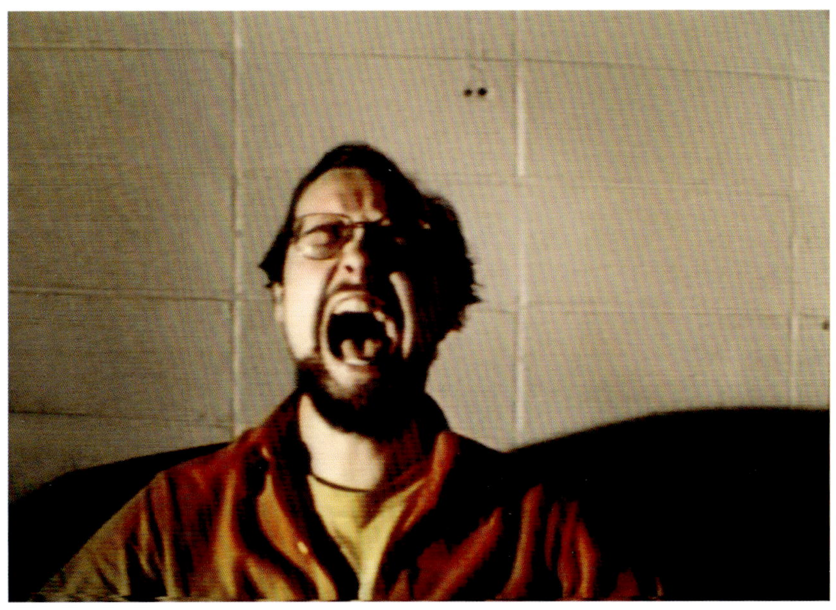

Bill Viola, *The Space Between the Teeth*, 1976
Part of *Four Songs*, 1976; video, color, sound, 9 min. 10 sec.

A drop of water is also at the center of *He Weeps for You* (1976), an installation that I first saw at documenta and selected for MoMA's Projects series. I was happy to commandeer a large, darkened gallery adjacent to the popular Andrew Wyeth painting *Christina's World* (1948). When viewers entered Viola's precisely calibrated environment, they came upon a long copper pipe originating at the ceiling and terminating at eye level in a small valve, from which a single drop of water slowly emerged. A color video camera, fitted with a special lens used for extreme close-up magnification, was set on this drop. The camera was connected to a video projector that displayed the swelling drop on a large screen in the rear of the space. The optical properties of the water drop caused it to act like a fish-eye lens, revealing the room and those within it. Gradually growing in size and swelling in surface tension, the drop eventually filled the screen. Then suddenly, it trembled and fell out of the image. A loud resonant "boom" was heard as it landed on a small amplified drum. Then, in an endless cycle of repetition, a new drop emerged and again filled the screen.

I chuckled when an ABC evening newscaster arrived to do a feature on Viola's show. The fellow opened his local report with "I'm sitting on the floor of MoMA next to a leaky faucet." As if on cue, the drop fell and landed on the drum with a loud kaboom that filled Viola's carefully tuned environment. Even inane press helps to build an audience.

Viola's early work drew upon Japanese aesthetics—in particular, the culture's respect for nature. I associated Viola with Kachou Fuugetsu (四字熟語), the idiom that literally reads "Flower, Bird, Wind, Moon" but means "Experience the beauties of nature, and in doing so learn about yourself." In 1979 Viola returned to Japan on a US/Japan Creative Artist Fellowship. He and his new wife, Kira Perov, spent eighteen months based in Tokyo, where they engaged with every imaginable artist, composer, writer, curator, Buddhist priest, and corporate executive.

Viola became the first and only artist in residence at the Sony Corporation's Atsugi research laboratories. *Hatsu Yume (First Dream)* (1981), which he created there, is a reflection upon the complexity of nature, representing both its glorious bounty and its terrifying power. The tape opens with a sunrise and the ebb and flow of ocean waves on shore. It continues with iconic Mount Fuji and goes on to a mysterious bamboo grove, a boulder with small rocks precariously set along its top, and a hot spring disgorging steam at a mountain shrine. On the deck of a brightly lit night-fishing boat, with mechanized lines slowly coiling and uncoiling like the tentacles of a monster, a solitary captain gazes out to the horizon, while near his feet rejected squid lie dying. Through the harsh nocturnal lights of Tokyo streets, at a protracted pace, a lonely figure approaches the camera and strikes a match, the flame suddenly filling the frame before he lights a cigarette. Rain cascades down a car windshield, through which shine the abstract, kaleidoscopic colors of the city.

Traditional Japan, with its pared-down simplicity and attention to craft, suited Viola's mode of operation at the time: ultraslow motion so that the viewer might sink into an image and connect with meanings contained within it. He also relished the harmony of opposites in Japan, what to Western eyes appears as a garish environment where kitsch and tastefulness coexist side by side. When I visited Japan for a conference, Viola took me to his favorite Mr. Donut coffee shop, rather than a rarefied teahouse.

Viola and Perov returned to the United States in 1981 and settled in Southern California to be close to nature—the Pacific Ocean and Death Valley—and the Long Beach Museum, with its then active video exhibition and production programs overseen by curator Kathy Rae Huffman. Viola joined the performance artist Suzanne Lacy, as well as another feminist artist, Sanja Iveković (b. 1949) from Zagreb, and a lively group of local and international artists whom Huffman had invited to produce and exhibit work at the Long Beach Museum.

By then, US federal and state funding for video was petering out due
to a conservative political climate. In 1983 Viola and I participated in the
low-budget "Media Arts in Transition" conference hosted by the Walker Art
Center in Minneapolis, which had been organized by the National Alliance
of Media Art Centers. The hardworking attendees came from community-
and university-based programs, museums, media centers, film festivals,
distributors, film archives, and community access television. Media artists
had progressed beyond their initial instinctive working style, as tools
advanced and video postproduction became more elaborate. Conversations
revolved around how to proceed, especially now that the PBS TV Labs
had come to an end. Sophisticated equipment necessitated expensive
maintenance—making it more difficult to work on the cheap for the polished
results that artists now sought. In some corners, social activism had lost
steam as glamour was on the rise.

Conference participants were restructuring their programs and
redefining what media art was. A frustrated Viola identified some of the
problems he was experiencing in exhibiting his art. Most museums, he complained, still relegated video to an isolated gallery without context. He often
found his videotapes shown on poorly adjusted monitors, which meant his
judiciously chosen color palette was skewed. Equally disturbing, he would
discover his carefully produced stereo sound set to mono, which obliterated
the spatial acoustics of a work. (This was the opposite of the attentiveness
of specialist media art curators to the particular aesthetics of each artist's
artwork that we exhibited.)

Media art's technical advances now meant that MoMA needed to
upgrade its exhibition equipment. With Film Department director Mary Lea
Bandy and MoMA director Glenn Lowry I made a pitch to Sony founder and
chairman Akio Morita, Mrs. Rockefeller's old friend, who soon joined her as a
museum trustee. Morita made a sizable donation of Sony's state-of-the-art
video equipment for the galleries and the new Titus 2 Theater, along with
sound equipment and a simple editing system.

The donation came at an opportune moment: I was able to utilize the
new equipment in Viola's 1985 retrospective, which featured three of his
installations and twenty-five of his videotapes. This was MoMA's first
solo exhibition to feature a video artist, and it was held in the contemporary
exhibition galleries instead of our usual video gallery. This exhibition proved
to MoMA and our audiences that video had reached a new stage, in which
it was the equal of painting and sculpture.

The exhibition's high point was the installation *Room for St. John of the
Cross* (1983), which is dedicated to the sixteenth-century mystical Spanish
poet and saint. MoMA carpenters built a black six-by-five-and-a-half-foot

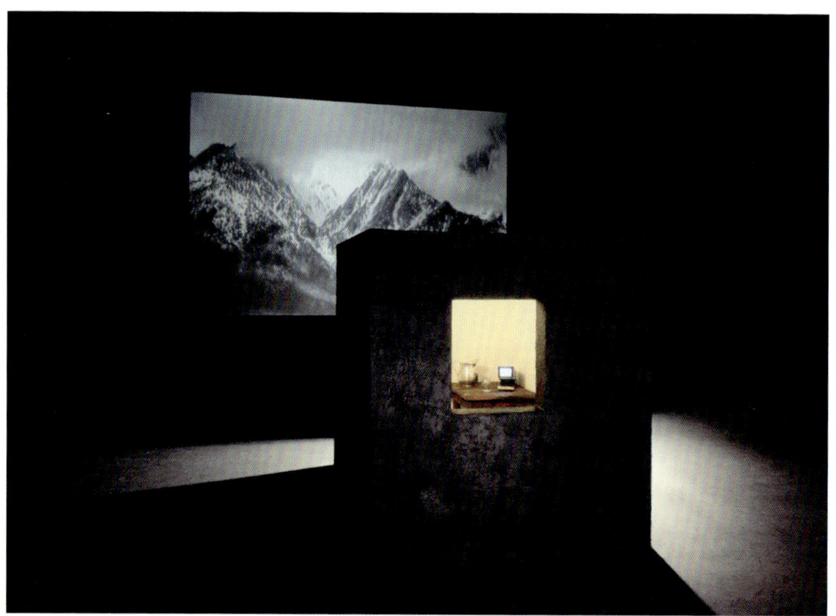

Bill Viola, *Room for St. John of the Cross*, 1983
Video and sound installation in a dark room, with a black
cubicle with window, peat moss, wooden table, glass and metal
pitcher with water, color video, and one-channel mono sound;
black-and-white video projection; amplified stereo sound; room:
14 x 24 x 30 ft. (4.3 x 7.3 x 9.1 m); projected image: 8 ft. 7 in.
x 12 ft. 8 in. (2.6 x 3.7 m); continuously running

(1.8 x 1.7 m) cubicle that approximated the windowless prison cell in which
St. John was confined for six months, a time when he was regularly tortured
for his heretical religious beliefs and he composed his ecstatic poetry. The
cubicle had a window, a dirt floor, and a small table on which was placed
a tiny monitor that bore the image of a beautiful mountain, flanked by a
pitcher and glass of water, and a just-audible soundtrack of the saint's
poetry murmured in Spanish, heard upon poking one's head through the
window. The cubicle stood in the center of a large, dark room with a grainy
black-and-white projection of the Sierra Nevada, shot with a camera held
out of a moving car's open window and accompanied by the loud amplified
sound of wind rustling by the camera microphone.

Viola came into his own with *Room for St. John of the Cross*. He had
used video, sound, and simple props to create an allegory about solitude
and anguish as sources of strength. Unlike the always-changing external

world, the rich, internal realm is always there, in fact becoming more accessible—Viola still believes—with curtailed physical activity and heightened concentration. In researching the show, he explained his goal to me: "I want to introduce an 'I' more extreme than in literature, a solitary position rather than a social discourse."[6] He was fully the master of his audiovisual tools, conceptual vocabulary, perceptual concerns, and spiritual studies that had begun in Florence.

Viola would move on to focus exclusively on video installation, with concerns that had more to do with transcendent beauty and raw emotional power, which grew out of an interest in Pontormo, a sixteenth-century Italian Mannerist painter known for complex compositions with brilliant-colored religious figures in twisting poses framed by ambiguous perspective and flattened space. Viola masterfully adapted this formula to video and went on to make painterly work that explores the phenomena of sensory perception as an avenue to self-knowledge. His subsequent installations became more institutionally accepted and have helped to raise video's overall status. This was demonstrated when in 2019 the Royal Academy of Arts in London organized *Bill Viola/Michelangelo, Life Death Rebirth*, an exhibition that looked at two artists who have interpreted human experience through their portrayal of the human body in order to give shape to otherworldliness.

Gary Hill

A technical virtuoso who rose to prominence in the 1970s and 1980s, Hill became known as a creator of single-channel videos and video-sound installations. His work with intermedia explores areas ranging from the physicality of language to synesthesia, perceptual conundrums, ontological space, and viewer interactivity.

Hill grew up as a skateboarder and surfer in Redondo Beach, California. He joined be-ins and frequented performances by such rock bands as the Doors, Jefferson Airplane, and the Grateful Dead. During high school, he took up sculpture and welding, fascinated by the brutal-seeming processes used by Giacometti and Picasso in the early twentieth century. In 1969 Hill headed east on a scholarship to the New York City–based Art Students League's summer session in Woodstock, New York. Settling into this rural Catskill Mountains hamlet, he encountered intellectuals, pacifists, and polemicists.

Sound was fundamental for Hill from the start. His predilection for being in the moment led to intuitive experiments in processing sounds generated by attaching a small synthesizer to his welded sculptures. He became absorbed by the different timbres and rhythms that were created from taut wire elements. While narrowing his focus down to the most elemental aspects of electronic sound, he came across the music of Terry Riley (b. 1935) and La Monte Young at a local record shop. The minimalist composers' interlocking modules and spare tones provided new inspiration. He still returns to their music.[7]

From his work with acoustics, Hill progressed naturally to video. Staying in and near the Catskills area, he was fascinated by the energy around Woodstock Community Video (WCV), an alternative production center founded in 1972 by Ken Marsh and his unconventional People's Video Theater that had moved upstate from Manhattan. Hill assisted Marsh in the making of spontaneous documentaries. In return, he received access to early consumer equipment at odd hours. He experimented alone late at night, lying on the floor, aiming the portable video camera down his naked body. In peering through the viewfinder, he found that his intimate world took on a heightened presence. With a restless curiosity, through trial and error he delved into the properties of an electronic signal, discovering how audio and video could affect each other and cause distortions in tandem or in opposition. An emerging artist, Hill perfected his technical skills, which soon included using synthesizers to experiment with image processing.

I first met Hill in 1975, when I attended the Woodstock Video Expovision, a short-lived grassroots festival of New York State–based media artists, where I stayed in a rambling old farmhouse in which dedicated guerrilla-style video makers lived communally. Wiry, with a mischievous grin and naughty demeanor, Hill revealed the devil-may-care attitude of an individualist.

Between 1974 and 1976, he continued to work with WCV as technical coordinator. Next, in nearby Binghamton, New York, he became an artist in residence at the Experimental Television Center (ETC), a pioneering production facility founded in 1969 by Ralph Hocking (b. 1931). At the time, the young engineer Dave Jones, with whom Hill would later collaborate, was designing an upgrade of ETC's processing hardware. ETC had been an early proponent of using a computer to create digital images and control systems for analog video imaging.

Hill spent several years at ETC working with Jones and plunging deeper and deeper into the phenomena of electronics, until he realized that he had become distracted from art making by technology. As he commented a few years later, "You can't sidestep the mechanics of the medium . . . but it's not what makes something."[8] Feeling that he had finally gained control over the construction of the analog video frame in real time, Hill moved on, in the manner of a linguist-philosopher, to analyze the relationships between words and electronic images.

In 1977 he and Jones moved to nearby Barrytown, where Jones built
a series of tools, which, later, in the early 1990s, included the first controller
that synchronized multichannel installations so that videos could start
simultaneously. The controller was sought after by installation artists
(such as Stan Douglas [b. 1960] and Judith Barry), who saw this as a big
step that made their work easier to present in museums.

Meanwhile, Hill connected with a group of local poets, which included
the poet-musician Charles Stein (b. 1944) and the poet and intermedia
artist George Quasha (b. 1942), who based his practice on "the principle
of free-moving order, liminality, and precarious, spontaneous configuration."[9]
Through the poets' encouragement, Hill started to challenge the visual
aspect of his own work by entwining his speaking voice with an image.
Soundings (1979) opens with Hill's commanding voice enunciating and
repeating over and over, "Imaging the sound/skin space . . . ," his words
emanating from an exposed loudspeaker the size of an open hand. In the
single-channel video's four sequences, the loudspeaker that continues to fill
the screen is deleteriously acted upon by what Hill described as "processual
rituals": Hill buries one speaker in sand, drives a spike through another, sets
one on fire, and engulfs the last with water.[10] With each ruinous action, his
prerecorded and weakening voice manages to seep out of the speaker that
is being obliterated for longer than seems possible. Working alone, Hill made
the video in his studio, funded by a grant funneled through WNET/Thirteen's
TV Lab. *Soundings* was never broadcast; PBS deemed it too stark and
abrasive for its audience.

As Hill persevered, supported by alternative spaces in cities scattered
around New York State, he often expounded upon how video evolved
technologically out of sound, explaining how the video camera bore a closer
relation to the microphone (with its electronics) than to the film camera.
He understood how cross-platform the electronic world was becoming with
synchronized networks of computers, communications equipment, and other
audiovisual devices.

On February 26, 1980, Hill premiered *Processual Video* as a lecture-
performance in MoMA's Video Viewpoints series. Declaiming a text in
a performance that became a single-channel video, Hill described his
changing practice, how his art had moved from a perceptual priority of
images toward a more conceptual method for developing idea constructs.
"Although my art is based on images," he went on to explain, "I am very
much involved in the undermining of those images through language."
He described the lecture-performance as "an attempt to circumscribe [his]
work and working methods, reflecting those ideas in the structure of the
'lecture' itself."[11]

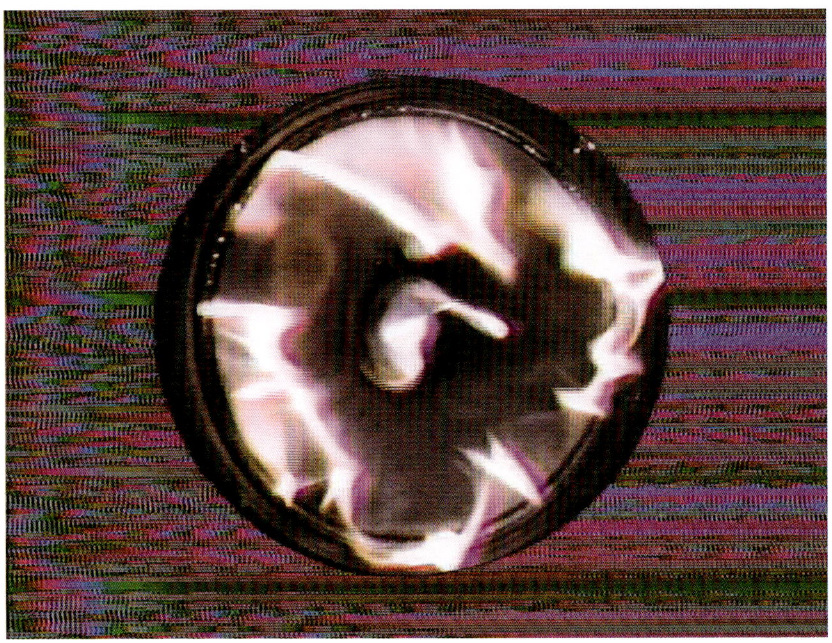

Gary Hill, *Soundings*, 1979
Video, color, sound, 18 min. 03 sec.

The video is a minimal black-and-white work that combines a compelling monologue with a single visual, a slowly revolving straight line that alternates between thin and thick as it rotates across the monitor screen. The spoken words convey thoughts that percolate through the speaker's mind—those of a surfer, an observer of airplanes at an airport gate, someone whose mouth forms the thread of an idea. The rotating line divides the frame into right and left, top and bottom, as the speaker's words allude to the split between the perceptual and the analytical sides of the brain. Quasha was an influence on this work.

Adapting the self-questioning texts of philosophers Martin Heidegger and Maurice Blanchot to his art, Hill increasingly questioned the place of language during a period when he was in and out of Paris, first in 1982 for a retrospective at the American Center and then again in 1988 when he made the installation *Disturbance (among the jars)* with the Centre Pompidou curator Christine Van Assche. Jacques Derrida, the French philosopher famous for developing a form of semiotic analysis known as deconstruction, is also an important figure for Hill.

In 1985 Hill moved across the country to Seattle, where he began teaching at the Cornish College of the Arts, the alma mater of John Cage and Merce Cunningham. Founded in 1914, it is well-known for its strong music program. Even though Hill would retreat into his studio in seclusion, we stayed in touch by phone, our paths crossing more often in Tokyo than in New York. In the late 1980s I remember once seeing him become stressed like a wild angry bear when he encountered technical snafus at the elegant Spiral building, near Shinjuku, where he launched an intimidatingly large and wildly whirling installation that appeared as if it were about to attack a viewer.

In 1989, when I expressed interest in his forthcoming work, he mentioned he would be at John F. Kennedy International Airport during a three hour stopover between planes en route to Paris. I made the effort to trek out to the airport. After years of camaraderie, I was comfortable with this wild spirit who could turn on a dime. We met for lunch near his departure gate, which was possible back then, when federal aviation security was more relaxed. Eating a quick sandwich, he enthusiastically outlined concepts for three new video sculptures. Poring over his diagrams, I became excited by one that I could tell would be a standout. I committed to this one and premiered the work four months later in a central location at MoMA.

Inasmuch As It Is Always Already Taking Place (1990), through its title, implies the impossibility of returning to the exact state we were in a split second ago. Life moves forward, never backward. The piece has the semblance of a deconstructed living, breathing being. Short video loops play on sixteen monitors that Hill removed from their protective shell. The bare TV tubes (called rasters) range in size from that of the tiny eyepiece of a camera to the dimensions of a human rib cage and are arranged on a shelf that is recessed five feet (1.5 m) into the wall. The shelf height compels viewers to bow slightly to meet the work on its own terms. The images on the various screens correspond to a particular section of a naked male body: a soft belly rises and falls with each breath; a quadrant of a face with an eye seems alive, peering out like a bird warily watching an interloper. Each loop inspires quiet contemplation. Despite showing body parts, the rasters are not organized in the manner of a skeleton: a tiny image of a finger, for example, is positioned in front of an image of a groin.

The depicted body parts fill the frames of their respective monitors, and, given their equivalent sizes, it seems that the image and the container are one and the same, similar to how a terrarium's sealed globe and living plants are unified. In many ways, the TV screen becomes part of the body: a holder, a closure, a vessel, no longer something that simply displays a picture. The raster and the image coexist as object and as representation, and as a living thing.

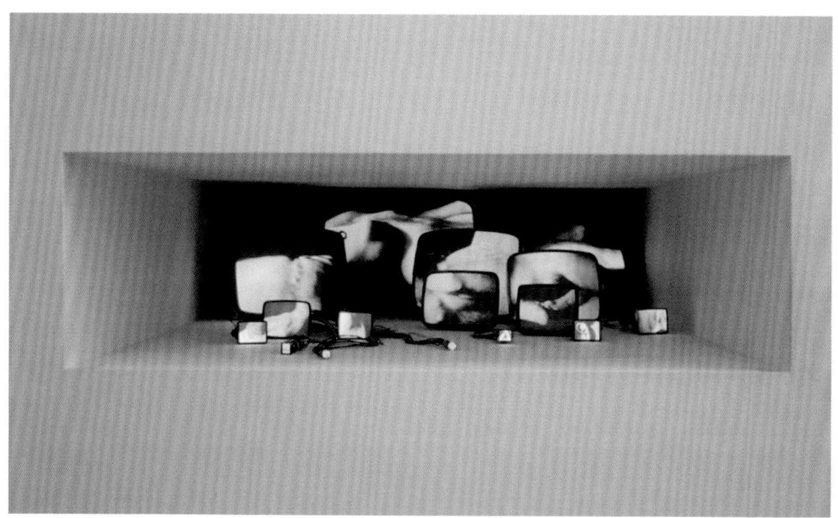

Gary Hill, *Inasmuch As It Is Always Already Taking Place*, 1990
Sixteen-channel video and sound installation, black and white

Thin black wires are attached to each monitor, and each bundle of wires snakes back along the shelf and drops out of sight, functioning as if they were the central nervous system of the separated body parts. It is as if neurons flow through this electrical network of wires, which connect to the hidden core of the body. This is Hill's metaphor for a human being's existential center, the soul.

Hill also orchestrated ambient sounds that create subtle texture for the installation. Sounds of skin being scratched or a tongue clicking inside the mouth, though barely recognizable, are combined with the lull of rippling water and soft mumbled phrases. The soundtrack creates a pulse that reinforces the living quality of *Inasmuch As It Is Always Already Taking Place*.

The body, in its plainness, suits Hill's endless loops, suggesting that its current state is not subject to the progress of a lifetime. This quality of continuous existence is essential to the living nature of the artwork and is what has kept viewers entranced by this piece. It is a high point in a career in which the artist has dedicated himself to mastering the technology of video and molding it to his ideas and intentions. Hill's life and self are the starting point for the eloquent metaphors he has constructed out of the protean medium of video. Incorporating the linguistic to generate multiple meanings and evoke a range of human feelings, he continues to exploit the uncharted terrain of electronic media for his art making.

When I first encountered Birnbaum's video work in the late 1970s, I recognized how her approach connected to facets of 1970s Conceptual and feminist art movements. The night we met as music mavens seeking relief from the colossal crowd at the club Danceteria, on West 21st Street, I got a sense of her critical mind and razor-sharp wit. She still challenges viewers and makes me laugh.

Birnbaum grew up in Queens and Manhattan and received a degree in architecture from Carnegie Mellon University in Pittsburgh. In 1970 she headed for Berkeley, where she thrived in the counterculture that in part grew out of the Free Speech Movement of 1964–65. While there, she worked in the office of the landscape architect, city planner, and environmentalist Lawrence Halprin. In 1973 Birnbaum completed a BFA in painting on a scholarship at the San Francisco Art Institute.

In 1974 Birnbaum moved to Florence, where she encountered a local art community. When out walking in the Renaissance city, she came upon a show of prints by the New York artists Vito Acconci and Dennis Oppenheim at the Centro Diffusione Grafica, Maria Gloria Bicocchi's small gallery (which later relocated and became Art/Tapes/22). Feeling quite alone in Florence, Birnbaum made the inviting environment her hangout. Conversations there propelled her in the direction of video, which the gallery also explored and specialized in.

Returning to New York in 1975, Birnbaum borrowed a portapak from an artist friend and experimented alone at home. Then she took a video production class with Global Village—a video collective and school founded by John Reilly (1939–2013) with Rudi Stern (1936–2006) and Ira Schneider (b. 1939)—in what was becoming SoHo. Interacting with the downtown art and music scene and the people in it, she felt a growing appreciation of video's double roots: contemporary art, specifically the unconventional forms of Land art and body art, and television.

At the time, many of Birnbaum's artist friends were reading the French psychoanalyst and psychiatrist Jacques Lacan, who believed that mirroring was central to the formation of one's ego. She developed an approach to self-inquiry that was the opposite of Acconci's and other male artists' early videos in which a kind of seduction was directed toward an anonymous female viewer. *Mirroring* (1975) was Birnbaum's attempt to replace a mirror self with a real self, through a repeated set of actions and manipulations of the camera. The piece begins by showing the artist's serious face, which in fact is her reflection in a large mirror. She gazes out toward the viewer, toward the unseen camera. The camera captures what is both her mirror reflection and her out-of-focus body as she stands directly in front of the mirror. When I first saw the work, it took a moment before I could distinguish which was her physical self, captured live by the camera, and which was her nearly identical reflection.

I associated Birnbaum's purposefully repeated actions in *Mirroring* with the work of choreographer Trisha Brown (1936–2017) and composer Steve Reich, who structured their elegantly pared-down compositions with repetition. However, Birnbaum's process had a closer connection to the work of her colleagues known as the Pictures Generation, a term coined by critic Douglas Crimp when he organized the 1977 *Pictures* exhibition at Artists Space. Jack Goldstein (1945–2003), Robert Longo (b. 1953), Cindy Sherman (b. 1954), Louise Lawler (b. 1947), and Sherrie Levine (b. 1947) all, in various ways, appropriated and critiqued images from the saturated everyday environment of mass media culture. Whereas Pictures Generation artists largely translated what they purloined from mass-media film or photography into other formats, Birnbaum approached pirating differently—she stayed within the medium of video. She critiqued the commercial side of the medium on its own terms.

Birnbaum was following the work of French-Swiss New Wave filmmaker Jean-Luc Godard, whose 1978 experimental TV series made with Anne-Marie Miéville, *France/tour/détour/deux/enfants*, had been produced through the Institut national de l'audiovisuel and Antenne 2, one of France's public television stations. The series had a strong impact on Birnbaum. It cast a critical eye on the impact of mass media on everyday life. Utilizing what can be called a "televisual language" for their investigation, Godard and Miéville employed precise formal devices—slow motion, the extended take, a fixed camera, on-screen text, and intertextual collages of photographic, cinematic, and television images. The documentary format and the direct interview are applied (and subverted) throughout. Focusing on the theoretical, the philosophical, and the quotidian, the series is largely devoid of professional actors; the subjects are ordinary French people: school-children and Godard himself, who conducts all of the interviews off-camera and is thus heard but not seen, a purposeful ploy.

As Birnbaum and I watched the twelve-part series on monitors at the Kitchen, we lamented that commercially minded American network television would never touch the likes of such radically experimental and intellectual work. In fact, it was fifteen years before ABC undertook the noir TV series *Twin Peaks*, by the maverick film director David Lynch (b. 1946).

By the late 1970s, most artists had come to see television, especially cable, as a desirable outlet for their work. While Birnbaum would aspire to reach TV viewers at home through cable television, she started out with the goal of putting broadcast programs under the microscope for formal analysis. Since it was nearly impossible at the time to get her hands on professional recording equipment, and because home-recording devices had not yet quite infiltrated the market, Birnbaum quietly gained the support of several broadcast engineers, who discreetly supplied copies of the programs she wanted. She created a series of works that dismantled television's conventional codes of representation in a powerful critique. Annoyed that commercial television's representation of women did not fit her view of herself or of other women, she focused on Wonder Woman, who had come to life in the 1940s as a DC comic-book hero.

Birnbaum analyzed the character of Wonder Woman, seeing her as a male creation in the TV series that originally ran from 1975 to 1979. In her videotape *Technology/Transformation: Wonder Woman* (1978–79), a business-woman spins around and around to become a powerful, albeit skimpily clad, superhero. Birnbaum relished how gender roles reverse when her heroine encounters a less-than-heroic male friend, who during a shoot-out ducks again and again behind a column as she defends him. A soundtrack with a chorus singing "Shake thy wonder maker" punctuates Wonder Woman's moves as the lyrics, performed by the Wonder Woman in Discoland Band, scroll across a blue screen. Hearing the band's song "Wonder Woman in Discoland" on the radio for the first time, Birnbaum had realized how closely the record and television industries were keeping pace with and capitalizing on each other. Appropriating the disco song as soundtrack, she forged what became a new vision of Wonder Woman.

Birnbaum's art was in line with the interests of *October*, an academic journal known for its critical interpretations of art, cinema, and popular culture, based on a progressive viewpoint that in the 1970s was shaping the debate around postmodernism and contributing to the adoption of French theory. My own perspective on her work was more straightforwardly feminist. I considered Birnbaum's Wonder Woman character an alluring, healthy-looking heroine, the likes of which could be found on the pages of Helen Gurley Brown's women's magazine, *Cosmopolitan*. Wonder Woman fit right in with the health and fitness craze *Cosmo* promoted by featuring articles on Jane Fonda's aerobics tapes, the hottest health club trainers, and the toned amateur runners competing in the New York, Boston, and Tokyo marathons. Purportedly wholesome recipes espoused by Dr. Atkins and *Diet for a Small Planet* were becoming the latest fad, having expanded far beyond the gastronomy of back-to-the-earth communes. I believed Birnbaum was asking, why is it that women are cast again and again as subjects of so many new compulsions?

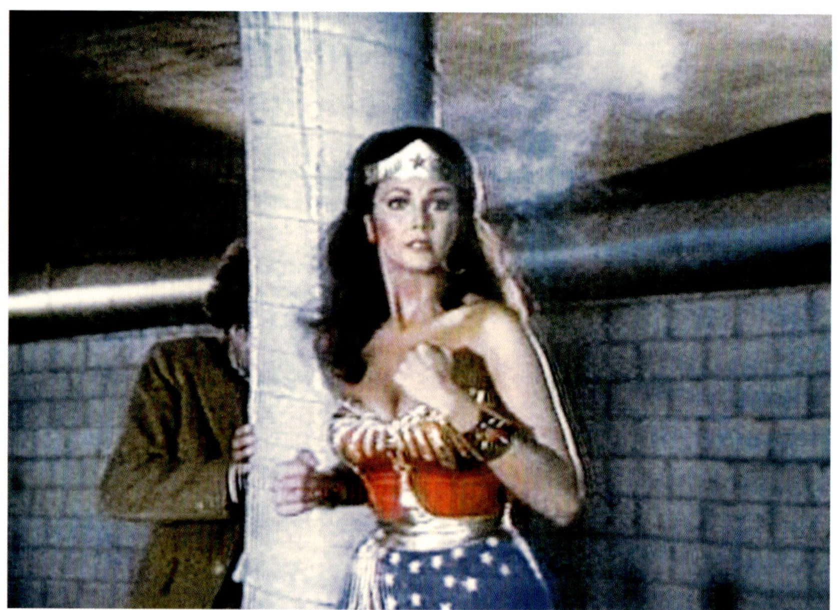

Dara Birnbaum, *Technology/Transformation: Wonder Woman*, 1978–79
Video, color, sound, 5 min. 50 sec.

Birnbaum's next video had a sardonic edge. For *Kiss the Girls: Make Them Cry* (1979), she modified imagery taken from the popular TV game show *Hollywood Squares*. Minor celebrities—washed-out actresses and actors—sat confined in a gridlike set of cages, illuminated by the staccato beat of the kind of brightly flashing lights that might also indicate slot-machine jackpots or a disco dance floor. One by one, each figure inanely greets the millions of TV viewers by saying hello, with a staged smile and toss of the head. Birnbaum turned their nervous laughs, the paranoid darts of their eyes, and their erratic hand gestures into a baroque, neck-snapping sequence of triple takes. Removed from their television context, the actors are exposed making stereotyped gestures of submission.

A keen aficionado of all sorts of music, Birnbaum energized her video by pairing her appropriated *Hollywood Squares* images with the latest hits that were being heard on the disco dance floor. With her levelheaded sharp-mindedness, she incorporated Ashford & Simpson's song "Found a Cure" with its repeating refrain, "Love will fix it." Birnbaum recognized the deception behind love as a Band-Aid, especially as AIDS was starting to emerge as an epidemic within the gay community and was being ignored by public health services.

Birnbaum edited *Kiss the Girls* while teaching in Halifax, Canada, at the Nova Scotia College of Art and Design (NSCAD), which was then a hotbed of experimentation cultivated by the artist-president Garry Neill Kennedy (b. 1935) and the artist-professor Gerald Ferguson (1937–2009). For more than a decade, Kennedy and Ferguson tilled the fields of Conceptual art, and each year allocated one faculty salary toward the travel expenses of ten artists invited from places such as Vancouver, New York, London, and Paris. Visiting artists discussed their practices and their local scene, and, at times with students as unpaid labor, made new work. Prominent German intellectuals—the curator Kasper König and then the art historian Benjamin Buchloh, who was also involved with *October*—oversaw NSCAD's publication program of artists' books, including one by Birnbaum.

While teaching at NSCAD, Birnbaum connected with James Coleman (b. 1941), Michael Asher (1943–2012), and other eminent visiting international artists who also challenged the notions and systems of art as a collectable product. Whenever any part of that group landed back in New York, I joined them for Sunday afternoon dim sum brunches in Chinatown. Conversations often turned to no wave bands heard the night before. It was easier to discuss music than art, especially because no wave music embraced everything from experimental film and video to underground art. Vernaculars overlapped.

At the time, both Birnbaum and Coleman were making work that scrutinized popular culture. I saw that connection when I came across Coleman's installation *So Different . . . and Yet* (1978–80) at Nigel Greenwood's gallery in London. I became part of the "setting" as I sat on an elegant chaise lounge on the parlor floor of a grand Edwardian house and watched the fifty-minute video unfold on a monitor in front of me. Shooting in one take, Coleman skillfully navigated around early analog video's technical limitations. He used the simple techniques of switchers and chroma-key and brought two spatially separated characters together in one frame. It was unclear whether the pair occupied the same pictorial space or simply the same temporality. Front and center, an actress wearing a décolleté evening gown performs and delivers lines, as she rearranges herself on a settee similar to the one I was seated on. She converses with a shadowy figure dressed in a tux playing a mélange of cocktail-lounge music on a grand piano, far off in the background behind her. Coleman was tackling questions that had to do with the nature of reality, and the impact of social stereotypes represented in the mass media upon the construction of one's own identity.

I exhibited Coleman's new work a few months later in MoMA's video gallery. Whereas Birnbaum carefully edited her material, which she copied directly from popular television shows, Coleman adapted stock poses and

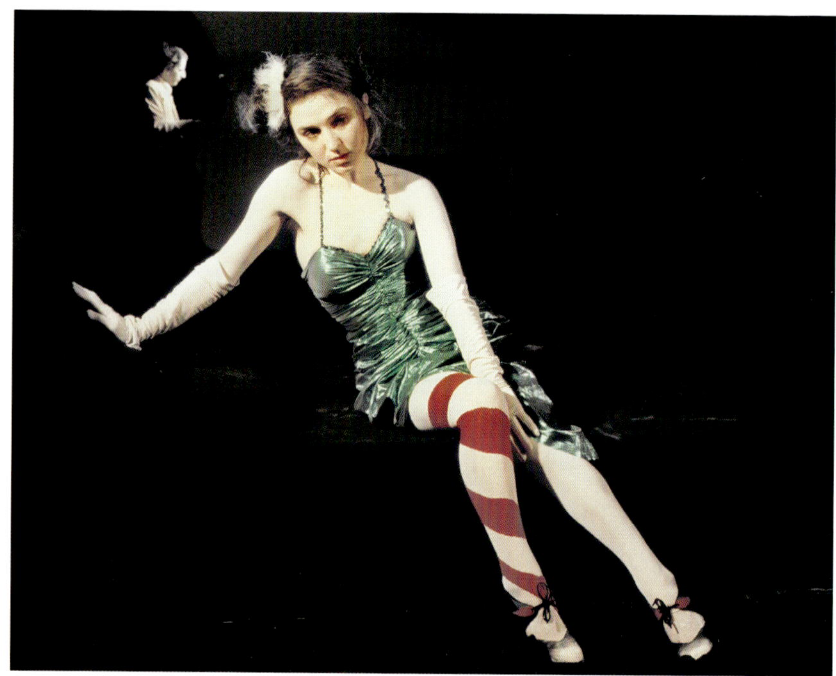

James Coleman, *So Different . . . and Yet*, 1978–80
Video installation, performed by Olwen Fouéré and Roger Doyle

stories he took from local soap operas, lurid pulp fiction thrillers, and romance novels, all of which appealed to a banal emotionalism. Although some erudite, established art writers and collectors might have assigned low status to the source material of both artists, critics and most curators considered their video work to be fresh, profound, and exceptional technically.

Many artists—whether in New York, London, Berlin, or Tokyo—had come to regard rock clubs, rather than museums, as the ideal locations for their intermedia inventions. In 1980 Danceteria opened on its third floor a "video lounge," designed and produced by John Sanborn (b. 1954) and Kit Fitzgerald (b. 1953). Artists including Birnbaum, Paik, and Juan Downey screened their works and held special evening events there. Some evenings I danced for hours on the Palladium's light-up Plexiglas dance floor as I watched Birnbaum's new videos projected large on the two twenty-five-monitor video-walls that came down from the ceiling on pneumatic supports and practically surrounded the dance floor.

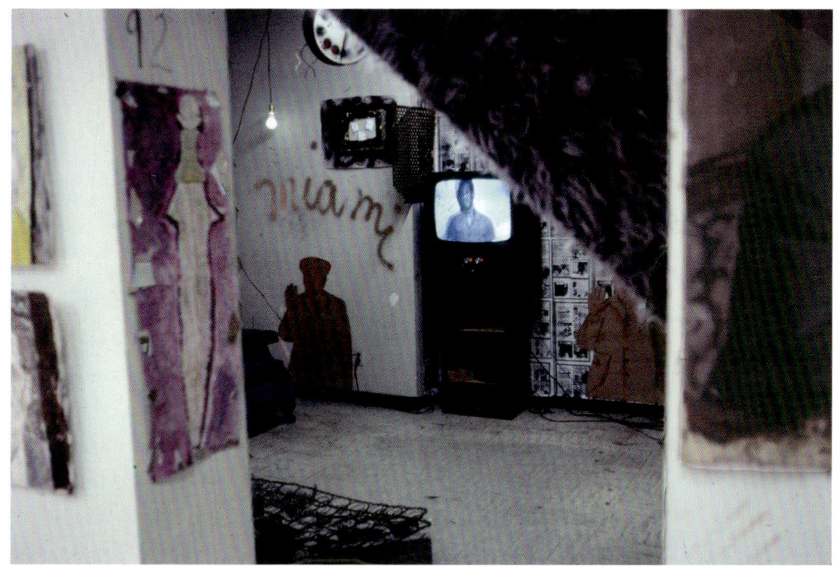

Exhibition view: *The Times Square Show*, New York, 1980

In June 1980, Birnbaum and I joined the large crowd tromping up and
down dingy narrow stairs to see *The Times Square Show*. The exhibition
had been organized by Colab, a group of artists that had recently become
a quick-and-dirty, strong underground force, responding to the repercussions
of Reagan-era economic policies, particularly the gentrification of the
artists' Lower East Side neighborhood, which had caused a wave of illegal
evictions. Crammed into a small, grimy three-story building that once
operated as a notorious massage parlor, Colab's sprawling and dynamic
hodgepodge of an exhibition displayed the same confrontational edge as
the graffiti painting style of New York artists Jean-Michel Basquiat, Fab 5
Freddy, Lee Quiñones (b. 1960), and David Wojnarowicz (1954–1992), all
of whom were in the show. I returned several times and caught the daily
activities, which included fashion shows and video screenings. I convinced
the MoMA Library to buy the LPs of Basquiat's and Wojnarowicz's short-
lived bands, and years later I featured the album covers in my *Looking at
Music: Side 2* show.

Well over one hundred artists from all five boroughs were featured
in *The Times Square Show*. That June the critic Richard Goldstein wrote
an article in the *Village Voice* promoting the show as a watershed for what
would become the art of the 1980s, the interaction between art and

creativity in the streets. One of the show's organizers, Colab member Joe Lewis (b. 1953), later commented that Colab captured a moment just as everything started to diverge.[12] Artists that dealers thought they could make money with were beginning to be cherry-picked, while others who were die-hard Marxist/Leninist/manifesto-ists remained active within the alternative community.

At that point, Birnbaum could be considered part of this underground. She forged ahead with video as painting recaptured the art world's imagination. In a Video Viewpoints talk at MoMA in 1981, she reflected upon how the art world had become vehemently antimodernist. She pointed out that intellectuals considered it bad form if an artist admitted a love of the medium they were using. Or heaven forbid that they mention the influential critic Clement Greenberg, champion of Abstract Expressionism. The domain of painting had reverted to the idea that the image was all about crudeness. She hoped that artists working in video would be allowed more freedom and not be limited to art-world trends. If artists wanted to make a comment about the media industry, they would have to keep a rawness and fresh edge to their work, especially if they lacked access to broadcast-quality tools. On the flip side, she believed that artists should be free to develop video with refinement.[13] MoMA was slowly coming around to acknowledge this new point of view.

Birnbaum went on to explore what she could do beyond appropriation and began shooting her own material that she altered with special effects and recalibrated as large-scale tableaux. This was during the first half of the 1980s, when video editing transitioned away from analog systems, which used two three-quarter-inch (1.9 cm) U-matic cassette decks—one that played the tape and one that recorded—with edits done by a remote controller (RM-40) that would direct the machines back up, then speed up together in synchrony so the edit didn't roll or glitch. Later on, the arrival of digital technologies and software meant more complex but smoother video-editing systems that could do the synchronizing electronically. Birnbaum, like other artists, started to explore what the new digital equipment could do. She drew upon her architecture and design skills as she took her video and installation work to a grander scale.

Video was gaining attention in proliferating international contemporary survey shows. In 1982, the Dutch art historian and curator Rudi Fuchs organized documenta 7, claiming art as a medium of social change both within the system of art and in real life. Birnbaum's *PM Magazine* (1982) was one of the few video installations Fuchs selected. In that multichannel work, Birnbaum conflated images from a happy talk news program and a Wang computer ad, and devised a sharp, updated view of computers, which were

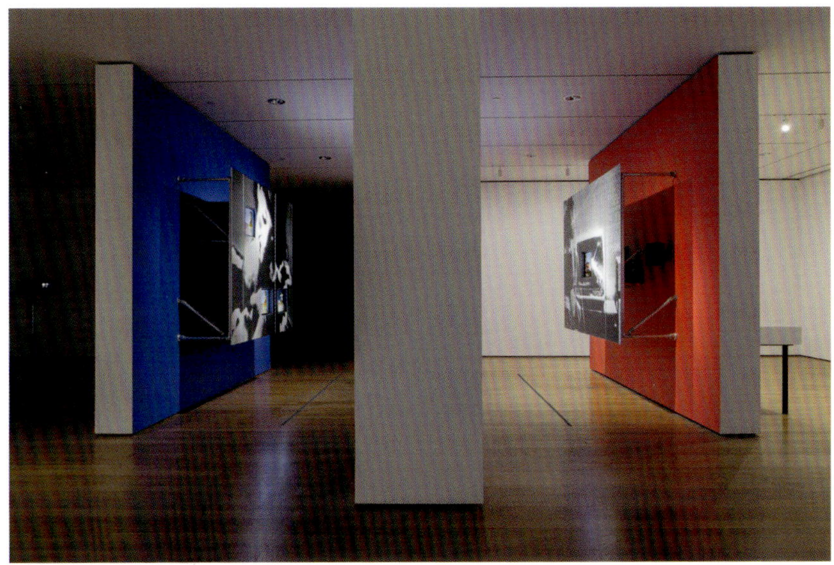

Dara Birnbaum, *PM Magazine*, 1982
Four-channel video (color, three channels of stereo sound, 6 min.
30 sec.), two chromogenic prints, Speed Rail® structural support
system, aluminum trim, wall painted Chroma Key Blue, wall painted
red; dimensions variable

now occupying our dreams, symbols of technology and information taking
over modern life.

In the early 1980s, Birnbaum launched her *Damnation of Faust* project,
which she based on Goethe's eighteenth-century magnum opus that Berlioz
had turned into an opera. She would go on to create two installations and
three single-channel videos as part of her *Damnation of Faust Trilogy*. Dorine
Mignot at the Stedelijk supported the production of the first of the *Faust*
installations for her exhibition *The Luminous Image*. Entitled *Damnation of
Faust* (1984), the installation is a panoramic two-channel wall installation,
an update of the Faustian myth as a free-floating dreamlike audiovisual
composition. The video begins at the local playground near Birnbaum's loft,
on the edge of gentrifying SoHo, which was closing in on a tight-knit,
well-established Italian community. Her characters are young local girls
who appear to be longing to break free of restraints in order to define
their own identity.

Birnbaum was one of twenty-four artists invited to present new
installations in Mignot's survey show. In addition to heavyweights such

as the theater artist Robert Wilson and the musician-artist Brian Eno
(b. 1948), Mignot included the bright-eyed, dreadlocked, now overlooked
artist Al Robbins (1938–1987). Allocated his own large space, this video
pioneer tinkered right up until the opening, arranging a tangled mess of
coaxial cables that snaked across the floor with dozens of monitors set on
top. Robbins had brought all his analog equipment with him and combined
prerecorded images of breaking waves and birds in flight with images
captured by live cameras in the gallery. True to the aesthetics of his
activist roots, Robbins's unkempt "sculptural" electronic environment
was the antithesis of Birnbaum's and the other artists' work.

Damnation of Faust was given a central position in the 1985 Whitney
Biennial, adjacent to billboard-size polemic artworks by Barbara Kruger
(b. 1945) and Jenny Holzer (b. 1959), among others. This marked the first
time a video-sound installation had coexisted with other art mediums in
a group exhibition. Before that, anything with sound was relegated to an
isolated room, so as not to contaminate the hushed galleries dedicated
to painting and sculpture. The change occurred with the introduction
of directional speakers, and as exhibition budgets expanded to include
expensive soundproof materials. Museum administrators had become more
relaxed, or simply were younger and more amenable.

Birnbaum was now a key player in the domain of contemporary art
museums and international biennial exhibitions. Her second installation
derived from the *Faust* series, *Will-O'-the-Wisp* (1985), is a sweeping
panorama based on a still from the project, with three videos displayed
on monitors slotted within the panorama. At billboard scale, her multi-
sectioned panels were flanked with swaths of color reflective of the larger
encompassing environment, on which she positioned an enormous blown-up
still from the video. Languorously paced, the videos emphasized her young
characters' feelings of detachment and anxiety about urban changes going
on around them. By now Birnbaum was devising techniques that she called
diagonal rain wipes and transitional fan wipes, formal structures inspired by
seventeenth-to-nineteenth-century Japanese ukiyo-e prints.

In 1987 Birnbaum and I traveled together to Tokyo, where Birnbaum
participated in an exhibition at the Spiral gallery. We joined an outspoken
group of international artists that included Tony Conrad, Klaus vom Bruch
(b. 1952), Tony Oursler (b. 1957), and the Kyoto performance group Dumb
Type, who designed the catalog. Over breakfast our conversations revolved
around the interface of technology and art. At that point, independent video
in Japan had reached an impasse, and the field had morphed into emerging
media, as artists there were breaking with convention. Tatsuo Miyajima
(b. 1957) had recently transitioned from sculpture to elegant installations

that used digital LED counters, out of an interest in the function and significance of time and space. Masaki Fujihata (b. 1956), who had been using stereolithography, a technique in which a laser polymerizes a liquid resin as it sweeps its surface, was now on to sophisticated interactive network installations, using multimedia technology to examine the possibilities for communication within virtual spaces.

During a break at the conference, several others and I walked to meet the fashion designer and performance art patron Issey Miyake (b. 1938) at his stylish store in the nearby Omotesando area. We went on to grab a five-dollar lunch of *tonkatsu* (the Japanese variant of schnitzel), followed by an expensive fifteen-dollar coffee in the fashionable Spiral building restaurant.

During the opening of documenta 9 in 1992, Birnbaum and I stopped by to see Piazza Virtuale, a TV project carried out by Swiss-American artist Mike Hentz (b. 1954) and Kathy Rae Huffman in a rigged-up van parked next to the popular outdoor cinema designed by the sculptor Franz West (1947–2012). We navigated the gear-filled van to chat with Hentz and his fellow members of Van Gogh TV, a group founded in 1986 by artists and technicians in Germany. The Van Gogh TV team and Huffman demonstrated how, on a shoestring budget, Piazza Virtuale technically (and miraculously) for each of documenta's one hundred days would be transmitting a different live performance carried out by artists in far-flung places, including Poland, Russia, Slovenia, Latvia, Finland, Czechoslovakia, France, Italy, Switzerland, Holland, Austria, Germany, and Japan. Out of grassroots gumption, Van Gogh TV's media project was seen around the world and proved to be the first artist-operated interactive television. Birnbaum and I anticipated that in the near future, artists would be connecting and spreading the word about their internet art, and we became among the first to have a personal email address.

What I have always admired most about Birnbaum is her curiosity and sagacity, and her ability to navigate the rising tides of new developments. She once pointed out that as tools and terminologies change, generations do too. In the 1970s, she appropriated images. In the 1980s, she stole images. In the 1990s, she sampled images. An artist who laid the groundwork for the media art that was just around the corner, Birnbaum always stays several steps ahead and in the game.

5

Everyone has a story, and video proved to be an ideal medium to convey one. Aim the camera at something meaningful, record, scrutinize, and engineer the edits—and out of the mix would emerge a narrative that was subjective, objective, or something in between. I organized several early shows that looked at how fact and fiction blurred in artists' videos, and I often contextualized work by studying precedents—film, television, radio, music, theater, literature, and so on—that video makers drew from.

In the 1980s, technology was becoming smaller and more flexible, and artists continued to mold video, performance, and digital technologies into art, especially storytelling. They often functioned as their own cheap subject, the spinner of a story, no matter how arcane or abstract. I had been watching narrative video evolve according to artists' individual predilections. The veteran avant-gardist George Kuchar (1942–2011) relished video for its low cost and the immediacy of instant replay. A younger Tony Oursler plucked stream-of-consciousness narration from the hallucinogenic 1960s and '70s and created emotive videos that he projected onto little rag dolls, using new miniature projectors.

By the late 1980s, there was a generation of media artists who had established themselves with institutional and critical recognition. I began to discover bold work from a younger generation of artists, including Pipilotti Rist (b. 1962) and a group whom several colleagues and I dubbed the "young and restless"—Cheryl Donegan (b. 1962), Kristin Lucas (b. 1968), and others who came of age watching the recently launched music video channel MTV. This under-thirty generation was opposed to the sumptuous postproduction of more established media artists and found inspiration in the technical limitations of consumer video. They pointed the camera at themselves and upheld the assertive performative spirit of early portapak days.

Miranda July (b. 1974) began with a similar ethos that came from her association with the DIY spirit of "riot grrrl" bands and zines in Portland, Oregon. July had a different path in mind. Driven to professionalize, she worked her way through indie music and performance and theater, and developed community internet projects, as preparation for a career in Hollywood and popular fiction.

George Kuchar

New York–born Kuchar was the unassuming elder statesman of the first-person narrative, active as an experimental filmmaker before he turned to video. This colorful, upbeat doyen of the diary-like home movie made roughly two hundred exemplars of the subjective form during his lifetime. He and his fraternal twin brother, Mike, who were revered for their lo-fi, campy aesthetic and childlike sense of wonder, began collaborating at age eleven, borrowing their aunt's 8 mm home-movie camera and their mother's nightgown and makeup. Using their weekly allowances, they produced quirky, ultra-low-budget, over-the-top stories of lust and angst, with such titles as *The Devil's Cleavage*, perfecting how to shoot and edit by scrutinizing the films of Hollywood veterans Alfred Hitchcock (1899–1980), Douglas Sirk (1900–1987), and Roger Corman (b. 1926) at nearby movie theaters in the Bronx.

In 1964, while still in their teens, the Kuchar brothers garnered the attention of *Village Voice* writer and filmmaker Jonas Mekas when they showed their work in New York's underground along with such notable artists as Andy Warhol, Kenneth Anger (b. 1927), Jack Smith, Stan Brakhage, and Ken Jacobs. In a November 1964 *Village Voice* review, Mekas proclaimed: "The Kuchar brothers have arrived on the movie scene. Here is the most macabre sense of humor at work. . . . Here is the Pop Cinema at its best pop. . . . Here are banality and corniness transposed into their grotesque opposites."[1] The brothers remained close, as they went on to pursue separate art film careers.

From 1971 until his death, George Kuchar taught at the San Francisco Art Institute. With a self-effacing disposition, an infectious exuberance, and a resolute work ethic, he inspired younger artists to pursue narrativity. Kuchar once wrote: "Teaching to me . . . filmmaking to me . . . is always some sort of loose script outline that I hope will develop into something visible and concrete, even if that concrete remains wet and vulnerable to foot-stomping and critical graffiti. It is my hope that the slab of concrete will never metamorphose into something hard and brittle."[2]

In the early 1980s, Kuchar switched from 8 mm film to video. He had given up on 8 mm due to his frustration with the way his films kept coming apart in bits and pieces during his feverish editing process. He would often be left holding grocery bags stuffed full of detached film splices. Once he became immersed in video, he grew into an even more prolific diarist, now that he was able to work on his own without an unruly student film crew to direct. Wielding his small, portable video camera, he captured beauty in the intimate details of his everyday life. His droll tapes were not for the faint of heart; they often bordered on the grotesque, and sometimes on the scatological. The Chaplinesque candidness in his vividly crafted ruminations in video captivated viewers and brought him attention among a small group of adherents of the art world.

Kuchar would always greet me with a winsome smile and a big bear hug. Right away he would have me in stitches, as he related his recent exploits. I remember his lamenting on one occasion that he had just put to rest his faithful partner, a worn-out old video camera. He expressed the same affection for it that he had for his beloved dog, perking up, however, as he elatedly described the personality of his new device.

Although a city boy at heart, Kuchar had always dreamed of capturing the rugged beauty of America's Wild West. In San Francisco, Kuchar relished the vicissitudes of life and landscape of Northern California. But he especially longed to confront the dramatic weather changes out on the majestic plains. During his childhood in New York, he'd had only limited experience of nature's ferocity, such as the torrential rains that sometimes flooded and shut down his local subway station. In fact, climate was behind a job at NBC in his early twenties. There he feverishly drew meteorological notations in pen and ink onto clear acetate sheets that then were super-imposed over a map of the United States, forming the backdrop for Frank Field's evening weather reports.[3]

Kuchar was able to witness the almighty fury of prairie thunderstorms and tornadoes by traveling around Oklahoma and Nevada. His *Weather Diary* series chronicled his pilgrimages to El Reno, Oklahoma, during tornado season. For many years, between 1977 and 2011, he'd traveled there alone to sit in a motel room or in a rental car, tracking weather reports on the radio, his anticipation building as he waited for a twister to appear.[4] As he chatted away by himself, he would record his monologue using his handheld camera. In his videos, he can be seen in profile, musing as he wistfully looks out through rain-doused windows toward the horizon.

Kuchar had remarkable timing and technical skills and an unusual amount of dexterity that enabled him to do several things at once, like a one-man band. For each one of his works, as he videotaped himself excitedly philosophizing, he hit the rewind button of a small audiocassette player belted to his waist and switched some upbeat music to a better song for his soundtrack. He edited each *Weather Diary* chapter entirely on location "in-camera," without postproduction later. The videotape would leave his camcorder just once—as a finished work.

Kuchar explained his methodology to a hard-core experimental film and video audience in a Video Viewpoints lecture at MoMA in 1989:

> At each stage I am constantly reviewing, going back right there on
> the spot, seeing where I can punch in new things and seeing what
> I have to get rid of in the scene I just shot. Then I punch in [and
> record] a new picture. It's like making a collage, laying scenes on top
> of one another. I don't even have to remember the scenes. All I got
> to do is remember a bit of dialogue that will last seven seconds.
> I know I got seven seconds; I say it in my head. You got to concoct

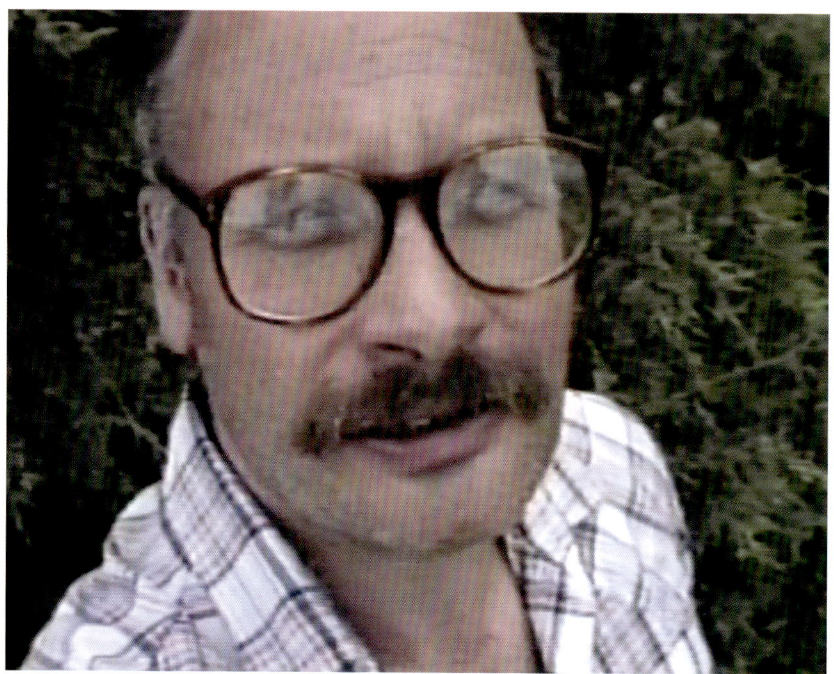

George Kuchar, *Weather Diary 5*, 1989
Video, color, sound, 38 min. 17 sec.

the words and say it in your head and depict the image that you
need and then just shoot it. And at the same speed. That is the only
thing you got to remember.[5]

Kuchar's prodigious skill lay in his ability to create his antic videos completely in the moment. His humanism, the poignancy of his work, and his
humble spirit call to mind the great nineteenth-century American writer
Henry David Thoreau. Whereas Thoreau ruminated on a simple life within
natural surroundings, Kuchar expounded upon the mundane and the mira-
culous in a less pristine setting for all the world to see, anticipating a world
fueled by listservs, chat rooms, and later forms of social media. Kuchar's
candor and truthfulness were especially noteworthy in contrast to the inane,
artificial TV banter not only of TV game-show hosts but also of newscasters
who performed as entertainers.

As a talented narrative video practitioner who came up through
the school of hard knocks by making genial, low-budget narratives, he

understood what it meant to contest the supremacy of the commercial industry. Kuchar was a sympathetic teacher who knew what younger artists were facing. In his Video Viewpoints lecture, he described them as

> castrated refugees from Jurassic Park because of the meteoric impact of new, electronic and digital mediums. We stand firm in the quicksand of a changing landscape, flinging that mud at all who dare to grab for dear life at the dangling video cables that swing above our heads like the sword of Damocles. That sword has already cut the hair of the student body down to the scalp. They wander about the catacombs of creative cadavers practically bald, looking like fetuses in bondage.[6]

Kuchar is revered by younger artists who have followed him as narrative innovators. They appreciate his infectious love of and campy use of the artificiality of cinema, and the genuineness of the bold adventures he carried out on camera. What mattered most to him were ideas, which is how he mentored his students, artists who have gone on to adapt technology's latest changes to their own narrative visions. He died of cancer in 2011.

Tony Oursler

Oursler was one of a younger generation of artists who took a DIY approach to video. He emerged in the late 1970s as the prolific virtuoso of madcap narratives that deviated from the products of broadcast television and the Hollywood film industry. Oursler grew up in a family of gifted storytellers that included distinguished science-fiction writers. His grandfather Fulton Oursler was known for writing the bestseller *The Greatest Story Ever Told* (1949), about Christ's childhood, public ministry, passion, death, and resurrection, and for having supported the magician Harry Houdini in an early crusade against fraudulent mediumship. It is not surprising that Oursler became preoccupied with phantasmagoria during a childhood spent north of Manhattan in the town of Nyack, close to his parents' offices at *Reader's Digest*, a popular general-interest family magazine.

Aspiring to become a versatile painter in the manner of Michelangelo, Oursler headed to CalArts in Los Angeles for his BFA in 1975. But identifying as a storyteller, he quickly realized that he would never be able to express himself as a painter, lacking sound and motion. Fortunately, he was learning how to be an artist at a progressive school founded by Walt Disney, the entrepreneurial pioneer of the animation industry. Oursler thrived at school in the charmed, easygoing atmosphere of what he once described to me as the soft twilight of the underground populated by hardworking nonconformists.

CalArts provided a foundation in Conceptual art, performance, video, and music, along with interdisciplinarity. Through an independent study with John Baldessari, Oursler discovered he shared a sense of humor and an interest in exploring the vernacular with his teacher. Baldessari suggested that Oursler think in terms of video projection, long before the technology was available. Baldessari was supportive of the younger artist's early videotapes, which through his connections were shown at the Kitchen in New York, and at the Los Angeles Institute of Contemporary Art in the late 1970s.[7] In the presence of John Cage, who was an artist in residence at the school, Oursler absorbed chance strategies that would become part of his methodology. He was immersed in contemporary music through his roommate, the puckish artist Jim Shaw (b. 1952), who had a vast record collection.

Oursler was delighted when a vintage portapak, initially bought for Hollywood-bound students but by that point sitting idle, landed in his lap. He experimented with painting in real time, one arm outstretched holding the portapak as he applied his paintbrush to big sheets of paper while looking through the camera's viewfinder; after hitting the record button, he took on the perspective of his audience. His videotapes evolved as moving pictures in which he performed, animating and endowing them with the attributes of life. He made his images move by using whatever material was available— for the most part, his own body. If a scene needed a hand or mouth, he cut a hole in his canvas and recorded the body part as he stuck it through. If a section called for sounds or words, he spoke or drew them into the story line. He incorporated music, which added to the atmosphere of the drama he was concocting. Working live as he looked through the camera and painted and recorded, he felt like a magician who could change the laws of physics and do almost anything—transform matter, space, and time; animate inanimate objects; and miraculously populate the theatrical worlds he devised.[8]

Video was the perfect medium for Oursler's hyperactive attention span, as well as for his rough-and-ready aesthetics. He liked the grainy, low-resolution, monochrome images he captured with the old CalArts camera. He zeroed in on the fuzzy, spotty fusion of the two-dimensional surfaces of his canvases and the monitor screen, and, more important, the three-dimensional physical space of his stage sets.

One day, Oursler stumbled upon a Paik-Abe synthesizer, a big, unwieldy, difficult-to-use analog image manipulation apparatus, which sat abandoned in the school's basement. Here was the tool Nam June Paik had developed and used to colorize his videos, including *Global Groove* (1973). Inspired by Paik, Oursler paused to consider art's role in assuaging the societal angst wrought by the radical advances of technology. Through the experiences of his own family and studies, he understood how the paranormal often blooms in tandem with shocking new technologies. A century ago, the wizardry of early cinema had made it possible for spiritualists and conjurers to perform sleight-of-hand tricks using the newfangled apparatuses.

Oursler saw how he could bring the transfiguring capabilities of the Paik-Abe synthesizer to punk's raw, ecstatic audiovisual improvisations using makeshift instruments and other electronic devices. Consumed by the no-holds-barred performance and video art developing around him, Oursler joined with kindred spirits Shaw and Mike Kelley (1954–2012), as well as other mischief makers who, as CalArts students, were critiquing Hollywood's slick production values in their experiments. They aggressively searched for taboo subject matter and designed their lo-fi work to disturb, baffle, and even amuse.

Starting in the late 1970s, Oursler was concocting histrionic narratives, each intentionally rough-edged and bizarre and made with expediency. His narrative odysseys are as funny as they are paranoid. With zero funding, he devised stage sets outfitted with funky props made of construction paper. He populated the environments with spare, handcrafted puppets and would spin a mesmerizing stream-of-consciousness tale through voice-over about the oddball eccentrics' lives. Once completed, his work gradually made its way out into the experimental art world either as an unlimited-edition single-channel video or as an installation, with the cardboard sets he constructed for production now on display and activated by his video running on a TV screen shoved into a make-believe window frame.

For his videotape *The Loner* (1980), Oursler devised a bizarre character by painting eyes and a nose onto his closed fist. His pliant thumb functioned as the character's lips, which mouthed his words in the manner of a ventriloquist's garrulous dummy. The Loner moves through the cardboard setting of a seedy bar, where the abject character is rebuffed by paper doll barflies. Preoccupied with the human face, Oursler managed to communicate strong emotional states with a few sketched lines and a cajoling voice-over. As the story unfolds, it conjures up the puerile, darkly twisted sexual awakening that Oursler has told me he experienced as a Catholic teenager, the kind of subject matter that also appeared in the work of his CalArts friends.

Eager to improve the soundtracks of his videos, Oursler studied how the early film composers Bernard Herrmann (1911–1975) and Nino Rota (1911–1979) worked. At the same time, he assiduously gathered subject matter, collecting urban legends and folktales from a combination of sources that included supermarket tabloids, pulp fiction, and overheard conversations.

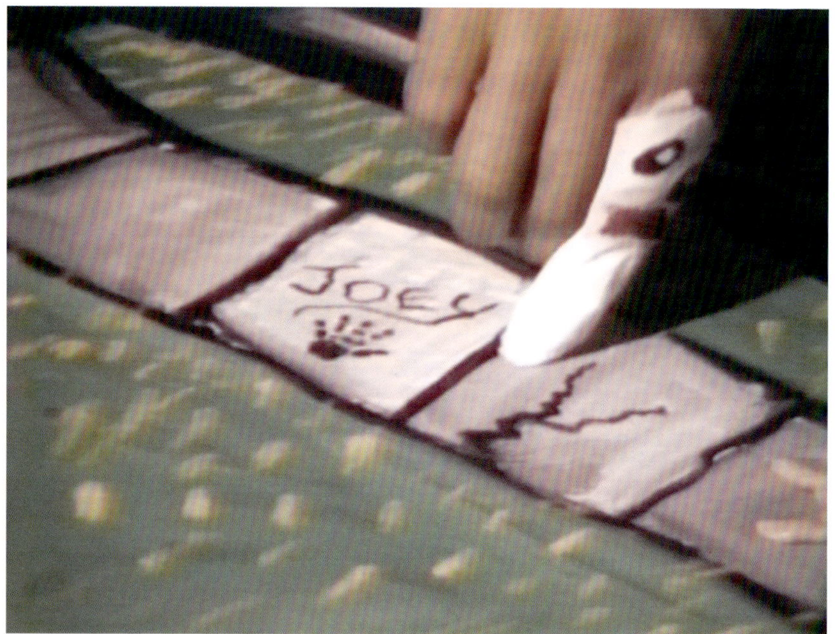

Tony Oursler, *The Loner*, 1980
Video, color, sound, 29 min. 56 sec.

Between 1977 and 1983, Oursler and his artist pals Kelley and John Miller, sometimes with Shaw and others,[9] collaborated as the Poetics, a self-described "art rock band" launched at CalArts, performing on and off together at venues in such cities as LA, New York, and Tokyo. With great aplomb and insouciance, they adapted music from various sources and traversed the punk, psychedelic, no wave, and noise genres in their raucous performances. They worked together and crisscrossed mediums on a few other projects, including a radio show and a performance involving dancing mops with the sardonic title *The Pole Dance* (1977).[10]

Around this time Oursler met the inventive intermedia artist and teacher Tony Conrad, who became a good friend. Conrad was a mutable artist, changing radically from project to project following the trajectory of his ideas. Oursler and Conrad shared interests in research-oriented multimedia.[11]

After graduating in 1979, Oursler left LA and returned to New York, where he and I would often meet to discuss the latest developments in music. Together we followed the artist Kim Gordon as she switched from painter to musician and began to perform in various downtown clubs. One night, Oursler offhandedly mentioned his unfinished feature-length student video, *Life of Phillis*, which he had abandoned. Excited by what he told me, I was able to secure for him MoMA's first video preservation grant from the NEA, which for years had been supporting MoMA's film preservation program. The grant enabled Oursler to carry out the months-long, labor-intensive, remastered final edit and complete his opus, using much better equipment than he had at CalArts. The video entered MoMA's collection and went into distribution as an unlimited-edition single-channel work through Electronic Arts Intermix. In a nascent field with limited resources, this is an example of how video professionals worked together on preservation projects so that early work could have the possibility of surviving into the future.

Life of Phillis (1979) is an offbeat, low-tech feature-length narrative that captures the ribald world publicized by tabloid newspaper headlines. Oursler's outrageous story weaves together such unsavory topics as child prostitution, necrophilia, macabre mutilations, religious visions, and weird science. The video revolves around the eccentricities of pitiful Phillis. She is both the quintessential victim and the avenging perpetrator, who carries out unspeakable acts directed largely at her miserable illegitimate child. Made from pipe cleaners and scraps of paper, Oursler's misfits perform in the tiny tabletop environment of Phillis's living room. The episodic soap opera is intensified by the programs that appear on Phillis's television, spasmodically scrolling down the make-believe screen, which is none other than a roll of toilet paper with Oursler's drawings on it. *Life of Phillis* is a benchmark for the artist's later work, featuring his signature dark humor, drawing strategies, and fascination with the psychosexual, including fetuses and pop psychology.

In November 1981, Oursler discussed his methodologies at MoMA in a Video Viewpoints talk that he titled "The More You Take Away from It, the Bigger It Gets." The title, a riddle that refers to a hole, describes the character from *The Loner*, whose deepening isolation serves to amplify his namesake quality.[12] Oursler pointed out that the title also refers to the squalid dark void that would engulf the character of his next video, *Grand Mal* (1981). He went on to refer to a fetus as a homunculus, what alchemists in the sixteenth century described as the representation of a human being in miniature. The homunculus suited Oursler's fascination with what I understood as his darker, stranger views of life, sex, and death—themes in his work that verged on the dreamlike and creepy. For me his vision and reasoning are as disconnected—or connected—as a hallucination. Oursler also noted: "I think anyone who's a Catholic knows that you're brought up to believe things you can't really see. Kind of in the same way science shows you things you can't see, but you know they're really here."[13] As his talk helped me understand, Oursler's fictive worlds possess the same credible magic he encountered in childhood—religion along with mediumship.

In the late 1980s, Oursler gradually advanced beyond his simply edited single-channel video narratives and diorama-like, handcrafted installations. He began a productive collaboration with the performance artist and writer Constance DeJong (b. 1950), who helped to sharpen the prose of his scripts. He also occasionally teamed up with the film artist Joe Gibbons (b. 1953), who then was teaching with Oursler at the Massachusetts College of Art. They shared a hippie-style communal house in Jamaica Plain, a run-down suburb of Boston. When I visited Oursler there, I saw how the ramshackle environment reinforced the abject side of his art.

During the same period, he was also making music videos with Gordon and her fellow members in the noise rock band Sonic Youth, who were Oursler's good friends.[14] One of their collaborations, the low-budget music video *Tunic (Song for Karen)* of 1990, which parodies the stereotypical interplay of celebrity, gender, and body image, is a rock-and-roll drama based on the life of Karen Carpenter and her struggles with anorexia. Gordon played the lead and sang on the track, which described the dying Carpenter as saying goodbye to Hollywood and hello to other dead rock stars, like Elvis and Janis Joplin. Oursler and Sonic Youth found the story extremely interesting, because "the Carpenters were whitebread middle-class people and Karen was somebody who was supposed to be so perfect. It was a heavy slice of Americana."[15] I was able to acquire the video for MoMA's growing collection.

Oursler's leap into art-world acceptance came in the early 1990s, when tiny, inexpensive LCD video projectors reached the consumer market. He transitioned from prolonged narratives intended for viewing on monitor screens and moved on to succinct stories that took a physical form and became sculpture. In a compelling series of works, he converted Raggedy Ann–like dolls from soothing children's toys to rowdy adult sculptures. Oursler fashioned the diminutive bodies of his dolls out of calico scraps that he bought at tag sales, and he used white fabric to make heads. Setting an unobtrusive projector on a tiny tripod on the floor directly in front of each figure, he brought his sculptural characters to life by projecting video faces onto the blank white fabric. Oursler manipulated the videos so that the animated faces on the dolls appear scrunched and their voices cry out in whimpering squeals.

Each of the pint-sized emoting characters in this new series appears to be trapped. In *Crash* (1994), one natters and peeks out of a barely open suitcase; in *Good/Bad* (1995), the figure looks out from under a mattress, where it lies pinioned on the floor. One pair of dolls is sewn together, conjoined like Siamese twins as they sit on a pedestal at viewers' eye level in *The Troubler* (1996). The sisterly pair are stuck together forever, as they chatter and argue nonstop, much like the id and superego in one's head.

In the series, Oursler's sympathetic firebrands deliver wild and crazy monologues, several enacted by Oursler himself, a few by DeJong, and others by the actress Tracy Leipold (b. 1965), who was then part of the Wooster Group theater troupe. Each character is presented as a slightly unhinged adult, who loudly declaims in an extreme mental state that seems to stem from a disastrous childhood experience. Oursler directed his critical eye at pop psychology's suspect labeling of new mental disorders, and in each of the doll works Oursler finds a balance between humor and reason and madness. Viewers have cathartic moments, grateful that a catastrophic situation is Oursler's art rather than life itself.

A few of the beguiling and horrifically cute dolls epitomized newly defined mental psychoses that fascinated Oursler, such as multiple personality disorder (now known as dissociative identity disorder). I remember Oursler saying at the time that some psychologists believed the illness resulted from excessive TV soap opera watching. The artist intended his dolls to become the embodiments of a link between the media and the psychological states it is capable of arousing—empathy, fear, and anger. Oursler's interest in mental disorders in many ways related back to his fiction-writer grandfather, who recognized that an illusionist's awe-inspiring stage tricks wowed an audience that had become spellbound by the latest magic, cinema.[16]

With *System for Dramatic Feedback* (1994), Oursler brought his doll methodology a giant step forward. Standing at the entrance to Oursler's installation, one of his tiny, hyperventilating dolls shouted, "Oh no!" over and over, as if to dissuade the visitor from entering the space. Inside, occupying the center of the gallery was what Oursler called his "mutation pile," composed of his life-size, scarecrow-like stuffed characters made of old clothes. Piled one on top of the other, the figures formed a large, tall mound, each one trapped forever by its own horrific psychotic memory, represented by a video projected onto a specific body part. One figure endured nonstop spanking; another's worried face was wedged at the bottom of the pile. On the far wall, a large projection showed viewers intently watching a movie in a theater. But whom were they watching and reacting to? Museumgoers in Oursler's installation, his artwork, life today?

The doll sculptures facilitated Oursler's transition from experimental video on the fringe to center stage in the limelight with a solid position as

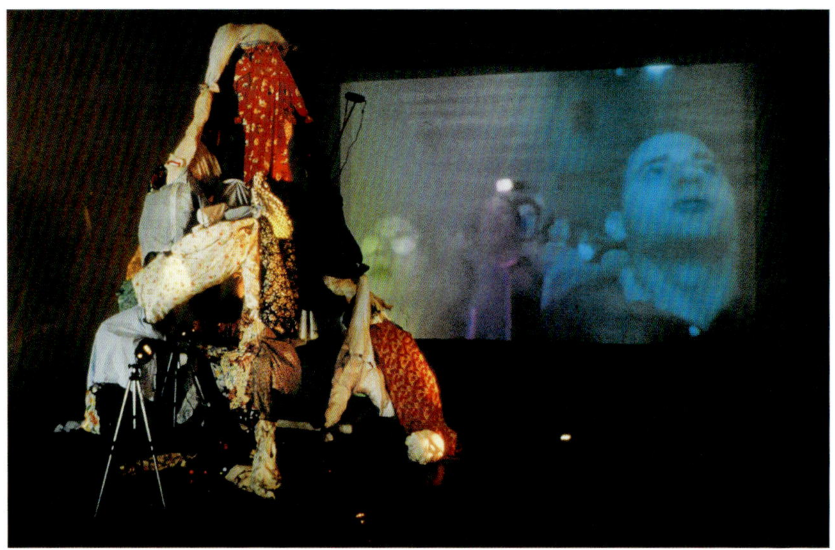

Tony Oursler, *System for Dramatic Feedback*, 1994
Ten-channel video and sound installation, with video projectors
and rag dolls

a contemporary artist. He now had salable, unique video sculptures that collectors and museums quickly snapped up. While several artists before him had created film objects that were considered largely uncollectable—such as Robert Whitman's *Shower* (1964) and Michael Snow's *Walking Woman* (1965)—Oursler had devised a new form during a transitional time for the newly marketable medium of video. Having found a niche with the miniature projector, which he continues to use, he went on to experiment further with narrative, using tools such as the then new CD-ROM (compact disc read-only memory) and in 2001 he created an internet artwork, *TimeStream*, that lived on MoMA's website with this note:

> The moving image has been transformed from medium to medium throughout its history; now it has coopted the hard drive. In this Web site specially commissioned by the Museum, Tony Oursler, an artist known for constructing phantasmagorical video tales, mixes intricate research with idiosyncratic information. The timeline tracks the evolution of virtual technologies and their relationship to what Oursler calls the spirit world.[17]

Personable and calm, the opposite of his dolls that emote nonstop
and recount untoward life experiences, Oursler continues to engage viewers
with fractured video narratives on an intimate scale as well as in large-scale,
outdoor public projects. He remains a dyed-in-the-wool storyteller who
continues to stop us in our tracks and make us ponder and also smile.

Pipilotti Rist

When I first met Pipilotti Rist in 1986, I quickly learned that vibrant color
infused both her wardrobe and her art—hot lipstick pinks, the vivid
synthetic tones of photocopiers and plastics, and tie-dyed T-shirts. Her
bright colors, which she often described as her "theology," evoked the
sixties, especially psychedelia and hippie subcultures that were open to
sensorial experience and the unconscious mind. Fearlessly receptive to the
unknown, in person and as the subject of her narrative videos, Rist radiates
the openness and innocence of childhood, which she elicits in others. I find
this to be refreshing in a rather jaded and conspiring world.

That year Rist and I were both in Bonn at the Videonale, a biannual
festival where I served on the jury and she presented an artwork. I can
still visualize the dark screening room where I spent long days previewing
videotapes and where I had heated conversations about the future of video
art with fellow jurors. They included René Pulfer (b. 1949), who had ample
experience as artist, curator, and program director at the Basel School
of Design, where he was one of Rist's video and media art professors.

Born in Grabs, a small Swiss village close to the Austrian border, Rist
is best known for her video-sound installations. She studied video and
animation at Pulfer's school, where the electronic equipment she had access
to was bulky, set in consoles, and too costly for a young artist to purchase.
Rist began by making Super 8 animation films and designing stage sets
for local rock bands. She invited audiences into her staged three-dimensional
pictures, which she thought of as dreaming bubbles that everyone could
experience together.[18]

In Bonn, the Videonale jury awarded Rist first prize for her lively, well-
crafted *I'm Not the Girl Who Misses Much* (1986). She had made the inventive
video using a clunky, stationary analog camera and a three-quarter-inch
(1.9 cm) video-editing system, which involved copying one section of a
prerecorded tape to another tape for the final version. Wearing a low-cut
black dress with her breasts exposed, she danced manically before the
camera, which she kept out of focus. Despite the video's being blurry, grainy,
and speeded up, Rist's radiant beauty shines through. She subverted the
porno-pop genre of MTV by singing a section of the lyrics from the well-

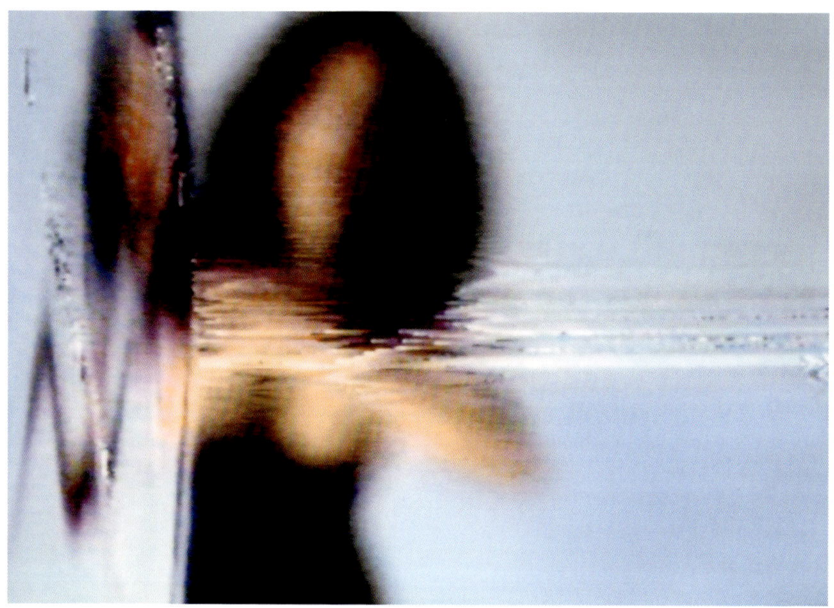

Pipilotti Rist, *I'm Not the Girl Who Misses Much*, 1986
Video, color, sound, 5 min.

known Beatles tune "Happiness Is a Warm Gun" in a Chipmunks-like falsetto.
The exuberant and sensual playfulness of the video belied the artist's serious
questioning of macho words and male posturing, which in style diverged
from the harder-edged performance videos of her sterner predecessors—
VALIE EXPORT, Joan Jonas, Shigeko Kubota, Hannah Wilke (1940–1993), and
Marina Abramović (b. 1946)—who also addressed issues of womanhood,
especially notions of beauty.

In following her videos and installations, I realized that the kindhearted
Rist always marches to her own drum. I came to see her as a deft user of
technology and a flea market devotee who is well-read and keenly aware
of how popular media promulgates gender constructs in what she considers
the parts of female society that sometimes feel pressured to the brink of
nervous breakdown. As curator Marius Babias observed in a 1996 article in
the journal *Parkett*, Rist takes a long, hard look at the accoutrements of
feminine culture, such as makeup, self-adornment, and the compunction to
masquerade with a cosmeticized identity. Her construction of self refers
to norms of taste and ideals of beauty, but, as Babius notes, it "is distorted
into a delirious filmic travesty of [beauty's] function—'personality appeal'

refracted through the prism of her own body."[19] An example is Rist's video *You Called Me Jacky* (1990), in which the artist lip-synchs to music and mimes in imitation of Madonna.[20] Through these acts, Rist undermines the typical music video's promotional appeal of polish and craft, as well as the industry's purported truthful portrayal of musicians.

Rist brought her open-mindedness to the all-women folk-punk band and performance group Les Reines Prochaines (the Next Queens), which she joined in 1988. Members wore outlandish outfits—garish dresses made of tacky fabric, synthetic wigs in jarring tones—and played on sets in the glow of brash lights. The band would swap their instruments in order to maintain a level of creative spontaneity. Although Rist played the flute, the bass, and occasionally a set of baby drums, she felt uncomfortable performing in public and instead assumed the role of designing the group's brightly colored, attractive sets. She stayed with the group until 1994.

Influenced by her experience with Les Reines Prochaines, Rist went on to merge music and performance in her own videos, with some electronic maneuvering. In 1992 she shot her video *Pickelporno* in a fanciful set that she had devised. The video opens as a young woman in high heels moves slowly through a maze of potted plants and heads toward a handsome Tarzanlike male. The pulsating soundtrack, composed by Les Reines Prochaines (Muda Mathis, Teresa Alonso, Gaby Streiff, Regina Florida, and Rist) and Peter Bräker, propels the action forward. The video alternates between the perspectives of the sexual partners, as they languidly circle around each other with rapt attention and eventually connect. Rist shot with a miniature camera attached to a stick, which she adjusted to slowly zoom in and capture close-up pans across the couple's body parts. Slowing down the footage considerably, Rist managed to put the camera into positions that would have been impossible for a bulkier, professional one. Eyes, toes, nipples, and pubic hair are transformed into a strangely luxuriant landscape. The shooting style resembles a kind of dance, as if Rist's goal were to encourage the viewer to enter the image and join the performers. With an infectious joy that honors sensual pleasure, the video counters the wantonness of a porno film, in keeping with Rist's desire "to propose images of sexuality rather than to analyze the pros and the cons of pornography."[21]

Another motivating influence behind Rist's merging of image and sound is her study of the early work of Paik and Yoko Ono, two artists who were open to chance. Their practices exposed Rist to the Fluxus movement's antielitist emphasis on incorporating the viewer into the artwork and the erosion of boundaries between art and everyday life.

Chance and a sense of wonder are at the heart of Rist's minuscule installation *Selbstlos im Lavabad* (Selfless in the Bath of Lava) (1994). The piece was brought to New York in 1995 at the invitation of Alanna Heiss, the inspired founder (and, at that time, director) of MoMA PS1. In this work, installed inside the building near the entrance, startled viewers could hear Rist yelling, seemingly from out of nowhere. As viewers would suddenly discover, the artist looked up at them from a tiny flat screen that was inconspicuously embedded under the floorboards they stood upon. Visible through a round peephole that measured approximately three by four by two inches (7.6 x 10 x 5 cm), cut into the floor, Rist appeared naked, engulfed by menacing flames, as if in hell. With arms outstretched, she cried out imploringly and yelled with absurd élan in several recognizable languages: "I am a worm and you are a flower. You would have done everything better." Her insectlike size naturally reduced the Good Samaritan instincts of the viewer. Using a now much refined, relatively inexpensive consumer video camera, she had recorded herself with all of the vernacular of a colorful music video, which is displayed pint-sized.

Rist's sense of humor aligned with what she saw of Paik's and that of her fellow Swiss artist Roman Signer (b. 1938), a sculptor, photographer, and video maker who records poignantly off-kilter experiments, using humble everyday objects paired with gunpowder to suddenly explode or collide with graphic results. In conversation with Rist in 2007 on the occasion of her show at the Museum of Contemporary Art in Houston, I learned that what she particularly appreciated was Paik's and Signer's seemingly effortless use of low-end generic technologies that were being integrated into noncommercial forms of communication, such as educational television. She also admired their informal approach. Like many of her generation, she relished the gap between home videos made with consumer gear and the polished promotional music videos made by the record industry.

Keeping up with Rist's career, I caught *Ever Is Over All* (1997) when she premiered the work in 1997 at the Venice Biennale, where she won the Premio 2000 Prize for it. The stunning installation grabbed the attention of unsuspecting viewers with its dynamic soundtrack that used Rist's voice, designed by the artist and Anders Guggisberg (b. 1966) and played through a first-rate sound system. Two large adjoined projections stretched across contiguous walls, spilling onto the floor and ceiling. The immersive double projection radiated the insouciance of summer. In the left-hand projection, at a slightly slowed-down speed, a woman wearing a diaphanous blue dress and red heels gracefully lopes along the sidewalk of a tidy Zurich street, holding a metal replica of the tall flower known as a red-hot poker. The flower suggests an ancient priapic wand, typically associated with springtime fertility rituals. The camera captures the woman's carefree movements as she merrily smashes the side windows of cars parked on the street with the

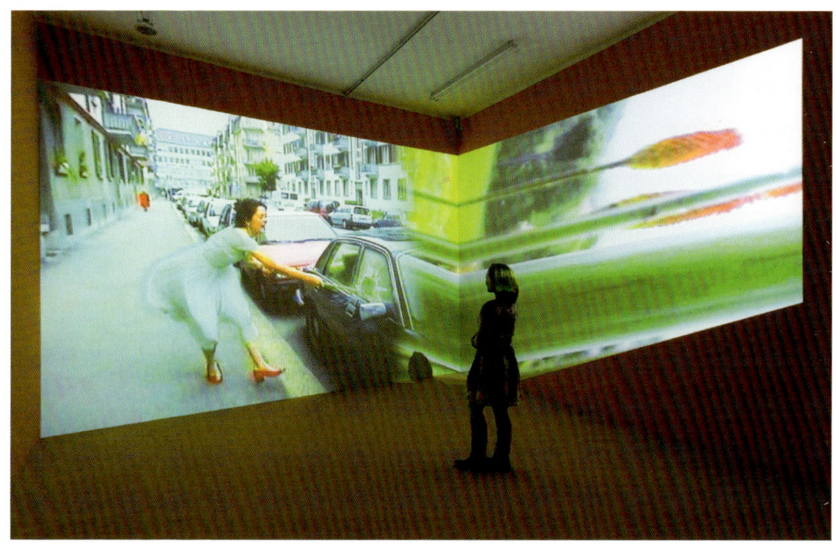

Pipilotti Rist, *Ever Is Over All*, 1997
Two-channel video installation, color, sound, 8 min. 25 sec.

metal flower. As if indulging an innocent child, passersby smile at the blatant transgression, including a policewoman, who salutes the perpetrator.

As a counterpart, the projection on the right side portrays a vivid field of actual red-hot pokers, expanding off into the distance on a sunny day. Shooting from the point of view of an insect on the ground, with her now customary technique of a camera attached to a stick, Rist leads viewers through a verdant field that exudes the warmth of grass on a summer day. Finding oneself immersed in Rist's high-spirited two-channel installation, its audiovisual components so naturally woven together, the viewer is transported into a magical realm of the artist's making.

For the complex production of *Ever Is Over All*, Rist came up with practical technical solutions. She pulled off the smooth dolly shot in the left channel by sitting in a supermarket cart as she was wheeled backward, shooting with two mini-DV cameras bunched together with gaffer tape. (One camera recorded close-up, the other at a wide angle.) Holding another camera, a friend shot in front of her as he walked backward.

Rist almost always works with a team, which often includes her four siblings. Her DIY roots and whimsical love of life bolster her canny ability to improvise a solution to any problem. Mistakes are welcomed. The process of editing is Rist's mise en place or setup phase, which occurs before she begins "cooking" the material: slowing it down into what she calls a soft motion or working on the colors and contrast. In the end, she adjusts her work to fit the particular exhibition space, which in the case of *Ever Is Over All* includes MoMA, as the work entered the collection.

Rist has explained that back in 1997, video-art production was generally low budget, especially when compared with filmmaking.[22] Her working conditions have since improved, and she has been offered larger production budgets since being taken up by the gallery and museum system, but she continues to use consumer tools, even though that means she often must wait until certain new technologies reach the consumer market before she is able to use them. She likes how consumer tools give her work a raw quality, because that rawness gives viewers more opportunity to form their own interpretations and feelings.

As digital video cameras have grown smaller, cheaper, and faster, they have become more democratic, at least in potential, and they require less brute strength to carry around. In the near future, when high resolution will dominate, Rist predicts that her videos will have a somewhat vintage look that is akin to aquarelle, the style of painting that uses thin, transparent watercolors.[23] The blurry vagueness leaves space for fantasy.

Rist compares audiovisual installation to a woman's handbag. The format has room for everything—painting, sculpture, technology, language, music, movement, flowing pictures, poetry, sex, premonitions of death, and sociability.[24] Out of this amalgamation emerge her imaginatively orchestrated installations, which viewers can bask in. Rist believes that the role of art is to encourage its viewers to open their minds in order to consider change with profound social consequences. A gifted audiovisual storyteller, her narrative installations, for me, open new doors of perception.[25] Rist turns a cold, technical medium into something joyous and warm and revelatory.

Young and Restless

By the early 1990s, I had begun to see the outlines of a new generation of artists, who were brazenly facing the video camera, mostly alone, and were using irony in frank narratives that explored female identity. Dubbing them the "young and restless" seemed fitting, since that was the name of a soap opera that was the first to deal on air with explicit sexual themes. The artists' tongue-in-cheek vignettes were smart, funny, and uninhibited. The young-and-restless video makers' role models were pioneering feminist artists who had been intrepidly addressing disenfranchisement, beauty, and sexual abuse in their work for decades, including Hannah Wilke, Karen Finley (b. 1956), Suzanne Lacy, Marilyn Minter (b. 1948), Howardena Pindell (b. 1943), and Tracey Emin (b. 1963). I followed the young artists' work whenever it was shown in alternative venues and the galleries sprouting up in Williamsburg and in Manhattan's Chelsea neighborhood, where the Kitchen had already resettled.

Cheryl Donegan

Donegan came of age in the 1990s, as fellow Generation Xers were questioning everything mainstream culture put in front of them. She and her artist peers began expressing themselves through the underground feminist, punk riot grrrl movement, along with grunge, slacker, and DIY aesthetics and forms. Politics were at the forefront of just about everything, as artists examined the efficacy of feminism, identity politics, and other political currents in art.[26]

Starting out in art school as a sculptor, Donegan realized that the process of manipulating physical materials, which evoked some degree of permanence, was uninteresting to her. She began sculpting with food, a more ephemeral medium, but it would rot and attract rats into her studio to dine. She turned to video, which allowed her to continue to use food as she investigated the ineffability of existence through the intangibility of time, which is at the core of her work.

A work that had a strong impact on Donegan early on was *Jeanne Dielman, 23, quai du Commerce, 1080 Bruxelles*, the 1975 film by Chantal Akerman (1950–2015). The hypnotic real-time study of a middle-aged widow's stifling routine of domestic chores and prostitution was much discussed during Donegan's studies at the Rhode Island School of Design and later as she pursued an MFA at Hunter College. The artist heard that the film was extraordinary and very long, with a surprise ending. (This was before the internet, when it was difficult to collect information.) She understood Akerman had zeroed in on simple, everyday movements; the fictive Jeanne Dielman can be seen scrubbing a bathtub for twenty minutes, before moving on to make a veal cutlet for dinner.

When Donegan learned about a screening of the film at the Alliance Française de New York in 1991, she dropped everything and raced uptown to see it. Donegan at the time was into the videos of Bruce Nauman, William Wegman, and Martha Rosler, and she realized that this film by Akerman was different, especially in the way the narrative was based around the tasks of daily life that were so familiar to her own growing up—household chores, babysitting, the mundane back-and-forth tasks of a housewife—all filmed practically in the dark. The closing of the doors between the rooms of the apartment seemed to create little boxes that limited the woman's life.

Moreover, the prostitution the woman carries out was presented as a part of the services she performs routinely. Donegan recognized the mundanity and the rage, shame, and violence mediated by housewifery.[27]

Moved by Akerman's film, Donegan went on to create her own works, in which she impishly—instead of solemnly, like the actress Delphine Seyrig in her role as Dielman—performed over and over a series of banal actions, carried out with a straight face, which she captured in her videos.

Donegan became known for videos that address clichés of how the female body is portrayed in art. In her early video *Kiss My Royal Irish Ass* (1993), viewers watch as she mass-produces paintings of shamrocks by dipping her bare buttocks into green paint and pressing them onto paper. As she was working alone in her studio with a camera, her interest in the idea of feminist labor was reinforced. Each video unfolded simply, the only edits being the moment she began performing an action and when she stopped and turned off the camera.

Donegan's videos from the early 1990s hark back to ones made with rudimentary video equipment and bare-bones effects by an earlier generation twenty years prior, such as *Now* (1973) by Lynda Benglis, in which the artist is seen saying, "Do you wish to direct me?" and repeats commands such as "Start the camera" and "I said, start recording"; and *Vertical Roll* (1972) by Joan Jonas. Both developed out of the respective artists' interest in real time, and the distinction between the presently unfolding "now" and the prerecorded past. These artists were both also well aware of their good looks but played them down. Donegan's work, by contrast, has everything to do with beauty and the carnal, as she tweaks the sensuality in the relationship between a painter (which she is) and her paint as befits a feminist agenda.

Donegan is more sexually explicit in her gestures than either Benglis or Jonas. With the grace of the well-known actress and celebrity fitness guru Jane Fonda, in her videotape *Head* (1993), Donegan surprises her viewers with an autoerotic workout that she performs in a neutral setting, showing only her upper body wearing a purple exercise bra. She appears in profile, facing a large green laundry detergent–like container placed on top of a pedestal. To a soundtrack of pop music, she unplugs the jug's spout, causing a stream of milk to spurt out. She leans forward and catches the liquid in her mouth, pauses, shoots the liquid back into the container, replaces the plug, and licks the spout. For the duration of the two-and-a-half-minute tape, she repeats the action, which brings to mind the titular sex act. When she splatters the liquid over the pink backdrop, she makes an irreverent parody of action painting. Toward the end, when she exits the frame, the empty setting suggests the location of a lurid crime or the aftermath of an illicit act of passion. In many ways, *Head* is a riposte to the

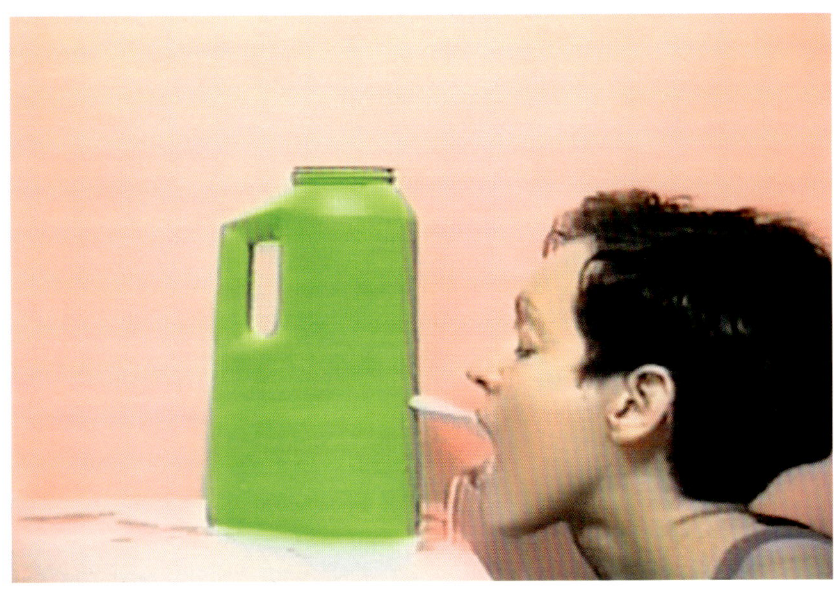

Cheryl Donegan, *Head*, 1993
Video, color, sound, 2 min. 49 sec.

somewhat belligerently masculine performance videos by Vito Acconci
and Paul McCarthy, created in the 1970s and much discussed for decades.

Donegan explained to me how during her first decade of working
with video, she often referred to Rosalind Krauss's essay "Video: The
Aesthetics of Narcissism," which appeared in *October* in 1976.[28] Krauss
begins by stating that narcissism can be a genre, which makes narcissism
seem to be a general theme of video art. (For many it wasn't, but at the
time, narcissism fit Krauss's interests.) The text seemed to be a sort of
shaming of the narcissistic video artist—at least, that is how Donegan's
Catholic-raised mind processed it, and it troubled her. Donegan considered
Jeanne Dielman—which revolves around an actress who carries out
Akerman's direction—a counterpoint to Krauss's criticism of video
makers' narcissism. What did excite her, instead, were Krauss's seminar
lectures at Hunter College (1988–90) that became chapters in Krauss's
The Optical Unconscious,[29] which were Donegan's introduction to "the
index" and semiology.[30]

As Donegan remarked in a 2016 *Art in America* interview, she was
also reading other critiques by second- and third-wave feminists, who were
known to say about work like hers, "You're performing for the male gaze;

you're showing your body" and "What are you going to be doing when you're 55? Rocking a G-string? How feminist is that?" Donegan would exclaim to herself, "Fuck you!" while another part of her was filled with Catholic guilt about exposing erotic underpinnings.[31]

She thought about being pigeonholed as a single-channel video artist, in particular a woman who performed with her body. She would be classified as making that type of work forever. Even if the labeling was biased, it made Donegan think seriously about what she was doing knowing that eventually she would evolve and change. She knew that art making is a perpetual rehearsal—current work would evolve into something yet to come.[32]

Donegan's video *Whoa Whoa Studio (for Courbet)* (2000) exudes the moxie that permeates her art and her life. The three-minute video unfolds in snippets of the outlandishly dressed artist moving about a sliver of her studio. Her face is concealed by a headdress made of shiny fabric and a laundry detergent bottle that protrudes like a pelican beak from the back of her head. She wears a sports bra and panties made of plastic bags and exposes her very pregnant belly. She stands between a video camera and her studio wall, which is painted in stripes of hot pink, coral, blue, and green, on which she draws outlines of her body. At times she raises her hand, which is covered by a gargantuan cardboard rendition of a hand with a pointing index finger. She hurls gooey globs of brown gook onto the wall, then leans over a monitor that sits off to one side and proceeds to draw black lines on its screen, which at other moments glows with computer-drawn lines. Her "whoa whoa" in the title and in her singsong soundtrack seems to question, what is reality? The title of Donegan's video also references Gustav Courbet (1819–1877), the nineteenth-century painter who invited the world into his studio to observe and comment on how he painted. Donegan's video displays her world and her practice, in which she is both object and subject.

Through her art, Donegan looks at the personal and the private, the highbrow and the tabloid, with a good sense of humor that tinges on irony. Compact, brainy, and visceral, her work asks questions that are difficult to answer.

Kristin Lucas

Like Donegan, Lucas came of age in the 1990s, when the grainy VHS cassette was the prevailing consumer video recording and storage format. She received her BFA from New York's Cooper Union for the Advancement of Science and Art, where she studied with Hans Haacke (b. 1936), a serious-minded artist known for work that critiques social and political systems, especially the system of exchange between museums and corporations and corporate leaders. His encouragement led her toward the uncanny overlaps between virtual and lived realities, as she explored the fast-changing mediascape that reconfigures perception and personal identity.[33]

The artist Perry Hoberman, another teacher, taught that the computer could function as both a programmable interface and a performative tool.[34] He was an avid user of early computers with custom chipsets (integrated circuits) that could handle audio, video, and direct memory access independently of the central processing unit, the part of a computer in which operations are controlled and executed. Hoberman, who had been a creative producer for Laurie Anderson's early performances, presented video documentation of Anderson and his collaboration with her to the class, so Lucas learned how a performative story can be put together in video.

Laura Cottingham (b. 1959) and her course on feminist art, plus the research for Cottingham's film *Not for Sale: Feminism and Art in the USA During the 1970s* (1998), had a strong impact on Lucas, as did Jennifer Montgomery (b. 1961), who screened the films of Maya Deren and Su Friedrich (b. 1954). Lucas began exploring such issues as how gender and the gaze were being addressed, the role of cameras in society, gender and technology, and how the personal was brought into institutional and technological frameworks.[35]

Through Oursler, also one of her professors, Lucas came up against tragicomedy through the droll performance video work of Michael Smith (b. 1951), among others. Like many of her professors, she had an ability to carry out technical details on low budgets, which gave her great freedom to experiment.

After graduating in 1994, Lucas spent several years working as Oursler's assistant, which is how we met. Although she appeared innocent and quite naive, she was plucky and rather tough. She lived rent-free in a squat on a drug-infested block near Tompkins Square Park. I attended many of the quirky VJ performances in which she dexterously translated technical know-how from media art to carry out performances in clubs around the East Village. Standing alone in the spotlight before a table loaded with gizmos and wires, she became lost in operating the low-resolution, video-intensive applications of chiptune music (the coarse electronic tones made with programmable sound chips used in vintage computers and arcade machines) and modified computer games. Lucas developed a low-key, loose approach to media, never conforming to one signature style. There was always something fresh to her work that showed how she experimented with electronics and examined aspects of the everyday.

Lucas had several residencies at the Experimental Television Center in Owego, New York, where she availed herself of a treasure trove of early analog video equipment, especially image processors. While there she made *Cable Xcess* (1996), which she describes as a public service announcement about how sustained exposure to electromagnetic fields—e.g., staring nonstop at computer or TV screens—can have deleterious effects. Poker-faced, she taped herself addressing the viewer both as a specialist and as a victim, then applied special effects to her dual performance. Meanwhile she claims to be transmitting a TV broadcast through her body, as if she were a satellite, wryly bringing together health, science, and hacker-ism.[36]

The street is the setting for Lucas's video *Host* (1997). The artist stars as a distrait individual adrift in a vague, panoptic digital network. In the opening scene, she ambles up to what appears to be a sidewalk ATM. As instructed, she swipes her card to begin a seemingly routine bank transaction. Lucas is presented from two points of view: as she stands out on the street, seen close-up on camera from the point of view of the ATM; and as she might exist from inside the machine, as if she were controlling the surveillance camera monitoring the cash machine. She proceeds to issue orders. "Just put it on my account," the sidewalk Lucas says, and in a confidential tone she starts to discuss her technical and emotional problems as if the cash machine were her therapist. She then internalizes herself into the system and begins to process an "upgrade." In a virtual conversation with the system she describes a difficult relationship. The dialogue seems to become a mix of "daytime television and tabloid," so that the ATM surveillance camera plays the role of both a shrink and the well-informed media.[37] As she strives to reach a higher level, an alter ego system operator inside the machine barks orders in computerese. From the street, Lucas asks if she can join a group therapy session but then quietly adds, "Are you paying attention to me?"

Lucas performed an action one evening for a Video Viewpoints program in conjunction with MoMA's *Young and Restless* exhibition in 1997, which I organized with curatorial colleague Sally Berger and sound artist and composer Stephen Vitiello (b. 1964).[38] Wearing a pith helmet with a tiny camera attached to it and connected to the theater's projector, she chatted in a sweet, unassuming voice and cast imagery on the big screen and made believe that instead of a brain, she had a computer processor within her, in a manner similar to the action that unfolds in *Host*. Around the time of the lecture Lucas commented: "As a woman, I am creating a discourse within which to elucidate my relationship toward the electronic dream. I unravel the complexity of this relationship by setting up virtual interactions with mediated devices, such as automated tellers, public access television, computer games, and the World Wide Web."[39]

While Lucas is tech-savvy, she does not indulge in naive technophilia. The cutting edge, she recognizes, is always in the process of becoming

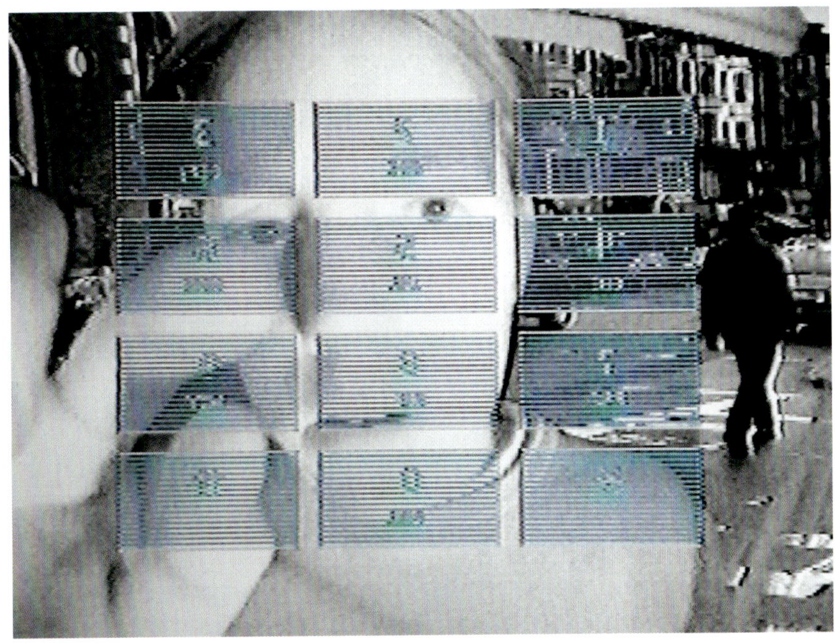

Kristin Lucas, *Host*, 1997
Video, color, sound, 7 min. 36 sec.

dated, and her work melds the familiar with the faddish. She always chooses the form that best communicates her ideas. She gravitates away from the monotony and stillness of work that exists strictly on a computer screen. There the rectangular frame is so persistent that she is compelled to destabilize it. As images and data become increasingly mobile, it seems anachronistic to be tethered to a contained rectangle. Over the last decade, she has turned to making art that comments on screen space without necessarily being bound by it. She has explored augmented reality, interactive technology that superimposes a computer-generated image onto a user's view of the real world, thus providing a composite view. Meanwhile, she has maintained a refreshing aw-shucks, homespun vibe.

Miranda July

July (née Miranda Jennifer Grossinger) set off on a young-and-restless-like path on the West Coast, where she assumed the surname of July because, as she once told me, she considered it the month that most facilitates her creativity. Our connection began in 1999, when I exhibited and acquired for MoMA's collection *Nest of Tens*, her narrative video that uses children to examine the behavior of adults. At the Kitchen a year later, I saw *Love Diamond* (1998–2000), July's solo performance in which she adeptly controlled slide and video equipment and imagery as she carried out a story about a girl and her mother.

Tracking where art and technology seemed to be heading, I went to Philadelphia and saw July's new performance, *Swan Tool*, which was part of "The Role of Live Theatre in a Digital Culture" conference in June 2001. July had upped the ante by combining video, performance, live music, and helium to tell the story of a woman (played by herself) who cannot decide whether to live or die. Later that year, when she performed *Swan Tool* at the Kitchen, we spoke together as part of the TV Dinner series before the evening performance on December 6; I caught her off guard by asking at what age she had run away from home. In February 2003 at MoMA, I programmed her flawless performance-demonstration of *How Will I Know Her* (2002), a web-based project about being far from the one you love for reasons that are out of your control.

From a family of new age writer-publishers who founded North Atlantic Books, July was often left to her own devices as a child in Berkeley, where she and an older brother invented their own entertainment by writing and putting on plays in a small playhouse they built in the backyard.[40] July and her best friend from high school, the musician-writer Johanna Fateman (b. 1974), were rebellious girls. They joined the Committee in Solidarity with the People of El Salvador, marched in gay pride parades in San Francisco, and listened to the indie bands Bikini Kill and Heavens to Betsy. In 1991 they launched the fanzine *Snarla*, which was punk by association and style, but, as Fateman once noted, in place of the usual scene reports, reviews of records, and travel diaries, they asserted a more abstract world of memory and self-reflection filtered through their new, unforgiving feminist analyses.[41] About *Snarla*, Fateman also said, "There were no rules: we went freely between prose and poetry and collage. There were no censors."[42]

As budding Bay Area writers, both women were inspired by the feminism of Oregon's alternative riot grrrl movement, which complemented the assiduous self-reliance they had grown up with. The six issues of *Snarla* aligned with the raw, confessional feminist writing associated with the Riot Grrrl Press that pulsated in the early 1990s. Feminism and punk were con-verging. Female zine artists adapted the machismo and swagger of hard-core male punk to spotlight feminine steeliness in the face of misogyny. That freedom fostered a stream-of-consciousness style that was a forerunner of blogging, which was to blossom on personal websites.

July dropped out of the University of Santa Cruz after two semesters, just before she would have had to declare a major and she followed Fateman (then a student at Reed College) north to Portland. Trusting she would be able to forge her own way within the accommodating punk underground in the Northwest, July joined Fateman's circle of friends. The small, easygoing city was a haven for offbeat artists and musicians who were dealing with gender issues and their concerns as marginalized subcultures. Many young artists were intersecting with the cult around independent filmmaker Gus Van Sant (b. 1952). As July pursued her writing and performed stand-up in clubs, she found odd jobs, including one at a driver-training school.

July briefly joined the queercore band the Need, formed by singer-drummer Rachel Carns and guitarist Radio Sloan, and meanwhile performed her own short talk pieces in music clubs, sharing the bill with the indie rock bands Sleater-Kinney, Chicks on Speed, and Dub Narcotic Sound System. Much of this early work was recorded and is still available on seven-inch (17.8 cm) records and CDs, published by the label Kill Rock Stars with such inscrutable titles as *Margie Ruskie Stops Time* (1996), *Ten Million Hours a Mile* (1997), and *The Binet-Simon Test* (1998). July was defining her disarming style of lyric writing as well as her elegantly low-key method of delivery, which often included intentionally scratchy, otherworldly noise. Her content usually touched on the strange and the libidinous.[43]

As July honed her dual literary and time-based art practice, the more public side of her work centered around finely tuned performances—events she carefully composed and staged live in local clubs. She designed words and actions specifically for the camera, released as short videos before she later moved on to more polished productions. In an interview in the *Believer* magazine, she said, "The level of control, that's part of what's so appealing about filmmaking—you have so much control over what the reader, the viewer, is noticing from moment to moment."[44]

She continued to be a committed social activist. In 1995, believing she could start a revolution of newly empowered young women who would make short movies and share them with each other, July launched *Joanie 4 Jackie*, initially called *Big Miss Moviola*. She began by placing notices in popular zines for girls and distributing a zine-like pamphlet, *The Missing Movie Report*, which declared, "A challenge and a promise: Lady, you send me your movie and I'll send you the latest Big Miss Moviola Chainletter Tape."

Marginalized young women from all over the United States heard the call and responded by using readily available, inexpensive consumer video tools to make short works, which they mailed in to July on VHS cassettes. Every movie July received was accepted, the opposite of juried festivals that rejected most entries. July assembled groups of recent submissions on cassettes. Each compilation comprised ten diaristic movies made by women and girls.

The compilation sent to each contributor arrived with an offset booklet containing letters written by the other filmmakers on that cassette. Word spread when American teen magazines—*Sassy*, which was geared toward indie rock fans, and *Seventeen*, which encouraged self-confidence in young women—published articles on the project. *Joanie 4 Jackie* empowered young women, who might otherwise have felt isolated, to express them-selves. The nineteen *Joanie 4 Jackie Chainletter* compilations made over the next decade went on to be screened at film-video festivals and DIY art events. Young artists, as well as teachers, librarians, and curators, bought subscriptions to the series. The loose underground network that formed around *Joanie 4 Jackie* taught July what she needed to know as an aspiring indie filmmaker. She also discovered in making the compilations how much she loved the process of video editing.[45]

When July made her video *Nest of Tens* in 1999, she applied everything she had learned as a performer, as an orchestrator of *Joanie 4 Jackie*, and as a denizen of the liberal, gender-bending environment of Portland. With video morphing from analog to digital, she adapted the more compact video production gear to intimate scenarios. Her twenty-seven-minute video— the appropriate length required should PBS wish to air it—consisted of four peculiar and obliquely connected stories. July performs as an awkward businesswoman stuck at an airport. She talks on a pay phone, looks down at her shoes, and interacts with a young girl who stares and innocently makes erotic gestures. In the following segment, a teenager brings a sleazy older man with her to a babysitting job, where he slyly exposes an erection. In the next story, a young boy silently collects cleaning supplies from around a house and proceeds to smear them on the chest of a naked baby girl, perhaps his little sister. He encircles the infant with cotton balls in a strangely naive and erotic fashion. In the final segment, a developmentally disabled man haltingly gives a lecture on phobias to an attentive audience. Woven together, the vignettes point to incongruities that lurk behind mundane interactions between elders and innocents. July pulls back the curtain of purported normalcy in everyday life that obscures anything aberrant. The refuge of home, the "nest" in July's title, is the secure place that we create for ourselves, as the "tens" or countless others like us do.

July's video entered the experimental video and film festival circuit, and at the same time, she went on tour and became active on the World Wide Web. In 2002 she had just launched *Learning to Love You More (LTLYM)*, a crowdsourced art project she devised with Harrell Fletcher (b. 1957), a Portland-based colleague who is a major figure in the development of

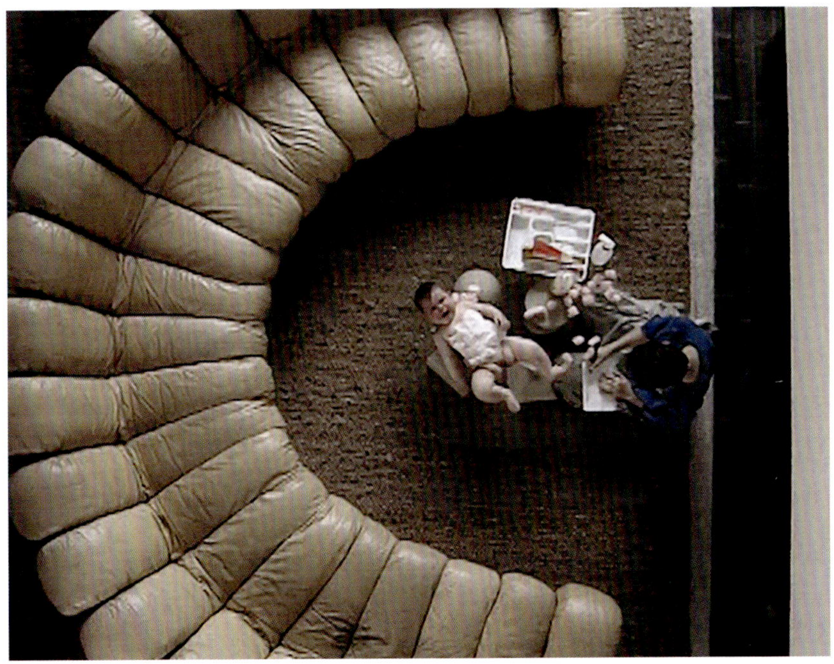

Miranda July, *Nest of Tens*, 1999
Video, color, sound, 27 min.

what became known in North America as social practice, or relational art.
Working on the principle that being creative enriches everyone's life, July
and Fletcher attempted to build a community on the internet through a
collaborative work. *LTLYM* began as an open call that spread virally, as July
and Fletcher posted weekly assignments that anyone online was invited to
accept and complete. Participants would carry out various tasks, following
simple but specific instructions. This is one example of an *LTLYM* assignment:

Assignment #8. Curate an artist's retrospective in a public place.
Select an artist whose work you really like and make black & white
Xerox copies of their work from books and magazines. Find a
public place, a bulletin board, a fence, or a wall, and post the Xerox
retrospective. Write a curatorial statement describing the artist
and your feelings about the work and post that with the exhibition.
(Don't make "art" from the artist's work—no collages. Just display
the images as if you were a curator at a museum.)

DOCUMENTATION: Take a picture of your exhibition, and a close up
of your curatorial statement so that it is readable.[46]

Once a task was completed, participants would send in their report
with their related text and their own photographs and/or video. Contributors
had the immediate gratification of seeing their work appear on the *LTLYM*
website, which was organized by assignment with a list of names and links to
each report. The online archive of intimate images, thoughts, and experiences
grew to more than eight thousand contributions from around the world.

LTLYM fit perfectly within what became known as relational art,
according to the definition of the French critic Nicolas Bourriaud. He defines
the concept as "a set of artistic practices which take as their theoretical
and practical point of departure the whole of human relations and their
social context, rather than an independent and private space."[47] In his terms,
July and Fletcher functioned as catalysts of their community artwork that
spanned the physical, digital, and emotional facets of regular people, who
took time out of their daily lives to produce acts of creative expression,
many of which required interaction with a stranger.

LTLYM demanded the attention and coordination of July and Fletcher,
just as *Joanie 4 Jackie* had for July. After an expansive seven-year run,
LTLYM was acquired in 2010 as a website by the San Francisco Museum of
Modern Art; the museum now hosts it as a static archive on its server. This
ensures that despite changing technologies, the vicissitudes of the internet,
and the artists' busy lives, *LTLYM* will continue to be studied as a step in
July's varied art career and the history of internet art.

July gained wider public attention in 2005, when she released *Me and You
and Everyone We Know*, an idiosyncratic indie feature film that is accessible
to a broad audience and won awards at international film festivals, including
Sundance and Cannes. Thus, July crossed over into mass media, not unlike the
trajectory of Steve McQueen (b. 1969), who started out as a serious-minded
artist known for video installations, such as his classic *Deadpan* (1997), before
he made his award-winning movie-industry film *Hunger* in 2008.

After finding celebrity status as a feature filmmaker, July gained
further attention as a novelist, and she also occasionally joins art biennials
and performance festivals. Eyes, like camera lenses, are on her. After
success, she faces a balancing act of figuring out where she belongs.
Competition is steep, now that the smartphone has turned everyone into
a moviemaker and blog writer, with new kinds of narratives being formed
almost faster than we blink. Everything is fair game—what is old and what
is new. Being out on the edge is still what makes art and artists interesting.

The Rise of Installation

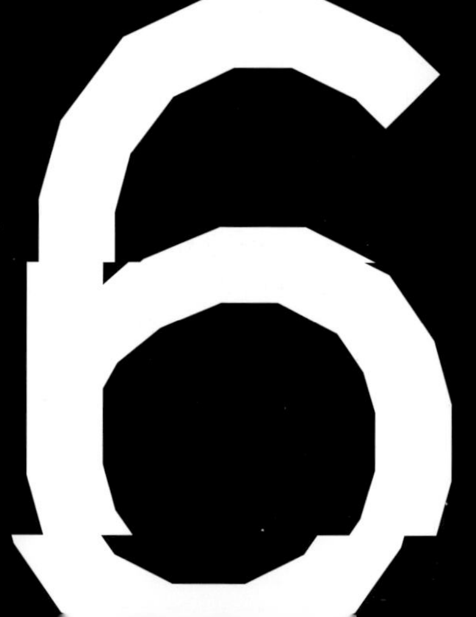

During the 1990s, media art started to be taken more seriously by professionals in the art world. The shift came about as artists incorporated the latest video projectors with markedly improved visual quality into their practice. The most successful of the new projection works were more than video images shown on the walls of dark rooms; rather, they were carefully planned audiovisual compositions based on complex content and exacting uses of space.

Enticed by astute marketing and PR, art enthusiasts hastened to the now proliferating biennials and contemporary blockbuster shows, aware they would find at least a few unorthodox forms and some surprises. In 1992 documenta 9 in Kassel, Germany, featured Bruce Nauman's *Anthro/Socio (Rinde Spinning)* (1992), the multifaceted artist's return to video and audiovisual installation after a hiatus of over fifteen years. The software publisher and philanthropist Peter Norton brought a group of American curators with him to the opening of the second (and last) Johannesburg Biennale in 1996. The curators' exposure to the projected video animations of William Kentridge (b. 1955) kick-started the career of this South African artist, who spent his early years with Johannesburg's inventive Junction Avenue Theatre Company, which addressed the social injustices, exploitation, and racism that black South Africans faced. Ten years before the visit, many of the same curators had given Kentridge the cold shoulder when he knocked on their doors during his first visit to Manhattan.

Over the course of the 1990s, *media art* became the term that museums, foundations, art schools, and critics adopted as the generic classification for any art that depended on a technological component to function. As the handy grab-bag name for a diverse and expanding field with many subdivisions, the term was so generic it sometimes led to confusion. On the other hand, as installation became an acknowledged form, it strengthened media art's position in the art world and is what quietly moved the term *video art* into the domain of art history. Media art's trajectory put emphasis on content over electronics and brought incisive allegories by multigenerational artists who responded—politically and emotionally—to the times. This was evident in the installations of Thierry Kuntzel (1948–2007) and the work of artists featured in my 1995 exhibition *Video Spaces: Eight Installations*, the first show to address these developments. The exhibition showcased the work of Stan Douglas, Teiji Furuhashi (1960–1995), Gary Hill, Chris Marker (1921–2012), Marcel Odenbach, Tony Oursler, and Bill Viola, as well as a collaboration between Judith Barry and the writer-artist Brad Miskell (b. 1964). My selection was based on a desire to present strong examples among a range of recent work.

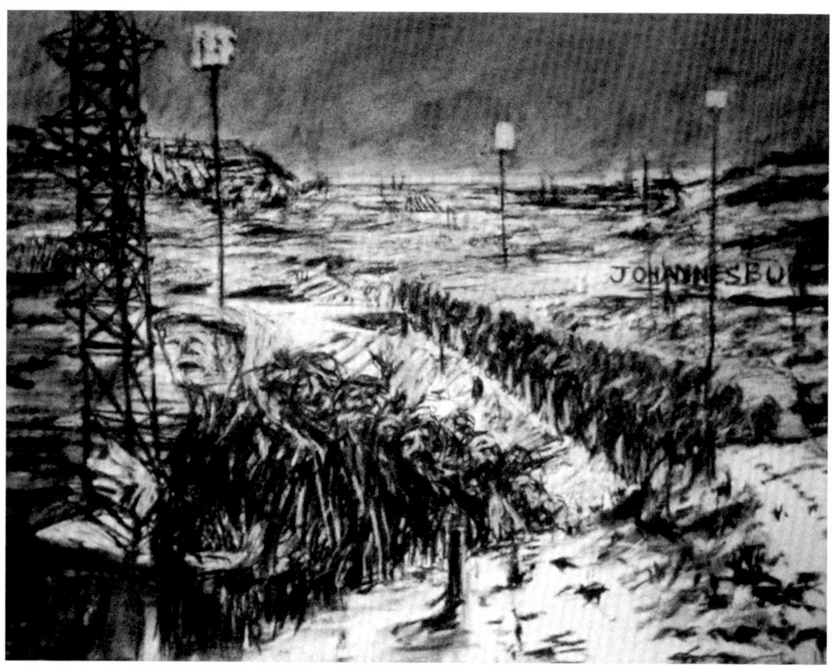

William Kentridge, *Johannesburg, 2nd Greatest City After Paris*, 1989
Video and laser disc transfer of 16 mm animated film, color, sound,
8 min. 02 sec.

The media artist and writer Thierry Kuntzel studied philosophy at the
Sorbonne, before he shifted to linguistics and semiology with theorists
Christian Metz and Roland Barthes. I was fascinated by how Kuntzel tackled
weighty issues—life, death, rebirth—in his art through minimal slivers
of light and shadow, turning his abstract videotapes and installations into
emotionally charged works.

In May 1983, this analytical thinker with a sharp wit discussed his work
in a Video Viewpoints lecture entitled "Screen Memory." Kuntzel explained
how his video work grew out of a scholarly investigation of cinema and
psychoanalytic theory. He discussed how he disliked representation but
always seemed to hover between repulsion-revulsion and fascination with it.
He went on to explain that his interests lay in the moment when the viewer's
perception of what is represented in the moving image is on the edge of
disappearing into the past as memory.[1]

A few years later, research brought me to Paris, where I stopped by Kuntzel's studio to learn what he was up to. The sun was setting over the Musée National d'Art Moderne at the Centre Pompidou as I walked two blocks over and climbed dark winding stairs up to the artist's luminous attic apartment furnished with refined flea market finds. The carefully orchestrated, contemplative space reminded me of the exactness in Kuntzel's early essay in which he analyzed the landmark film *La Jetée* from 1962, by the writer, photographer, and filmmaker Chris Marker, who tells the story of a post–nuclear war experiment in time travel. In the essay, Kuntzel describes the process of analysis as a "promenade dans un film," a walk that results in evanescent memories, in which something is always lost.[2]

Over tea, we chatted about Marker and other mutual friends, especially those Kuntzel knew from his days as a professor at the University of California, Berkeley, including his brilliant student, the Korean-born artist-writer Theresa Hak Kyung Cha (1951–1982). Cha had moved to Manhattan in 1980, and I often caught up with this eloquent, multilingual artist whose videos were grounded in performance, speech, and text. Her spare work explored the interactions of meaning and memory, similar to Kuntzel's. I was the one who sadly had to break the news to him about Cha's horrific murder in the basement of the Puck building, where she had gone to meet her husband, who was photographing the building.

While at UC Berkeley, Kuntzel had spent many afternoons in a small building that housed a camera obscura. There, his immersion in observing numinous live projections of the outdoors, cast on interior walls through a pinhole, stimulated his interest in perception. "In my work as a theorist," Kuntzel later said, "I quickly felt that I was moving away from writing and discourse to focus on my fundamental preoccupation: being with or in the image."[3]

Kuntzel, who had a melancholic nature, encouraged me to read the Swiss author Robert Walser, a fragile being who in an early essay had foretold his own solitary death in the snow. This was the inspiration for Kuntzel's three-channel video installation *Hiver (La mort de Robert Walser)* (Winter [The Death of Robert Walser]) (1990), which I soon presented as a Projects exhibition adjacent to MoMA's main lobby. The dissolving images of the expansive triptych were projected directly onto the long wall of the gallery.

Video was the perfect medium for Kuntzel to craft his silent, almost ecclesiastical portrayal of an entombed, yet breathing, sculptural figure. The central projection depicted a male figure lying motionless on his back. The naked body silently conveys the anguish of an encounter between life and the afterworld. During production, a broadcast-quality camera had followed a calculated path in the shape of an infinity symbol over the prone

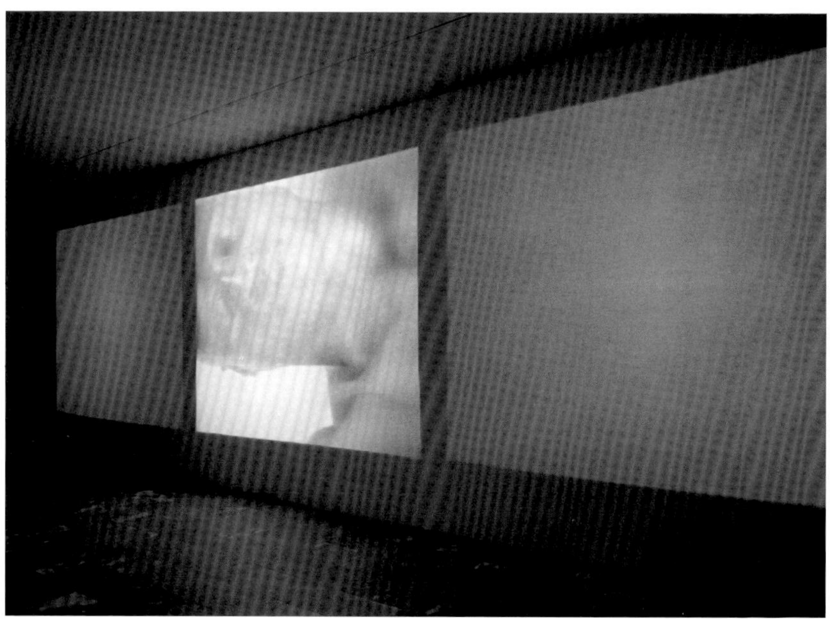

Thierry Kuntzel, *Hiver (La mort de Robert Walser)*
(Winter [The Death of Robert Walser]), 1990
Three-channel video installation, 5 min. 30 sec.

body. Slowly repeating the pattern four times, the camera subtly moves
both toward and away from the figure. Covered at first with thin fabric,
which at times takes on the texture of crystalline snow, the features of the
body begin to emerge. The actor was Ken Moody, who had been a frequent
subject of the late photography of Robert Mapplethorpe (1946–1989).
Kuntzel positioned this projection between two rectangular fields of cobalt
blue, which dissipate by fading to gray, only to reappear again.[4]

A day after the opening, friends and I drove Kuntzel to Coney Island in
search of the kinds of "freaks" he had seen in the legendary 1932 horror
film by Tod Browning (1880–1962) about circus sideshow characters. Unable
to locate any, although Kuntzel had been convinced we surely would, we
decamped to a Russian restaurant along the boardwalk in nearby Brighton
Beach, where our small group of revelers joined a voluptuous belly dancer
onstage. From that time on, Kuntzel and I often went dancing. In Paris,
I enjoyed many late-night, epicurean dinners that he prepared for me and
some of our friends—the video and film curator-scholars Raymond Bellour,
Anne-Marie Duguet, and Christine Van Assche. We laughed and swayed,

162

singing along to the songs Kuntzel played from his vast collection of LPs; Edith Piaf and Lou Reed were his favorite singers.

Nearly thirty years later, my memories of certain images in *Hiver* remain even stronger than those of our wild evenings. It is a work that occupies a special place in my mind, distinct from but parallel to the large-scale installation *Play Dead; Real Time* (2003) by Douglas Gordon (b. 1966), who also deals with memory and critiques and deconstructs media technology. In *Play Dead* Gordon filmed a circus elephant obeying a series of commands—repeatedly lying down and then awkwardly struggling to rise. Like Kuntzel's male figure at the center of *Hiver*, the elephant is subject to greater forces, beyond its control. Whereas Gordon plays with video art's old trope of real time and with the tedium of everyday life, Kuntzel plays with what goes on in the unconscious mind—the ineffable processing of the psychical and the real, which is the stuff of his and Walser's poetry.

Video Spaces, MoMA

My goal as a curator continued to be to decipher the many overlapping categories that video and other media were taking, especially artworks that were created away from the global capitals of culture. Less trodden paths still suited my nature, and I avidly pursued what was emergent and lesser known. At MoMA throughout the 1990s, video maintained a resilient position, as I continued to organize an ongoing series of exhibitions that showcased the perspectives of artists who worked with electronic gear in different parts of Asia and the Pacific, and Eastern Europe before the Soviet Union fell and Germany reunified.

I had been seeing artists explore three-dimensionality in increasingly expansive installations that used video. By the mid-1990s, I felt the time was right to tackle a survey with recent video installations made by artists from around the world, to showcase their distinctive approaches and points of view. When MoMA's then director Richard Oldenburg gave the exhibition *Video Spaces* a green light and allocated a good budget and the entire temporary contemporary exhibition gallery, I first settled on a group of artists and then selected which of their works to feature. I thought about the show as an engaging totality that would establish an informative introduction for the public. The final list included eight three-dimensional works that were shown together for the first time. The two years of preparation required me to spend hours with MoMA's lead exhibition designer in his subterranean office across from the carpenters' workshop. We came up with a layout that gave each installation a spacious area with soundproofed walls and transformed the formidably austere, cavernous

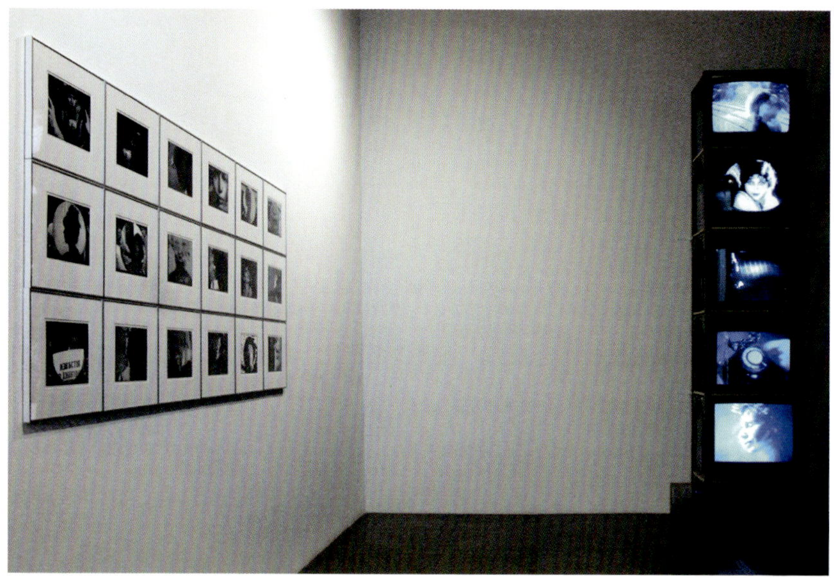

Chris Marker, *Silent Movie*, 1995
Five-channel video and sound installation, 20 min. (looped) each

galleries into a handsome arena for this innovative new art. The works were situated as a progression so that museumgoers readily moved from one work to another and looked and listened and interacted with the storylines and tactics specific to each installation.

The first piece visitors encountered was *Silent Movie* (1995) by the venerable Chris Marker. I had just worked with this reclusive elder statesman of film and media on a show that featured all of his single-channel videos—television series, video essays, and music videos—including one in which his cat plays the piano, and another in which an elephant dances to Igor Stravinsky. Whenever I had to fax Marker a technical question, his eloquent answer would always come back to me with a charming anecdote and a drawing of his cat.[5] (Marker was an observant and elusive person. It may have been the alertness, idiosyncratic nature, and unreadable intelligence of cats that appealed to him.)

Silent Movie consists of a sculpture—a tower of five oversize cube monitors carefully placed one on top of the other—surrounded by a series of classic-looking film posters, created by the artist and hung on the walls. The black-and-white video images of a beautiful woman—Marker's friend, the young actress Catherine Belkhodja—shown on the screens appeared to have been taken from the golden age of silent film, a passion of Marker's. He brought the visual effects of the early era—dissolves and subtitles—up to date by including his computer-controlled images on the five screens.[6] His moving images ran through a computer interface that assembled an ever-changing array of sequences. At any given moment, each scene was in a unique juxtaposition with the other images passing across the surrounding monitors. Thus, the viewers' perception of coloration, tone, and association was governed by chance contiguities.

In the exhibition website, I included texts by each artist. Marker wrote:

> To give an installation the name of something that never existed is probably less innocent than the average cat may infer. There was never anything like silent cinema, except at the very beginning, or in film libraries, or when the pianist had caught a bad flu. There was at least a pianist, and soon an orchestra, next the Wurlitzer, and what contraptions did they use, in the day of my childhood, to play regularly the same tunes to accompany the same film? I'm probably one of the last earthlings—the "last," says the cat—to remember what themes came with what films: "A Midsummer Night's Dream" on *Wings* (the dogfights), Liszt's "The Preludes" on *Ben-Hur*. A touch of *humour noir* here, to think that the saga of the young Hebrew prince was adorned by Hitler's favorite music, which in turn explains why you hear it more often than Wagner on the German war newsreels—but I get carried away.[7]

Nearby, I positioned Hill's *Inasmuch As It Is Always Already Taking Place* (1990). This was the second time we presented the installation. To set up the work, MoMA's technical crew had to cope with the fragility of the sixteen TV tubes that Hill had meticulously taken out of their protective outer casings in order to elongate the wires of each one so that they would seem nervelike. The collective experience of handling Hill's piece and the detailed documentation we made later became critical, when the museum acquired the installation in 1997.[8]

As the viewer progressed further into *Video Spaces*, Viola's *Slowly Turning Narrative* (1992) occupied a dark gallery in which an oversize panel rotated on its vertical axis two times every minute. One side was mirrored; the other was matte. Two video projectors faced the panel from opposite sides of the room. One projected a black-and-white video of a man's strained face seen in close-up in harsh light. The other projected a series of chaotic scenes in color—young children on a moving carousel or outdoors playing with fireworks, a house on fire, a carnival at night—that were full of nonstop

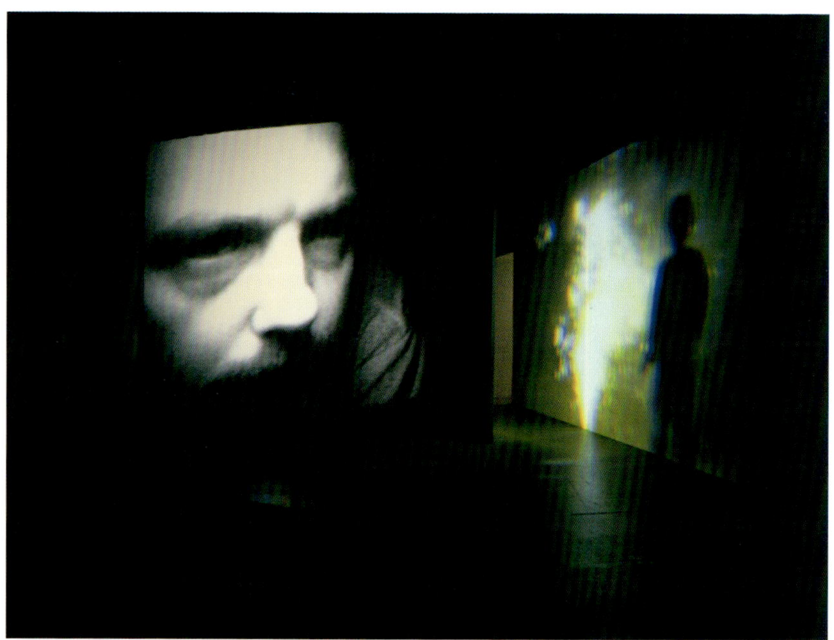

Bill Viola, *Slowly Turning Narrative*, 1992
Video and sound installation, with central rotating screen, mirrored
on one side; two channels of video projections, one color, one black
and white; amplified mono sound, one speaker; amplified mono sound,
five speakers; projected image: 9 ft x 12 ft (2.75 x 3.7 m);
room: 14 x 20 x 41 ft (4.3 x 6.1 x 12.5 m); continuously running

motion and tumultuous light and color. The imagery of the man's face was
accompanied by the sound of his voice rhythmically chanting a long list of
phrases descriptive of mental states and individual actions, while the color
images were complemented by ambient sounds related to each scene.

As the panel rotated, its position in relation to each projector by turns
narrowed and widened, warping the projected beams and splashing images
onto the surrounding walls. The mirrored side sent distorted reflections—
indistinct shards of light—spilling onto every surface in the room. Viewers
also caught fleeting images of themselves and the room around them in the
mirror as the screen revolved.[9]

Viola noted:

Slowly Turning Narrative is concerned with the enclosing nature of
the self-image and potentially infinite (and therefore unattainable)

states of being, all revolving around the still center of the self. The room, and everyone in it, becomes in effect a continually shifting projection screen, encompassing images and reflections, all locked into the regular cadences of the chanting voice and the constant rotation of the screen. The entire space becomes an interior for the revelations of a constantly turning mind absorbed with itself. The confluences and conflicts of image, content, emotion, and intent perpetually change as the screen slowly turns.[10]

With this work, I was interested in how Viola composed with time, prioritizing conceptual concerns over technical. Here media technology was not at odds with our inner being but was a reflection of it. Viola starts out with what might be considered impossible goals. Never compromising, he goes to great extremes to develop art that portrays images and emotions that had begun as a precise image in his mind.

For the artist Judith Barry, the impetus for any new work—including the sculptural installation I featured in *Video Spaces*—begins with philosophical underpinnings. Back in the mid-1970s, when Barry and I first met in San Francisco, she lived in a loft building that she shared with the performance-video artists Terry Fox and Howard Fried, as she fended for herself as a woman outside the old-boys network. She had to be strong-willed as she developed her singular practice, which paralleled that of nearby feminist activist-artists Lynn Hershman and Suzanne Lacy, who have used media and performance to examine issues around beauty and aging.

Barry supported herself and her art by working as a corporate events manager at a nearby five-star hotel. This experience affected her subject matter, an analysis of corporate hierarchy. Always pragmatic, she had turned Super 8 film and slide carousels—the inexpensive display devices she used for the business meetings she orchestrated—into the media she used for her art in *Echo*, which I featured at MoMA in 1986. The two-sided slide/film/sound projection examines the promise of the glass skyscraper as transparent skin and reflective space, which became a site for her to interrogate notions of subjectivity, refigured through the myth of Echo and Narcissus set in a grand shopping arcade. Jean Fisher, one of the most distinctive British art writers of her generation, wrote back then, "Barry explores the way public space intervenes in private fantasy."[11]

In the early 1990s, many of Barry's peers were intrigued with the body and cyborglike prosthetics, and were reading essays by feminist thinkers Sandy Stone, Eve Kosofsky Sedgwick, and Elaine Scarry, in particular *Fragments for a History of the Human Body*, a three-part academic series published by MIT's Zone Books in the late 1980s. Barry saw many of these

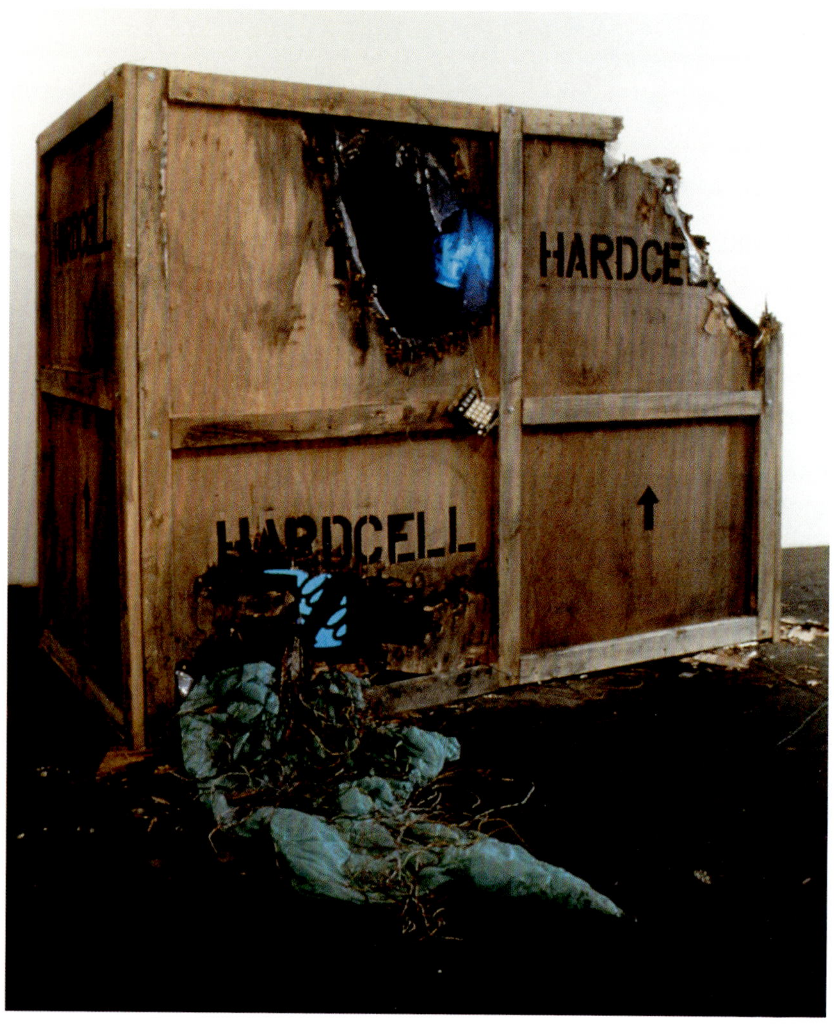

Judith Barry in collaboration with Brad Miskell, *Ha@dcell*, 1994
Sculpture/installation, with crate including pages from a narrative,
computer discards, three video monitors, surveillance camera, three
video projections, thirty-seven various other technological devices,
programmed "random motion" board, sound; 6 x 6 x 4 ft. (1.8 x 1.8 x 1.2 m)

body iterations as building on the existing foundation of "feminisms" and
poststructuralist thinking, especially the impact Michel Foucault and Gilles
Deleuze and Félix Guattari had on the concepts of "formlessness" and "form"

and the concept of the "monads" as described in books written by theorists Manuel DeLanda and Brian Massumi.[12]

Barry stood out in pursuing what she deemed an important discipline, one that combined art, science fiction, and technology. One outcome was her collaboration with Brad Miskell, *Ha®dcell* (1994), which added a light note to *Video Spaces*, whose other installations had a more somber tone. The pair seemed to ask, what if old abandoned technologies happened to be sentient? How would this happen and what orders would they impose? They answered by using the metaphor of dumpster diving—a necessity for some city dwellers and a sport for others. Whereas urban denizens sort through a mass of debris in hopes of discovering treasures among the cast-off appliances and furniture, the viewers of Barry and Miskell's installation encountered a weather-beaten wood crate that appeared as if it might be harboring life inside. The simple black letters stenciled along the sides suggest that the crate once belonged to the supposed HardCell Corporation. Inside sat musky computers and keyboards, abandoned disk drives, and other electronic debris, including a defibrillator, everything connected by a nervelike network of wires. Trembling and groaning, with lights and hints of a story darting across the screens, the worn-out components suggested that a cyborg made of secondhand parts lived inside.[13]

With the most modest of means, Barry and Miskell had constructed a highly formalized installation in which ideas, cultural artifacts, and implied narrative were explored. At the time, Barry explained to me that she identifies this as a punk rock video-jamming version of Nam June Paik.

Around the corner from *Ha®dcell*, I placed Oursler's similarly circumspect view of the marketing around technology, *System for Dramatic Feedback* (1994). Next, in a room of its own, I positioned *Eine Faust in der Tasche machen* (Make a Fist in the Pocket) (1994), a three-part allegorical installation by Odenbach. I had been tracking the work of this refined Cologne-based artist since the late 1970s, when he first arrived in New York and worked at the SoHo outpost of Berlin dealer René Block. All of Odenbach's art—which includes single-channel videos, installations, drawings, and prints—reflects an ambivalence about his own background as a German born shortly after the Second World War, during what has been labeled a period of "economic miracle." He tends to position identity in a fraught relation to history, culture, and gender. Indeed, the title of the work I included in *Video Spaces*, "Make a Fist in the Pocket," is a German expression for hiding one's rage—here a reference to the anger that lurks behind an expressionless face.

As an introduction, in bold letters drawn directly on the outside wall at the entrance to the installation, Odenbach placed a quote from Ingeborg Bachmann, an Austrian feminist writer and activist who was influential in the

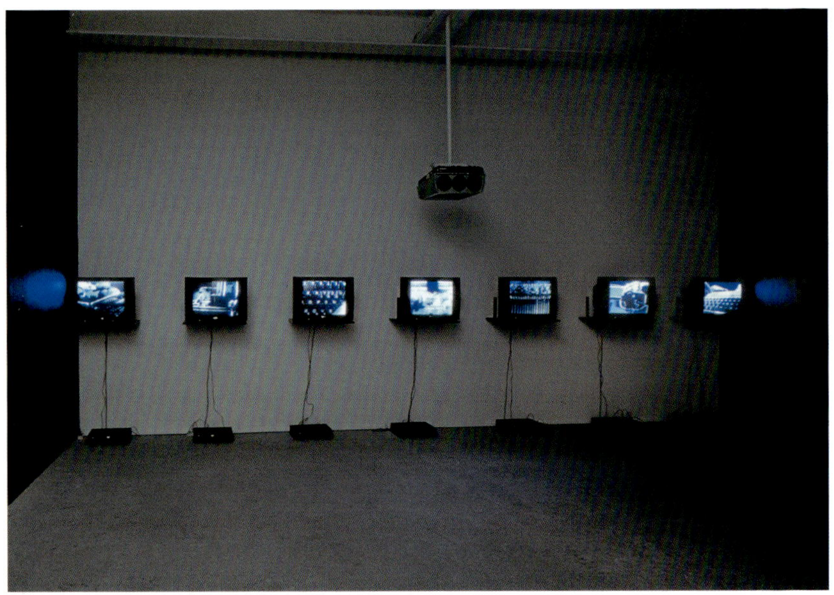

Marcel Odenbach, *Eine Faust in der Tasche machen* (Make a Fist
in the Pocket), 1994
Eight-channel video and sound installation; one video projection:
4 min. 57 sec.; seven videos on monitors: 2 min. 50 sec.

stormy 1960s. The text reads, "I am writing with my burnt hand about the
nature of fire." In this context, fire is symbolic of the organized violence seen
throughout German history. That history and the artist's attempt to situate
himself within it are Odenbach's subject matter.[14]

Inside the installation's front wall, Odenbach projected a video with
images of a Thai kickboxer that he had seen on TV in a seedy bar in Bangkok,
which for the artist was a reference to the men with prurient interests
who vacation in Southeast Asia in search of a quick dalliance, regardless of
sexual orientation.[15] Seven monitors with footage of 1968 student protests
in cities including New York, Paris, Mexico City, and London were lined up at
eye level on the opposite wall. This archival footage was intercut with images
of vintage typewriter keys clacking, as if being operated by newspaper
journalists. With an economy of means—the monitors and the projection—
the artist created a cogent dialogue that situates his work within a historical
context. Odenbach is to video art what prominent German artists Gerhard
Richter (b. 1932), Sigmar Polke (1941–2010), and Anselm Kiefer (b. 1945) are
to painting. Those artists probe the construction of the self in relation to the

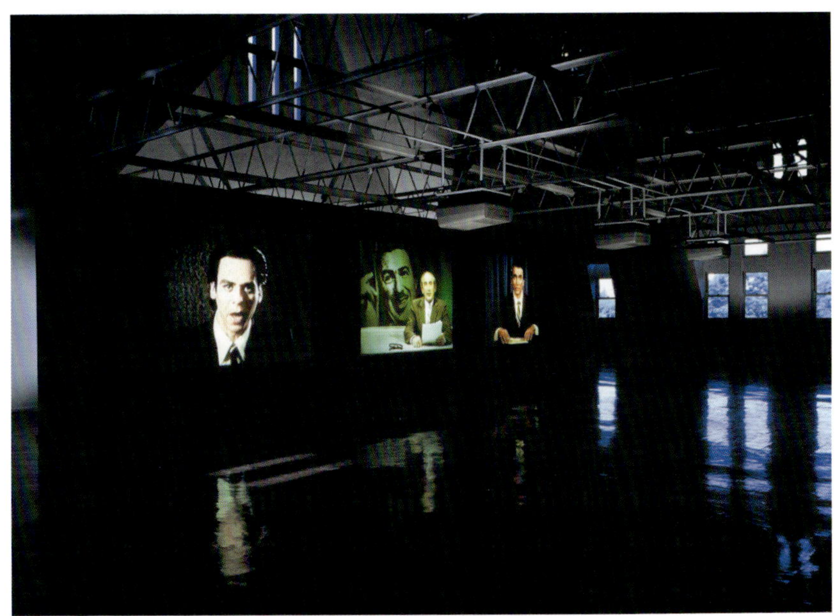

Stan Douglas, *Evening*, 1994
Three-channel video installation, color, sound, 14 min. 42 sec.
(looped). Installation view: Renaissance Society, Chicago, 1995

psychological and the cultural, and they have untiringly explored memory
and the traumas of history through their work.

Near Odenbach's installation, I placed *Evening* (1994), the work of
Vancouver-based Douglas, who took a somewhat different approach to
history and mass media. Having followed artists in the Northwest, I was
intrigued by how staunchly independent and informed Vancouver artists
are, with eyes looking across the Pacific toward Asia and also toward Europe.
I knew that since the mid-1970s, the well-organized alternative spaces
Western Front and Video Inn had been contributing to the definition of and
theories around video, installation, performance, and new music. Their early
programs embraced experimental activity in New York and London and
other European cities, more than exploits in easterly parts of Canada. Early
on, New York artists Dan Graham, Robert Smithson, and Joan Jonas, and
the French Fluxus artist Robert Filliou (1926–1987), frequented Vancouver's
alternative art centers and art schools. Perhaps more important was the
impact of the internationally recognized local photography artist Ian Wallace
(b. 1943), who maintained a strong conceptual and analytical approach to his

work. He had a significant influence on his and the subsequent generation—
artists Rodney Graham (b. 1949), Jeff Wall (b. 1946), and Douglas—all of
whom were intellectually formidable.

A profound thinker, Douglas defined his position as a person of color
based in Vancouver by explaining:

> Cultural appropriation is how one learns a foreign language, and it's
> maybe even how one learns one's own language. This is especially
> true of people who are not of a given majority culture, because the
> dominant languages and customs will constantly imply that the
> outsider's presence is either irrelevant or dangerous. So someone,
> like myself, who is born into a culture as the majority's "minority,"
> will often learn to think and act from two positions at once because,
> even though it might be the only culture you know, you can come
> to understand how you are constantly objectified or excluded.[16]

In *Evening*, Douglas looks back on American television in the late 1960s,
when commercial stations started to prioritize the stardom of their anchors
over editorial content. The installation features three stations: WCSL, a
staged reconstruction based on the Chicago station that instigated the
form known as "happy news," which is joined by two other fictional local
news stations—WAMQ, a station moving away from serious reporting to
happy news, and WBMB, a restaging of one that retains its paternalistic
approach. Each is featured in a large video projection and is shown on a
separate screen, installed side by side. Douglas follows nine news stories
from 1969 and 1970, obtained through assiduous archival research. The
restaged footage is in color; the archival material shown behind each
anchor is in black and white.

Performing as newscasters, actors read scripts written by the artist.
They begin in unison with "Good evening, this is the evening news," and
continue with their separate stories. Each anchor has the same impassive
face, regardless of whether the content is horrific or pleasant.

Douglas designed a complex sound component, heard through an
umbrella (parabolic) directional speaker suspended from the ceiling in front
of each screen. Standing under the speaker dome in front of WCSL, a viewer
heard: Abbie Hoffman is a buffoon, Adam Clayton Powell Jr. is a thief, and
the heart transplant surgeon Dr. Christiaan Barnard is a savior. Visitors
standing on the periphery, at a distance from the screens and speakers,
heard an abstract score. Names and words merged together, in the manner
of concrete poetry: "J. Edgar Hoover," "radicals," "murderer." In this way,
experienced from a distance, both in time and in space, the catchwords

were a fitting distillation of the watered-down journalism that is presented on regular television.

In *Evening* Douglas treated advertisements with restraint. Instead of castigating advertisers for their effect on the news—turning it into a ratings game—he conveys commercial time slots with the simple words "PLACE AD HERE." The phrase lets viewers develop their own thoughts about the billion-dollar industry of paid advertising. The artist appears to posit the question, what contributes to a more humane and rational world?[17]

While Douglas's title refers directly to the evening news, I recognized another important allusion: the "evening out" of ethnic distinctions, especially the homogenization of social and racial ones.

The eighth installation in the show occupied its own room—Furuhashi's *Lovers* (1994), which added a touch of lyricism to *Video Spaces* and exemplified the seamless melding of performance, music, and architecture. I first met Furuhashi in Kyoto during a research trip in 1984. He was then an art student when I acquired *Conversation Styles: Dumb Talk, Balance*, a tape he had just completed. He appears in the video, jerkily looping along to electronic sounds, in front of a barren landscape. (The site happened to be the monkey house of the local zoo.) Furuhashi was a Kyoto native, whose parents designed exquisite kimono fabrics. His babysitters were *maiko* (apprentice geisha) trainees at his grandmother's geisha house. Accustomed to dressing up since childhood, he considered costumes to be transformative sculpture. Throughout his life, the many guises he assumed did more to conceal than reveal his character.[18]

Furuhashi and I often connected during my subsequent trips, especially when I lived in Tokyo during a sabbatical that began in the late 1980s. He became an important mentor, who elaborated on how Japanese culture naturally divides itself between Tokyo and the Kansai region. He told me how he had visited New York on his own in 1985 and hung out in Lower Manhattan. During his stay, he had sewn costumes for *Book of Days* by Meredith Monk (b. 1942) and frequented experimental theater. At the Pyramid Club in the East Village, he had performed with a friend as the "Kookie Kabuki Sisters." The duo had vamped doing ikebana (Japanese flower arranging) and the tea ceremony, or daintily holding chopsticks and nibbling sushi. Furuhashi had become friends with performance artists Stuart Sherman (1945–2001), John Kelly (b. 1959), John Epperson (a.k.a. Lypsinka, b. 1955), and Ethyl Eichelberger (1945–1990), who took him under their wing.

After returning to Japan, Furuhashi met Shimonu "Simone" Fukayuki, the queen of drag queens. Together, they launched monthly Diamonds Are Forever parties in Osaka and Tokyo nightclubs, where Furuhashi performed glamorously done up as any outrageous character he could invent with makeup and clothes—as a space cowboy, an invader, or one of his regular drag characters, such as Barbra Streisand, Barbarella, or Julie Andrews,[19] which I saw him do wearing a blond wig. Fukayuki explained that their performance work had Japanese rather than Western roots, and he referred to *angura bunka* (underground culture), which evolved in the 1960s and 1970s, mainly in refutation of modern theater.[20] Carried out in the ill-lit shadows, it was completely at odds with the cool, calm, sleek image of postwar skyscraper megalopolises.

Furuhashi's radically innovative, multidisciplinary performances and installations distinguished his short but exceptional career. As an undergraduate, he had teamed up with fellow students in their early twenties: Toru Koyamada (b. 1961), Yukihiro Hozumi (b. 1963), Shiro Takatani (b. 1963), Takayuki Fujimoto (b. 1960), and Hiromasa Tomari (b. 1963), all eager to move art beyond museum and gallery walls. Attracted to technology but suspicious of the information-age dream, in 1984 they founded Dumb Type, a collective of architects, designers, choreographers, actors, artists, and computer programmers, adding members when needed for new large-scale projects. They were aware of multimedia performances in the West by Robert Wilson, Laurie Anderson, and Pina Bausch (1940–2009). In the late 1970s when Wilson, Anderson, and Bausch came to Japan, performance art became the rage, and the young Japanese artists hoped to create something new with their own skills. Dissatisfied with the master/apprentice relationships in Japan's traditional theater companies, Dumb Type's members decided to have equal voices in decision-making. The brainstorming they did was intuitive rather than logical, and it resulted in projects that used visuals rather than words as their main means of communication. As I frequented the group's bustling studio in a timeworn Kyoto building, I observed how Furuhashi was the de facto leader, the one who kept the disparate parts of a new performance-installation project together in his head.

Whenever I was in Japan, I took the train to Nagoya, Kyoto, or Fukuoka to catch Dumb Type's latest performance, such as *036-Pleasure Life* (1987). The set resembled a gargantuan integrated circuit, featuring a bristling grid with thirty-six pedestals supporting ordinary household objects: electric fans, glasses of water, and TV sets depicting images of sky and grassy fields. Within the top of each of the open metal-frame pedestals was a round, white, neon kitchen light that progressed through a rhythmic sequence of turning on and off. Performers moved silently among the pedestals accompanied by mellifluous yet commanding voices and TV-jingle music. In android fashion, they mimed brushing their teeth, heading to work, picnicking, and channel surfing.

Afterward, I would go with the artists for a late dinner, before we all continued on to the fringiest of the music clubs. Much like a rock band

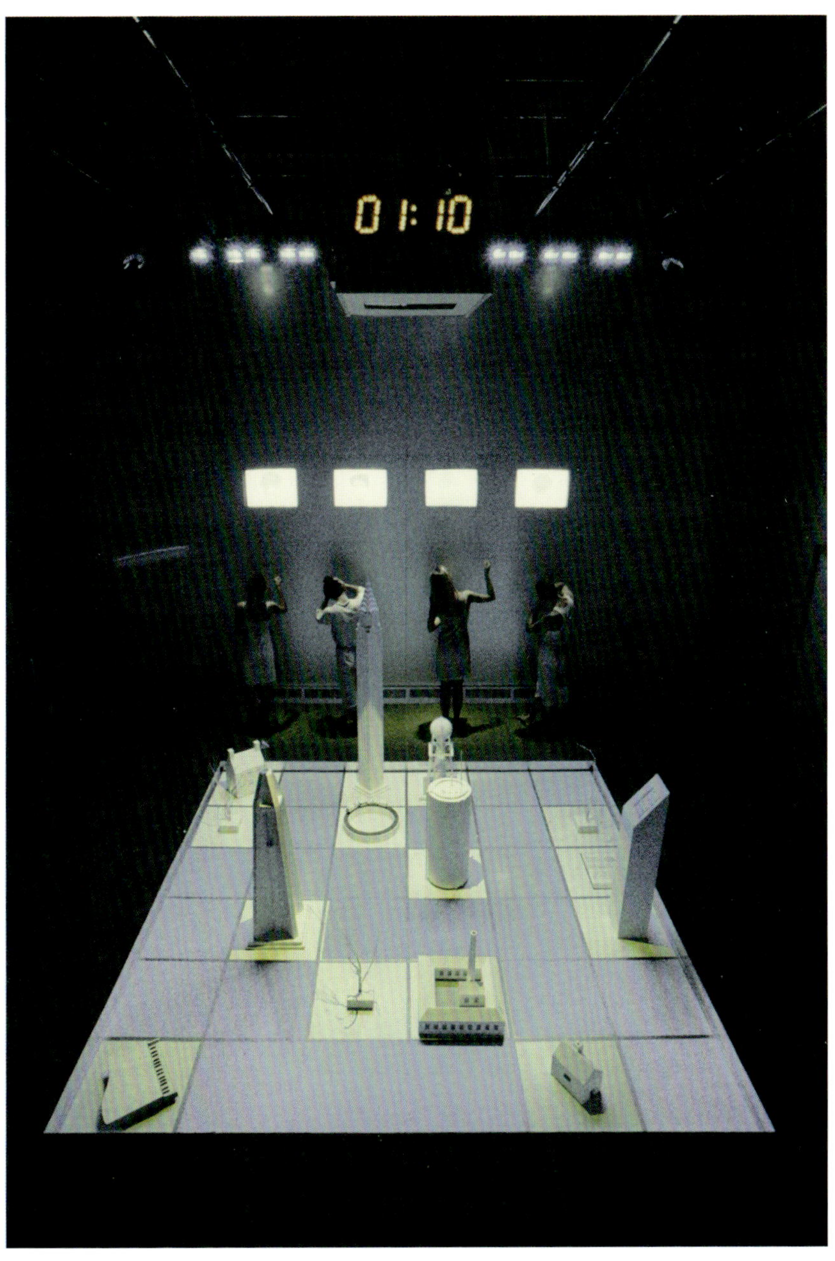

Dumb Type, *036-Pleasure Life*, 1987
Performance at Art Space Mumonkan, Kyoto, 1987, 77 min.

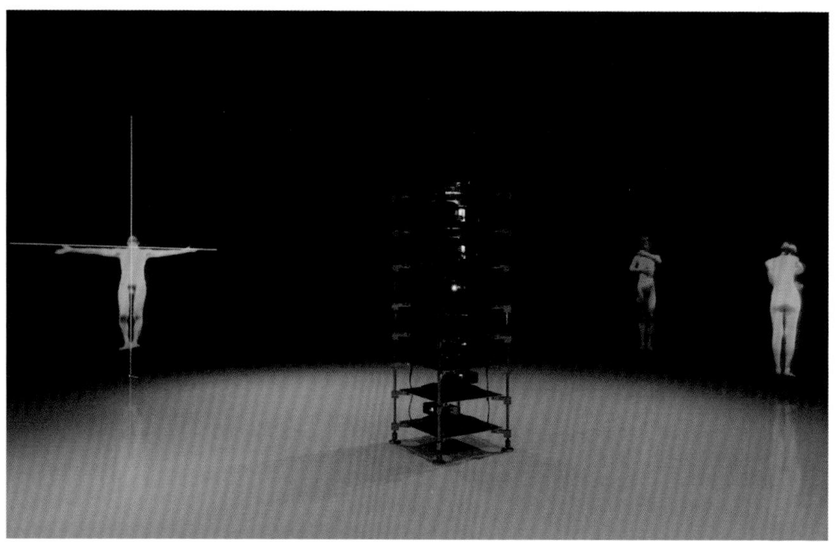

Teiji Furuhashi, *Lovers*, 1994
Computer-controlled, five-channel laser disc and sound installation, with five projectors, two sound systems, two slide projectors, and slides (color, sound); 32 ft. 10 in. x 32 ft. 10 in. (10 x 10 m). Installation view: *Teiji Furuhashi: Lovers*, Museum of Modern Art, New York, 2016–17

groupie, I basked in their presence, enjoying their lively, quick-witted, and warm-hearted company. We would usually be joined by a good friend of Dumb Type, Alfred Birnbaum, a Tokyo-based American writer and translator who collaborated on many of their scripts that merged Japanese and English spoken words. Birnbaum helped me understand why the better my Japanese became and the better I understood the culture's intricacies, the more uncomfortable some of my older non-art acquaintances would be with me, because they considered their own culture to be impenetrable.

Furuhashi often described Dumb Type's work as being political in nature, something that set it apart from other Japanese performance art. "Japanese audiences don't want to see [politics]," he once explained in an interview. "They want to avoid it. They just want entertainment. Yes, I think we should always have a political view. We should represent that this is Japan."[21] Dumb Type were to become activists who asserted their opinions.

As Japan's bubble economy burst in 1991 and the worldwide AIDS crisis escalated, the government refused to acknowledge that the disease had invaded the country. Local grassroots activism rose to deal with AIDS, and with issues of sexuality and gender identity. Dumb Type was thrown into the thick of it when Furuhashi publicly came out as HIV positive and became an outspoken AIDS activist.

In response to public debate, the group premiered their performance *S/N* in 1994. Gifted as a composer as well as a visual artist and performer, Furuhashi spent many hours intuitively selecting each and every electronic tone for the score, assisted by the young, talented sound artist Ryoji Ikeda (b. 1966). The most personal work in the career of Furuhashi, *S/N* opened with him wearing placards reading "male," "Japanese," "HIV," "homosexual." Other performers wore similar signs. The group then turned and addressed the audience, saying, "We're sorry to tell you that we're not actors. We are what we're labeled." From a conference table, the celebrated postmodern writer-theorist Akira Asada imparted gravitas and authority, reporting hard facts about AIDS in Japan.

If *S/N* burned like the sun, Furuhashi's solo installation *Lovers* (1994) glowed with moonlight. "Lovers is very soothing and hopelessly romantic. *S/N* is more direct, more sweaty and bitchy somehow," he commented.[22] The installation of *Lovers* was spartan. A metal tower with five synchronized video and slide projectors on rotating shelves occupied the center of an otherwise empty, twenty-nine-foot-long (9 m) square gallery with a white linoleum floor and walls painted black. Technology operated like a dutiful stagehand.

Produced by the short-lived entity Canon ArtLab,[23] *Lovers* allows visitors to interact with life-size, lifelike images of dancers projected onto the gallery's black walls. Accompanied by a brightly pinging, gentle sonic score, the specter-like projected figures move gracefully across the installation walls, appearing so real and spontaneous that they seem to cohabit the space with viewers. The naked figures are also detached and, despite their movements, seem drained of life. Their flowing choreography becomes so familiar that it's surprising when two of the figures suddenly come together in a brief virtual embrace.

Lovers has two kinds of sound. When the moving figures pause, the room fills with whispers, indistinguishable phrases that make it seem as if an audience had clustered somewhere. The second part consists of gentle tings, reminiscent of the bleeps of diagnostic machines that Furuhashi heard while briefly hospitalized.

By means of an inconspicuous motion detection device placed above one wall, a subtle occurrence happened when one of the videotape's figures, Furuhashi, stopped and sought out one viewer, and faced this person with his arms outstretched. The artist assumes a beatific pose, vulnerable and exposed. Then he falls backward into the unknown, as if he were accepting his fate. Through this action Furuhashi challenged the notion that technology overwhelms the human spirit.[24] For him, technology was a circuit that enabled the artist to explore himself. As the culmination of his extraordinary career, *Lovers* is a transcendent ode about love in the time of AIDS.

A week after *Video Spaces* closed, Furuhashi passed away in Kyoto. He was thirty-five. Many of my friends were reeling, having lost close friends like Furuhashi and family members to the AIDS pandemic.[25]

In 1996 I was grateful when Canon donated *Lovers* to MoMA. I knew that because the installation had a big footprint and was technically complex, it would be complicated to get the tour de force on view again. For the next twenty years, *Lovers* sat in storage. In 2017, when MoMA decided to exhibit the installation, the media conservation team upgraded its controller software. Fortunately, Furuhashi's Dumb Type colleagues who originally worked with him on developing *Lovers* were able to help.[26] MoMA ended up using hardware from the original Canon donation.

Where does the problem of outmoded technology leave the future of technically complex works of early media art? What if there is no viable solution without a larger investment in the preservation of this art? Do we present work that is compromised, or do we sadly admit its demise? The responsibilities of collecting and archiving media art are daunting, but worth every bit of the effort.

A Collector Base Grows

Meanwhile, I followed several intrepid contemporary art collectors who started to tackle video and media as art in earnest, even though the conservation of video had yet to be developed, unlike painting, which has centuries of preservation formulas. The actions of these early collectors assuaged others' fears, so over time they, too, became patrons of this contemporary art.

In Munich, Ingvild Goetz was an impassioned investigator of the work of emerging artists. During the 1960s, she was among the first to acquire the postwar work of "dé-coll/age-ist" and video pioneer Wolf Vostell (1932–1998) and Arte Povera artist Giovanni Anselmo (b. 1934). In the 1990s, she believed that artists finally had the tools to achieve greatness through work with multiple channels of precisely edited videos, and she wholeheartedly turned to the medium. Bjørn Melhus (b. 1966) was one of the young artists whose multichannel flat-screen installations Goetz collected in-depth.[27] For each of his colorful multichannel works with syncopated edits and beats, Melhus performed every role, wrote and delivered every word, and made every edit.

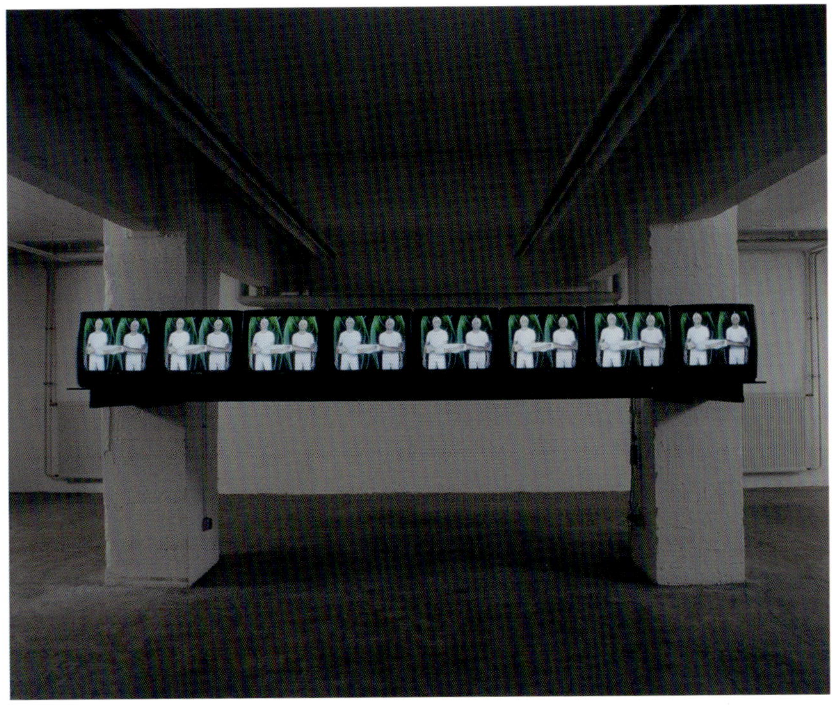

Bjørn Melhus, *Again & Again (The Borderer)*, 1998
Video installation for eight monitors, color, sound, 8 min. (looped)

As the author Stefan Heidenreich put it, at the core is how Melhus sees "our character as something forced upon us by external relations of media and power, regardless of who we are."[28]

In 2014 Goetz donated her extensive holdings of video art to the state of Bavaria, exasperated that the Munich museum Pinakothek der Moderne had ignored the medium and therefore missed the boat. Her donation of 375 media artworks included pieces by a stellar international roster: Francis Alÿs (b. 1959), Janine Antoni (b. 1964), Matthew Barney (b. 1967), David Claerbout (b. 1969), Nathalie Djurberg (b. 1978), and Kimsooja (b. 1957).[29] Still passionate about the new, Goetz continues to avidly collect the works of up-and-coming video artists, including Nira Pereg (b. 1969), Teboho Edkins (b. 1980), and Cyrill Lachauer (b. 1979).[30]

Toronto-based Ydessa Hendeles opened a state-of-the-art contemporary exhibition space for her carefully chosen collection in 1988. The ultimate perfectionist, with distinctive taste, she had flawless rooms constructed for each video-sound installation included in her intelligently curated shows. I observed her installers put soundproof materials inside the specially constructed walls and around the carefully gusseted entrance doors, which kept sound from bleeding into adjacent spaces. Hendeles's high standards raised the bar for many museums, whose finance departments were far too ready to slash already bare-bones exhibition budgets. Unfortunately, Hendeles closed the doors of her space in 2012 and subsequently dispersed her collection. In 2009 she had donated thirty works to the Art Gallery of Ontario in Toronto, including media installations by James Coleman, Gary Hill, and Bill Viola.

Pamela and Richard Kramlich are two rare collectors who have focused exclusively on installation, both video and film. Based in San Francisco, they have acquired over 150 media art installations, which they showcase in a brand-new, carefully designed museum-like home by the architecture firm Herzog & de Meuron in Napa Valley. Committed to maintaining the art of today for future generations, the Kramlichs established the New Art Trust in 1997, with a collection of over two hundred single-channel videos, for the serious advancement of time-based media scholarship and preservation. The trust has worked closely with the San Francisco Museum of Modern Art, the Tate, and MoMA; their curatorial, conservation, and registrar staffs collaborate to establish practices and methodologies directed at understanding an artist's intention, with the goal of preserving the aesthetics of a work. The New Art Trust shares what it continues to learn about best practices for media art collecting by uploading useful information to a robust website, Matters in Media Art.[31] The documents include templates for a range of key materials that include loan forms, cataloging procedures, and advice for conducting an interview in order to understand an artist's aesthetics.

How a media artwork lives on into the future will be determined by the completeness of information gathered today. Recently a new organization joined the efforts of Matters in Media Art: Voices in Contemporary Art is engaged with critical dialogue around the production, presentation, and preservation of contemporary art.[32] Media art stands a strong chance of surviving into the future.

Media Art Diversifies

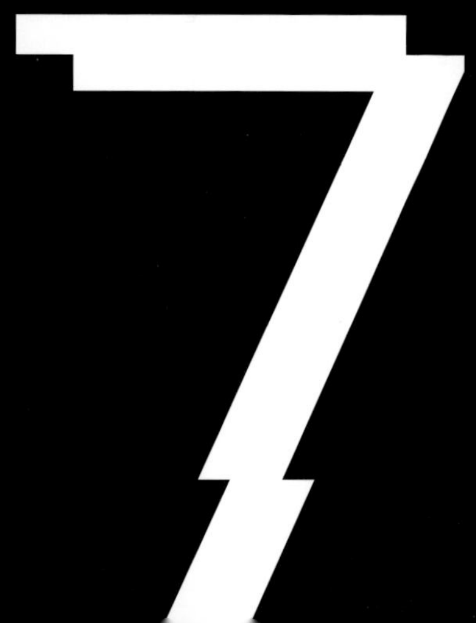

Long before Edward Snowden leaked classified documents and exposed surveillance programs run by the US government with the support of telecommunication companies,[1] artists had been asking, how do the prying eyes of security cameras installed in banks, at bodega cash registers, and even in massage parlors affect ordinary life?

As early as 1983, the German filmmaker Michael Klier (b. 1943) had released his feature-length video *Der Riese* (The Giant), made with scenes appropriated from the in-situ surveillance cameras he called his "Giants" that were positioned around Hamburg and Berlin at airport landing strips, mansion gates, and intersections congested with rush-hour traffic. In the following decade, the topic of surveillance was investigated in great depth by younger media artists troubled by the ominous consequences of personal computers and software advances, especially the ease of clandestine observation of a person's daily life with the new devices.

Surveillance grew as a serious topic of civic concern with the expansion of the internet. The history of the internet dates back to the 1950s, with the development of large-scale computers and the auguring of wide area networking. It wasn't until the 1970s that the internet emerged as an experimental and academic system with limited means of connection. In 1989, British computer scientist Tim Berners-Lee began working on creating the World Wide Web, which linked all sorts of digital files in a point-and-click information system that was accessible from any node or point on the global network.

In the early 1990s, once a number of pioneering international artists accepted both the World Wide Web and the internet as mediums and as means of distribution, they found that net art offered them unforeseen opportunities. Net art was a relatively small field at its start and was characterized by diverse practices, unrestrained collaboration, and evolving formal and aesthetic standards. As a genre, it relied on the internet to exist and took advantage of such aspects as an interactive interface and connectivity to multiple social and economic cultures and microcultures.

Ever curious about the cutting edge of technology, I visited artist and media pundit Wolfgang Staehle (b. 1950) one day in 1991 in his small Tribeca basement office. Staehle and his friends foresaw what the internet would become today. I clambered down a metal staircase, under sidewalk grating. Staehle had just launched the Thing, the first international art community online. He demoed for me his bulletin board system, a text messaging system accessible to a burgeoning coterie via the telephone network. In the mid-1990s, I regularly visited the Thing's sprawling new Chelsea office, where a diverse group of media artists from around the world congregated to converse, collaborate, discuss software, and critique the latest net art.

Whereas the stereotype of net artists might be one of solitary, nocturnal geeks possessed by their computers, the Thing's office flourished as a lively social space. These face-to-face meetings and impromptu encounters raised the level of discourse and contributed to net art's development.

It is worth noting that the World Wide Web's debut in the early 1990s coincided with the end of the Soviet Union. The former Eastern Bloc became an active region for net art, powered in part by media labs funded by philanthropist George Soros, and in part by the fact that formerly isolated artists—including Olia Lialina (b. 1971), Vuc Ćosić (b. 1966), and Alexei Shulgin (b. 1966)—were able to experiment and connect with international peers through the electronic superhighway.

Museums in the early 1990s were, for the most part, sidestepping the question of how to exploit the internet. Urged by me and two curatorial colleagues—Paola Antonelli and Sheryl Conkelton—MoMA agreed to a provisional institutional website in 1995, before the museum finally bit the bullet and launched an official, albeit rudimentary, site a year later. MoMA is international, art is international, and the web was the new international.

I regularly spoke with the artist and curator Mark Tribe (b. 1966), who in 1996 launched Rhizome as a LISTSERV (an electronic mailing list that distributes messages to subscribers) that sent tips about the latest net art to some of the first artists to work online. Rhizome eventually grew and expanded to champion digital art and culture through commissions, exhibitions, digital preservation, and software development, and it has played an integral role in the history of contemporary art engaged with digital technologies and the internet.

Blossoming in the 1990s and 2000s were several notable trends that had started as early as the 1970s as artists created work with new (digital) technologies, including personal computers (hardware and software), the internet, surveillance systems, and gaming and other devices. The development of the interactive media art made by innovators during this period coincided with the increasing acceptance of digital art practices.

Attracted to a field that perpetually upgrades, media artists figure out how to persevere through steady technical transitions. A good example is Julia Scher (b. 1954), whose childhood experiences in a Los Angeles household where she "was always being watched but wasn't being protected" led to her interest in surveillance as a theme.[2] Out of a built-in need "for watching," she developed an aesthetic centered on vigilance and being in the present. Bill Horrigan, founding media curator at the Wexner Center for the Arts in

Columbus, Ohio, once accurately described the artist this way: "Julia Scher was born under the sign of Security. Lightly, or laterally, and always with explanation, alibi, and persuasion, her work enforces that sign's wishes."[3]

In looking back, Scher recently explained that a major problem today is that the industries of protection and threat have merged. She quoted such examples as Tyco, Lockheed Martin, Raytheon, and Honeywell, corporations that provide control gyroscopes for intercontinental ballistic missiles and materials for biowarfare—technologies that are then adapted to create protective devices such as smoke detectors for hospitals, control mechanisms for home security systems, dog tracking collars, and tests for analyzing food safety. The line between guarding the public's safety and endangering it becomes blurred.[4]

In 1984, after graduating from the University of Minnesota with an MFA in studio art, Scher spent two years back in LA. In Venice Beach, she surfed and connected with innovative artists, including Chris Burden, Alexis Smith (b. 1949), Ed Ruscha (b. 1937), and Lynda Benglis. She gravitated toward filmmaking, doing art production for educational films, and then engaged in sound engineering and, later, cutting special effects tracks. In 1986 she returned to Minneapolis, where street crime was rampant, and took a job as a janitor-handyman at an aerobics studio. She augmented her earnings by installing security locks for some of the female patrons.

In 1987 her investigation of security technology led to her first installation, *Safe & Secure*, which she presented at the local Rifle Sport Gallery. For the exhibition, Scher devised a surveillance system with cameras aimed at the street and monitors inside, connecting indoors with outdoors so that viewers in the gallery could determine whether it was safe to go back outside. That same year, Scher participated in a group show devoted to surveillance at LACE, an alternative gallery in LA. Co-curated by the artists Branda Miller (b. 1952) and Deborah Irmas (b. 1950), the show featured the work of artists who either utilized surveillance methods used by spies, private investigators, and security companies, or who adapted the latest surveillance technologies into their work.[5] As Scher moved her practice forward, she added a small live camera to her site-specific art, which had as much to do with particular locations and situations as with watchfulness.

Living again in LA, Scher formed a security-equipment company called Safe and Secure Productions and supported herself by installing burglar alarms, electronic security systems, and locks in the homes of women. Alternating between her company and her installations, she began performing in the pink guard uniform she had devised for her business. The color—Pantone number 1765—had special meaning for Scher: she saw it as the color of innocence, children, virginity, queerness, strength and power, and ACT UP,[6] the international direct-action advocacy coalition that had formed in 1987 as a diverse, nonpartisan group committed to ending the AIDS crisis.

In 1989 in LA, Scher presented her installation *Security by Julia VI* at the Video Festival of the American Film Institute (AFI). Entering the lobby of AFI's main building, I came upon a row of nine small monitors hung slightly above eye level, individually connected to dangling coaxial cables. Each screen displayed a live feed that came directly from one of the eight cameras placed in different locations around AFI's sprawling campus, and from a ninth camera installed in the lobby. Next to each of the outdoor cameras, Scher had posted a sign, warning visitors they had entered an area monitored by closed-circuit television. An art student in a pink uniform stood guard nearby. Below each camera was a kiosk with a small monitor, on which individuals were able to observe and tidy up their live images. The kiosk also housed a printer, which allowed viewers to leave with "souvenir" printouts of their images captured from the live video camera.

I caught up with Scher at AFI, and in talking with the affable, keen-witted artist, I sensed a naughty side. I learned that surveillance in Scher's installation was a deft convergence of narcissism and voyeurism—both the preening that goes on alone in front of mirror reflections and candid cameras, and the illicit pleasure that comes from covert peeping as others disrobe, engage in sex, or stumble. (Some of her work that followed was more sexually explicit.) Scher explained that narcissism and voyeurism were things naturally added on by people and attributed to her work—an easier pill to swallow than hard-core world topics. "My sources are all about power and control," she has said.[7] I thought back to Barbara Kruger's *Surveillance is your busywork* (1983), a bannerlike artwork that pointed to how people seem reconciled to the symbols and gestures of surveillance, and how it had become an omnipresent part of our lives.

During the 1990s, while living and teaching in Boston and New York, Scher based a group of new installations on an idealized version of a corporate office for her security business. Wearing the company's pink security officer's uniform, she (or a young intern) would stand at attention guarding the gallery space as monitors in the ostensible work area displayed live camera feeds from the gallery and from nearby stairwells, interspersed with prerecordings of naked figures scampering through the same spaces. With considerable panache, Scher, during this phase of her work, also incorporated bondage into her voyeuristic settings, especially installations with live cameras positioned at the four corners of a spacious bed.

In an interview in *Frieze*, she explained:

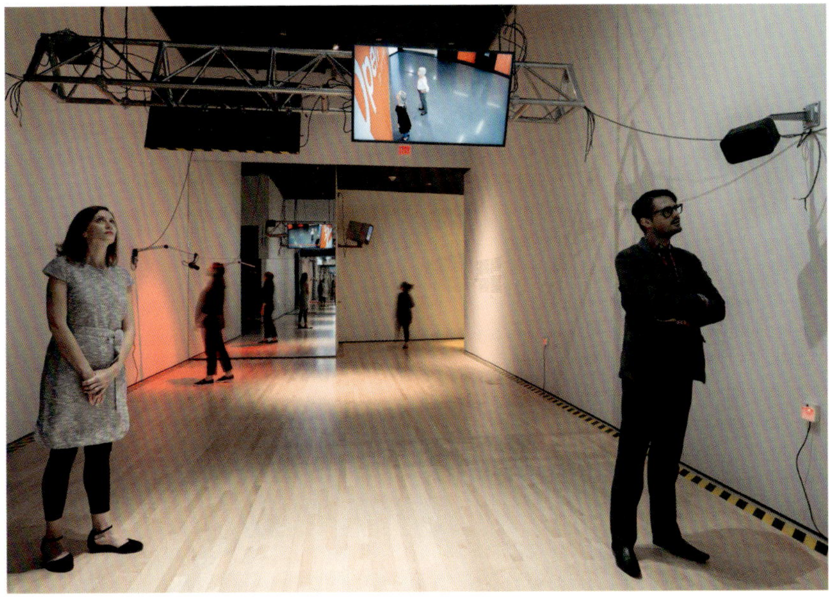

Julia Scher, *Predictive Engineering³*, 1993–present
Multichannel video and sound installation, with live cameras,
sensors, microphone, mirrors, tape, plastic balls, drone, and
text-messaging service; dimensions variable. Installation view:
San Francisco Museum of Modern Art

My interest in the bed did not come so much from its association
with privacy; rather, I was interested in it as the site for various
transitions. In bed, you move from being awake to sleep, from
control to no control, from consciousness to the unconscious. In
addition, the bed is *the* location of domestic drama. My first "bed"
work, which was shown in 1994 at Andrea Rosen Gallery, New York,
was created to investigate this zone of transition, but of course,
also to monitor the sexual activities of a couple who totally knew
what was going on. The electronically loaded bed could record
everything and play it back as well. Under the bed there was
something like its "memory": the recording device.[8]

Prescient about how technology exists in a perpetual state of upgrade,
Scher describes her long-term project commissioned by the San Francisco
Museum of Modern Art (SFMOMA), *Predictive Engineering³* (1993–present), as
an "episodic, self-documenting and self-consuming work" that "gobbles up"

previous iterations of itself.[9] The surveillance-based installation incorporates recording and display devices that respond to visitor movement in the galleries and is a playful yet unsettling commentary on the ubiquity of surveillance in our daily lives. *Predictive Engineering[3]* was originally tailored to SFMOMA's 1993 galleries, and years later, Scher spent months working closely with the museum's staff on two technically and conceptually complex upgrades, in 1998 and again in 2016.[10] Each of the enriched iterations is relevant to the aesthetics of the work (both past and present) and is a commendable case study of media art preservation. The carefully considered upgrade phase of a media artwork's life is one step toward survival.

Today Scher holds a professorship for Multimedia and Performance and Surveillant Architectures at the Academy of Media Arts Cologne. She continues to do research and to create web, installation, and performance works that explore issues of power and expose the dangers and ideologies of monitoring systems.

Grahame Weinbren

An experimental filmmaker and renowned pioneer of interactive cinema—and by nature a sardonic philosopher—Grahame Weinbren (b. 1947) has published and lectured on cinema, interactivity, and new media for over thirty years. As the tireless senior editor of the *Millennium Film Journal*, which is dedicated to avant-garde cinema and media theory and practice, he occupies a catbird seat with an overview of moving image art history that provides insights into where the field is headed.

In the late 1970s, while teaching critical theory at art schools around LA, he began to use the film production equipment that sat idle in the institutions where he was a visiting professor. Quickly finding linear storytelling too tedious and film theater seating too regulated, he picked up computer programming skills and switched over to the emerging field of interactive narrative, in which users create or influence a dramatic story line through their clickable actions. In 1982 he was hired by the exhibition and graphic design firm Ramirez & Woods to develop thirteen user-friendly, interactive monitor and keyboard display consoles for the US Pavilion at the Knoxville World's Fair. In the process of pulling off the complicated undertaking with a postproduction team he brought in from Manhattan and technologists from MIT's Architecture Machine Group, Weinbren became a skilled specialist himself.

Adapting his newfound commercial skills to his art making, he began working with a friend, the filmmaker Roberta Friedman (b. 1948), and together they created one of the first interactive video artworks, *The Erl*

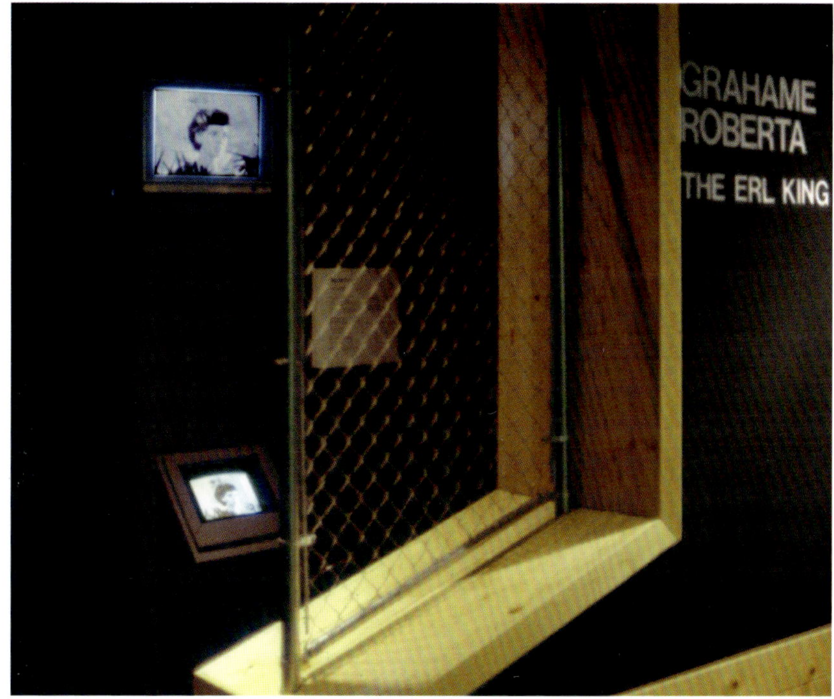

Roberta Friedman and Grahame Weinbren, *The Erl King*, 1983–86
Analog/digital interactive cinema installation.

King (1983–86). The title, story, and music came from the well-known lied *Erlkönig* (Erlking), composed by Franz Schubert in 1815, which itself was based on a 1782 poem by Johann Wolfgang von Goethe. The four characters in the song—narrator, father, son, and the Erlking—are sung by a single vocalist, Elizabeth Arnold. The one voice provided the unifying strategy for Weinbren and Friedman's use of present-day technologies to convey the flowing streams of a complex story: Goethe's about a supernatural being, one that is partly good but mostly evil, who haunts the Black Forest, luring children to their destruction, which the artists coupled with Freud's 1914–15 case study of his patient the Wolf Man.

For the *Erl King* installation, Weinbren and Friedman devised an inviting setup—a comfortable seat for one active viewer and handsome armature-cabinetry that concealed the reservoir of hardware. Those awaiting their turns could listen to the music and watch the evolving story on a screen attached to the exterior of the unit. At the premiere of the first iteration,

I hunkered down in the one seat and interacted with the touch screen. Response time was immediate—contact with the screen brought up images and sounds from three inconspicuous laser disc players that were connected to a then powerful eight-megahertz computer. I had control over my experience of the arcane story, clicking on words or segueing off in a different direction, determined by my interest and attention span. I pursued the main action, as it unfolded in a nineteenth-century-style, upper-class parlor and moved off into various landscapes, including the Wolf Man's nightmare of howling animals perched in a tree in a wooded setting. I followed the lied's libretto by reading the graffiti-like text, shown as words spray-painted onto the walls of an abandoned building. Old and new were conflated.

The Erl King had two additional texts that sometimes appeared as overlays, complex passages selected from the early twentieth-century philosopher Ludwig Wittgenstein and the more recent theorist Jean Baudrillard. The superimposed texts conveyed the serious academic and philosophical underpinnings of the work. Whether I understood the theoretical texts or not didn't matter. The work's relevance was in how the viewer gets caught up in *The Erl King*'s curious lair. I followed the multiple story lines as they continued until one, some, or all of them came to an end. That's when I was left to ponder, interpret, and reflect upon my own experiences and the ongoing narrative that continued to spin nonstop in my mind.

I once heard Weinbren chortle irreverently as he explained how *The Erl King* had converted him from filmmaker to installation artist. He was well aware of the shaky ground beneath the feet of anyone who promotes a conclusive definition of *media art*. His own conception of what a moving image is or can be is expansive because of his multifaceted practice as artist, media studies professor, and editor of the *Millennium Film Journal*. For him, the computer is a chameleon, the universal tool whose qualities can be defined and redefined from project to project and from use to use. When art becomes software and vice versa, aesthetic qualities become indeterminate, undefined until fixed by code. He regards this as both the liberation and the burden of computer-based art.[11]

When the Guggenheim Museum acquired *The Erl King*, the museum also became responsible for the installation's future. Over the years, the Guggenheim's conservation staff has worked closely with Weinbren and Friedman, along with computer programmers and technicians, to determine the best practice for *The Erl King*'s preservation. This is no simple matter, given the work's combination of obsolete hardware (both off-the-shelf and custom-made) and artist-written software. There is no "miracle cure" for the conservation of any electronic artwork. Responsibility resides with both the artist and the collector, who need to be astute. Fortunately, today media art is a congenial field that readily shares technical information and tries to stay up-to-date as best it can.

Perry Hoberman

Some artists have a tongue-in-cheek approach toward technology's rampant change. Perry Hoberman (b. 1954) playfully addresses obsolescence, the bane of media artists. I first discovered the artist in the late 1970s, when I caught one of his witty performances at Artists Space. I donned 3-D glasses—the kind with one red lens and one green one—as the burly artist stood in the middle of the raw space, operating dual slide projectors as he spun a crazy, autobiographical story, with a whimsical but decidedly critical spin on gadget-consumed life. Although the performance had the appearance of spontaneous improvisation, I knew it had been planned down to the minutest detail.

I kept up with Hoberman and regularly saw his shows, which sometimes involved singing along to a Beatles song at one of his karaoke nights that he organized in clubs near his Williamsburg, Brooklyn, studio. Years later, in 1990, I saw one of his most memorable madcap installations, *Faraday's Garden* (1990), which evoked the happier and simpler times when the American Dream was symbolized by the General Electric Home. Laid out on two long tables parallel to each other was Hoberman's arrangement of a raft of old appliances—hair dryers, fans, mixers, blenders, record players, movie projectors, radios—each of which made individual sounds when a viewer stepped on electronic foot pads concealed under the carpet. Viewers had a sense of control as they created their own musical scores out of the activated appliances. If the audience expanded, pandemonium ensued. If left alone, *Faraday's Garden* was silent.

Hoberman and I formed a reading group with our media art friends, who sometimes grieved about the obsolescence built into their recently purchased hardware. Hoberman soon launched another interactive work with an open call that he sent out through the internet. He invited people to submit images, sounds, or texts and vent their frustration with digital tools that had failed and gripe about the electronics industry's nonstop release of seductive but pricey upgrades. Hoberman took the candid written-and-drawn responses and turned them into the playful content shown in the unruly projection of *Cathartic User Interface (CUI)*.

In 1995 *CUI* premiered at Postmasters Gallery, the leading gallery in New York dedicated to challenging media artwork.[12] At the opening, an enthusiastic crowd stood before a wall with row upon row of cast-off computer keyboards, the most dilapidated ones missing multiple letters.

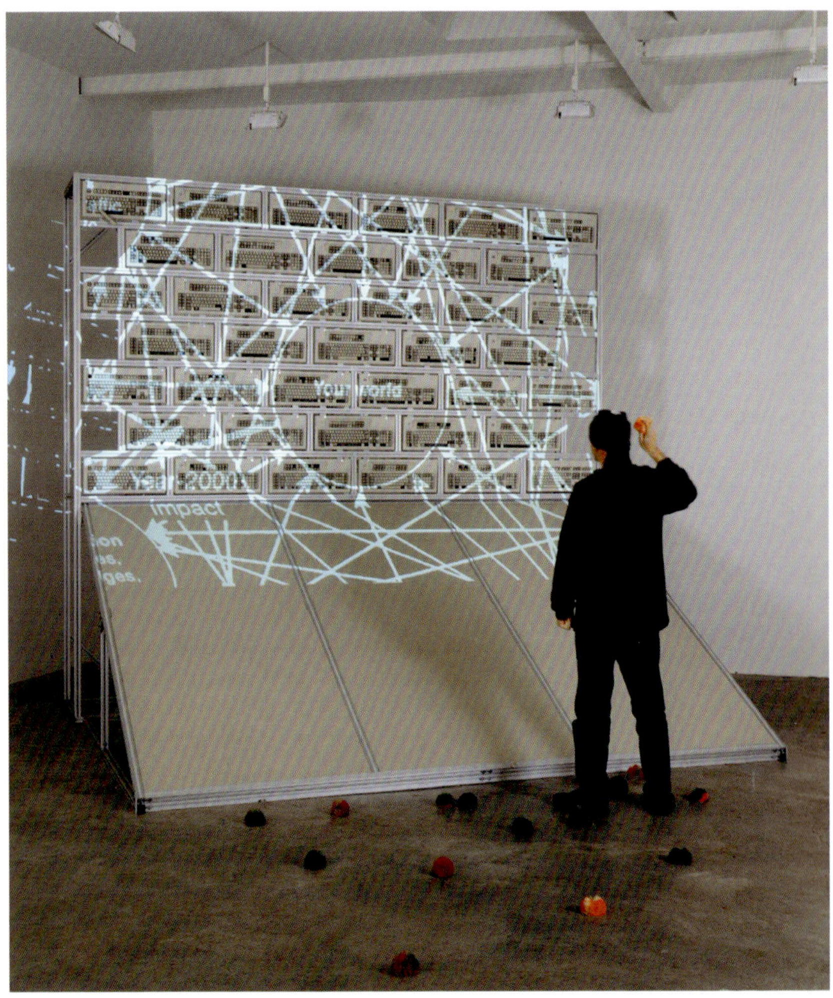

Perry Hoberman, *Cathartic User Interface (CUI)*, 1995
Interactive installation

Viewers grabbed one of the nearby soft, plushy balls, which they pitched
at the cavalcade of keyboards. When a ball—a stand-in for a mouse—made
contact with an active key, it triggered a visual and sonic response, in the
manner of a raucous game of chance played at a fairground. Cacophonous,
winner-take-all sounds accompanied a comical jumble of smiley faces,
stick figures, and texts—the solicited submissions—in a projection that

spread out over the wall of keyboards. The balls made their way back to the feet of viewers for further cathartic action. Eliciting from its audience the high spirits of arcade game players, Hoberman's multiuser artwork cannily addressed the inevitable obsolescence of consumer electronics and the fact that sooner or later, everyone gets stuck with a dud.

Hoberman was one of quite a few media artists who hurled invectives at the electronics industry, annoyed by the way a fabulous, recently purchased device would soon be on the market in an upgraded—and coveted—new version. My own feeling was that artists and equipment makers were driven by the same goal: progress. Artists were intent on creating relevant artwork, while manufacturers were just as intent on creating better gear, understandably with an eye toward greater market share.

Ericka Beckman

With a relaxed attitude about tools and a can-do spirit, media artist Ericka Beckman (b. 1951) began her career in the late 1970s, at the epicenter of experimental action. She received an MFA in 1976 from CalArts, *the* place to be in LA, where she pursued her interest in music and performance, studying with other experimenters, including Mike Kelley, Tony Oursler, James Welling (b. 1951), Barbara Bloom (b. 1951), John Miller, and Jim Shaw. She saw a lot of Kabuki theater and Tibetan dance, along with gamelan concerts and puppet theater. She screened her early films at Hallwalls Contemporary Arts Center, an interdisciplinary artist-run venue in Buffalo, New York, in 1977, and at Artists Space. Beckman and her peers pursued representational imagery that referenced and quoted from overlapping sources, television in particular.

During the 1980s in New York, she was a part of the downtown art and music scene, when it seemed that everyone either played in a band, hung out with a band, or followed a band. Beckman focused on the moving image. Her work dealt with causal sequences, the way shots are temporally linked to other shots in film and how meaning is created through repetition and developed systems, systems that related to the work of her musician friends.[13] An inveterate investigator, she was interested in arcade gaming in the late 1980s, an era when it seemed that social interactions within computer game playing were as meaningful as those in everyday life.

In the late 1980s, artists and curators like me were sponging up technical information by frequenting SIGGRAPH (Special Interest Group on Computer Graphics and Interactive Techniques), the gigantic annual show-and-tell of the computer graphics industry. At the 1989 event, Beckman encountered virtual reality (VR) for the first time. She talked at length with Ron Reisman, a specialist in the fields of artificial intelligence and artificial neural networks, based at NASA's Ames Research Center in Silicon Valley. Reisman invited her to spend several days at Ames, where she met with the gifted software scientist-engineer Scott Fisher and his team, who were developing VR for missions on Mars. Their simulators were designed so that astronauts could rehearse space station maintenance. Beckman donned prototypes of the in-development tactile data gloves and head-coupled displays (goggles) associated with VR and 3-D audio. She discussed the technologies in depth with Reisman, Fisher, and the VR guru Jaron Lanier.

Back in New York, she began developing the visual vocabulary for *Hiatus* (1999/2015), her video inspired by the proto–virtual reality headgear she had just tried at NASA. Galvanized by what she saw as the paucity of video games geared toward girls,[14] Beckman developed a work with a female hero that emulated the high-tech look of an interactive video game, while managing to compensate for her lack of access to sophisticated tools. (An ingenious craftsperson, Beckman has always been a wizard at finding low-tech solutions to making high-tech-looking art.) The story opens with a young woman, in her apartment, who inserts a floppy disk into her computer. She then dons a special corset, one that teleports her instantly into an online virtual game, Hiatus. In the game, the woman's avatar is Wanda, who discovers other players in the fantastical place. Wanda starts to tend a virtual garden where she stores her memories, her corset functioning as a memory device. Evil appears in the form of a profiteering cowboy, none other than the proprietor of a pharmacological startup, who tries to make her part of his enterprise. She resists as he tries to entice her: "I've decided the two of us should be partners." In a world where startups rise and fall and women hit their heads against glass ceilings and face innumerable obstacles, *Hiatus* is an engaging representation of women and technology.[15]

When I asked Beckman about the stunning, effervescent colors in her work, including *Hiatus*, she answered that they come from the illustrated books she read as a child, and also the color codes used in video games, hardware store labels, and commercial advertising.[16]

Through ingenuity, pragmatism, and hard work, Beckman has prevailed and stayed at the top of her game, managing to take big steps forward rather than stand in place. Her latest one-person exhibitions—at the Secession, Vienna (2017), KW Institute for Contemporary Art, Berlin (2018), Zabludowicz Collection, London (2018), and MIT List Visual Arts Center (2019)—have allowed her to expand upon earlier work, adding what she initially intended but didn't have the means to do. *Hiatus* became a dual-screen installation; another installation, *Tension Building* (2014–16), gained a set of bleachers. Her next piece, its working title *Lost Productivity*, will explore 360-degree video, an up-and-coming technology. She will create

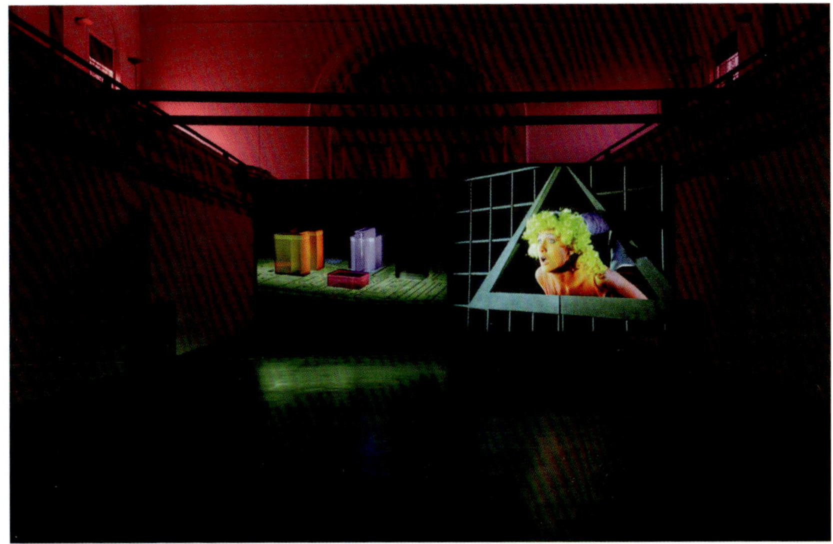

a wraparound four-screen installation that viewers can enter, and inside of which they will navigate around the "background collateral," the term some curators apply to ancillary sculpture. Beckman always manages to drive storytelling in inventive ways.

Jim Campbell

Jim Campbell (b. 1956) is one of those artists whose deft programming skills enables them to move between the worlds of culture and Silicon Valley startups. After graduating with degrees in electrical engineering and mathematics from MIT, where he also studied film, Campbell moved to San Francisco in 1978. There he began to apply his programming skills not only to his jobs with startups but also to his own singular art. His original goal was to get away from both the conventional computer screen and button-pushing interfaces, and move toward making media art that had a more intuitive level of interaction, in which technology would be in the background.

During the 1990s, I would frequently run into Campbell when we were speakers at the same media art festivals in Japan, where the craft of technology was respected. Often we paid visits together to Itsuo Sakane,

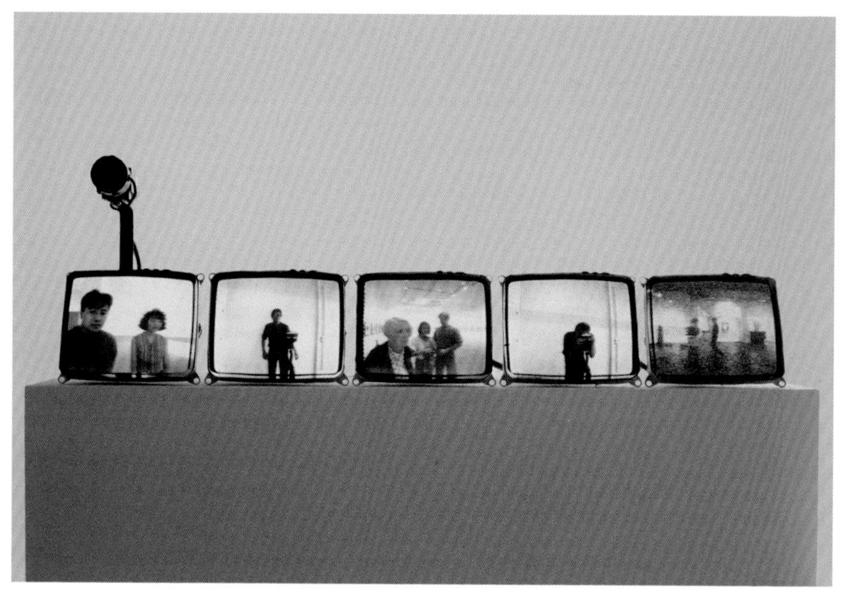

Jim Campbell, *Memory/Recollection*, 1990
Black-and-white video camera, five CRTs, PC computer, custom
electronics; dimensions variable

the eminent art and science newspaper writer who became president of the
Gifu prefecture's International Academy of Multimedia Arts and Sciences
in Ogaki, and to the NTT InterCommunication Center, an exhibition and
conference space in Tokyo founded by the telecommunications giant Nippon
Telegraph and Telephone. Japan's passion for art and technology matched
its manufacturing prowess.

In a 1996 Video Viewpoints talk at MoMA, Campbell explained, "I have
tried to create installations that are less about a viewer dominating a work,
and more about viewers participating in the developing personality of a
work."[17] *Memory/Recollection* (1990) epitomized his approach. The installation
has five stripped-down monitor screens that sit on a long plinth at roughly
the height of a person's torso. Viewers standing before the work encounter
images of themselves captured in real time by a camera positioned at the
far left. The live images of the present environment first appear on the
leftmost screen and shift to the right, onto the adjacent monitor screen in
time delay. Thus, the present becomes the recent past and subsequently
will appear (in a seemingly random way) in the future on the other screens.
Campbell goes even further, merging the very recent past with images

from the unfamiliar distant past—that is, from every room in which the installation has previously been shown. Viewers see images of themselves in the present conflated with prerecorded images of years ago, culled from the work's electronic memory. The further back in time, the grainier the past appears, emulating the deterioration of memory that comes with age.

About his practice Campbell noted, "Using technological tools and scientific models as metaphors for memory and illusion, my work seeks to interpret, represent, and mirror psychological states and processes, and their breakdown. Time and memory, individual and collective, electronic and real are the elements of my work."[18]

Memory/Recollection has both charm and complexity. It presents installation challenges going forward, given that TV tubes have become obsolete and the computer hard drive and the software that was used will always need upgrading. Still, the future for this masterful, pioneering work should be promising, now that media art has become a specialized area of conservation.

Jeffrey Shaw

The visionary software artist Jeffrey Shaw (b. 1944) has been ahead of the curve for decades. He was part of the Artist Placement Group, an artist-run organization established in 1966 by artists seeking to refocus art to situations outside the gallery. Each of the original members was firmly committed to an intermedia practice that challenged traditional notions of art making.[19] Shaw gradually shifted away from his training in sculpture and architecture and turned to media, in 1969 becoming a member of the Eventstructure Research Group in Amsterdam. I first met the Melbourne-born artist in the late 1980s, when he was teaching at the Städelschule's Institute for New Media in Frankfurt, right before he became the founding director of the Institute for Visual Media at ZKM in Karlsruhe, Germany.[20]

In 1993 Shaw came to MoMA to discuss his inspired interactive installation *Legible City* (1989–91), which he had recently completed at ZKM. He explained how he had collaborated with a team of engineers (Dirk Groeneveld, Gideon May, Lothar Schmitt, Charly Jungbauer, and Huib Nelissen) in rigging up a bicycle so that it would connect to a computer system. Sitting on a stationary bicycle, the viewer-user of the work pedals and navigates the system by turning the handlebars, a clever interface that replaces the standard mouse or gaming joystick. Two overhead projectors cast simulations of a city onto the flanking walls. The seated user drives through the enveloping cityscape of buildings that are created by computer-generated three-dimensional letters, which form words and

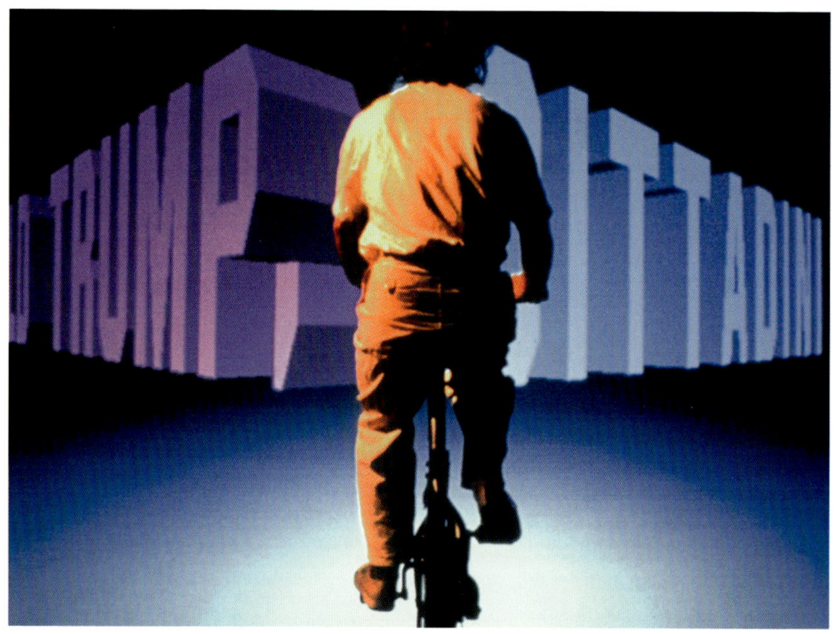

Jeffrey Shaw and Dirk Groeneveld, *Legible City*, 1989
Video and computer-based installation, with bicycle interface,
Mac mini computer, operating system (Linux), custom software,
custom-made electronics, TFT monitor, projector, and concave
projection surface; dimensions variable

sentences adapted from purported conversations and published articles
by the city's inhabitants. The pace of the user's pedaling controls both
the speed at which the text unfolds and the direction through the cityscape.
Others at the installation can observe the landscape as they mill about
the room.

At MoMA Shaw demonstrated the Manhattan version of *Legible City*,
which had eight distinct scenarios that were based on supposed monologues
by former mayor Ed Koch, architect Frank Lloyd Wright, developer Donald
Trump, a tour guide, a con artist, an ambassador, and a taxi driver.[21] The
monumental letters of each story line were distinguished by a specific
color so that the viewer–user on the stationary bike could select a person
and follow the path of that narration that he or she had selected. I opted
for the taxi driver, who, in this case, was a friendly, mischievous soul
with encyclopedic knowledge of the city. Shaw anticipated today's global
positioning system, better known as GPS, by placing a small LCD monitor

in the center of the handlebars that showed and displayed the ground plan of the city plus the cyclist's location from moment to moment.

Over the years, I've kept in contact with Shaw, at annual events like Ars Electronica in Linz, Austria, where creative denizens of augmented and mixed reality, immersive visualization environments, navigable cinematic systems, and interactive narrative all gather to present and discuss their innovations. Shaw is now an esteemed professor in Hong Kong, where he holds multiple research appointments.

Masaki Fujihata

In 1984 I visited Seibu Digital Communication Inc. (SEDIC), at that time a bustling computer graphics design studio in Roppongi, a hip area of Tokyo. Wearing big round, black-rimmed glasses that gave him frog eyes, Masaki Fujihata (b. 1956) peered out from behind a large computer screen to say hi. The young virtuoso had just completed *Maitreya*, a lively three-minute video that opened with a Buddhist text. Accompanied by a buoyant soundtrack composed by Haruomi Hosono (b. 1947)—a member of the popular Yellow Magic Orchestra—rotund, cute, cartoonlike figures would totter and make sexually suggestive gestures, then suddenly multiply and divide at a prodigious rate. I immediately decided to feature the work in the 1986 show *New Video: Japan* and acquired it for MoMA's collection.

In the early 1990s, the adroit artist headed the media department at Keio University, where he honed multimedia strategies, scrutinizing virtual space and physically building interactive communication environments. The complex installations he created grew out of his prowess as a formidable programmer and drew upon his sophisticated sense of design.

I was back in Japan in 1995 for the premiere of Fujihata's *Beyond Pages* (1995–97). I entered a cozy room, where what appeared to be a large book with blank pages lay open on a table. I approached and sat down on the one available chair. Then, I ran my fingers over the virtual book as if it were a touch screen and spontaneously began turning the pages that had appeared. The movement of my fingers had triggered an overhead projector to cast coquettishly romping words over the page. When I flipped to another virtual page, another cluster of words was set in motion. Meanwhile, on the wall directly in front of me, a life-size projection of a screen door emitted the bright outdoor light of a fine summer day, accompanied by the sound of chirping cicadas. Suddenly the screen door swung open, and a young girl peeked in, as if she were about to join me in the room. There was a truly magical moment in this stunning work when she giggled and left.

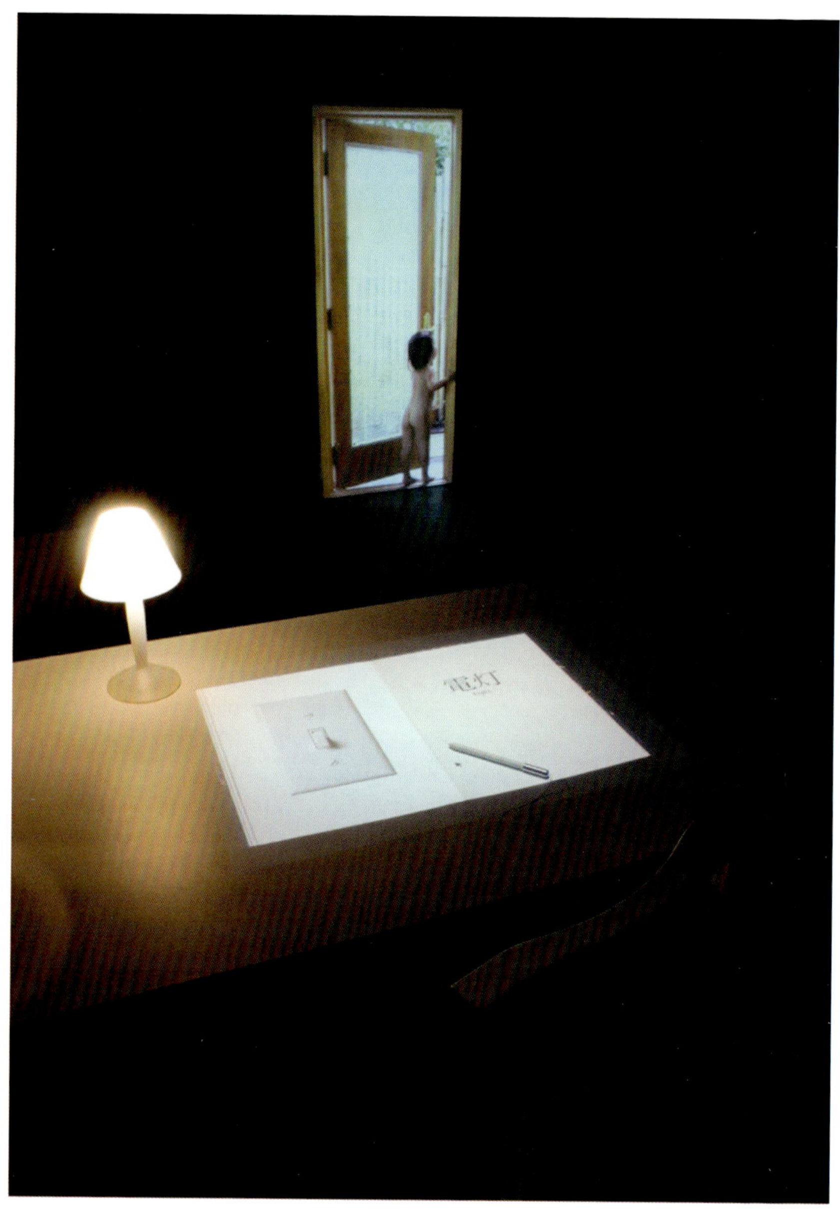

Masaki Fujihata, *Beyond Pages*, 1995–97
Interactive installation, programmed using Macromedia Director,
with a room, table containing digitizer tablet, wireless tablet pen,
chair, and two projectors; room: 13 ft. 2 in. x 18 ft. (4 x 5.5 m)

Fujihata continues to approach technology with an easygoing attitude, and he still makes me smile with the way he plays with tactility to charm viewers, and sometimes challenge their comfort level. This was clear when I came across his installation *Private Room/TV* (2009–10) at a collateral event of the 2017 Venice Biennale. The work consisted of 150 white fluorescent tubes combined in the shape of a radiant little house, in the middle of which sat a similarly constructed lightweight folding chair, glowing amid a nest of wires. *Private Room/TV* seemed to allude to the golden age of early television, when families gathered together around a glowing TV set, each family separate but watching the same TV network showing nearly the same content. Fujihata seems to ask, might we still be lonely in this age of supreme connectivity as we embrace our always-present devices?

Cory Arcangel

Cory Arcangel (b. 1978) is well-known for playful, ironic artworks that explore the culture of everyday technology, in particular button-pushing video games. When the congenial, self-effacing young artist first stopped by my office in 2000, he talked enthusiastically about growing up in Buffalo, a run-down city where a stellar group of artists—professors and students— connected to SUNY Buffalo had contributed to the definition of media art. The experimental art scene at SUNY had included video pioneers Woody and Steina Vasulka, avant-garde filmmakers Paul Sharits and Tony Conrad, and pop culture thinkers Cindy Sherman and Robert Longo. Arcangel grew up taking workshops with these media art veterans and following their films and videos at home through local public access cable TV programs. During high school, he was a "heavy metal suburban wannabe shredder" who analyzed cassette tapes of "neo-classical axe-wielders," such as the composer-guitarist Jason Becker. Meanwhile, he was fixated on arcade games and practiced the guitar eight hours a day.[22]

We met just as Arcangel was graduating with a bachelor of music degree from Oberlin Conservatory of Music, at the moment when user-friendly personal computers began to permeate the consumer market, along with artificially intelligent robotic pets, personal digital assistants (electronic handheld information devices known as PDAs), and virtual worlds (computer-based simulated environments) on the internet. Eschewing the latest gadgetry, Arcangel gravitated toward discarded low-resolution, user-activated Game Boy devices that he picked up while dumpster diving or at thrift stores for next to nothing. He would take apart the crude eight-bit handheld game consoles, with their simple operation buttons labeled "A," "B," "SELECT," and "START," and directional pad. He figured out how to modify the programs of eight-bit chiptune devices. Arcangel also spent hours poring over hefty computer programming manuals and taught himself to write code, afraid he would be unemployed after college.

At Oberlin Arcangel had gained access to a high-speed internet connection and at the same time was inspired to explore music technology. He had been a member (with his sister Jamie and friends Paul Davis, Joe Beuckman, and Joseph Bonn) of the short-lived programming music ensemble BEIGE, which evolved into an electronic DIY art collective. Their first release was the 1998 EP *Tardy Tracks*, based on rowdy eight-bit synthesized electronic music they composed using the programmable sound generators found in Atari and Commodore home computers. The collective went on to produce videos, web projects, and other albums of chiptune music, using real-time computer graphics and modified computer cartridge games. Their eight-bit computer aesthetic grew out of a fascination with process.

Arcangel was well versed in music theory and the history of twentieth-century composition, having majored in electronic music composition, with a minor in classical guitar. His passion for music in all forms led him to explore sound—incessant repetition that seemed either exhilarating or mind-numbing—and melodic structure in projects that engaged the culture of music at large.[23] He avidly studied the work of the 1960s electronic Minimalist composers La Monte Young, Terry Riley, Steve Reich, and Philip Glass (b. 1937), who focused on the processes of their music composition. At Oberlin he met Pauline Oliveros. "I was kind of a punk back then, but Pauline transcends authority," he recalled. "She told us about a piece she did in the sixties, when she hooked up sine-wave oscillators to speakers and tuned them to the resonant frequency of the concert hall. The waves match up and amplify each other, so the sound gets louder and louder inside the hall. That's when it clicked for me. I'd learned about Stockhausen. I'd learned about Schoenberg. But Pauline made it all come alive and I finally could see that this history really did have an edge."[24]

Arcangel's programming and hacking of computer systems paralleled his interest in minimalistic electronic sound. Indeed, a legacy from his years at Oberlin is the way in which many of Arcangel's works foreground the repetitive labor of dismantling his gizmos and soldering parts[25]—the intensity, focus, drive to perfect, discovery, and breaking down of image and sound to its parts. "That whole idea that I could practice the same [music] piece for a year influenced the way I look at computers and my competence and patience with them as a tool," he once remarked.[26]

Going on tour to give lecture-performances, at such venues as Harvestworks Digital Media Arts Center and the American Museum of the Moving Image, among other institutions, Arcangel captivated audiences with his affable explanations of how he arrived at the new work he presented. As he often describes, the process would always begin by carefully checking to see if the insides of a newfound item had any personality. Should there be something interesting in the obsolete gear's programming—which to him corresponded to the notation system in music—he would tinker with the grammar of the device, its sequence of symbols and patterns, searching for ways to improvise and tell new stories with it. Sometimes his new treasures included old VHS tapes with tacky sitcoms and hard drives containing obsolete software. He would fiddle around with the once popular material, searching for ways to tell new stories with it.

Interested in the archaeology of game aesthetics, his early Nintendo-derived works fit the category of generative art, in that they were generated, composed, or constructed through computer software algorithms. His modus operandi was to create theater out of the journey through the obsolescence cycle of his found gear.

When Arcangel was starting out at Oberlin, it had been enough to simply put his artwork on the internet, because then the contemporary art world was not part of the dialogue. This gradually changed once he moved to New York, where his audience grew to include like-minded souls who were also smitten by computer technology and who were congregating at the fringier music-art venues, where they showed their funky intangibles.[27] Still, Arcangel did keep one eye on what was selling in the art market, and he participated in group shows at offbeat galleries, such as that of Daniel Reich, who operated out of his minuscule studio apartment.

Arcangel attained underground acclaim with *Super Mario Clouds* (2002). Taking a still-functional vintage Nintendo game cartridge from 1985, he hacked the software and was able to remove every visual element of little plumber Mario from the microchip, leaving only the background of blue sky and animated clouds. The piece was released first as an online technical tutorial on his folksy website, where he described each step necessary for someone to re-create the work, thereby empowering his audience. Arcangel's techie fans were ecstatic.

In 2001 the artist told me he was about to submit something to the curators of the upcoming Whitney Biennial, a work that he believed was sure to be a shoo-in. What better choice than an abstract digital landscape of beautiful rolling clouds. His stand-alone, projected version of *Super Mario Clouds* was immediately accepted and prominently featured on its own in one of the Whitney's main galleries. Arcangel's digitally rendered abstract clouds had a lighthearted sense of infinity and a cartoonlike novelty that enchanted museumgoers and garnered acclaim from art critics who spotted the wit of a Warhol and the color field abstraction of Helen Frankenthaler (1928–2011).

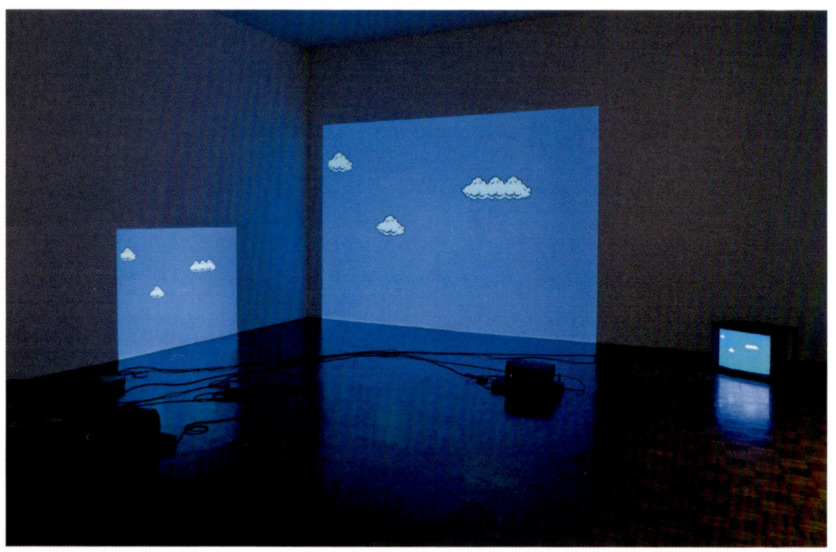

Cory Arcangel, *Super Mario Clouds*, 2002
Handmade hacked Super Mario Bros. cartridge, Nintendo NES video
game system, artist software; dimensions variable

Arcangel took a step further by combining humor with critical theory in
Totally Fucked (2002), a projection derived from another modified Nintendo
game cartridge. Hacked right out of his legendary game, Super Mario Bros.,
the normally bustling, diminutive Super Mario stands in place, pinioned on a
block emblazoned with a question mark. The ingenuous plumber floats in the
vast blue sky, unable to relocate. He looks right, then left, then right again.
Because it would be the end of the artwork if he were to jump off his perch,
little Mario is doomed, stuck forever confronting his imminent demise. The
stranded gnome epitomizes the dynamic eight-bit, low-res computer game
culture, and yet, at the same time, *Totally Fucked* contradicts the gamer's
usual fixation on achieving a perfect score. Tinged with disconcerting humor,
Arcangel's work, on one level, is tragicomedy for the masses. On another,
the work is intriguingly rigorous, befitting an art audience. Unlike Sisyphus,
the legendary king of Corinth who is forever pushing a boulder uphill, Super
Mario, Nintendo's mascot, stands eternally perplexed, without a gamer's
conviction that practice makes perfect and without the power to advance.

204

I stayed in touch with Arcangel, who by 2010 had become the de facto poster child of digital art. Whenever we caught up, he would explain that he saw humor as the currency of the internet. As I pondered the question of which net art works would have the legs to survive, Arcangel introduced me to jodi.org, the scruffily dressed husband-and-wife duo Joan Heemskerk (b. 1968) and Dirk Paesmans (b. 1965), who had been active in Holland since the mid-1990s. Maintaining the activist spirit of their antiauthoritarian student days, the pair made the cleverest—and for some the most disturbing—classic web artworks with an ironic aesthetic. After clicking on the jodi.org URL, users were startled to see what appeared to be a virus with meaning-less text and glitches streaming nonstop across their computer screens. Only upon a close read of the virus's HTML source code could one recognize detailed diagrams of hydrogen and uranium bombs.

About the same time, I met Mark Napier (b. 1961), a pioneer of digital and internet art, in addition to being a software designer who worked as a senior technical specialist at Reuters, the international news agency. His early web artwork *The Shredder 1.0* (1998) exposed the unprotected and protean nature of the web. Grabbing the raw material of the web, Napier tore it up and tossed it onto a virtual heap—markup, text, code, images, and links that got scattered across the screen, resulting in what looked like an instant Jackson Pollock.

According to Napier:

The web browser is an organ of perception through which we "see" the web. It filters and organizes a huge mass of structured information that spans continents, is constantly growing, reorganizing itself, shifting its appearance, evolving. The Shredder presents this global structure as a chaotic, irrational, raucous "action painting." By altering the HTML code before the browser reads it, the Shredder appropriates the data of the web, transforming it into a parallel web. Content becomes abstraction. Text becomes graphics. Information becomes art.[28]

I appreciated how Napier and his work addressed the then much-discussed issues of authority, ownership, and territory in the world of the web.

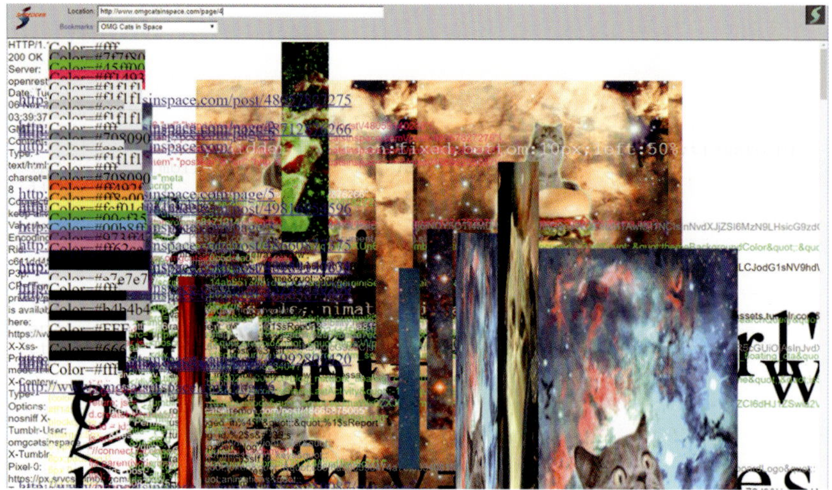

Mark Napier, *The Shredder 1.0*, 1998
HTML, JavaScript, and PHP

John Simon

In 1997 a bowling team of media artists welcomed me into their monthly night out. I met their reigning champion, John Simon (b. 1963), during my first bowling evening. His website (numeral.com) featured an online store where interested mavens could buy editioned copies of his artwork that he released as protected digital files.[29] He had just released *Every Icon*, a work of software based on a Java applet, a downloadable program that ran on a user's own computer rather than a web server. Meant to be displayed vertically on a flat screen, installed on the wall, or even framed, *Every Icon* never-endingly chugged along, as it enumerated the multitudinous patterns that can be computed in a thirty-two-by-thirty-two grid of black-and-white square pixels. In the late 1990s Simon told me that if one used a reasonably fast Pentium-powered personal computer that could flash one hundred different combinations per second, it would take about sixteen months to display the 4.3 billion variations on the top line of the grid in *Every Icon*. Because the number of possibilities expanded exponentially, the second line would be completed in about six billion years.

Simon had spent years studying the celebrated geniuses who paid homage to the square—Paul Klee (1879–1940), Piet Mondrian (1872–1944), and Josef Albers (1888–1976). While their paintings sell for many millions, Simon's *Every Icon* can be purchased for twenty dollars. The edition is still

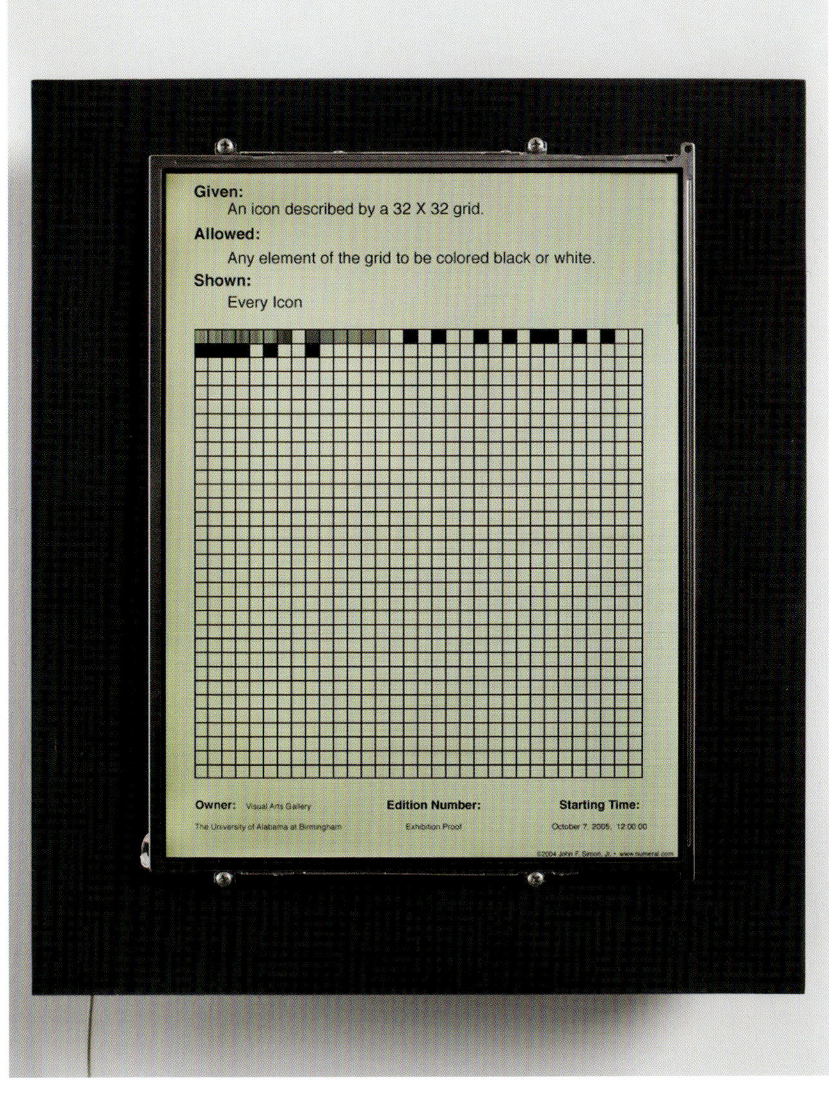

John Simon, *Every Icon*, 1997
Software, Macintosh PowerBook G3, acrylic plastic, 11¾ x 8 x
2½ in. (29.8 x 20.3 x 6.4 cm)

available in numbered but unlimited copies; to date, 160 collectors have
acquired *Every Icon*.

Simon had been envisioning the artwork since the late 1980s, when post-modernism was emerging and there was talk about how we had reached the end of representation. He wanted to show that as opposed to painting, even in a simple thirty-two-by-thirty-two-pixel space, the conceptual possibilities for imaging were infinite. As opposed to saying, "This is my image," he wanted to present the conditions in which an image could come into being.[30]

I came to understand Simon's work as far more than a clever mathematical exercise or a modest electronic meditation on the eternal nature of the creative urge. I recognized the elegant poetry that came from his philosophical underpinnings. With *Every Icon*, he asks: "Can a machine produce every possible image? What are the limits of this kind of automation? Is it possible to practice image making by exploring all of image-space using a computer rather than by recording from the world around us? What does it mean that one may discover visual imagery so detached from 'nature'?"[31]

Automatic Update, MoMA

The quasi-revolutionary aura of the dot-com era dissipated with the financial crash in March 2000. Still, technology and art continued to ride together on a tidal wave of imagination. In 2007 I organized the exhibition *Automatic Update* so that the diverse languages and ecumenical interests of media artists would reach a broad art audience. The exhibition featured recently acquired installations, mature works with entertaining agendas that lightened the somber mood of the times. Each of the artists had a unique approach to incorporating technology into his or her work. The artists' humor did not soften their biting commentary on our social milieu. The exhibition included work by Arcangel, Rafael Lozano-Hemmer (b. 1967), Xu Bing (b. 1955), Paul Pfeiffer (b. 1966), and Jennifer and Kevin McCoy (b. 1968 and 1967).

Rafael Lozano-Hemmer

The Mexican-Canadian electronic artist Lozano-Hemmer holds a degree in physical chemistry. A cyclone of energy, he exudes the passionate congeniality of a reveler combined with the incisiveness of a top scientist. He not only creates showstopping, huge outdoor installations, but also makes small, equally dynamic work by joining everyday objects with simple electronic tools and off-the-shelf programming software. When I saw his installation *Caguama* (2004), I had to laugh as thirty thirty-two-ounce brown beer bottles twirled in sync on a tabletop as if they were the Rockettes.

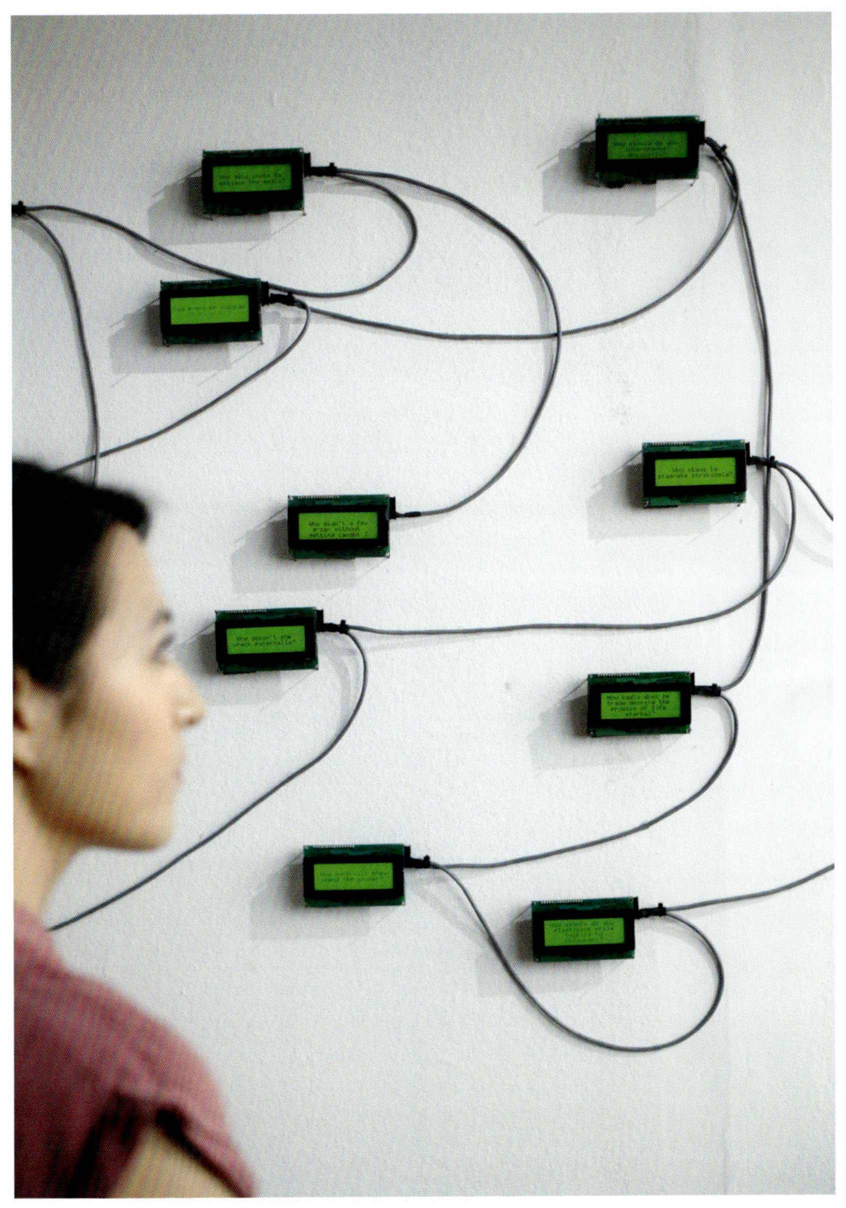

Rafael Lozano-Hemmer, *33 Questions per Minute*, *Relational Architecture 5*, 2000
Computer, custom software, and twenty-one LCD screens; dimensions variable

Lozano-Hemmer's ability to turn complex ideas into elegant, under-standable systems is what drew me to his *33 Questions per Minute* (2000). The interactive installation consists of a computer and twenty-one tiny LCD screens, each the size of a cigarette pack. The work is based on a computer program that uses grammatical rules to combine random-access words from a dictionary and generate fifty-five billion unique questions. The automated questions are presented at a rate of thirty-three per minute—the threshold of legibility—on the LCD screens mounted either on the support columns of the exhibition space or on a wall. The system will take over three thousand years to ask all possible questions. By means of a keyboard, members of the public can introduce any question or inject a comment into the flow of automatic questions. Their participation shows up on the screens immediately, and words or questions entered by viewers become part of the program's database.

Whether a chimpanzee pecking randomly at a typewriter could repro-duce Shakespeare's *Hamlet* is a question that gave twentieth-century philosophers, mathematicians, and sundry other academics a platform on which to strut their erudition. Today the question would need an update, because by now a computer would be able to simulate all the random typing. An ambitious simian scribe might start a successful writing career with Lozano-Hemmer's grammatical software program.

Xu Bing

For decades, Beijing-based Xu Bing has studied how words shape our under-standing of the world. He has become world-renowned for his printmaking skills and for his ingenious fabrication of Chinese logograms. Having followed Xu's career for a long time, I quickly responded when at last he turned to media. In *Automatic Update*, I included the initial installation version of his *Book from the Ground* (2007–13).

The word *icon* once denoted objects of worship—images or sculptures. Now the word refers more commonly to company logos and the thumbnail images on computer screens that users double-click to activate an appli-cation. Icons are ubiquitous symbols providing information without words, antidotes to misunderstanding in the enveloping sphere of world languages in the global electronic network. With *Book from the Ground*, an ongoing project, Xu's intention is to foster communication through a common language of icons.[32]

A massive undertaking, Xu spent four years painstakingly compiling, reading, arranging, and revising a copious number of pictograms—incl-uding the familiar icons used to indicate stop and go, identify gendered washrooms, or prepare airplane travelers for an emergency landing—that provide serious information that anyone can decipher. Out of his assembled icons, he created a bittersweet story about a day in life of a white-collar office worked named Mr. Black.

The story opens as Mr. Black awakens from the calls of a nearby chirping bird and the sounding of his alarm clock. He brushes his teeth, makes coffee, watches TV, and feeds his cat before taking the subway to work. Once at the office, he investigates fast-food options for lunch, uses the bathroom, daydreams, and sends flowers, and then he socializes after work. Back at home, he kills a mosquito, gets into bed, sleeps, and the next morning starts his routine again.

With the simplicity of a children's illustrated storybook, Xu's narrative can be understood by anyone, without translation. It is an elegant parable about everyday modern life, always in transit and with adequate signs so that we hopefully stay out of harm's way.[33]

At MoMA, the installation of *Book from the Ground* consisted of two workstations—two desks, each with its own mouse and keyboard and flat screen—separated by a tall Plexiglas panel covered on both sides with a Mylar skin on which the story was written. Nearby, a hidden computer contained a software database with what Xu referred to as an "alphabetory" of icons. When seated at one of the workstations, a visitor could look up and read the short story spread out over the Plexiglas panel or use the keyboard to type a message, which would appear in a text bubble on his or her own screen and on one used by another person, translated into Xu's icons. Even without understanding each other's language, two people were able to engage in a conversation of icons. The results were social and in some cases romantic, leading to dates, which I learned about from the guards.

Jennifer and Kevin McCoy

Jennifer and Kevin McCoy met in Paris in 1990, as students of the great theorist of cinema Raymond Bellour. I met the pair back in New York, as they began a collaborative practice. They were engaged in analyzing television and commercial film, breaking works down according to the sounds, images, symbols, characters, and words as bits of information that they categorized and organized in their computer. Their art was the perfect embodiment of what is called "database aesthetics," art that explores the database as a cultural and aesthetic form.

The McCoys spent long hours chopping up into short clips such popular TV series as *Starsky & Hutch*. When they exhibited *Every Shot, Every Episode* (2001) as an installation at Postmasters Gallery, I was able to choose from

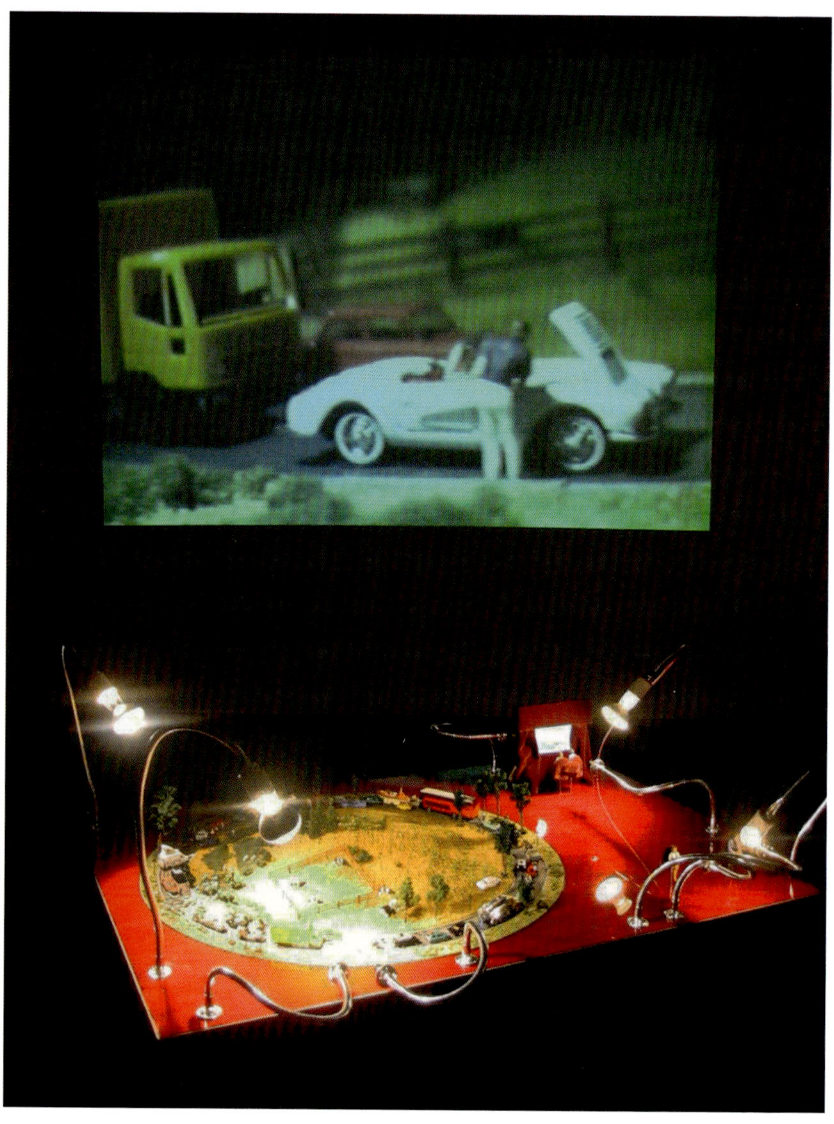

Jennifer and Kevin McCoy, *Our Second Date*, 2004
Tabletop installation, with six miniature cameras, computer, LCD
monitor, and one projector; 42 x 56 x 50 in. (106.7 x 142.2 x 127 cm)

a library of carefully labeled DVDs and insert one into a player to watch.
My selected DVD might contain every occurrence of the color blue in an
episode, or every extreme close-up shot. Each DVD had nothing to do with
story line but everything to do with the attributes of data and the computer.
Whenever I changed my selection, I would rearrange the viewing order
according to metadata: a set of data that describes and gives information
about other data.[34] The McCoys explained all of this in a lecture at MoMA
in 2001.

For *Automatic Update*, I selected *Our Second Date* (2004), the
installation that refers to the McCoys' second date in Paris, when they
went to the movies and saw New Wave filmmaker Jean-Luc Godard's
black comedy *Weekend* (1967). Based on their memory of that experience,
they reduced the film classic to intimate dimensions. In their hands, the
famous car accident scene is the size of a model train set. A brief stroll
around the tabletop installation gives the viewer the full impact of Godard's
masterpiece. In their version, the McCoys are seen as tiny plastic figurines
seated together on a couch, facing a tiny LCD monitor screen. The pair
watch a "live" movie that is being edited on the spot in the space adjacent
to them. In the circular diorama of the highway accident and traffic pileup,
small plastic figures represent the angry travelers who have gotten out
of their toy cars and are milling about on the road. The figurine McCoys
watch a movie that is a continuously changing view, a live feed that switches
between six teeny endoscope surveillance cameras inconspicuously
nestled within the setting.

Our Second Date looks at the role that media has played in the
development of the McCoys' personal relationship and in their collaborative
work. MoMA visitors who saw their installation and read the wall texts
accompanying each work in *Automatic Update* understood that the show
reflected the artists' simultaneous interest in and skepticism about
technology, revealed through their comical and absurd use of technologies
in ways that that suggest how these tools are mollifiers that smooth rough
edges and not a panacea. The installations anticipated the big changes
that lay ahead for media artists in a world where feature-length films are
watched on smartphones. Ideas still matter but scale is less relevant. Media
as a field goes on and continues to encompasses disparate cross-platform
art practices, as medium specificity becomes irrelevant.

Media Art, Globalism, and Identity Politics

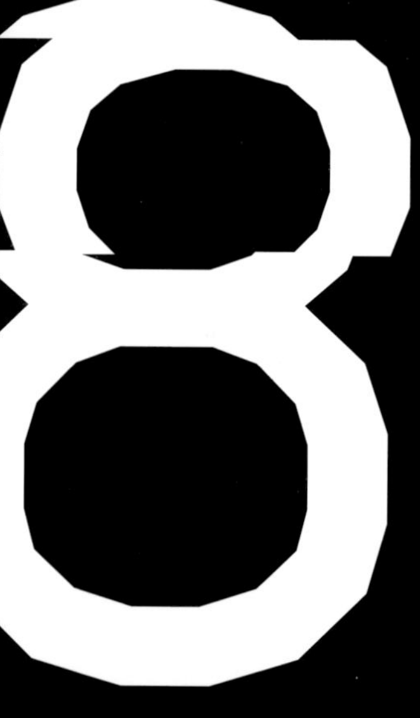

The prevalence and global spread of technology during the late 1990s and early 2000s meant that the arts embraced it more than ever. I watched the administration at MoMA give growing acceptance to digital tools, from versatile management software for large museum databases to the increasingly user-friendly technologies utilized in fine art. Encouraged by broad-minded professors at music and art schools, especially in Western parts of the world, budding interdisciplinary artists adapted miniaturized and cheaper personal devices to their visions. These young self-starters mapped out trajectories that included personal home pages on which they presented their downloadable CVs and gave web surfers access to their media art.

A community of media artists and thinkers was convening internationally for specialized events. Ars Electronica, founded in 1979, was a well-regarded annual showcase for media art in Linz, Austria. Ars went on to establish a prominent research center, Futurelab, with an extensive archive and a staff of twenty. The Inter-Society for the Electronic Arts launched in the Netherlands in 1990 to bring together individuals and organizations from around the world for a biannual (now annual) symposium and exhibition, held each time in a different host city.[1]

As a classification, multimedia became more expansive through its upgrading components—proliferating laptops, faster hard drives, and advancing video game software. The diversified field had many subsections. The programming, software-driven facet of new media had a lot to do with function and form, and was closer in spirit to commercial art and design. During the 1990s, image sharing—both official and illicit—allowed artists to share content and became fodder for art. Website links were shared among friends, some with go-to bookmarks on such sites as popdex.com, founded by Cameron Marlow, and memepool.com, founded by Joshua Schachter; both were multiple-author weblogs active from the late 1990s that offered links to interesting entities on the web with annotated comments.[2] By the late 1990s new intermediaries appeared between contemporary art and the public: bloggers, who endorsed and spread the word about new trends but were often careless about fact-checking.

Identity politics, the subject of no-nonsense media art veterans who had emerged in the 1970s, such as Howardena Pindell and Martha Rosler, intensified as artists grew more critical of gender and racial inequalities, as well as class divides. At the same time, artists' worldviews became more global as they took advantage of inexpensive airfares and traveled overseas more frequently, often to study. Foreign students poured into art schools in London, Frankfurt, and New York. Simultaneously, in some areas of the world, artists defiantly honed political agendas and developed theoretical and critical art practices with strong convictions that sometimes smacked of propaganda. To some extent festivals and biennials tempered regional distinctions, at the same time that international films and music streamed out via internet platforms. Vimeo was one: founded in 2004, it gives creators the tools to host, distribute, and monetize their videos.

The art scene became more globally inclusive and quietly shifted away from the preeminence of the West. The first performance and video artists to appear from what were then still considered by some in the West as faraway places with ancient cultures, like China and India, had operated for years on their own without support, and were situated tenuously between the fine arts and the commercial world. As part of the underground, they were fortunate in often being overlooked by those in power and therefore were able to enjoy some freedom in making work that, for an outsider like me, required careful study in order to understand the wider cultural context and allusions.

Technology's perpetual upgrades keep media artists agile, always open to experimentation and new challenges. As a curator engaged with an art form that is readily disseminated (especially work suited to the internet), I am mindful of how media art is affected by both regional history and global trends. Artists from several different continents, some of whom started out on the fringe and went on to have a major impact on the field, helped to define what media art is.

Media Art in China

In the late 1990s, I became aware of the media and performance art clandestinely unfolding in China, outside of mainstream art practices. I quizzed my European cohorts who had visited the country already, and also read every article I could find that shed light on the developing scene there. At that point I decided that I need to get a firsthand look at how such artists were working. I knew that artists who engaged in performance or managed to make a video there did so somewhat surreptitiously. They would present their provocative work often for just a few hours to a small coterie of supportive friends and peers in unsanctioned places, and promoted it by word of mouth. They were responding to local politics and to the goings-on in foreign art, which they learned about through exhibition catalogs and magazines hand-carried into the country by the few individuals granted visas to travel, or through books with postage-stamp-size images of early Warhol and Beuys artworks leafed through at the rare government-sanctioned book fair.

In 1997 I secured a travel grant from the Asian Cultural Council, which supports cultural exchange between Asian countries and the United States.

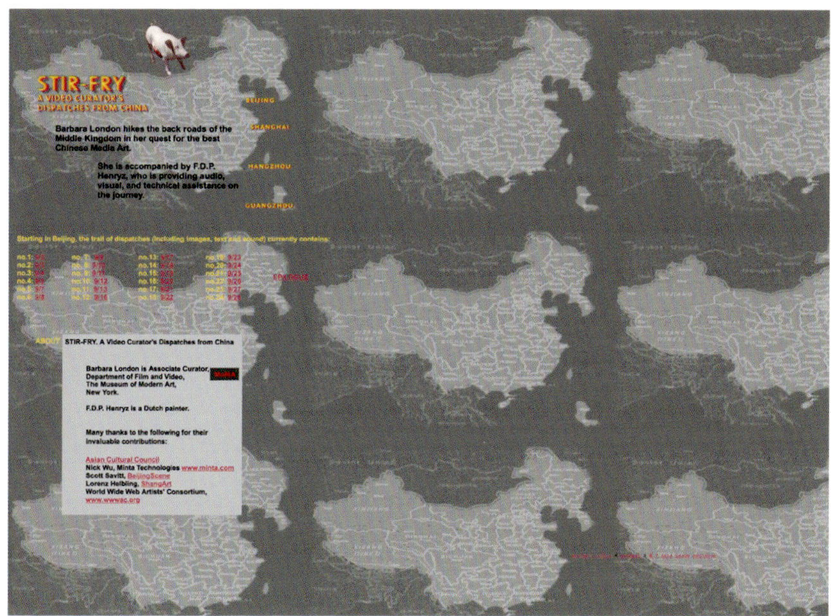

Barbara London in collaboration with the Museum of Modern Art
and äda'web, *Stir-Fry: A Video Curator's Dispatches from China*, 1997
Website (screen capture of home page)

My objective was to do the same kind of research in China that I had been
doing for years in North America and Europe—visiting artists' studios,
gathering documentation, and methodically organizing the information
in manila file folders. But now I had the idea to make my files public by
putting the content on the internet, rather than squirreling away information
that would go toward an exhibition many years down the road. This was just
before blogs took off on personal web pages.

Two weeks before my departure, I obtained approval to turn my research
into daily dispatches that would appear on MoMA's recently launched
official website. Because the museum had a skeletal web staff, I met with
äda'web, a nonprofit research and development group founded in 1994 by
the discerning media art curator Benjamin Weil to pair nonmedia artists
with dot-com web designers and producers to experiment with and reflect
on the web. A web journal we called *Stir-Fry* about my subsequent trip
and the thirty-five artists I met in China would develop from our informal
conversation. (Although äda'web folded in 1998, *Stir-Fry: A Video Curator's
Dispatches from China* is still online.[3])

Lugging a backpack stuffed with a laptop, a video camera, a tape recorder, and cables, I set off on my trip, accompanied by F. D. P. Henryz (b. 1937), a computer-savvy former documentary filmmaker, who was going to record my studio visits. Each night in my hotel room, Henryz and I would write up that day's report, and early the next morning from the hotel business center, we would email the text and images, which would appear on the museum's website the following day, after äda'web's designer-artist Vivian Selbo (b. 1971) assembled our latest dispatch into an engaging form. Back then using the internet in China was next to impossible, but with some hard work, we never failed to send something out. In 1997 only one of the artists I met had a computer—unlike today, when everyone does. Indeed, since 2008, China has been the country with the largest number of internet users worldwide.

As soon as I landed in Beijing, the renegade conceptual artists Wang Gongxin (b. 1960) and Lin Tianmiao (b. 1961) invited me to an informal dinner in their small courtyard home, where they had gathered a group of video-performance artists, whose studios I would visit over the coming days. Wang showed me his *The Sky of Brooklyn—Digging a Hole in Beijing* (1995), an early example of installation art in China. The artist had dug a ten-foot-deep (3 m) hole in a small room just inside the front door of his home. At the bottom he had placed a belly-up video monitor, which glowed with footage of the Brooklyn sky that he had recorded from the roof of a building where he and Lin had previously lived for several years. Reversing the American childhood fantasy of "digging a hole to China," Wang had combined this notion with the Chinese saying "Look at the world from a well," an aphorism encouraging introspection.

Over the next few days, armed with a rented clamshell mobile phone, I moved about Beijing in battered private vans that seemed as flimsy as tin cans. Taxis did not exist. One of my first visits was to the East Village courtyard houses, where the intrepid artists Ma Liuming (b. 1969), Zhang Huan (b. 1965), and Rong Rong (b. 1968) lived. They gave me a full description of some illicit midnight events they had recently carried out there, in front of an impromptu audience gathered by word of mouth; they dreaded being reprimanded by officials for the perceived inappropriateness of the transgender or masochistic actions they performed naked. By their implicit references to a discomfort with long-held traditions, their disquieting work addressed the anxieties that accompany progress.

My next stop was Shanghai, where Wang had helpfully called ahead and set up a few meetings for me. There I visited the young Swiss dealer Lorenz Helbling at his new ShanghART gallery, which occupied a small area of a mezzanine in the new Portman Shangri-La Hotel. I made use of the practical overview offered by this generous, multilingual insider as I continued on

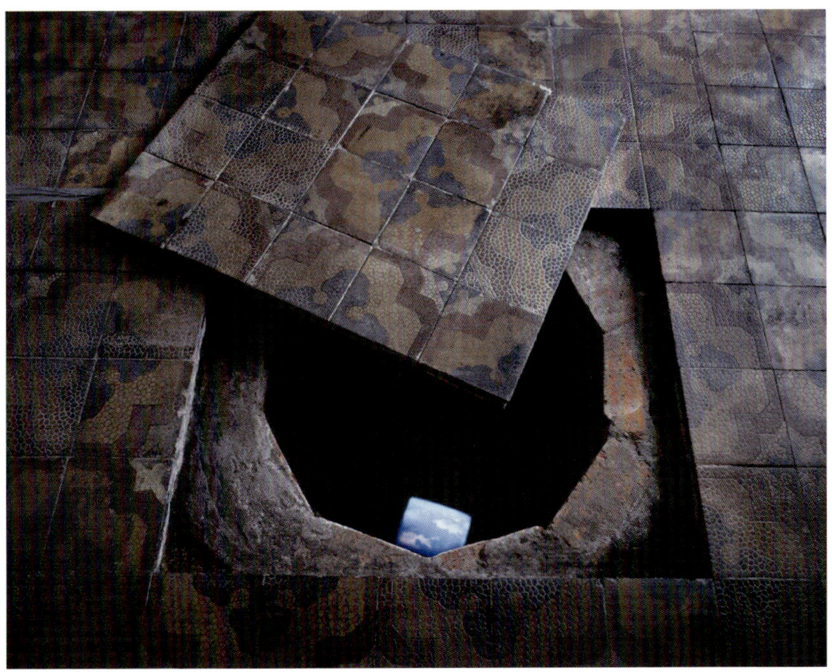

Wang Gongxin, *The Sky of Brooklyn—Digging a Hole in Beijing*, 1995
Installation, with TV set and audiotape, 11 ft. 6 in. (3.5 m)

and navigated my way through the contemporary art scene in China.
(Today an éminence grise, Helbling has multiple warehouse-size gallery
spaces in Shanghai, Beijing, and Singapore, and a roster that includes the
best artists in China.)

I also went to see the savvy artist Zhou Tiehai (b. 1966), from whom
I picked up more insights into the scene, especially in terms of local politics.
Zhou's work documents the hammering that noble ideals have faced in an
age completely changed by consumerism and skyscrapers. Zhou was born
at the onset of the Cultural Revolution and grew up believing the party
line that called upon Chinese youth to be patriotic and ration the little
they had to help the people starving in other parts of the world. It was
the opening to the West in 1978 that demolished Zhou's enthusiasm to be
of service to humanity. He discovered that Western populations were well
fed and that the capitalist countries were rich. Observing others of his
generation, he saw how money overwhelms idealism. He scornfully declared,
"Money is all that anybody cares about"—a mantra of modern China. His

work pointedly reminds viewers that material acquisition can never be as meaningful as people coming together for a cause.[4] Through Zhou, I gained helpful background for the small and dispersed group of media artists I discovered on the research trip.

During my visit to his city, Zhou hosted a Yunnan-style dinner in his home, where he discussed his work with me, Helbling, the Swiss collector Uli Sigg, the abstract painter Ding Yi (b. 1962), and the trailblazing Swiss curator and art historian Harald Szeemann. As commissioner of the international survey to be held in the Italian pavilion of the next Venice Biennale, Szeemann was also interested in meeting new Chinese artists. Zhou had just completed his sardonic series of large Joe Camel tableaux, drawings done mainly on newspaper. In *Joe Camel, Are You Lonely?* (1996), Joe with his gargantuan proboscis wears a halo of words—*Glory, Splendor, Wealth, Rank*—indicating that he has achieved high status. The implication is that, despite his fame and success and having his face on the cover of *Art in America*, Joe is lonely. From a window in Zhou's studio, we looked out over the Huangpu River, toward farms that would soon be demolished and replaced by Pudong skyscrapers. The race to succeed would have serious consequences for everyone, including artists, as I lived to see.

From Shanghai, I went on to Hangzhou, via a packed local bus, and met Zhang Peili (b. 1957). One of the first to work with video in China and still one of the most active media artists there, Zhang creates candid videotapes and installations that critique the stern political system. His single-channel video *Document on Hygiene No. 3* (1991) features a close-up of the artist's hands as he laboriously washes a live, disgruntled chicken in a basin of water nonstop for thirty-six minutes, a not-so-subtle parody of indoctrination. His three-channel video sculpture *Eating* (1997) contains three monitors stacked vertically, each with a different perspective on the same scene. The top monitor shows the image of a cheek chewing; the middle one shows a black-and-white, surveillance-like view of a fork's movement between plate and mouth, recorded by a small camera strapped to the diner's arm; and the bottom monitor shows Western food (a hardboiled egg, tomato, and layer cake) disappearing from the porcelain plate. It's as if a sentence has been parsed into subject, object, and verb, as in an English language class.

During my meeting with Zhang, I explained the distinction between a singular work (a one-off) and works that exist as an edition with a limited number of copies. I also told him how MoMA maintained and preserved its video art collection. At the time, the archival format used for videos was tape, which had segued from open-reel in 1965 to Digital Betacam in 1997, with longevity boosted through storage at stable temperature and humidity conditions. Zhang and several of his peers in China had recently

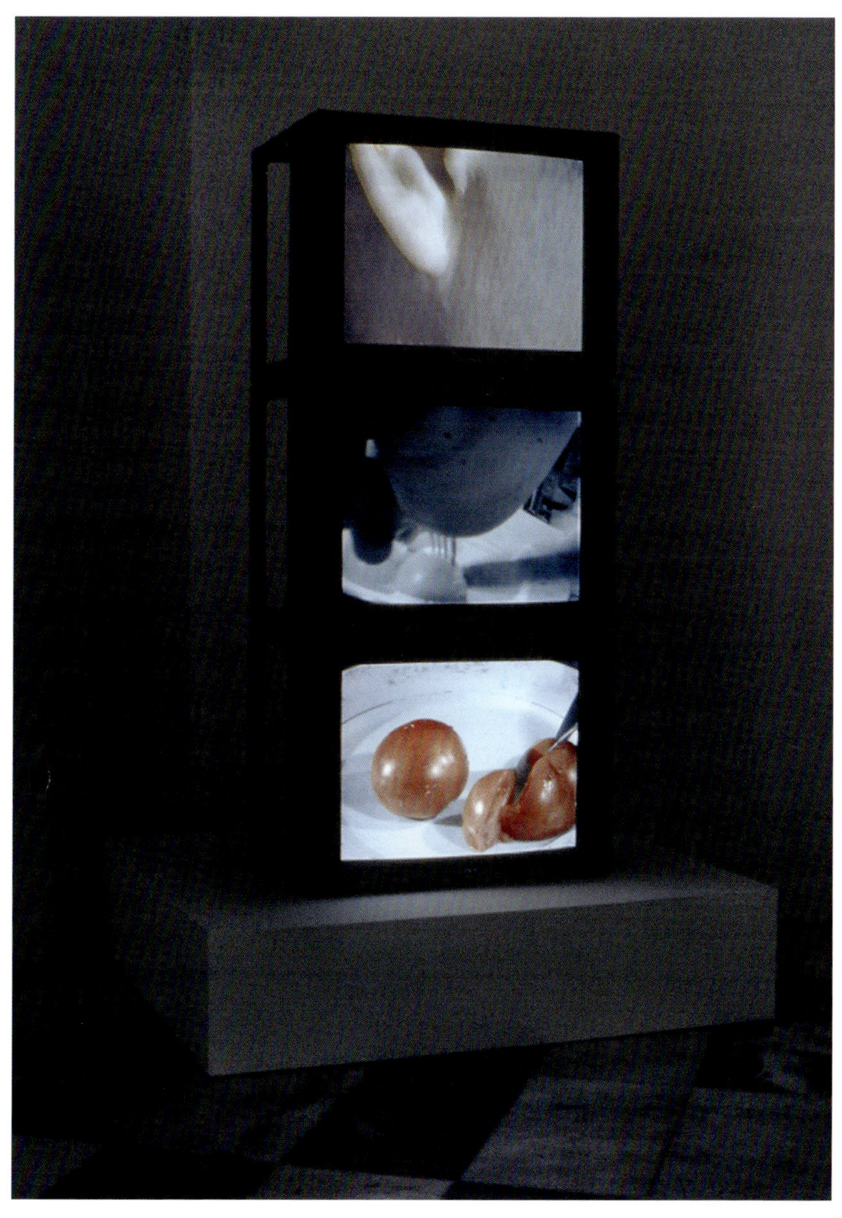

Zhang Peili, *Eating*, 1997
Three-channel video, color, sound, 27 min. 43 sec.

made trips abroad, where dealers had been eager to take on these art-world neophytes, as well as to take advantage of them. After my explanation, Zhang understood that although editioning would make finite the number of legitimate copies of an artwork, pricing for each individual video work, regrettably, was still less than that for most paintings. I promised to send him an example of an artist's contract, which spelled out the acquisition process. This was important, since I intended to raise the funds to bring two of his single-channel videos, along with *Eating*, into the MoMA collection. I did, and in 1999, we exhibited *Eating* adjacent to a large Jackson Pollock retrospective.

I was surprised by how remarkably well-informed the artists I met during my *Stir-Fry* research seemed; several had even just returned from documenta X in Kassel, Germany. Even so, digital art was a minor presence on their radar screens, since available computers were few and far between, generally limited to art school graphic design departments, where artists slaved for bigwig professors and learned the ins and outs of the commercial design industry.

On the recommendation of a German colleague, after days of searching I managed to track down the Big Tail Elephant group, a loose collective of four congenial Guangzhou-based artists who showed work together in ad hoc exhibitions, finding strength in numbers for the sake of their subversive work. The easygoing ringleader, Xu Tan (b. 1957), met me at the airport and shepherded me to a meeting with the other members, who included Chen Shaoxiong (1962–2016), Liang Juhui (1959–2006), and Lin Yilin (b. 1964). Visiting their individual studios in a run-down warehouse, I saw their artwork —photographs, ink drawings, videos, and documentation of their performances and installations. I went with the group to Libreria Borges, a bookstore that engulfed owner Chen Tong's modest apartment.[5] The bookstore was supported by the French cultural attaché, important moral support in this southern city far from the capital.

In Guangzhou I was also able to see an early version of *San Yuan Li* (2003), a documentary video essay by writer Ou Ning (b. 1969) and artist Cao Fei (b. 1978) about the local riverbank, where a back-street opium exchange had been taking place since the time of the Boxer Rebellion (1899–1901). The filmmakers' thorough research methods led to piercing observations.

On my return to Beijing, I caught up with Feng Mengbo (b. 1966), then the only artist in China who was lucky enough to have his own computer. He revealed that in the early 1990s, he had taught himself English to learn how to program, and he eventually obtained a computer of his own by working for an American company. He based his first interactive CD-ROM work, *My Private Album* (1996), on his family's photo album. He sought to break free of the constrictions of a linear narrative and move closer to reproducing the palimpsest nature of memory. He wanted to give his audience the freedom to manipulate his work, the story of a multigenerational Chinese family.[6] He created another interactive CD-ROM work, *Taking Mount Doom by Strategy* (1997), a conflation of *Taking Tiger Mountain by Strategy*, a famous Beijing opera about Mao's life,[7] and the first-person-shooter video game Doom. The New York dealer Holly Solomon would soon present Feng's work at her gallery. The following year I ran into Feng in England, where his work was featured at ISEA98 (the 9th International Symposium on Electronic Art): Revolution98, which took place in both Liverpool and Manchester. After seeing that artists such as Keith Piper (b. 1960), Nina Fischer (b. 1965), and Moroan el Sani (b. 1968) and the artist duo Granular-Synthesis (Kurt Hentschläger [b. 1960] and Ulf Langheinrich [b. 1960]) approached their multimedia installations in far more complex and nuanced ways than appeared on international art magazine pages, Feng returned home and expanded upon his methodology.

This was evident at the third Guangzhou Triennial in 2008, where I saw his *Long March: Restart* (2008). Acquired by MoMA in 2009 and shown at MoMA/PS1 in 2010, viewer-users entered the gargantuan panoramic installation and stood between two parallel, big-pixel, computer-generated projections of approximately eighty by twenty feet (24 x 6 m) each. One viewer held a Game Boy and controlled the movement of the avatar on the screen, a diminutive Red Army soldier, a stand-in for Nintendo's mascot, Mario. The viewer dashes in front of but in tandem with soldier-Mario within the action-packed panorama, as if on Mao Zedong and the Red Army of the Communist Party's Long March (October 1934–October 1935), fighting enemies—here ghosts, demons, and deities with cans of Coca-Cola instead of guns. Mengbo effectively continued his conflation of history, popular culture, and art.[8]

I gained considerable recognition because *Stir-Fry* had an interested audience that followed my daily postings at the time. Subsequently, researchers continued to turn to the site for information about media art and artists in China. Philippe Vergne, then at the Walker Art Center, and several other curators followed my lead and went on to make art blogs during their own research trips. I have stayed in touch with most of the artists who welcomed me into their studios in 1997 and whose careers in the meantime have soared. *Stir-Fry* remains an important chronicle and offers insight into a formidable time of change in China.

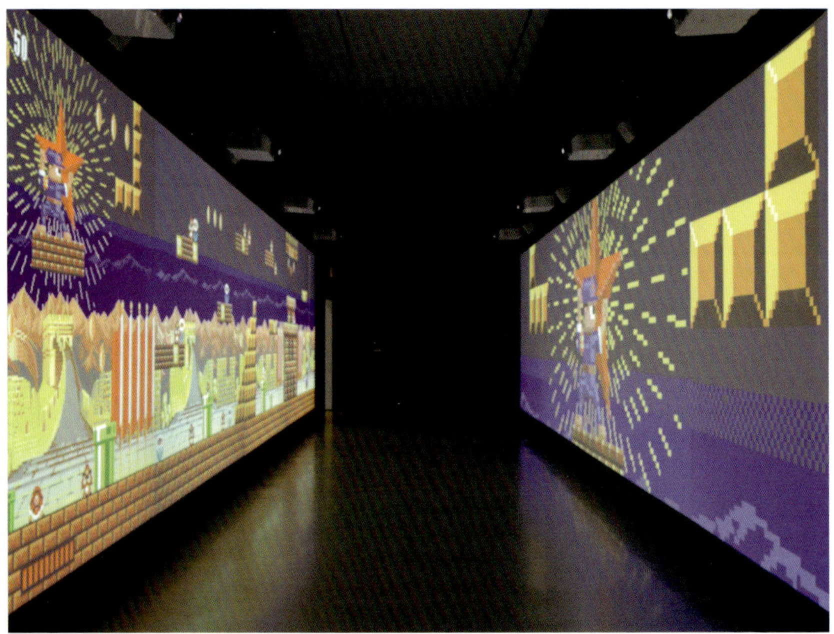

Feng Mengbo, *Long March: Restart*, 2008
Video game (color, sound), custom computer software, and wireless
game controller; dimensions and duration variable

Yang Fudong

I returned to China in 2000 for the Shanghai Biennale,[9] where I met Yang
Fudong (b. 1971), a tall, unassuming media artist whose work had been featured in group shows in China during the late 1990s. After working on the
margins, he was on the cusp of gaining attention abroad, working in the area
I call the "camera arts," a studio practice involving the mediums of video,
film, and photography. At the biennial, his collateral exhibition, *Useful Life*,
was presented in an off-site space, with his own work alongside that of his
Shanghai cohorts, the artists Xu Zhen (b. 1977) and Yang Zhenzhong (b. 1968).
The 2000 Biennale gave Chinese artists a bit of hope about a new openness
shown by the government and about the opportunity to exhibit with foreign
artists for the first time. I stopped by Yang's tiny apartment, where he
showed me recent work, including the photography complement of his video
installation *I Love My Motherland* (1999), which had recently been featured
in the exhibition *Love: Chinese Contemporary Photography & Video* at the
International Arts Festival in Tachikawa, Japan. The portrait-like project in

224

black and white features forlorn twenty-year-old youth, who embody the malaise of a generation that grew up post-Mao in a culture that saw itself in competition with the West.

Yang had honed his visual art and cinema skills on his own. In 1993, while studying social realist oil painting at the Zhejiang Academy of Fine Arts (later renamed the China Academy of Art), he had come across a translation of Jack Kerouac's *On the Road*. Inspired by the novel to forge his own way, Yang took a vow of silence as his senior art project, for which he was nearly expelled. Throughout his *Three Months of Silence* (1993), Yang communicated by writing on his hands or on other parts of his body. The performance boosted his sense of autonomy.

In 1996, when Yang enrolled in the Beijing Film Academy, China's tightly controlled propaganda machine regarded nonsanctioned film as illegal and a threat to the country's leadership. As an underground artist working outside of the official system, Yang was not permitted film stock for his own work. His recourse was to sit at the doors of successful so-called fifth-generation filmmakers, a group of filmmakers whose work had official approval and sometimes made it into foreign film festivals. They were among the first in China able to see the innovations of foreign directors Michelangelo Antonioni (1912–2007) and Akira Kurosawa. (Others would later see the films on bootleg DVDs, which Yang referred to as his education.) Begging for expired reels and extraneous bits of unused film, Yang completed his underground feature *An Estranged Paradise* (1997–2002) five years after the shooting, due to lack of funds. The film reflects the anxiety he and his classmates had felt as they confronted the challenges of life as they were being unmoored from the principles of Communist orthodoxy, as well as their own uncertainties as they dreamed about the possibilities that would come with what they felt was impending freedom.[10]

I brought *An Estranged Paradise* into MoMA's collection as a film transferred to video. I had hoped MoMA would be able to preserve the original film version of Yang's classic and restore the uneven, rich black tones. Unfortunately, the many kinds of outdated film stock he had used made preservation too expensive an undertaking for our rationed budget.

Over the following years, Yang slowly gained international recognition. Prada and other corporate brands commissioned him to make sumptuous commercials. Museums began awarding him budgets that enabled him to produce large-scale multichannel works, including *East of Que Village* (2007), to me his greatest installation. During a trip in 2007, when I sat with Yang in Shanghai for the premiere at the ShanghART Gallery, he told me how he had filmed the imagery of the immersive, six-channel installation, working in the rural area north of Beijing, where he had spent

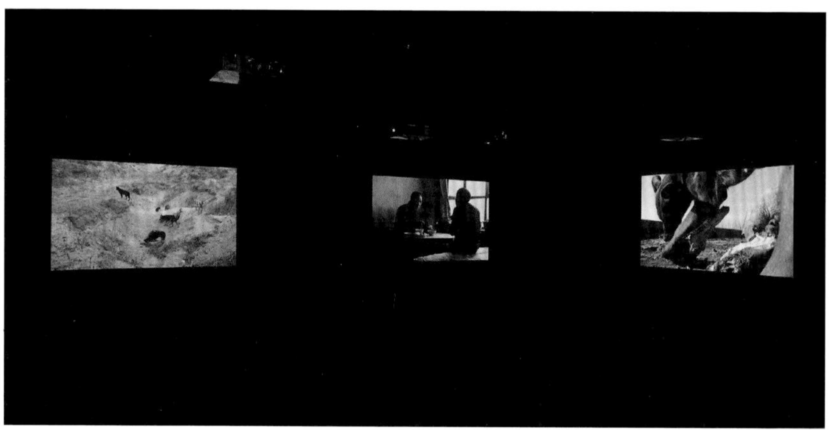

Yang Fudong, *East of Que Village*, 2007
Six-channel video installation, filmed with HDV, black and white,
sound, 20 min. 50 sec.

his childhood. The once-thriving industrial area had become a depressed,
barren landscape populated by senior citizens living in shabby homes and
by mangy feral dogs foraging for food, fighting over animal carcasses, and
occasionally standing on their haunches to peer through open windows
and stare hungrily at what was on the elders' meager dinner plates. The
work opens with haunting, dissonant music that accompanies the funeral
procession of a town elder. As I listened, the mournful indigenous sounds
got under my skin; they set the tone of authenticity. Out of a grim scenario
that symbolized the cycle of death and rebirth, Yang made a beguilingly
profound composition. He skillfully managed to express the foreboding
sense of fatalism that moviegoers experience when immersed in film noir.

Yang had painstakingly studied film history—Eastern and Western—
by watching classics on bootleg DVDs that cost the equivalent of one dollar
each, which he shared with artist friends. He once noted:

> I am very interested in the methods of documentaries, and also
> mockumentaries. This kind of documentation is like a sharp blade
> presented in front of the audience. . . . *East of Que Village* is a
> fictitious documentary, because within this reality, those stray
> dogs are in fact actors in this film, either acquired or captured; is
> this then a real documentary? Here are many interfaces between
> narration and documentation. . . . Theory and reality shouldn't be
> out of touch with each other.[11]

I regularly returned to China, eager to better understand the context for Yang's art practice and that of other artists I had met earlier. On subsequent trips I became impressed by Yang's pragmatism in adapting the subject matter of his installations to photography. He understood that the market for photography was well established, unlike the market for video. His counterparts in the West had been taking similarly shrewd pathways toward developing their media art practices. The adaptability of tools allows him and other artists to move fluidly and successfully between formats, and between the fine art and commercial sides of their careers.

Shirin Neshat

Shirin Neshat (b. 1957) navigates the taut line between Western and Middle Eastern cultures. She does this as an eloquent artist with gracious diplomacy. She came to my attention in 1995 as she segued from painting into a studio practice in the camera arts.

Neshat grew up in a progressive household in Qazvin in northwest Iran. In 1975 she set off for California for her final year of high school, then the University of California, Berkeley, where she studied painting and received both a BA and an MFA. She stayed in California when the 1979 revolution and the Iran-Iraq War prevented her from returning home. Supported by a strong network of friends, Neshat moved to New York in 1983. From 1988 to 1998, she codirected the Storefront for Art and Architecture, a downtown nonprofit gallery and forum devoted to exploring issues involving the built environment. She put her art making on hold during this period, which is when her art education really took place. Storefront was flourishing as a hub of new ideas.

In 1990 Neshat returned to Iran for the first time, a decade after Ayatollah Khomeini came to power and a year after his death, and she discovered a changed country. Later she would comment on how she was really taken by everything she saw and wanted to belong to the Iranian community again. Back in New York, in 1993, Neshat returned to art making. She worked in photography before moving on to film and image-sound installation, and in her words, her new work dealt with issues that belonged to the present and revealed a new sense of intimacy and familiarity with the way in which Iranian society functioned.[12]

Neshat's focus then was on women in relation to Iranian society and the revolution, so she produced a series of photographic works that explored the topic.[13] Through her *Women of Allah* (1993–97) series of thirty-eight photos—shown initially in 1993 at Franklin Furnace in New York—she portrayed women as strong sources of resistance and strength, inspired by female

writers in post-revolution Iran.[14] I remember being struck by the work when
it was featured in 1995 at the gallery of Annina Nosei, who also exhibited
the early work of Jean-Michel Basquiat, Barbara Kruger, Robert Longo,
and Ghada Amer (b. 1963).[15]

Neshat would explain in interviews that her visions were subjective,
fictional, and poetic. Gradually, identity politics became a central and
charged topic of exploration in her work. Even after decades spent living
abroad, Neshat at times still felt like a cultural outsider in America. In the late
1990s, some Western critics considered her early photo-calligraphic works
to be disingenuous. They criticized what they saw as an Orientalist approach
in their erroneous perception that it was religious texts she was writing on
images of herself in traditional garb, some of those images including gun
barrels nestled between body parts and aimed at the viewer. In fact, she
used poetry by the protofeminist writer Forough Farrokhzad (1934–1967),
who was not at all religious and died more than a decade before the
revolution. Neshat also quoted from the work of the female fundamentalist
poet Tahereh Saffarzadeh (1936–2008), who concentrated on the collective
public interest and eulogized martyrdom. In this way, Neshat's work could be
said to point to contradictory impulses within Iranian society itself.[16]

Belonging to a small expatriate community of Iranian-born filmmakers,
visual artists, and musicians living in New York, Neshat was inspired by the
second wave of Iranian cinema, which evolved as various directors adapted
to the revolution's purge of Western influences. Abbas Kiarostami (1940–
2016), a pioneer of second-wave filmmaking in Iran, was a friend and a huge
idol for her. Indeed, it may have been Kiarostami's mixture of simplicity
and complexity that imbued Neshat's approach with the almost melancholic
romanticism it often displays. Neshat once noted that while his work seemed
to capture social realism in Iran, in reality, it was deeper—universal and
timeless; his character and art went beyond his nationality.[17] It's interesting
to note that when Kiarostami finished making his film *The Wind Will Carry
Us* in 1999, he stated that he wanted to make films like Neshat's.[18]

On a cold November afternoon in 1998, I saw Neshat's installation
Turbulent (1998) when it premiered in the branch of the Whitney then on
the ground floor of the Philip Morris headquarters, across the street from
Grand Central Terminal. Neshat had made the piece with an almost entirely
Iranian crew,[19] shooting in a high school auditorium on the Lower East Side
of Manhattan, not far from Storefront. In a dark, simply designed installation
space at the Whitney, I sat down on a bench beside several midtown office
workers, positioned between the large projections of two black-and-white
videos, playing simultaneously on opposite walls. We twisted around, looking
one way and then the other.

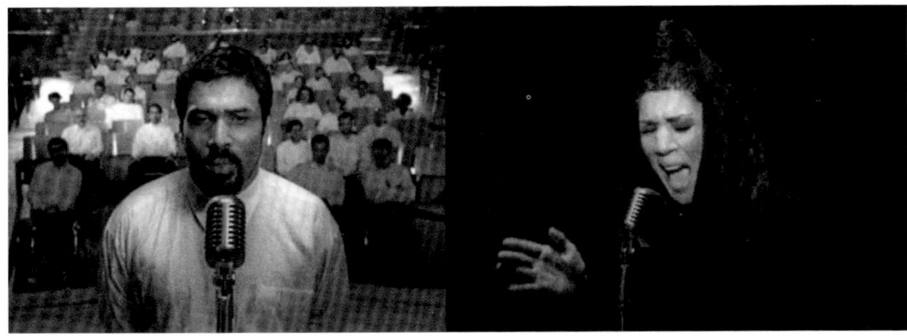

Shirin Neshat, *Turbulent*, 1998
Two-channel video and audio installation, shot in 16 mm black-and-white film, 9 min. 31 sec.

The film is a sandwich of formidable opposites. In the projection on one side of the installation stands a confident, handsome man who sings a love song written by the thirteenth-century Sufi poet Rumi, a celebrated transnationalist who wrote in multiple languages. The man faces the camera (the viewer), with his back to a group of solemn men seated in a theater. The man sings and, once finished, turns and bows to the men seated in the audience, then turns again and silently faces the camera. At that moment, the woman on the other screen starts to sing, with her back to the camera. She is shown standing alone in the same theater, now empty. By being in a theater (even if empty), she violates Islamic conventions. She sings an improvised, emotive scatlike song that soars like a lark reaching new heights. Gradually, the camera starts to revolve around her. I listened to the soundscape of alternating mellifluous voices—his tightly controlled, hers clearly ecstatic.

Later, by doing a bit of research, I learned that in 1979, at the start of the revolution, Khomeini had criticized music for being like a drug: whoever acquires the habit can no longer devote himself to important activities.[20] Women were banished from the music scene until after Khomeini's death in 1989, when the composer Hossein Alizadeh (b. 1950) formed an ensemble, Hamavayan, with musicians who performed with classical instruments and with a chorus of both male and female vocalists, thus reintroducing women's voices in public.[21]

Neshat often explains that *Turbulent* took off in various directions and brought about other important questions about the male and female contrast in relation to the social structure. The ultimate question was how each would go about reaching a level of mystical expression inherent in the Sufi music.[22] The title *Turbulent* implies that the work is a reflection of the woman's state of mind; she is clearly not at peace. She is a strong, magnificently unfettered woman, who wears a crownlike mantilla, which, unlike a chador—the garment that covers the head and upper body, leaving only the face exposed, worn especially by Muslim women—is Spanish and therefore not traditionally part of the Islamic world. That is the strength and challenge of Neshat's deeply felt installation, with its dualities and paradoxes tightly woven together: male-female, East-West, conformist-rebel, oppressive-mystical.[23] Neshat's compelling installation probes the meaning of roots and rootlessness as intercontinental life is experienced today.

Turbulent became the first chapter of a trilogy, each work based on the idea of opposites, visually and conceptually, in which women appear as the unpredictable force. The second part is *Rapture* (1999), in which men maneuver inside a citadel and women in the desert, moving toward the sea, where some board a small boat and head out onto open water. In *Fervor* (2000), Neshat focuses on the clash between sexual and carnal desire and social control—what is effectively at the heart of each part of the trilogy and what is at odds throughout most of her work.

Nalini Malani

In 2002, the pioneer of video art in India, Nalini Malani (b. 1946), arrived in New York from Mumbai, to set up her *Hamletmachine* (2000) at the New Museum. In creating the work, she had adapted fragments of a play written by Heiner Müller (1929–1995) in 1977, when Germany was divided into east and west. She had turned to Müller as she looked beyond the India/Pakistan conflict, in search of a more universal viewpoint. I stopped by a few days before the exhibition's opening and watched her assemble a pure white bed of salt, which glowed on the floor below her video projections that portrayed the bloody violence that grows out of myths of victimization and redemption and causes disenfranchised groups to turn against one another, with horrific results.[24] I learned that Malani's focus has been the plight of women in times of conflict. For her, violence is a persistent subject—both its unfortunate presence and its universality.

Malani was born in Karachi, Pakistan, at the time of the country's battle for independence. Her family fled to India, where she grew up. Her practice evolved within a committed cross-national community of Mumbai artists. She trained as a painter at the Sir J. J. School of Art, receiving her diploma in 1969. While at school, she obtained a studio at the Bhulabhai Memorial Institute, which thrived on discourse as well as on interdisciplinary art making. She had become an accomplished printmaker and was determined to maintain a hands-on practice. At the Vision Exchange Workshop[25] starting in 1969,[26] she had access to a darkroom that she shared with the artist Nasreen Mohamedi (1937–1990), and together they experimented with process. In 1969 she made a series of experimental 16 mm films in tandem with artist friends, including Vivan Sundaram. With a grant from the French government to study printmaking, she spent the years 1970 to 1972 in Paris at Atelier Friedlaender and at the Sorbonne. She has said that she was "keen to be out there and expose [her]self to all these other winds that were running through Paris at the time."[27]

Upon returning to India in 1972, she chose to work in the impoverished Bandra slum in Mumbai, next door to a mosque. Whenever she could, she shot film, which at the time simply went into storage. It wasn't until the 1980s that independent media in India was bolstered by the arrival of consumer video and by the cable television revolution, twenty years later than in the West. Due to her country's complex, turbulent history characterized by violent actions resulting from antagonistic religious factions, Malani and her peers were instilled with a sense of political urgency. They made strong activist films and videos, inspired by the earlier documentary work of local photographers and filmmakers, who had become active following India's independence in 1947.

Malani has a strong interest in literature, and she sees herself as part of a tradition of narrative sustained as a living form in Indian art. It was the actor Alaknanda Samarth who introduced Malani to the work of Müller, considered one of the great dramatists of death, who sees history as an "unending slaughter, the work as a scene of devastation."[28] Malani spent a month developing paintings that were an interpretive rendering of Müller's play *Despoiled Shore Medea Material Landscape with Argonauts* (1981). (They were intended to be shown as an installation in 1992, but the project was delayed a year when bloody riots broke out after Hindu fundamentalists bombed and demolished the Babri Mosque in Ayodhya.) The resulting piece—a fifty-six-minute single-channel recording of her and Samarth's interpretation and reenactment of Müller's play, which Malani titled *Medeamaterial* (1993)—marked a turning point in her career, as she now concentrated on video as an alternative to her painting practice.

In 2003 I traveled to Turkey for the 8th Istanbul Biennial, where I saw the first iteration of Malani's *Gamepieces* (2003/2009). The installation occupied a magical location—the underground, Roman-era Basilica Cistern, which still collects rainwater a thousand years after it was built. The grand, colonnaded cistern sits next to the Hagia Sophia mosque, built as a cathedral in 537 AD. For Malani, the cistern was an ideal setting, a convergence of different histories and religions.

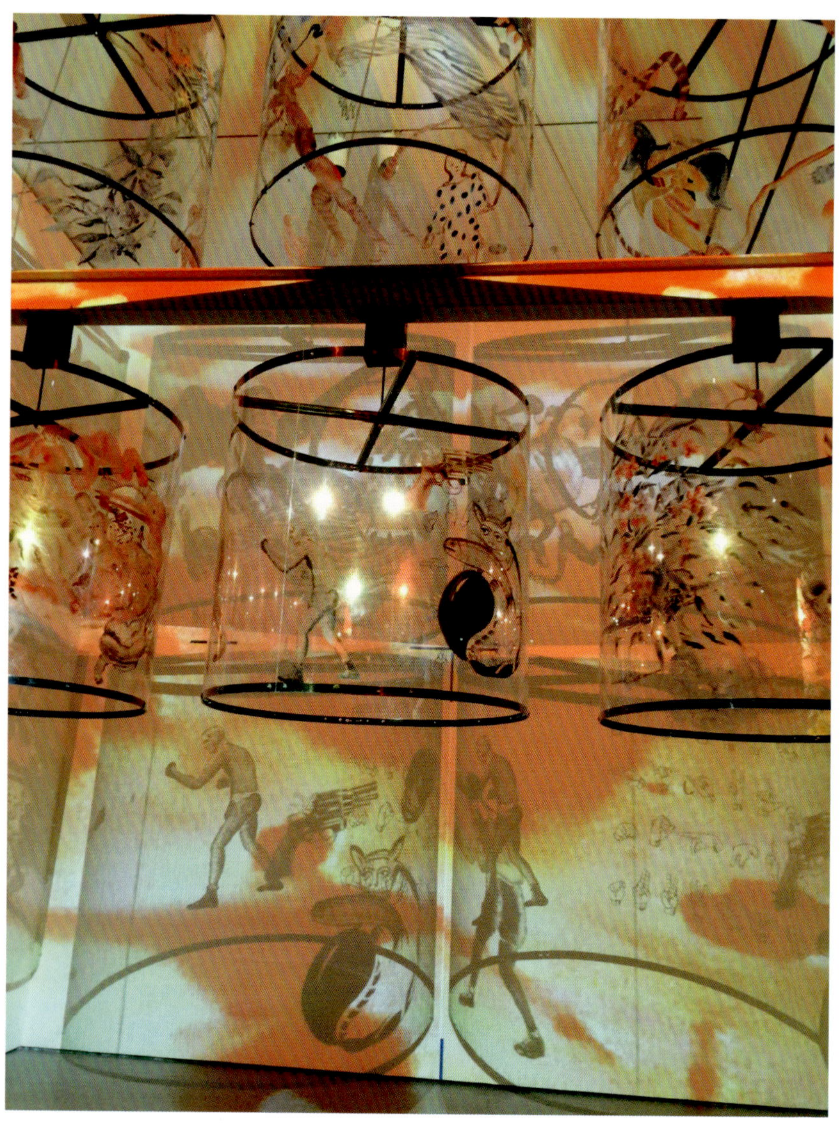

Nalini Malani, *Gamepieces*, 2003/2009
Four-channel video/shadow play (color, sound, 12 min.), with six
reverse-painted rotating Lexan cylinders; dimensions variable.
Installation view: *Scenes from a New Heritage: Contemporary Art
from the Collection*, Museum of Modern Art, New York, 2015–16

The installation made me feel as if it were a sort of détente between fractious religions, as *Gamepieces* was all about the healing powers of myth. The installation consisted of rotating Mylar drums, each just under four feet (1.2 m) high. On the interior surfaces of the six seamless, translucent cylinders, Malani had painted chaotic battle scenes with Byzantine angels, boxers ready to fight, monsters, warplanes, guns, and human skulls—familiar symbolic images from different cultures and periods—which functioned as metaphors for an embattled world. Malani's painting style reminded me of another female artist, Nancy Spero (1926–2009), who looks at aggression and victimization with an unflinching eye. Both artists paint floating, deceptively delicate figures.

Malani projected videos of nuclear bomb explosions and other disasters through the painted Mylar drums, which produced enigmatic effects. The light the four videos emitted illuminated her quirkily painted figures and sent their shadows dancing over the cistern walls. As the drums rotated, images of the mushroom clouds of nuclear bomb explosions in vivid reds and yellows splashed across the walls, momentarily obliterating the shadows of the painted creatures. Weaving together traditional and contemporary materials and storytelling methods, Malani produced a dynamically layered environment where the past collided with the present in an ever-unfolding cycle.

When I returned to New York, I met with MoMA's conservators and discussed what needed to be considered if MoMA were to acquire *Gamepieces*. Should the acquisition go through, I would have to encourage Malani to use a Mylar that better withstands aging for her drums. As we moved ahead, she provided MoMA with paint samples so if any element flaked off in the future, new paint could be matched to the original and repairs carefully made. We determined that it would be best to store the painted Mylar flat rather than as standing sculptures. Appropriate storage crates were built for this unique artwork.

In 2015, nearly a decade after the acquisition, *Gamepieces* was in excellent condition when it was finally shown. At the artist's suggestion, the work was installed in a novel way. Instead of hanging the six cylinders in a row, which would require considerable space, they were piggybacked in MoMA's contemporary gallery with its generous, nearly twenty-one-foot-high (6.4 m) ceiling. The museum had upheld Malani's aesthetic vision, which should be the mission of every owner of media art.

By this time, throughout the art world, the one-of-a-kind or limited-edition installation was finding its way into museum collections. MoMA, SFMOMA, and the Tate had each added in-house preservation specialists to their staffs. As installation artists were being taken on by committed gallerists, prices began to go up.

During a visit in 2014 to London's Frieze art fair, I stopped by Hauser & Wirth's gallery on Savile Row and saw a new work by the French artist Pierre Huyghe. I formed an immediate connection to the video *(Untitled) Human Mask* (2014), in part because I once made a pilgrimage to Tōhoku, a remote area in northern Japan where Huyghe had filmed the work.

Ostensibly straightforward, *(Untitled) Human Mask* consists of a large video projection in a dark environment with finely calibrated ambient sound. The work opens with a tracking shot, which moves slowly down a gloomy, deserted street, taking viewers into an abandoned town scarred by the tsunami and nuclear disaster that devastated the areas around Fukushima, in 2011. Suddenly the scene cuts to the interior of an abandoned restaurant, occupied by what appears to be the only survivor—a young girl wearing a sailor dress and a long, black wig. Her face is obscured by a white Noh-like mask that is frozen in a beatific smile. I sat transfixed, watching as the diminutive figure moved automaton-like through the restaurant's forsaken rooms. Alone, except for a cat, the girl carries out what appears to be the regular duties of a food server, as she gracefully goes in and out of the kitchen, where a few vermin are seen crawling around.

When the camera zoomed in on the girl, as she stroked and picked at her arm, I realized the fingers were not human; moreover, the arms were covered in fur. The figure was none other than a monkey. Huyghe had been inspired when he heard about a pair of trained, costumed macaque monkeys that serve and entertain patrons at a traditional sake house outside of Tokyo. Learning about the monkeys, the artist managed to get hold of one to perform as the peculiar actor in his work.

Huyghe's installation made me ponder and question the motions and emotions we go through every day, as nature cycles through the four seasons. The work evoked nature's mournful beauty and elicited foreboding and a sense that at any moment disaster may be about to settle in. I thought about the work of Naoya Hatakeyama (b. 1958), an artist who grew up in Tōhoku near Fukushima and through photography captured exquisite beauty in the devastated landscape of his hometown after the disastrous 2011 earthquake. Of roughly the same age, Huyghe and Hatakeyama are global figures who are simultaneously rooted in their local environments and aware of the universalities in the world at large. They harness technology and devise work that transcends cross-cultural theory and addresses how ordinary people, in the face of adversity, have the strength to move on.

In October 2018 I was again in London, eager to see Huyghe's much discussed installation *UUmwelt* (2018) at the Serpentine Galleries in

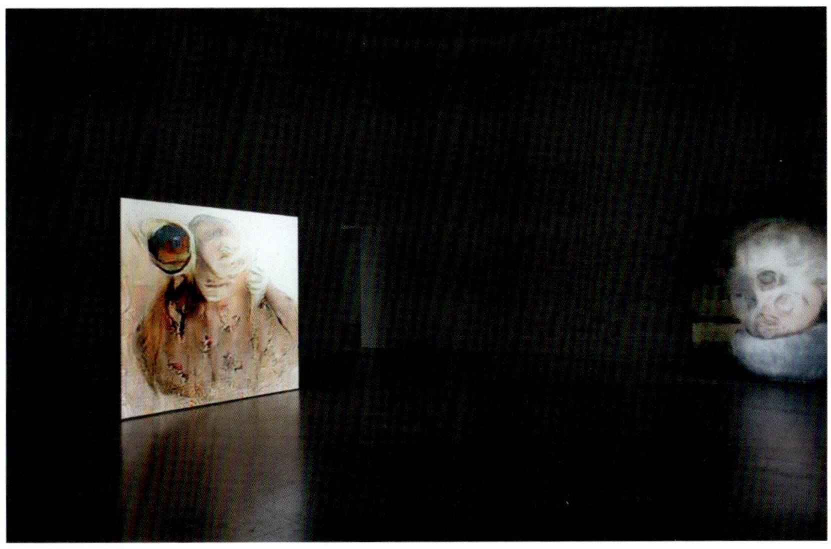

Pierre Huyghe, *UUmwelt*, 2018–ongoing
Installation view: Serpentine Gallery, London, 2018–19

Kensington Gardens. I thought it fitting that a major new work that connected art with the latest in neuroscience research would premiere at a venue
that has championed cutting-edge art since 1970, when it took over a
charming tea pavilion built in the 1930s.

Upon reaching the Serpentine, I went straight into *UUmwelt*. This
impressive and mystifying installation was culled from the ever-changing
elusive present and anticipates how in the future we should be able to
download and visualize our own thoughts. Making my way slowly through
the dimly lit, contiguous galleries that wound around the compact building,
I felt flies whiz by my face and noticed dead ones scattered about the floor.
They lay on a blanket of plaster dust, the result of Huyghe's having sanded
down sections of the gallery walls to create map- and crater-like forms out
of old layers of paint.

Going from room to room, I heard a gently clicking ambient score (which
I later learned was recordings of brain waves). I paused before each of the
five imposing eight-by-eight-foot (2.4 x 2.4 m) LED screens and watched as
strange images trembled and shifted dozens of times per second, a rate
affected by the movement of visitors and the buzzing flies. The bulbous
entities portrayed on-screen were all positioned at the center of what
resembled an overcast landscape. Despite the hefty presence and physical

robustness of the forms, their trembling brought to my mind the notion of ectoplasm, the mysterious matter that psychics in the nineteenth century described as ineffable spiritual energy, the internal substance "exteriorized" by mediums. Huyghe's images simultaneously conveyed weightiness and weightlessness.

Circling back to the entrance, I read the wall text and program notes, and chatted with the young attendant. I learned that the images had been generated from actual workings of the brain, but, as the attendant explained, no one on staff knew what the cryptic digital images represented. It turned out that Huyghe had managed to access processes of the human mind in the informatics lab of the eminent scientist Yukiyasu Kamitani at Kyoto University. There Huyghe was able to work with a group of invitees who agreed to participate and became source material in his project. Participants entered the lab's MRI scanner, where they either looked at representational photographs or focused on images in their own mind. Applying Kamitani's software to the output from the MRI, Huyghe tweaked the visualizations of invitees' neural activity and arranged the imposing images together at the Serpentine.

Upon reentering Huyghe's dark environment, I recalled the feeling I had as a child when I stood awestruck before taxidermized, antediluvian animals arranged in convincingly realistic dioramas at New York's American Museum of Natural History. But instead of presenting picturesque views of primordial areas of the world, Huyghe was inviting viewers to consider something closer to home—the perplexing visualization processes of their own minds, those half-remembered, vivid dreams people struggle to recall upon emerging from a deep sleep.

Huyghe's title is a variant of the German word *umwelt*, which describes the outer world as perceived by particular organisms within it. The artist's choice of word for his title made sense, as we appear to be entering the decade of the brain, when we will encounter the work of other artists who see the brain as a site-specific surveilled, performative space.[29] My recent studio visits with artists Ellen Pearlman (b. 1952) and Maurice Benayoun (b. 1957) point in this direction.

Lisa Reihana

Lisa Reihana (b. 1964) came to my attention in 2006, when I read that the Museum of Archaeology and Anthropology in Cambridge, England, had invited her to create an installation. (I found it unfortunate that an artist with Maori roots was invited to exhibit in England in a science museum before an art institution.) Poking around the museum's archives, Reihana discovered a statue of an unidentified, but seemingly once revered, Maori elder. Originally given as a gift to the British explorer-navigator James Cook in the eighteenth century, the carved-wood figure had made its way from New Zealand to England as booty. Aware that the forsaken elder belonged to her ancestral Maori community, Reihana developed *He Tautoko* (2006), an installation that symbolically reunited him with his people. She positioned the figure in an old-fashioned vitrine, standing before a video screen that displayed a waterfall from his native land. Wearing headphones, he listened to current elders narrate the Maori history that had unfolded since his departure.

A few years later, I happened to be in Auckland, New Zealand, and visited Reihana's studio, where I saw examples of her *Digital Marae*, a project she began in 1995, in which she took photographs of Maori people and put them in imaginary ancestral landscapes. She turned these into powerful, large-scale totemic projections.

When Reihana represented New Zealand at the 2017 Venice Biennale, she created a colossal work. I sat for an hour and watched images scroll by in her panoramic installation *in Pursuit of Venus [infected]* (2015–17). The seamless thirteen-by-eighty-two-foot (4 x 25 m) ultra-high-def single-channel video was based on a well-known wallpaper created by Joseph Dufour between 1804 and 1805. The Parisian printer devised his twenty-panel *Les Sauvages de la Mer Pacifique* from drawings that Cook and several French explorers had made during their scientifically motivated expeditions. The wallpaper, which originally would have embellished the dining room walls of a wealthy few, portrayed a colonizer's view of the exotic landscapes and peoples around the Pacific. In Venice, however, Reihana's rendering of Cook's journey reached a massive audience of about six hundred thousand. What made the work particularly noteworthy was that Reihana had adapted the scenes to honor rather than show a lack of respect toward the cultures of Pacific Islanders.

During a seven-year period of research and production, Reihana had worked with a crew of about one hundred people to create the work. She harnessed film and animation technologies, and used high-resolution video (15K) and 7.1 surround sound, assembling images with a total of 3,168 trillion pixels.[30] In describing her objectives for the work, Reihana explained that she was concerned with the ethics of representation:

> I'm interested in what you think is important when you're working with other people's imagery. From my perspective, what I do is make images. I don't take them. Working in a studio makes this incredibly clear, it's not stolen moments I am after. This is my strategy for finding an ethical way of working through that.[31]

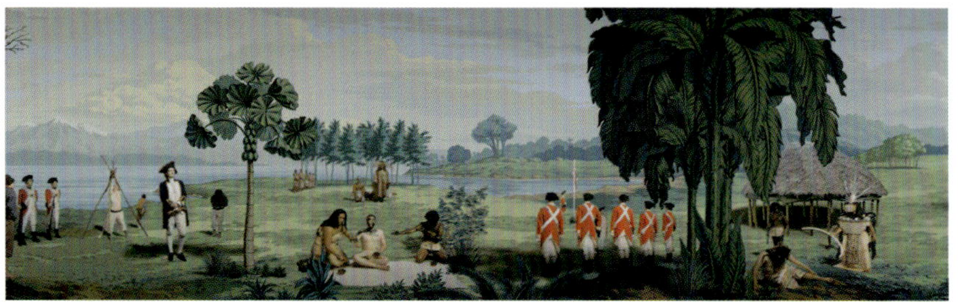

Lisa Reihana, *in Pursuit of Venus [infected]*, 2015–17 (detail)
Ultra HD video, color, sound, 64 min.

She brought life to her luxuriant landscape of emulated verdant greenswards and trees by incorporating live action performed by people from the different Pacific regions. Each figure was outfitted according to the period and a specific locale. Actors wearing the bright red uniforms of British soldiers brandished their rifles, strung up and thrashed a Maori man, or drew a Maori man in a journal entry. A group of women wearing grass skirts and dancing in a circle were Balinese. An Easter Island sculpture dominated one setting and a totem from the Pacific North Coast another.

A rich soundscape by the composer James Pinker (b. 1960) with Sean Cooper (b. 1967) wove together the live sounds of the performed actions with the winding of the actual clock that had accompanied Cook on his voyages and recordings of the indigenous instruments he had collected. Reihana created a looping visual and sonic world where time is cyclical according to *tā-vā*, the concept of time and space in Pacific Island cultures. In ancient times, the concept of *tā-vā* had spread as far as Japan, which has a word with a similar meaning, both having to do with a "gap" or "pause," the empty yet dynamic "space" between two structural parts. The concept of *tā-vā* sits at the heart of Reihana's installation with its uninterrupted pan of the landscape with a flow of intersecting entities of time and space.

One of my New York–based colleagues believed Reihana's installation was too close to Dufour's original wallpaper, whereas I saw something more nuanced in her reinterpretation. Reihana addressed how we describe people and culture from the past. She seemed to ask, who gets to tell their own stories and determine what becomes their history, and who rewrites it according to other agendas? Contemporary technologies had given Reihana the means to examine how the world operates and tell an elegant narrative.

When I first encountered *Of Dice and Men* (2011–16), a panoramic installation by Turkish-British artist Didem Pekün (b. 1978) that manages to be both lyrical and politicized, I thought back to the great American video maker, poet, and gay rights activist Marlon T. Riggs (1957–1994). His deeply personal and emotional work tested the conventions of the media essay, a form that attempts to unravel the complexities of current political events. In his thoughtful single-channel video made at the height of the AIDS crisis, *Tongues Untied* (1989), Riggs mixed expressive, poetic, and rhetorical elements and stressed positive thinking as opposed to narrow-minded prejudice. Pekün, like Riggs, has blurred the line between narrative essay and fact-based documentary. In her case, she crafted something both time-based and sculptural.

Produced and premiered at SALT in 2016, an important contemporary art space in Istanbul, Turkey, *Of Dice and Men* was presented in 2018 in a special exhibition that I co-organized at the Stavros Niarchos Foundation Cultural Center in Athens with Robert Storr, Francesca Pietropaolo, and Kalliopi Minioudaki. The piece is configured as a pair of towering LED screens that are positioned side by side like a gigantic open book. The fluidly edited web of visuals and sounds enveloped me as a viewer. The artist used video as a means of digging into the emotional quarry of memory, specifically with regard to events in her two home cities, London and Istanbul, which dominated international news at the time.

Thirty-five short diary entries, mini episodes in black and white with lengths ranging from one to four minutes, flow across the tall screens. Pekün opens the installation with footage she recorded as she joined the violent Occupy demonstration in London on November 30, 2011. *Of Dice and Men* then continues in Turkey, where the artist held up her camera and recorded her movement as part of an enraged crowd that was provoked by the murder of Hrant Dink, the Armenian human rights journalist. (She explained to me that the incident was followed by state cover-ups, which galvanized the activist minds of her generation.) She interlaced the footage of these events with images of more extreme experiences, such as the moment she saw young boys diving dangerously from a very high bridge into the water of the Bosporus, her first encounter with such a dramatic feat. Connecting so-called everyday events with political ones, she created an elegiac video installation that is drawn from four years of her life, from 2011 to 2014.

Each of Pekün's entries received its own formal treatment based on its content and became a poetic entity with its own tone, form, and length. Weaving across the screens, each section has a sense of authenticity in

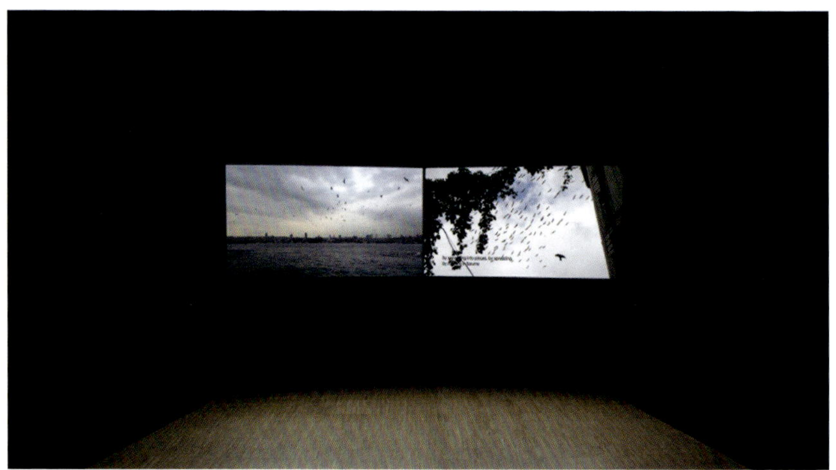

Didem Pekün, *Of Dice and Men*, 2011–16
Two-channel HD video installation, color and black and white,
sound, 43 min. 06 sec.

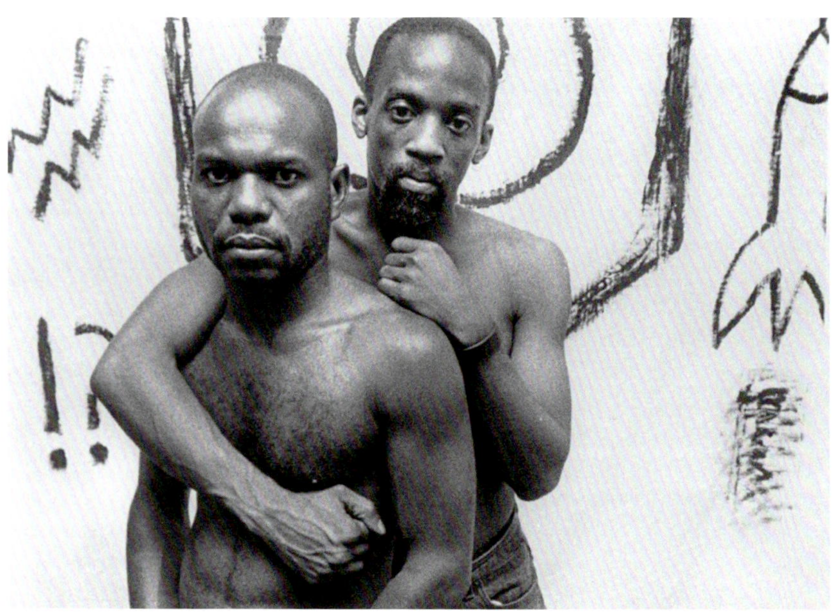

Marlon T. Riggs, *Tongues Untied*, 1989
Video, color, sound, 55 min.

its portrayal of events, unlike the blur of mediated network news that constantly spews out. Pekün's essayistic installation conveys the inexorable sadness that she describes as coming from the deflation her generation has felt, after seeing the world increasingly torn asunder and feeling unsure about the possibilities for betterment.[32]

Dice are a leitmotif of Pekün's installation, appearing as a recurrent image accompanied by the clattering sound of a woman throwing a pair. Symbolizing the random patterns of daily life, the roll of the dice also affirms how history has perpetual repetition, but with inconsistent variations.[33]

I sensed an aesthetic connection between Pekün's installation and the work of John Akomfrah (b. 1957), a respected British intellectual and media artist of Ghanaian descent, who investigates memory, postcolonialism, and temporality through work that explores the experiences of migrant diasporas. Pekün confirmed to me that Akomfrah was an unwitting mentor. His filmmaking had a profound impact on her, in particular his film *Handsworth Songs* (1986) and, later, his films *The Nine Muses* (2010) and *The Stuart Hall Project* (2013). She was emboldened by his political commitment, and the range of styles and formal strategies that he uses.

Like other global artists of our time, Pekün has managed to stitch together a peripatetic life for nearly two decades. She is from Istanbul, where she attended a French high school, and from an early age she was an avid music enthusiast and record collector. Starting in her teens, she worked as a DJ in Istanbul's underground music/dance club scene. Her early music experience had an impact on her fluid editing style, which is much like the mixing and matching she did in the DJ booth.

At twenty-five, she moved to London, and out of her love of jazz and soul music she pursued a BA in ethnomusicology at the School of Oriental and African Studies, where she explored the Yoruba language and culture of Nigeria. From 2006 to 2016, she studied at Goldsmiths, a research university in London specializing in the arts, design, the humanities, and the social sciences. She completed an MA and then a practice-based PhD in documentary film and visual culture, developing her research-based media art practice, which is rooted in topical geopolitical questions of identity, displacement, and statelessness. She studied with Tony Dowmunt (b. 1951), a first-person, autobiographical filmmaker and old-style community video activist.[34]

Pekün now lives between Berlin and Istanbul, where she remains attentive to what is happening further east. This was clear from her installation *Araf* (2018), which I saw in *Geometries*, a 2018 exhibition organized by Locus Athens[35] at the Agricultural University of Athens. I caught her work just as the single black-and-white projection began, as a lithe man stands high

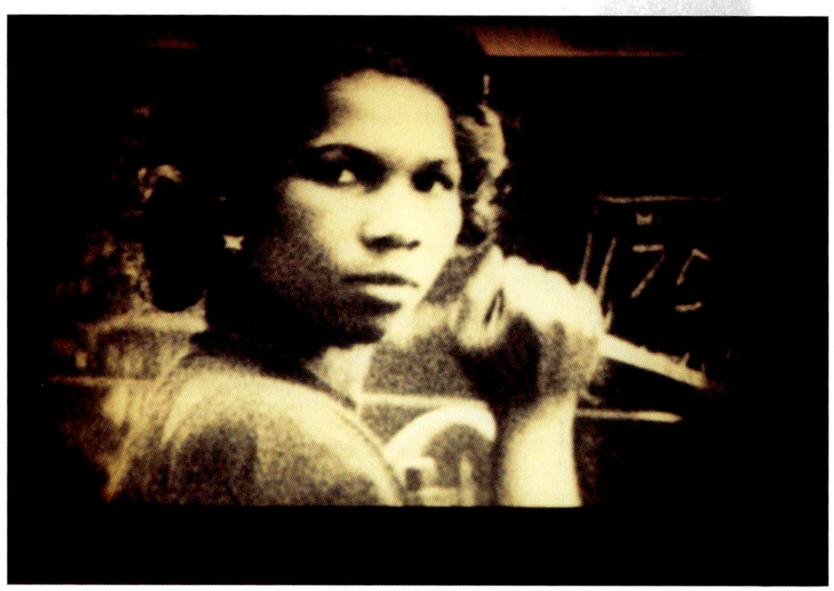

John Akomfrah, Black Audio Film Collective, *Handsworth Songs*, 1986
Single-channel 16 mm film transferred to video, color, sound,
58 min. 33 sec.

up in the middle of an Ottoman-era bridge in the old city of Mostar, in Bosnia
and Herzegovina. In very slow motion, he gracefully dives. When interviewed
about the work, Pekün references Icarus, who exists in the borderland between heaven and hell, where, she notes, humanity meets the future.[36] *Araf*
is a kind of road movie, derived from the purported diary of Nayia, a woman
who travels between Srebrenica and Sarajevo to Mostar, and who returns
from exile for the twenty-second anniversary of the 1995 Srebrenica geno-
cide.[37] As in her earlier work, Pekün seems to imply that discoveries will lead
to new interpretations of what were fractious situations and new optimism
brought on by technological change. It is a tall order but worth the effort.

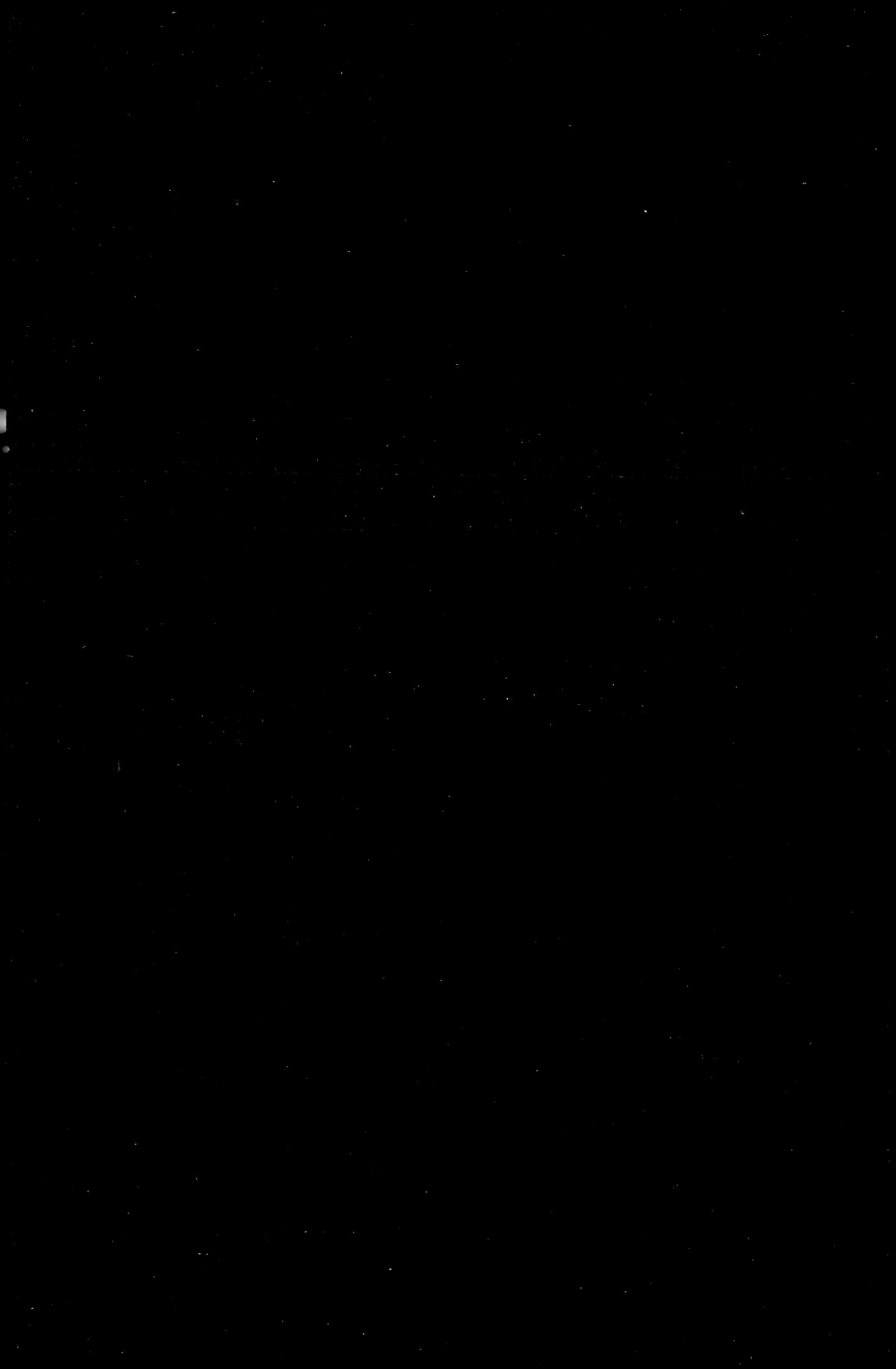

Facing the Future

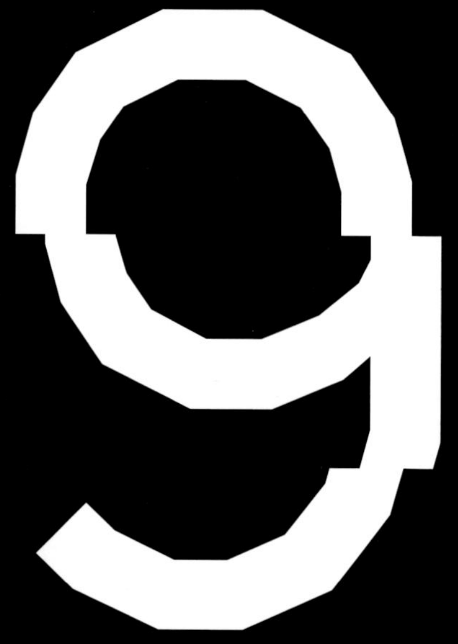

Media art continues to advance, often straddling the domains of fine art and popular culture as artists adapt new tools to their practice. A few directions have emerged in recent years. Momentum still persists in alliances between music and performance, between space and installation, and between the internet and virtual worlds. The new generation of work consists largely of digital files, constellations of faster tools that might include off-the-shelf software programs, or code specifically written for a project that operates in real time. This configuration of data available through apps, stored on smaller and smaller devices, and presented through an audiovisual cornucopia of screens and sound systems, has made media art mutable, adaptable to multitudinous outcomes. As a result, media artists now tend to be more relaxed about the formats a project may take, especially with regard to future upgrades. As a work and its content evolve, an artist's aesthetics are what remain more or less constant, their concept defining the relationship between image and sound and what layout their arrangement may take.

After more than fifty years of innovation, media art continues to divide into two all-purpose categories. The first is installation and performance. Artists devise their spatial layout using electronic components, in combination with live, prerecorded, or computer-derived video images that may include elements of voice, language, or movement. As projects have gained respectability as museum-worthy collectables and become more mainstream, some artists have garnered financial backing from the establishment, while others have eschewed that route and questioned the concept of media art that is easily possessable.

In the second category, media art is manifested as compositions that might unfold as live simulations in real time; they can be streamed online or downloaded as apps, or they function utilizing the same software that drives user-activated games. The digital art created by these makers defies easy categorization as media art.

Today's media artists are forging new methodologies for their audiovisual art practices. Ragnar Kjartansson (b. 1976) and Kahlil Joseph (b. 1981) have strong connections to music. Jana Winderen (b. 1965) transforms sounds that are inaudible to the human ear gathered from nature into audible, ambisonic installations. Sondra Perry (b. 1986), Ian Cheng (b. 1984), Wong Ping (b. 1984), Lu Yang (b. 1979), and Rachel Rossin (b. 1987) manipulate the synthetic and blur distinctions between reality and invention. All of these artists create hybrid work that has an impact on the viewer's body or mind, or both.

The performance and media artist Ragnar Kjartansson came to my attention when he represented Iceland at the 2009 Venice Biennale with his work *The End* (2009), for which he spent four months on the ground floor of a palazzo on the Grand Canal. I entered the majestic old building and became part of a convivial gathering. The artist was lounging about, surrounded by the expanding flotsam and jetsam of his daily life, which included stacks of just-completed paintings and a parade of empty beer bottles. When he wasn't talking to visitors, Kjartansson played his guitar or painted portrait after portrait of his artist friend who wandered about, dressed in a skimpy bathing suit. In an adjacent space, I saw his early euphonious looped videos, which played second fiddle to the live action. I thought about the Living Theatre and other experimental groups active in the 1960s that bridged theater, music, and film to challenge art conventions and viewers' sense of propriety. The earlier artists' mutable events had still managed to have some sort of beginning, middle, and end, whereas Kjartansson's work continued nonstop, like life itself.

Four years later, Kjartansson boosted New Yorkers' spirits when his installation *The Visitors* (2012) opened in Chelsea at Luhring Augustine Gallery in 2013. During its seven-week run, when word of mouth drew hordes of people each day, some viewers like myself stayed for all sixty-four minutes inside the rousing environment of the nine-channel, immersive audiovisual installation.

I was unwittingly charmed by the fluid coalescence of image and sound, which bore equal weight in Kjartansson's adroitly orchestrated installation. Eight nearly six-foot-tall (1.8 m) projection screens displayed images of carefully lit, frayed interiors, each a painterly tableau with a musician surrounded by the accoutrements of Rokeby, a once fashionable forty-eight-room mansion built by William Backhouse Astor in the nineteenth century. The run-down home in Barrytown, New York, is filled with sculptures, paint-ings, floral-print fabrics, domestic bric-a-brac. Each of the eight musicians—a pianist, an accordionist, a banjo player, a cellist, a few guitarists, and the guitar-strumming Kjartansson lounging naked in an antiquated bathtub—was in a separate room, isolated from the others, yet they sang and played the same song in harmony, nonstop and in unison. Their soulful, looping interaction was possible because all of them wore headphones, which conn-ected them by a digital sound system overseen by a sound engineer, who is visible only at the beginning during setup and at the end of the session.

A ninth screen showed a miscellany of family and friends gathered on the mansion's porch, with expansive views of the lush rolling lawns and bucolic

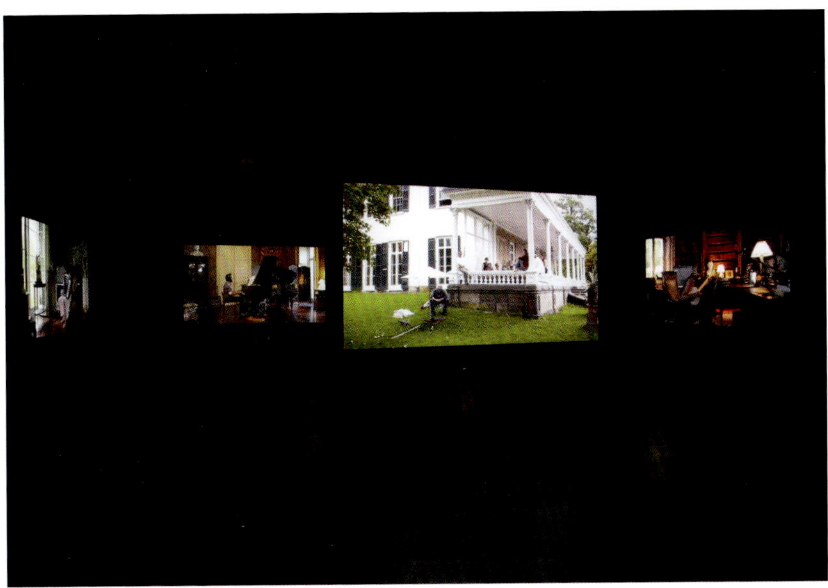

Ragnar Kjartansson, *The Visitors*, 2012
Nine-channel video, color, sound, 64 min. Installation view:
Luhring Augustine, New York, 2013

landscape nearby. In the gallery, viewers drifted around the installation,
often lured into staying with one screen, each flanked by a speaker, listening
carefully to the soothing sound of that individual's solo. The collective but
dispersed performance evoked the united actions of a well-rehearsed rock
band, such as Reykjavík's Sigur Rós, whose members are Kjartansson's
good friends.

Born into a theatrical family in Reykjavík, Kjartansson grew up playing
with local bands, including Trabant, well-known for its formidably flamboyant electronic, punk, and pop music, which was well suited to Kjartansson's
ebullience. He often says he felt like a poseur when he played music himself,
largely because he felt he wasn't good.[1] Visual art felt much more effortless
and more like total freedom—and that's what Kjartansson decided to con-
centrate on. Performance, however, remains central to his unconventional
practice, which he associates with his idol, the great American artist Carolee
Schneemann. When I attended the 2013 Göteborg International Biennial
for Contemporary Art in Sweden, I heard his public conversation with Schneemann. It was fun to see the dynamics of their friendship, clearly based
on respect for each other's work. A feminist since art school, Kjartansson

responded to the way Schneemann worked with what she considered lived time—performing sustained actions.

What distinguishes Kjartansson is his approach to repetition. His nonstop looped work belongs to a tradition that goes back to twentieth-century American masters—the early writer Gertrude Stein (1874–1946), John Cage, Allen Ginsberg, and more recently the American-Swiss sound collage artist Christian Marclay (b. 1955). Each has employed repetition and interlude to explore the sensation of passing time, and in Ginsberg's case, to reach a state of ecstasy. It is Ginsberg's use of repetition that comes closest to how Kjartansson harnesses collective emotion in his jubilant time-based media art.

Whether I'm ardently singing karaoke in a local bar with Kjartansson, as I did in Sweden, or am ensnared within one of his installations that are continuous, I sense that his candidness is real, which makes for a gratifying experience. His work is deeply felt, connected to the life he lives right now and to his innate ability to capture something magical that he offers viewers the chance to experience for themselves.

Jana Winderen

Sound is the building block of another artist with Nordic roots, Oslo-based Jana Winderen. She trained in mathematics, chemistry, biochemistry, and fish ecology before receiving a BA in fine art from Goldsmiths in London in 1993. Winderen investigates ecosystems and creates engaging sonic installations that are presented in both institutional and public spaces, as well as audio compositions that she releases as unlimited-edition works in the form of film, CD, cassette, or vinyl, usually through Touch, the experimental British music label. Winderen's sonic artwork has found global listeners interested in art and the natural environment.

We first met in Oslo in 2012, when I was researching a younger generation of media artists, in particular the long-standing sound art community in Scandinavia. Winderen caught my attention. I was struck by the intensity of her commitment to exploring aural dimensions of landscapes that are difficult to reach, and to accessing sounds that are imperceptible to most people. Often alone, she travels to the ends of the earth to capture sound with with an arsenal of the most sophisticated, professional recording gear. She might drop a microphone inside the crevice of a gigantic glacier or deep within the frigid Arctic Ocean—or even into the edges of Manhattan's East River, where shrimp noisily communicate in efforts to mate.

The sounds Winderen records in nature become the components of compositions she develops. Her repeating patterns have made me think about Steve Reich's early Minimalist music. The immateriality of sound suits her interests, especially the way sound tends to be perceived intuitively in advance of rational workings of the mind. I appreciated the simplicity of her stereophonic compositions. This led me to premiere her sixteen-channel, twenty-minute ambisonic *Ultrafield* (2013) at MoMA in the exhibition *Soundings: A Contemporary Score*.[2] Visitors entered the darkened environment of the installation, which was designed by the artist to be both inviting and perplexing. They sat on soft cushioned seating in the middle of the nineteen-foot (5.8 m) square space, surrounded by sixteen inconspicuous, approximately ten-inch-high (25.4 cm) black speakers mounted from floor to ceiling on the four walls, each painted black. Two subwoofers with low-bass frequencies were placed on the floor in corners. Without the visual stimuli usually encountered in a museum, Winderen's audience sat down and paid close attention to what *Ultrafield* had to offer, shushing anyone who dared to speak.

The installation aurally transported listeners down into the depths of the ocean to hear the vocal clicks of whales and the subtle drone of boat motors, before taking them up to the surface of a river where the rhythmic sounds of canoe oars could be heard; then the installation went skyward into the domain of chirping birds and echolocating bats. After a pause of a few seconds, the twenty-minute sonic cycle gently started over again. Listeners had space for imaginative readings of the aural realities unfolding around them, discovering the commonalities of the sounds, with some discerning the transition from underwater to midair, especially after reading the wall text on the outer wall adjacent to the entrance.

Winderen describes her compositional methodology as "blind" field recording, meaning she is open to chance. For *Ultrafield*, she used especially long cords and a range of sensitive microphones, including hydrophones, that she dropped hundreds of feet deep into the icy ocean at the Arctic Circle. After months spent carefully collecting the sounds made by different species of fish, insects, and bats, both audible and inaudible to human ears, she returned to her studio and reworked the material, especially in the ultrasound range above the hearing capacity of humans, as she slowly composed her ethereal work with its harmoniously joined biotic and abiotic elements.

With the technical proficiency of an ambient electronic composer, Winderen turned the intriguing crunches and cries that she captured outdoors into a compelling abstract sonic work that offered an intimate, shared experience. At MoMA, the piece interested museumgoers enough that they would slow down and pay attention rather than move by quickly, and listen rather than simply hear. As a curator, that was my goal: to disrupt

visitors' normal pattern of grazing, of moving quickly from one artwork
to the next, and to entice them to contemplate sound as a major area
of contemporary art. And many did, staying to hear all twenty minutes,
wrapped up in Winderen's cocoonlike installation. Winderen's insightful sonic
universes continue to direct her audience's attention to what are fragile
ecosystems in nature, circuits that all living beings are part of.

Lu Yang

I met the Shanghai-based Lu in Beijing in 2018, when she was nominated
for a prestigious art award. She was dressed in brightly patterned, intentionally mismatched clothes; I recognized an *otaku*, the word for a young adult
who is an idiosyncratic technology whiz, obsessed with computers, usually
asocial, and a bit strange. She grew up inspired to become an artist by the
Japanese cartoons she watched on local television as a child, and by the
burgeoning Chinese contemporary art she followed in the proliferating
Shanghai galleries. A promising young painter, she made it into the prestigious China Academy of Art in Hangzhou, where she made works that dealt
with mind control, many of which her professors considered too controversial
and discouraged her from completing at school.

After Lu graduated, the Fukuoka Asian Art Museum in western Japan,
well-known for showing and collecting the work of emerging artists from
nearby countries, helped produce her six-minute video *Reanimation!
Underwater Zombie Frog Ballet!* (2011). For the work, she used bodies of
dissected frogs that she connected to electrodes and zapped with electrical currents. She recorded the underwater ballet that resulted, and added
a soundtrack of electronic beats. To Lu, all bodies are interesting, and
she looks at them analytically, unbothered by anything that goes against
decorum.[3]

I first came across her work in 2014 in a small pop-up show in a storefront in Manhattan's Chinatown, and at first I didn't quite know what to
think. I sensed an inquisitive mind behind the strange, Ganesh-like deities
she portrayed in brightly designed posters and animations, which fascinated
the hip young locals with spiky neon-colored hair and thrift store clothes
who were hanging around the show. The highlight was her video *Uterus Man*
 (2013), about a strange hero inspired by the female reproductive organ,
which to Lu resembles both a cruciform and a caped figure with arms outstretched and its back turned. A fully conceived character with superpowers,
weapons, and a fancy mount—a pelvis chariot—it mirrored the female
organ's versatility. *Uterus Man* was performed by Mao Sugiyama, a gender-
less individual she met online, who became the star of her do-it-yourself

franchise that included a manga (comic book), feature film, and video game, all produced by the Fukuoka Asian Art Museum. Her superhero story about a sexless character grew out of her belief that society's gender divisions are absurd.[4]

Lu is a prolific artist who works in her studio alone, with the online collaboration of a diverse group of musicians with practices in opera, death metal, electronic and pop music, and hip-hop. She connects with them through such websites as SoundCloud. The internet is expedient for her, as someone who works at home alone and doesn't have face-to-face interactions with people that much. Now often on the road, especially in Japan, she is able to make art and connect with peers as long as she has access to a computer. As soon she completes a new work, she uploads it on her pulsating, bright website, making it downloadable and streamable through Vimeo for her avid followers. I see her as a free spirit, paying more attention to what people online think than to the impact she might have on people in the art world.

Lu finds labels and definitions to be limiting. She especially dislikes being called a "Chinese artist." When asked about her nationality, she explains that she lives on the internet, where nobody knows who you really are. She believes that what her online audience cares about is whether an artwork is any good; they're not thinking about who the person is behind it. By living on the internet, artists like Lu can abandon any concern for how they are pegged, whether by nationality or gender or another marker of identity.

From the first time I met Lu it was clear she is passionate about popular culture, especially sci-fi movies with sophisticated computer-generated special effects. Speaking about her work, she came across as serious, someone who determinedly works nonstop and with great conviction, as she makes connections among science, aesthetics, and technology, all with a strong sense of respect for other living beings.

Sondra Perry

Perry is a media artist who is as single-mindedly driven in her practice as Lu Yang. Curators, writers, and other artists are paying attention to what this young artist is up to. In 2012 Perry received her undergraduate degree in upstate New York from Alfred University, where she studied electronic media with the veteran image-processing artist Peer Bode (b. 1952). Interrupting her studies, she spent several semesters working at Electronic Arts Intermix in Manhattan. Through this formative experience, she learned the history of video art and became committed to the concept of unlimited-edition video. In 2015 she completed her MFA at Columbia University, where

she was one of relatively few students of color. This led to her considering
the role that digital technology has played in what she calls the systemic
oppression of black identity.[5] In 2018 she received the Nam June Paik Award,
the international media art prize awarded by the Kunststiftung NRW, a
Düsseldorf-based foundation that honors transdisciplinary artists who push
boundaries and bridge cultural divides, in the spirit of Paik's practice.

Exploring themes of race, identity, family history, and technology, and
what she calls the easy "slippages of identity" that shape self-image in
the digital realm of everyday experience,[6] Perry started out deliberately
positioning her work in opposition to what she considered high-end
commodification, whereby a small number of artists' unique projects are
given hefty price tags and sold at art fairs. Her antiexclusivity stance is
similar to that adopted by media artist Martha Rosler and other video
pioneers in the early 1970s. Upholding their utopian belief that electronically
reproducible experimental art should be affordable and accessible to those
interested, especially art students, Perry makes her unlimited-edition
single-channel videos available for educational and cultural use through EAI,
her nonprofit distributor. Perry has said that her work is leased—in other
words, licensed rather than sold—to institutions, which means they cannot
resell the work.[7] She started out providing links to nearly all of her artworks
on a personal website, and continues to do so. In this way, like the artist
Ryan Trecartin (b. 1981), she makes nearly all of her artworks previewable as
downloads for scholars and educators at roughly the same high resolution
as preservation files held by the artist. She purposefully participates in
the market by creating salable installations that include video, which her
gallerist, Bridget Donahue, sells as unique works. She is one of a few artists
who are deliberately challenging the notion of scarcity and ownership for
video work, by exploring both noneditioned and one-of-a-kind models.

In 2015 Perry captured critical attention for her work when her playful
yet serious installation *Lineage for a Multiple-Monitor Workstation: Number
One* premiered at MoMA PS1 in the museum's fourth iteration of its *Greater
New York* survey exhibition. Perry's structure was simple, consisting of
paired, perpendicular projection screens, one approximately five by nine feet
(1.5 x 2.7 m) and the second seven by twelve and a half (2.1 x 3.8 m), situated
in a small room with walls painted green. The work began with a short
sequence of Perry's family members horsing around as they staged a group
portrait on the sidewalk in front of her maternal grandmother's house, where
she grew up in Perth Amboy, New Jersey. From the point of view of the video
camera in Perry's hands, viewers saw her family outfitted in matching black
sweatpants and sweatshirts, their faces hidden under balaclavas that are
the bright chartreuse of chroma-key green.[8] For me, Perry's balaclavas bore

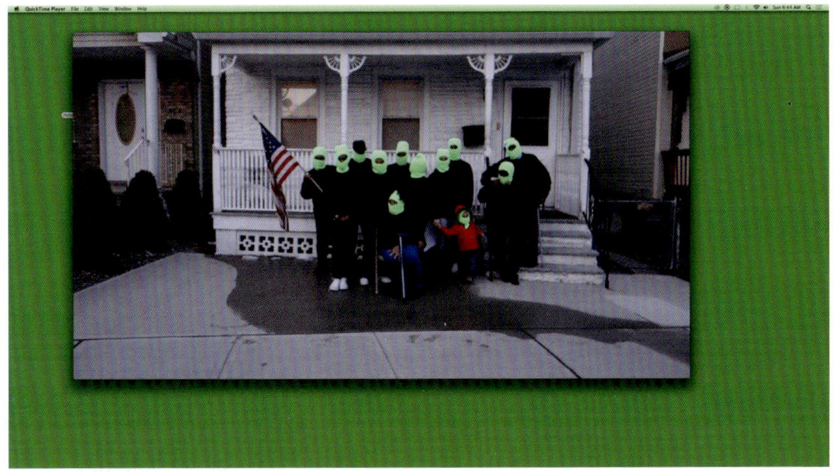

Sondra Perry, *Lineage for a Multiple-Monitor Workstation:
Number One*, 2015
Two-channel video, color, sound, 25 min. 24 sec.

a connection to the masks used by other art-world mavericks such as the
Guerrilla Girls and Pussy Riot. The masks and the identical leisurewear outfits
are what united her extended family.

In the following section, Perry's relatives stage the burial of an American
flag in the backyard. Her grandmother can be heard explaining the family
tradition that when an old flag becomes too worn to fly, it must be buried
and not tossed into the garbage. In the final scene, the entire family of
aunts, siblings, and cousins, again in matching black sweats and green ski
masks, gathers around a dining table. Having a good time as they peel sweet
potatoes, they sing a popular gospel hymn, "Somebody Prayed for Me."

Perry framed the video sequences in *Lineage* against a chroma-key-
green computer desktop backdrop, with the windows of various files shown
open and in use, revealing the software icons that she used during the
creative process of choreographing and editing her work. Her ulterior motive
was clear: Perry is subtly critiquing how video artists today all toil with
similar software and the same jumble of small windows and files on their
computer screens when they orchestrate a work. More to the point, she
is very much engaged with issues having to do with identity, stereotypes,
and the protean possibilities of constructing an online character, referencing
the artist-writer Juliana Huxtable (b. 1987) for her understanding of how
easy it is to cut-and-paste or morph self-representation digitally.[9]

Another question Perry raises revolves around the word *lineage* in her title. By engaging her family as actors, Perry looks at how identity—whether individual, family, class, or racial—develops out of the constant sorting of memories and personal narratives. The central video in the installation concludes with the artist's grandmother singing the words to the Clash's song "The Guns of Brixton": "You can crush us, you can bruise us, but you'll have to answer to . . . the guns of Brixton."

Effectively bucking the art world's lingering discomfort with art that is time based or computer derived, Perry remains active and on the move, delivering lectures and going from residencies to art colonies that pay per diems for stays of a month or two as she develops new installation work, her primary interest. She has said she likes to surround a viewer with multiple screens, with narratives that move from one physical place to another physical place.[10] From Perry's work I have learned much about the nuances of how black people have been portrayed throughout history, particularly how blackness influences technology and image making. Her message is serious, but Perry understands play as an effective way to bring about changes in awareness.

Ian Cheng

The American artist Ian Cheng has been fascinated by narrative since his childhood in the 1980s and 90s, when he often binged on four movies a day. Becoming dissatisfied with being confined to a theater seat, and longing to have a say in the forward direction of a film's storyline, he hankered for a different kind of cinematic experience. In 2000 Cheng's world radically changed when he discovered the Sims, a real-life-simulation computer game that was developed by a video game conglomerate in Silicon Valley (Maxis, the Sims Studio, and Electronic Arts). At last he was able to guide fictional characters through the stories of their lives in an environment that he managed as a player. The genius of the Sims, Cheng has said, is the "idea that intelligence is not just in your head. It's distributed between you and all the objects and other people that are around you" in the game.[11]

Cheng graduated from the University of California, Berkeley, in 2006 with a dual degree in studio art and cognitive science, the interdisciplinary study of the mind, a field that bridges psychology, philosophy, language, and computer modeling—a good fit for Cheng, who had become interested in artificial intelligence. As a next step, he spent several years working at Industrial Light & Magic, a motion picture visual effects company founded in 1975 by George Lucas. While there he was exposed to visual effects techniques that included motion capture, compositing, and 3-D modeling.[12]

By the time Cheng earned his MFA from Columbia University in 2009, personal computers and video games were ubiquitous, making it possible to experience interactive stories at home, in an arcade, or at a theme park through large computer systems. Inspired, Cheng began experimenting with the video game engine Unity, considered the ultimate video game platform that runs on C# (pronounced "C-sharp"), a multipurpose, multiparadigm programming language designed for the creation of what the industry calls real-time animation (in which computer-generated actions unfold at a lifelike pace). He went on to create an imaginative form of media art that he describes as a "neurological gym": work that stretches the mind.[13] This allowed him to simulate the behavior, actions, and population dynamics of living organisms, and concoct worlds inhabited by sentient beings with believable behavior.

In 2015 Cheng caught me by surprise at the Frieze art fair in New York, when he premiered the projection of sketchy, realistically in-motion, diminutive humanoids at Standard (Oslo)'s booth. For this immersive work, *Emissary in the Squat of Gods*, Cheng started with a simple narrative in his mind's eye and expanded it into a quirky situation. Cartoonlike characters moved and lived in an expansive landscape, where they interacted with people and animals, and responded to the weather in the arid environment. The entities' activity reminded me of hippie survivalists living off the grid in desert communities. It was hard to tell whether Cheng was exercising the minds of his viewers or his computer-generated creatures, or both.

Two years later, MoMA PS1 presented Cheng's *Emissary* trilogy (2015–17) as a solo exhibition. Each of the three chapters of the trilogy, which were shown in adjacent rooms, is an open-ended animation developed with algorithms, each with a general story line that plays out with unpredictable variations, a format Cheng describes as live simulation, meaning that the simulation is playing out as the viewer watches.[14] The first chapter, *Emissary in the Squat of Gods*, the piece I'd seen at Frieze, is set in prehistoric times and has a main character, the young daughter of a shaman, who gets hit on the head prior to a volcanic eruption. She then attempts to lead her people to escape from pending disaster. Cheng explained, "It's precisely this moment where it's the threat, and not the actual disaster, that humans find the most anxiety-provoking and the most stressful. . . . You don't actually know which way to go."[15]

The next chapter, *Emissary Forks at Perfection*, takes place thousands of years in the future. The volcano in the same landscape has become a crater lake, around which a tribe of Shiba dogs lives. The main character is Shiba (Emissary), a mutated offspring of a character from the first chapter. The dog, Cheng said, is "a means of talking about where consciousness can

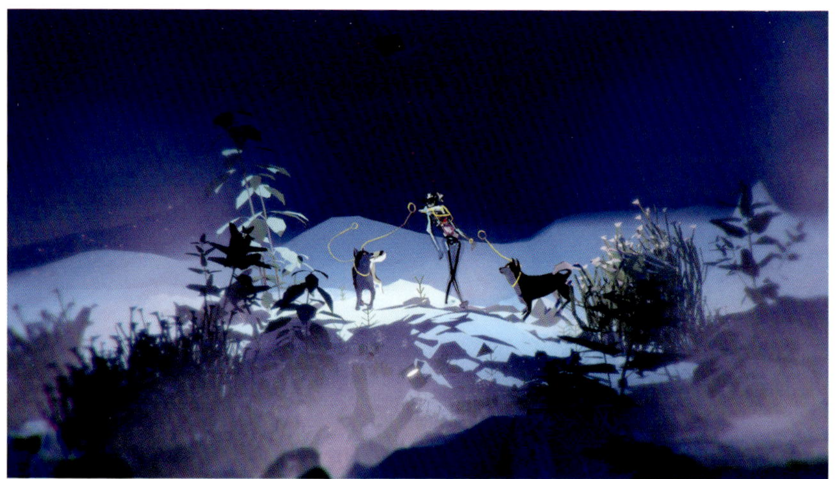

Ian Cheng, *Emissary Forks at Perfection*, 2015–16
Live simulation and story; infinite duration

go, without eradicating powerful emotions like fear and anxiety, which can be very useful."[16] The final chapter, *Emissary Sunsets the Self*, occurs in the same location billions of years later. In this future time, the sentient artificial being is an oceanic substance (resembling nothing other than a blob with a face) that has merged with the landscape to form what Cheng defines as a Sentient Atoll. The entity sends a diminutive chunk, or Puddle, of itself underground, where it eats a plant and gains something close to full-blown consciousness. Eventually, a population of blobby, rotund figures, shaped somewhat like the Michelin Man, scurry about the barren gray landscape as if to protect the environment from catastrophic change.[17]

Cheng's beings are computerized characterizations of entities that move jerkily about or go off alone into the distance, where a Darwinian struggle for survival is taking place. The artist often speaks about being inspired by Hayao Miyazaki (b. 1941), a masterful Japanese director of exquisite feature-length animations, in particular his portrayal of the complex relationship between culture and nature. Cheng sees nature as a container, a portal out of which he operates.[18]

At PS1, I lingered in the *Emissary* trilogy, first looking as I sat on a bench, then as I stood up close, fully immersed in each chapter. The way I managed to differentiate between each landscape, epoch, and character was by poring over the brochure available for free during the show. The brochure opened up Cheng's complex work to me and other nongamers.

For the *Emissary* trilogy, Cheng expanded his audience to include
remote viewers by offering a link to a live feed on PS1's website available
all hours of the day, via the popular streaming site Twitch, which is generally
used to watch real-time game play. The live feed brought Cheng's evolving,
unconventional artwork closer to a media event.

Although Cheng's work is watched in a gallery or on a home computer
screen, much like a film is, his artwork has no edits and no script that the
artist adheres to. He belongs to a young generation of media artists who have
grown up in a world where technology has become a user's coequal partner.

Kahlil Joseph

Modern life is lived in a kind of temporal collapse, a "digital now," as time
and space have continued to shrink since the early 1990s, through the use
of smartphones and other handheld and wearable devices. Kahlil Joseph
understands the new culture. He is known as a versatile artist, filmmaker,
and music video director, and an active, founding member of the collective
What Matters Most. This online Seattle-based cooperative, spearheaded
by a youthful group of creatives, seeks to improve their respective crafts
through collaboration. Their website hosts short films by Joseph and others
created through collaborations with music artists who have a similar taste
and style.[19]

Joseph grew up in a close-knit family in Seattle, and it was as a high
school exchange student in Brazil in 1998 that his interest in film arose.
Feeling homesick, he tuned in to the Academy Awards and watched *Good
Will Hunting* win for best screenplay. If two young kids from Boston can
write, he thought, then so could he. Joseph went on to study art, art history,
photography, and television at Loyola Marymount University in downtown
Los Angeles but never graduated. On his own, he delved into film history
through Netflix, the internet-based video-on-demand service launched in
1997. He discovered Andrei Tarkovsky (1932–1986), the Russian film director
who has been called a progenitor of slow cinema, which is characterized as
being observational with little or no narrative. At the same time he explored
Asian cinema. "I was living in a $500 a month apartment in Inglewood and
I'd get a different Asian movie every two days. . . . It blew my mind how
unconcerned they were with the three-act structure."[20]

After an internship with Doug Aitken (b. 1968), an artist who inventively
adapts cinematic video images to installations with fragmented tableaux,
Joseph worked for five years during the mid-to-late 2000s with the
Directors Bureau, a Los Angeles production company cofounded in 1996
by the filmmaker Roman Coppola (b. 1965). Next he took an editing job in

Texas with the Hollywood director Terrence Malick (b. 1943).[21] To me this makes sense, as both keep a low profile yet are deeply engaged with the world.[22]

When Joseph turned to making music videos, he remembered that someone had once asked him, "'Who do you wanna work for?' And, because I was black, they were like, 'Spike Lee?'" No, he wanted to work for Hype Williams, who had directed music videos for Missy Elliott, Kanye West, and Beyoncé. Joseph worked briefly as an assistant on one of Williams's shoots: "PA-ing is like being a gopher—you pick up the garbage. It's a high turnover rate because no one wants to do it forever, but that's how I started and it's the best thing I ever did."[23]

Joseph's four-minute video *Until the Quiet Comes* (2012) came about when the electronic musician, DJ, filmmaker, and rapper Flying Lotus asked Joseph to develop a work for his new song. The project was in tune with Joseph's commitment to community, in particular local black communities, where he feels the richness, honesty, and pain.[24] The video brought Joseph widespread acclaim, including winning the Grand Jury Prize for Short Films at the 2013 Sundance Film Festival and Video of the Year at the UK Music Video Awards in 2013. He was praised for his hybrid practice that navigated across cinema, visual art, fashion, and popular music.

The following year, I saw the video in *Ruffneck Constructivists*, an exhibition organized by the artist Kara Walker (b. 1969) at the Institute of Contemporary Art in Philadelphia. The exhibition focused on art that reflected a culture of policed bodies and self-confident identities.[25] Walker chose the title as a reference to Russian Constructivism, an art and archi-tecture movement that originated in 1913 around Vladimir Tatlin (1885–1953), geared toward art as a practice for social change.[26] In her essay for the exhibition catlog Walker stated, "It is my hope that the interaction between these very divergent works and methods could return a viewer to the questions of modernism, architecture, urbanism and the resistant bodies who reshape it."[27]

In *Until the Quiet Comes*, Joseph successfully matched his visuals to Flying Lotus's intricately nuanced soundtrack and style. The video revolves around the astonishing street dancer Storyboard P: At night in the Nickerson Gardens housing projects of Flying Lotus's native Los Angeles, Storyboard P gracefully falls to the ground in slow motion. His body is then shown lying dead, apparently from a gunshot. The emotional vertigo caused by the sight of the body is compounded by the way Joseph plays with time and narrative by showing a scene in reverse, of a man running backward past the dead body. Is he the shooter? Is he running before or after the gunshot? The critic Hilton Als wrote in the *New Yorker* that "it's as if Joseph's visual world were

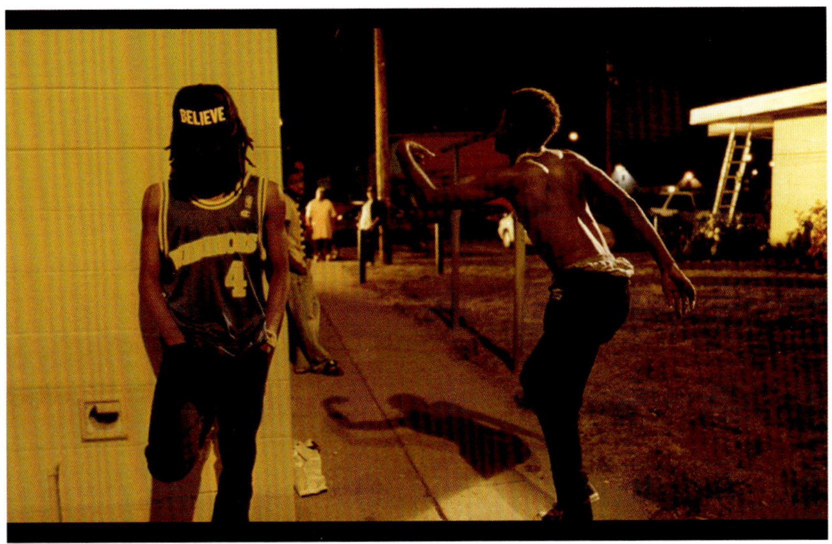

Kahlil Joseph, *Until the Quiet Comes*, 2012
Transfer of 35 mm film to digital video, color, sound, 3 min. 50 sec.

a vinyl record, complete with scratches that make the needle skip, thereby changing the flow of things."[28]

Joseph was close to his younger brother, Noah Davis (1983–2015), a painter of surreal, postracial images, as well as curator and cofounder of the Underground Museum in Los Angeles, a small yet bustling family-run nonprofit art collective in the neighborhood of Arlington Heights, near central Los Angeles. The founders focused on black excellence rather than struggle. Davis had helped Joseph realize his potential as an artist. "He saw something I was working on that was, in my mind, nowhere near art, and he said: 'You should make this into an installation.'"[29] Shortly after that, the rapper Kendrick Lamar asked Joseph to create a video installation to accompany his opening act for Kanye West's *Yeezus* album world tour in 2013. Joseph assembled an hour-long edit of material he shot in Compton, Lamar's LA neighborhood, juxtaposed with home movies from Lamar's life and simulated shootings. The video accompanied songs from *good kid, m.A.A.d city*, Lamar's 2012 autobiographical album.

In the middle of editing, Joseph's brother asked him to present the video at the Underground Museum. The project evolved into a two-channel work that premiered in a group show in August 2014. The following spring, the Museum of Contemporary Art, Los Angeles, exhibited *m.A.A.d.*[30] as an installation with the exhibition title *Kahlil Joseph: Double Conscience*, which referenced the phrase *double consciousness*, a term coined by the American writer, historian, sociologist, civil rights activist, and Pan-Africanist W. E. B. DuBois (1868–1963) to describe the internal struggle of African-Americans—namely, the divide between African heritage and an American consciousness.

In 2016 the Frye Art Museum presented a survey exhibition, *Young Blood: Noah Davis, Kahlil Joseph, the Underground Museum*, in the brothers' hometown of Seattle. In his catalog essay, their friend, the writer Maikoiyo Alley-Barnes, noted that Joseph's "film works are often accompanied by sound and also rely greatly on visual stillness. Stillness that can turn the mundane into the epic and the horrific into the sublime. . . . He is adamant about detail and slowing the viewer down in the point of visual mediation, but he is more fascinated with gestural particularities and individual physical elan."[31] He concluded saying that both Davis and Joseph "invite us all to think deeply about what sustains us and, perhaps more important, where we are headed as makers and consumers of art. As visual consumers of their work, we are invited into stories that are in the midst of being told. It is their gift to us."[32]

Joseph's next work was an installation that took the viewer on a profound audiovisual journey that captured the energy of Harlem. His video *Fly Paper* (2017) premiered in a one-person exhibition entitled *Shadow Play* at the New Museum in 2017. Joseph worked with a team of technicians and sound engineers to orchestrate how the audio content would exist spatially, carefully placing subwoofers and amps and sixteen special loudspeakers, ones usually found in dance clubs or at music festivals.[33] As word spread like wildfire among my art community friends, I hastened to the show and joined a crowd of about fifty people, who were hunkered down, lying on plump beanbag seats on the carpeted gallery floor, watching and listening to the twenty-three-minute black-and-white work, as they meditated on the slippery nature of memory and reverie, coupled with the candor of Joseph's insightful eye. A team of actors—including his own father, as well as the celebrated actor, dancer, and singer Ben Vereen (b. 1946), and Vereen's daughter, Karon Davis (b. 1977), wife of Joseph's late brother—appear as melancholic figures inside a Harlem brownstone and out on local streets.

Joseph's goal in *Fly Paper* was to create in film a black aesthetic, an articulate voice that speaks to the gains and setbacks of this century's New Negro, the term popularized during the Harlem Renaissance in the early twentieth century, indicating a refusal to submit quietly to the practices and laws of Jim Crow racial segregation and a goal of achieving a fuller participation in American society.[34] The artist Arthur Jafa (b. 1960) believes that Joseph achieves his humane representation of black sociality because "he's self-authorizing. He's not waiting for things to become canonical."[35]

For *BLKNWS* (2018–ongoing), his next work, he incubated ideas during a yearlong residency at Stanford University as part of the Presidential Residencies on the Future of the Arts program. As a visiting artist, he worked with faculty, students, and staff from a number of different fields, ranging from art history and law to business and critical race and ethnic studies, and held roundtable discussions with them and others invited from the Bay Area.[36] He started with the postulate that anything can be news.

I saw *BLKNWS* at the 2019 Venice Biennale, at the time about twenty minutes in duration (the artist plans to continue adding footage). A pair of side-by-side flat screens were positioned on a gallery wall on top of a blown-up photo of a group of nuns. Caucasian and black, they wore full-length habits and wimples, and stood in rows facing the viewer. The paired screens displayed videos with fast-paced clips, both archival and new—a remix of material that included YouTube videos and amateur film footage, Instagram stories, actual news clips, and in-studio interviews.[37] In one of the clips I recognized the collector and MoMA patron A. C. Hudgins, who was shown chatting with Joseph's friend, the Los Angeles–based painter Henry Taylor (b. 1958), in a split-screen, TV news–like format. The videos are an indication of what broadcast news could or will be, as Joseph and others pursue dimensions of truth from an understanding that truth exists as the foundation of ideology.[38]

I learned that *BLKNWS* was originally conveived of as a pitch to cable networks for a real news show. Turned down by the major networks, the proposal became an artwork. I believe that television and art will continue to evolve, intertwined, as artists seek new paradigms. Joseph's work is the harbinger of an image-oriented, posttext future, as audio and video gallop along together on the internet. Joseph seems primed for the future—a multimedia culture, in which text recedes to the background and audiovisuals take over.[39]

Wong Ping

A self-taught video animator with a sizable online following, Hong Kong–based Wong Ping casts his childlike characters in garish eye-popping colors in animations on risqué subjects. At the New Museum's 2019 triennial, *Songs for Sabotage*, I sat on a bench enchanted by the projection of *Wong Ping's Fables 1* (2018), the artist's slapstick thirteen-minute work that gives a rather wicked view of daily life in Hong Kong. The video tells the story of three somewhat crazy, dysfunctional characters: Elephant,

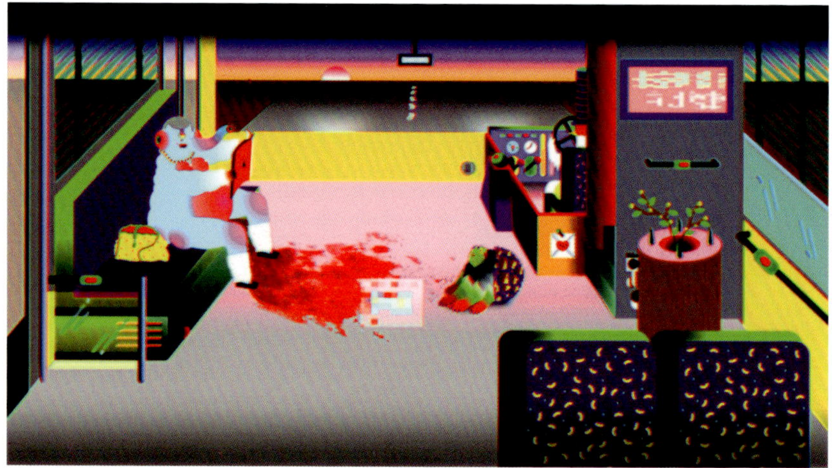

Wong Ping, *Wong Ping's Fables 1*, 2018
Video animation, sound, color, 13 min.

an intellectual who discovers that he has second sight; Chicken, a police officer with Tourette's syndrome who accidentally kills his family; and Tree, a bus passenger who rides and contemplates his worst fears of rejection and death. They are imperfect characters rendered in bold, idiosyncratic colors and wacky design.

Overlaying their actions is a soundtrack of electronic buzzes and blips and the sweet voice of a young female narrator. Subtitles divulge some of the economic anxieties that come from high rent and unemployment, which have fractured and isolated Wong's generation. Viewers might find his zany tale a bit too over-the-top were it not rendered in cartoon form with a good dose of humor.

The artist recently wrote: "The tradition of fables providing a maxim is like the tradition of the artist's statement. . . . It tries to explain work that often doesn't need it. But in the internet era, maybe we don't have the time for long fairy tales—we want everything to be short and pithy."[40]

Wong received a BA in design from Curtin University in Perth, Australia, after which he returned to Hong Kong. He bought and pored over how-to books on video postproduction and was hired by a local TV station. Becoming proficient in After Effects, the commercial industry's standard software, he realized he could adapt his computer programming skill to creating simple animations. In 2014 he set up the Wong Ping Animation Lab (he was the only staff member) and went on to work freelance for the Cartoon Network, an American cable and satellite TV channel that broadcasts animated shows. After a few years, when the job came to an end, Wong turned to the underground art scene and discovered that alternative gallery shows offered another route for him to experiment and be productive in Hong Kong. Finding the densely populated Hong Kong megalopolis uncomfortably crowded and loud, he would stay at home and work in his studio. His friends started calling him *otaku*.

I met the dapper, bespectacled Wong in May 2018 in New York at the opening of *One Hand Clapping*, the Guggenheim Museum's exhibition that looked at the ways in which meaning becomes destabilized in a globalized world. His featured work, *Dear, can I give you a hand?* (2018), tells the story of a young man and his wife who move into his infirm father's apartment, which they turn into a profitable, crowded home for the aged imbued with erotic titillation. The father encourages his fellow wheelchair residents to spin like dervishes so fast that their gold teeth spew out and pile up over him. I watched the rather raunchy work on a towering LED screen as it captivated an audience of adults and children. I had to chuckle when I discovered that on the floor behind the screen was a pile of kitschy, wind-up denture toys, their gold teeth chattering away. Some might consider the work a perverse look at family life, but it is spot-on about addressing what the artist describes as the generational divides, tensions, and alienation brought on by digital devices and the myriad forms of entertainment, savory and otherwise.[41] Imperiously, the daughter-in-law forces the old man to throw out his substantial collection of pornographic videos in the obsolete VHS format, but he triumphs when the videos are retrieved later in the story.

Wong wrote in the Guggenheim catalog about how he was affected by seeing so many destitute elderly people collecting garbage off the streets of Hong Kong. His animation installation presents a critical view of contemporary life, peering into the deepest—even shameful—traits of human nature.

Rachel Rossin

Rachel Rossin is an artist who uses the mediums of virtual reality (VR) and painting to operate in what she describes as the liminal space between the real and the digital.[42] She grew up in South Florida, where everyone lives with the threat of imminent disaster in the form of hurricanes and floods, which instills in people a dread of nature's ferocious side, an uneasiness that colors her work. At age eight she was painting and had already taught herself to write computer code (for MS-DOS), and like many other young people was a video gamer. It is not surprising that her art was reviewed in *Wired* magazine before *Artforum*. Based on her computer skills, she is able to hack action-adventure video games, such as Grand Theft Auto, as part of her research into understanding how big-budget special effects are executed.[43] The *New York Times* described Rossin as a VR outlier,[44] someone outside the industry. She works alone, without any connection to commercial VR developers, who today are soliciting famous painters and sculptors, eager to develop markets for their products.

Rossin pursues an independent path, much like another outlier VR artist, Jakob Steensen (b. 1987). Both artists bring VR together with painting, and work to go beyond the technical limitations of VR that are the result of its newness, especially the restraints of individual headsets that are aimed at the gaming world. They each create intricate installations that feature projections of magnificant animations, which viewers watch together while standing and moving about. Viewers can also opt to plunge deeper into an immersive visceral experience by putting on individual VR headsets, which enable them to turn with the sensation of moving 360 degrees in the virtual landscape. Rossin and Steensen are motivated by a new challenge—real-time sound, audio that is generated within the 3-D world and is fully "alive." It means that a plant can have one sound, a footstep another, and wind a third. Each of these is spatialized, so that the audio is interactive and each sound reacts to the others. The sounds mix and will send out a signal to whatever speaker or VR headset an artist sets up.[45]

Rossin spent several years developing *Stalking the Trace* (2019), which was commissioned by and premiered at the Zabludowicz Collection in London. For this work, Rossin began by thinking about the final scene of Michelangelo Antonioni's film *Zabriskie Point* (1970), the moment when an explosion of household goods flies through the air in slow motion, high above the desert near Death Valley, California.[46] Rossin's turbulent install-ation features cars floating along flooded streets and forests twisting in severe winds—drawn from NASA imagery of hurricanes seen from space[47]—and mammoth fireballs surging forward, one unfurling out of another as if they were Russian nesting dolls. Rossin explained to me that she is responding to the present moment, which she sees as a chaotic time of great acceleration.[48]

Viewers of *Stalking the Trace* are offered two levels of viewing experience. People standing in the gallery watch and listen to a virtual narrator deliver a text written by the artist, accompanied by a sound collage—a so-called tone poem that serves to illustrate her VR work.[49] Dense projections—scenes that give the impression of spectacle—cover the gallery walls. Some of the imagery is real and some is simulated from movie-effects software, the line between the two being blurred. The two longest gallery walls are punctuated by narrow slivers of eight-foot-tall (2.4 m) doorways that expose visitors walking behind them.[50] A nod to cinema history, the slim doorways reference the zoetrope, a nineteenth-century handheld optical toy made of a cylinder with slits in its surface. As the zoetrope was twirled, its viewer saw pictures on the inner surface come together as a continuously moving image.

Viewers of *Stalking the Trace* who wear one of four VR headsets are able to move about in both the virtual and physical space. While physically walking and moving within the gallery, the headset wearers experience the visual sensation of moving temporally forward and backward within the image, doing what the artist calls "scrubbing time." The viewer's body becomes the cursor that controls the progress (or "game time") of the piece. Their perception is what drives the work forward or back according to where they are in space.[51]

Afterword

Today when I walk along the urban sidewalk, I see pedestrians who are no longer confined to their physical bodies. They circulate among virtual communities, slipping in and out of their online lives using the latest software on their portable devices. As Rachel Rossin notes, the avatars we cultivate online bleed into our physical selves and act as peripherals for our cognitive processes—storing our memories and contacts, helping us navigate, and so on. The promise (and the delivery) of these virtual selves is that we can offload a lot of the work of becoming "more human" into this virtual space.[1] For Rossin, being human is starting to encompass things that we used to wholly attribute to machines.[2]

Although I stepped down from my position at MoMA in 2013, I remain as inspired as ever by the strides that art and technology continue to take. To understand the cultural flux, I still turn to artists, harbingers of what lies ahead. Teaching a history of media course at the Yale School of Art has given me access to emerging artists, who have a fresh approach to the advancing field of media art. VR catches the attention of some students; sound fascinates others who, like me, are intrigued by sound's ineffability as much as by the still-unsettled terrain that tethers art and music histories. This interest led me to organize *Seeing Sound*, an exhibition featuring recent audiovisual installations and sculptures that begin to sketch new definitions of how sound, music, and language become visible, physical forms. The show includes the work of eight artists—from North and South America, England, Singapore, and Hong Kong—and will begin a five-year tour in 2020, under the auspices of Independent Curators International.

Pondering the future is like writing science fiction, and I'm reluctant to prophesize, as the possibilities of video as art continue to shift. I felt it was important to seek the opinions of those who are intimately engaged with the new. I asked Julia Scher what she foresees, and she predicted that art will take another, as-yet-unknown form soon; current technology cannot handle the accelerating change.[3] When I posed the same question to the Taiwanese-born artist Shu Lea Cheang (b. 1954), who works in the fields of net-based installation, social interface, and film production, she pointed to the BioNet—her term for a fictional technology that is built inside the human body—as the next frontier where art will stake a claim.[4] The artist Heather Dewey-Hagborg (b. 1982) responded by describing her four-channel video poem, *T3511* (2019), which traces a biohacker's obsession with the cells and data profile of an anonymous DNA donor. The work shows a future that is already at hand. In this world, human cells and fluids are commodities for sale online, genomic information is omnipresent and linked to social media, and human connection unfolds over biotechnological networks. Desire and intimacy come from spending time with someone's data, holding their cells close.[5]

I remain intrigued by how artists such as Rossin, Scher, Cheang, and Dewey-Hagborg look beyond the borders of the physical body and beyond existing telecommunication schemes. Their explorations will lead to new art forms and new definitions.

In the time ahead, I know that media artists, art institutions, and cultural mass media will carry on with their lively dance and discover new steps, new languages, and new partnerships. Connections are there; it's all in the making.

Notes

Introduction

1 Siobhan Burke, "Artistically Inclined: Many Events Mark the Choreographer Merce Cunningham's Centennial Year," *New York Times*, February 24, 2019.

2 Roslyn Sulcas, "Dance: Freeing the Inner Childs: Talking Dancer," *Village Voice*, July 10, 2001, 67.

3 Lucinda Childs worked closely with Rainer and others in the collective of dancers, composers, and visual artists who performed at the Judson Memorial Church on Washington Square between 1962 and 1964. They were known for abandoning the proscenium; featuring pedestrian, ordinary movement; and shocking audiences.

4 Nam June Paik to Porter McCray (JDR 3rd Fund director), November 3, 1965, JDR 3rd Fund program files, Rockefeller Archive Center, Sleepy Hollow, NY. In 1980 the JDR 3rd Fund was transformed into the Asian Cultural Council, a nonprofit organization.

5 Rosalind Krauss, "Video: The Aesthetics of Narcissism," *October* 1 (Spring 1976): 50–64.

6 Nam June Paik, "Input-Time and Output-Time," in *Video Art: An Anthology*, ed. Beryl Korot and Ira Schneider (New York: Harcourt Brace Jovanovich, 1976), 98.

Chapter 1

1 Jasia Reichardt, "Cybernetic Serendipity: The Computer and the Arts," special issue, *Studio International*, reprinted 1970, 71.

2 Michael Shepherd, "Machine Mind," *Sunday Telegraph*, August 11, 1968, quoted in Rainer Usselmann, "The Dilemma of Media Art: Cybernetic Serendipity at the ICA London," *Leonardo* 36, no. 5 (2003): 391

3 Frank Rose, "The Big Bang of Art and Tech in New York," *New York Times*, November 6, 2015, www.nytimes.com/ 2015/11/08/arts/design/the-big-bang-of-art-and-tech-in-new-york.html.

4 Marita Sturken, "TV as a Creative Medium: Howard Wise and Video Art," *Afterimage* (May 1984): 7.

5 Barbara Rose, "Television as Art, 'Inevitable,'" *Vogue*, August 15, 1969, 36.

6 Kynaston L. McShine, ed., *Information* (New York: Museum of Modern Art, 1970), 1.

7 Ibid., 103.

8 "Identifications. Fernsehenausstellung II," LIMA, www.li-ma.nl/lima/catalogue/art/gerry-schum/identifications/1662.

9 "60 TV Sets," Luxonline, accessed May 20, 2018, www.luxonline.org.uk/artists/david_hall/60_tv_sets.html.

10 Calvin Tomkins, "An Eye for the New: A Private Woman's Pervasive Influence in the Contemporary Art World," *New Yorker*, January 17, 2000, 54.

11 Suzanne Muchnic, "Leo Castelli, Whose Legendary Career as an Art Dealer Is Being Honored at the Gagosian Gallery, Has Seemingly Seen It All. But at 88, He Still Has . . . : An Ageless Passion," *Los Angeles Times*, February 1, 1996, www.latimes.com/archives/la-xpm-1996-02-01-ca-30943-story.html.

12 Willoughby Sharp, "Nauman Interview," *Arts Magazine*, March 1970, 23.

13 Douglas Davis and Allison Simmons, eds., *The New Television: A Public/Private Art* (Cambridge, MA: MIT Press, 1977), 24.

14 Ibid., 26.

15 Global Village was a documentary-oriented space a few blocks away from the Kitchen on Broome Street. It was founded by John Reilly with Rudi Stern and Ira Schneider, who were joined by Stephan Moore and Julie Gustafson.

16 Davis and Simmons, *New Television*, 69.

17 Ibid., 61–62.

18 Ibid., 97.

19 Ibid., 202.

20 Ibid., 110–11.

21 Douglas Davis and Allison Simmons, eds. (Cambridge, MA: MIT Press, 1977).

22 Thomas Wilfred coined the term *lumia* to describe his art based on light. Wilfred's *Lumia Suite, Opus 158*, acquired by MoMA and on view between 1964 and 1980, is said to have inspired artists in the late 1960s to work with light. Stephen Petersen, "Lumia: Thomas Wilfred and the Art of Light," *CAA Reviews*, May 3, 2018, www.caareviews.org/reviews/3386#.XQqgpi2ZPOR.

23 While both 1945 and 1947 have appeared as Palestine's birth year, the artist confirmed the year as 1947, explaining: "When i was younggg i felttt tooo younggg and lied when abouttt 19 and became 21,,,therefore why sometimesss i've beenn 1945 and 1947,,,,,but noww that i'm so much olderrr i've taken backk my 2 ancienttt lie yearss,,,,,sooooo i'm actuallyyy born on August 15th 1947,,,, [*sic* throughout]." Charlemagne Palestine, email to author, March 5, 2019.

24 Bill Viola, "Artist to Artist: Peter Campus—Image and Self," *Art in America*, February 5, 2010, www.artinamericamagazine.com/news-features/magazines/peter-campusimage-and-self/.

Chapter 2

1 Nam June Paik to Porter McCray, letter dated December 5, 1966, sent with proposal dated November 30, 1966, JDR 3rd Fund program files, Rockefeller Archive Center, Sleepy Hollow, NY.

2 In addition to Nam June Paik's piece, video work by Allan Kaprow, Otto Piene, James Seawright, Thomas Tadlock, and Aldo Tambellini was also commissioned, created, and anthologized for the broadcast.

3 Nam June Paik to Porter McCray, February 17, 1971, JDR 3rd Fund program files, Rockefeller Archive Center, Sleepy Hollow, NY. For years the synthesizer Paik and Shuya Abe left behind intrigued later CalArts students. In early 2004 Tony Oursler told me that he needed a technician to use it, given the analog machine's complexity.

4 Josephine Reed, "Nam June Paik: The Artist Who Invented Video Art," National Endowment for the Arts, accessed June 11, 2013, www.arts.gov/photos/nam-june-paik-artist-who-invented-video-art.

5 Vito Acconci, "Words Before Music," n.d. Photocopy of a five-page text typewritten by the artist, Vito Acconci artist file, Museum of Modern Art Library, New York.

6 Steina and Woody Vasulka, "Origins of The Kitchen," 1977, www.vasulka.org/Kitchen/KRT.html.

7 The Kitchen is now based in Chelsea.

8 Wulf Herzogenrath went on to become director of the Kunsthalle Bremen from 1994 to 2011 and today is director of the Visual Arts Section of the German Academy of Arts, Berlin.

9 Not wanting to retain the name of either her father or her ex-husband, the artist devised her pseudonym in 1967, thereby refusing to cater to a "system that is defined by the masculine." She fine-tuned her public persona and made a strong political statement, as her name—which she emphasized by using all capital letters—became a manifesto. Sophie Delprex, "VALIE EXPORT: De-Defining Women," tr. C. Penwarden, *Art Press*, 293 (September 2003): 36.

10 The Lijnbaancentrum team—Henk Elenga, Wink van Kempen, and Frédéric Kappelhof—produced videos based on live performances carried out in the *Projekt '74* galleries by not only VALIE EXPORT but also the artists Taka Iimura, Doug Davis, Willoughby Sharp, Rainer Ruthenbeck, Vito Acconci, Joan Jonas, Dan Graham, Ulrike Rosenbach, Peter Weibel, and Heinz Breloh. The Lijnbaancentrum was an exhibition space of the Rotterdam Arts Foundation.

"Rotterdam Cultural Histories #6: Video at the Lijnbaan-centrum," Witte de With Center for Contemporary Art, accessed January 4, 2019, www.wdw.nl/en/our_program/exhibitions/rotterdam_cultural_histories_6_video_at_the_lijnbaancentrum.

11 Roswitha Mueller, *Valie Export: Fragments of Imagination* (Bloomington, IN: Indiana University Press, 1994), 219.

12 Vito Acconci, "Vito Acconci on Chris Burden," *Artforum*, September 2015, www.artforum.com/print/201507/chris-burden-54478.

13 Nam June Paik was sometimes unable to hide his anger that it took the museum twenty years to acquire one of his installations. My MoMA contemporaries were put off by how casually put together Paik's sculptural work often appeared. In fact, Paik did create lesser work to sell quickly. He was perpetually drastically short of funds to cover the expenses of his always-more-ambitious-and-more-complex next production. "I need money" was the mantra curators would often hear from Paik and other artists over the years.

14 Jom Tob Azulay, a filmmaker who worked for the Brazilian Consulate in Los Angeles at the time, also hand-carried a video camera to Rio, which Geiger and several other artists used. Anna Bella Geiger, email to author, July 17, 2019.

15 A good example is Elena Shtromberg, *Art Systems: Brazil and the 1970s* (Austin: University of Texas Press, 2016).

16 Into this group of early feminists I must add Shigeko Kubota, Mary Lucier, and Hannah Wilke in New York; Lisa Steele in Toronto; Gina Pane and Annette Messager in Paris; Susan Hiller in London; and Zofia Kulik in Warsaw.

17 "Media Burn," Electronic Arts Intermix, October 14, 2018, www.eai.org/titles/media-burn.

18 *Media Burn* was remastered in 2003.

19 At this time, the Whitney Biennial, for example, isolated video in small viewing rooms, because its curators were afraid of bleeding sound.

Chapter 3

1 Paul Bonner, "Broadcast Access Television and Its Future Development," British Broadcasting Corporation mimeo (London: BBC, 1976), 1–2, quoted in Ed Webb-Ingall, "Community Video/Community TV," Lux, June 25, 2015, lux.org.uk/writing/community-video-community-tv-ed-webb-ingall#sdfootnote8anc.

2 The exhibition featured sculptures by a group of international artists using ordinary construction materials that they employed to pare art down to the most fundamental level. The emphasis was on raw material and raw gesture, and most projects were realized in situ.

3 Joan Simon, "Scenes and Variations: An Interview with Joan Jonas," *Art in America*, July 1995, 75, quoted in Barbara London, "From Video to Intermedia: A Personal History," *Modern Women: Women Artists at the Museum of Modern Art* (New York: Museum of Modern Art, 2010), 356–57.

4 Joan Simon, "Scenes and Variations," 74.

5 "An Exchange between Joan Jonas, Susan Howe and Jeanne Heuving," *How2* 2, no. 3 (Spring 2005), www.asu.edu/pipercwcenter/how2journal/archive/online_archive/v2_3_2005/current/workbook/joans/exchange.htm.

6 Other members of Group Ongaku, which literally translates as "music group," included Mieko Shiomi, Mikio Tojima, Genichi Tsuge, and Yumiko Tanno.

7 Fujiko Nakaya, email to author, June 5, 2019. The core members of Video Hiroba included Sakumi Hagiwara, Nobuhiro Kawanaka, Hakudo Kobayashi, Masao Koura, Toshio Matsumoto, Shoko Matsushita, Rikuro Miyai, Michitaka Nakahara, Fujiko Nakaya, Yoshiaki Tono, Katsuhiro Yamaguchi, and Keigo Yamamoto, and also Morihiro Wada. The group's motto was always to be open to everyone. Anyone who wanted to use the Hiroba portapak joined the group; at the time it was the only equipment that anyone could rent at a very low cost of ¥1,000 per day. Members often helped each other and together instituted the name Hiroba.

8 Anne-Marie Duguet, "Anarchive n°5 - FUJIKO NAKAYA 中谷芙二子. FOG 霧 BROUILLARD," Anarchive, accessed October 13, 2018, www.anarchive.net/nakaya/fn_bio_eng.htm.

9 Between 1979 and 1981, *Video from Tokyo to Fukui and Kyoto* was shown in museums in fifteen cities, including Albuquerque, NM; Boston; Flint, MI; Long Beach, CA; Richmond, VA; Seattle; Vancouver; Amsterdam; Zurich; and, in Japan, Tokyo, Kobe, Fukuoka, Osaka, and Sapporo.

10 "Mark Mothersbaugh Looks Back at 9 Classic Devo Videos," *Rolling Stone*, February 11, 2014, www.rollingstone.com/music/music-lists/mark-mothersbaugh-looks-back-at-9-classic-devo-videos-11220/devo-corporate-anthem-230250/.

11 RoseLee Goldberg, *Laurie Anderson* (New York: Harry N. Abrams, 2000), 32.

12 Kate Horsfield and Lyn Blumenthal, "Interview with Laurie Anderson," *F newsmagazine*, April 2006, www.fnewsmagazine.com/2006-apr/interview_1.html.

13 Goldberg, *Laurie Anderson*, 40–41.

14 Ibid., 47.

15 Ibid.

16 Charles Amirkhanian, "Interview with Laurie Anderson," in *The Guests Go in to Supper*, ed. Melody Sumner, Kathleen Burch, and Michael Sumner (Oakland, CA: Burning Books, 1986), 226.

17 Robert Palmer, "3-Day Nova Convention Ends at the Entermedia," *New York Times*, December 4, 1978, www.nytimes.com/1978/12/04/archives/3day-nova-convention-ends-at-the-entermedia.html?searchResultPosition=17.

18 Goldberg, *Laurie Anderson*, 58.

19 Jessica Prinz, "It's Such a Relief Not to Be Myself: Laurie Anderson's Stories from the Nerve Bible," in *Interfaces: Women, Autobiography, Image, Performance*, ed. Sidonie Smith and Julia Watson (Ann Arbor: University of Michigan Press, 2005), 392.

20 Craig Owens, "Amplifications: Laurie Anderson," *Art in America*, March 1981, 25.

21 Laurie Anderson, "Control Rooms and Other Stories: Confessions of a Content Provider," *Parkett* 49 (May 1997), 132.

22 Bérénice Reynaud, "*Americans on the Move* by Laurie Anderson; *Solo* by Phil Glass," *Performing Arts Journal* 5, no. 1 (1979): 46.

23 Michael VerMeulen, "Say Hello to Laurie Anderson," *TWA Ambassador*, October 1982, 72.

Chapter 4

1 Details about Bill Viola in this section come from numerous conversations bewteen author and artist over many years.

2 David A. Ross and Peter Sellars, *Bill Viola* (New York: Whitney Museum of American Art, 1997), 21.

3 Bill Viola, "Artist to Artist: Peter Campus—Image and Self," *Art in America*, February 2010, 61.

4 Ibid., 60. Bill Viola offered these definitions of time: "'Real time' refers to an image existing in the present tense, parallel with unfolding experience, and it is distinct from 'recorded time,' 'past time,' 'delayed time,' 'slowed time' and other forms of time that were starting to accumulate in the media landscape."

5 Bill Viola, *Reasons for Knocking at an Empty House, Writings 1973–1994*, ed. Bill Viola and Robert Violette (Cambridge, MA: MIT Press, 1995), 44.

6 Bill Viola, conversation with author, June 1, 1985.

7 Stephen Sarrazin, "Surfing the Medium," in *Gary Hill*, ed. Robert Morgan (Baltimore: Johns Hopkins University Press, 2000), 71.

8 Lucinda Furlong, "A Manner of Speaking: Interview with Gary Hill," *Afterimage*, March 1983, 10.

9 George Quasha and Charles Stein, "Liminal Performance: Gary Hill in Conversation with George Quasha and Charles Stein," *PAJ: A Journal of Performance and Art* 20, no. 1 (January 1998): 21.

10 "Soundings," Electronic Arts Intermix, accessed August 28, 2009, www.eai.org/titles/soundings.

11 Gary Hill (Video Viewpoints lecture, Museum of Modern Art, New York, February 26, 1980), transcript, vv1980.4, Special Collections, Museum of Modern Art Archives, New York.

12 Shawna Cooper and Joe Lewis, "Joe Lewis," *Times Square Show Revisited*, accessed April 23, 2019, www.times squareshowrevisited.com/accounts/joe-lewis.html.

13 Dara Birnbaum, "Pop-Pop-Video: Reinvesting in the American TV-image" (Video Viewpoints lecture, Museum of Modern Art, New York, October 20, 1981), transcript, vv1981.3, Special Collections, Museum of Modern Art Archives, New York.

Chapter 5

1 Jonas Mekas, "Movie Journal," *Village Voice*, March 5, 1964.

2 George Kuchar and Mike Kuchar, *Reflections from a Cinematic Cesspool* (Berkeley, CA: Zanja Press, 1997), 85.

3 Ibid., 10–12.

4 George Kuchar cites his film *Wild Night in El Reno* (1977) as the start of his *Weather Diary* series. "George Kuchar's Weather Diaries," Harvard Film Archive, accessed August 2, 2018, library.harvard.edu/film/films/2011julsep/kuchar.html.

5 George Kuchar (Video Viewpoints lecture, Museum of Modern Art, New York, May 1, 1989), transcript, vv1989.3, Special Collections, Museum of Modern Art Archives, New York.

6 Ibid.

7 Tony Oursler, email to author, May 13, 2019.

8 Tony Oursler, introduction to *Tony Oursler: My Drawings 1976–1996* (Cologne: Oktagon Verlag, 1997), n.p.

9 Ann Goldstein, Michael Smith, Tony Oursler, Paul McCarthy, Jim Shaw, and Kim Gordon, "Image of the People: Mike Kelley (1954–2012)," *Artforum*, May 2012, www.artforum.com/print/201205/tony-oursler-30821.

10 Serena Bentley, "The Poetics Project," *Leg of Lamb*, January 9, 2015, lamblegs.wordpress.com/2015/01/09/the-poetics-project/.

11 Tony Oursler, email. Although Tony Conrad was of an earlier generation, he and Oursler would find common ground as collaborators.

12 John Minkowsky, "The Videotapes of Tony Oursler," September 1985, the website of Tony Oursler, tonyoursler.com/the-videotapes-of-tony-oursler-by-john-minkowsky/.

13 Tony Oursler (Video Viewpoints lecture, Museum of Modern Art, November 24, 1981), transcript, vv1981.7, Special Collections, Museum of Modern Art Archives.

14 Founding Sonic Youth members included Thurston Moore, Kim Gordon, and Lee Ranaldo. Steve Shelley joined in 1985.

15 Graham Reid, "Sonic Youth's Thurston Moore Interviewed (1990): Corporate Greed and the Politics of Music," Elsewhere, November 14, 2008, www.elsewhere.co.nz/absolute-elsewhere/2017/sonic-youths-thurston-moore-interviewed-1990-corporate-greed-and-the-politics-of-music/.

16 Tony Oursler, conversations with author at the time the artist first began making his dolls, in the early 1990s.

17 Tony Oursler, *TimeStream* (web page), www.moma.org/interactives/projects/2001/timestream/. A link to *TimeStream* is available via MoMA's website, but as an internet artwork, *TimeStream* is no longer active.

18 Mark Sanders, "Pipilotti Rist: Stay Metal," *AnOther Magazine*, Autumn/Winter 2006, 431.

19 Marius Babias, "The Rist Risk Factor: When Dreams Twitch Like Dying Fish," *Parkett* 48 (1996): 105.

20 Pipilotti Rist's title and the lyrics that she lip-synchs are derived from a 1973 song by Kevin Coyne entitled "Jackie and Edna."

21 "Pickelporno," Electronic Arts Intermix, accessed August 16, 2011, www.eai.org/titles/pickelporno.

22 Pipilotti Rist, email to author, January 31, 2019.

23 Pipilotti Rist, interview with Museum of Modern Art staff Barbara London, Sydney Briggs, and Glenn Wharton about the work *Ever Is Over All*, December 16, 2006.

24 Pipilotti Rist (Video Viewpoints lecture, Museum of Modern Art, New York, December 9, 1996), transcript, vv1996.15, Special Collections, Museum of Modern Art Archives, New York.

25 "Doors of perception" is an expression taken from the title of a book by Aldous Huxley published in 1954, and based on a phrase coined by William Blake in 1793 in his poem *The Marriage of Heaven and Hell*.

26 William J. Simmons, "Pattern Play: An Interview with Cheryl Donegan," *Art in America*, January 28, 2016, www.artinamericamagazine.com/news-features/interviews/pattern-play-an-interview-with-cheryl-donegan/.

27 Cheryl Donegan, email to author, January 30, 2019.

28 Cheryl Donegan, email to author, January 31, 2019, referring to *October* 1 (Spring 1976): 50–64.

29 Rosalind Krauss, *The Optical Unconscious* (Cambridge, MA: MIT Press, 1994).

30 The concept of index originates in the semiotic theory of Charles Sanders Peirce, in which indexicality is one of the three fundamental sign modalities by which a sign relates to its referent—the others being iconicity and symbolism.

31 Simmons, "Pattern Play."

32 Ibid.

33 Courtney Fiske, "In the Studio: Kristin Lucas," *Art in America*, September 3, 2013, www.artinamericamagazine.com/news-features/magazines/in-the-studio-kristin-lucas/.

34 Ibid.

35 Kristin Lucas, email to author, May 12, 2019.

36 "Cable Xcess," Electronic Arts Intermix, accessed June 30, 2017, www.eai.org/titles/3763.

37 "Host," Electronic Arts Intermix, accessed June 30, 2017, www.eai.org/titles/host.

38 The twenty-three videos by the seventeen artists featured in the *Young and Restless* exhibition were compiled into four programs. The artists included Alex Bag, Phyllis Baldino, Vanessa Beecroft, Cheryl Donegan, Anne Kugler, Alix Lambert, Kristin Lucas, Johnna MacArthur, Kirsten Mosher, Nurit Newman, Cara O'Connor, Kristin Oppenheim, Tatiana Parcero, Alix Pearlstein, Linda Post, and Jocelyn Taylor with Lisa Marie Bronson.

39 "Kristin Lucas," Electronic Arts Intermix, accessed June 30, 2017, www.eai.org/artists/kristin-lucas/biography.

40 Elizabeth Day, "Miranda July: 'I Had Some Rough Episodes When I Was Younger,'" *Guardian*, February 8, 2015, www.theguardian.com/books/2015/feb/08/miranda-july-had-some-rough-episodes-when-i-was-younger-first-bad-man-interview.

41 Lisa Darms, ed., *The Riot Grrrl Collection* (New York: Feminist Press, 2013).

42 Meredith Melnick, "Anatomy of a Zine: When Magazines Go Indie," *Time*, September 3, 2011, content.time.com/time/arts/article/0,8599,2091194,00.html.

43 Meanwhile, Johanna Fateman and activist Kathleen Hanna founded the all-girl electroclash band Le Tigre. The self-proclaimed "underground electro-feminist performance artists" combined visuals, music, and dance in their performances. Le Tigre became known for its left-wing sociopolitical lyrics and for dealing with issues of the LGBT community. The artist Sadie Benning was an early band member, who eventually left to pursue her video art.

44 Ross Simonini, "An Interview with Miranda July," *Believer*, October 1, 2015, believermag.com/an-interview-with-miranda-july/.

45 From the get-go, July has been a diligent archivist. When the entire nineteen-part *Joanie 4 Jackie* film series went to the Getty Research Institute in 2016 as a donation, she included the related ephemera she had saved—every poster, brochure, and postcard created for the project. She had also written to each contributing filmmaker to explain the donation and obtain their approval. As a result, the complete *Joanie 4 Jackie* archive is available for study purposes to scholars and researchers. July's

conscientiousness ensures that *Joanie 4 Jackie* is well understood as a part of video art's history.

46 Assignment #8, Learning to Love You More, www.learning toloveyoumore.com/reports/8/8.php.

47 Nicolas Bourriaud, *Relational Aesthetics*, tr. Simon Pleasance and Fronza Woods with Mathieu Copeland (Dijon, France: Les Presses du Réel, 2002), 113.

Chapter 6

1 Thierry Kuntzel, "Screen Memory" (Video Viewpoints lecture, Museum of Modern Art, New York, May 2, 1983), transcript, vv1983.7, Special Collections, Museum of Modern Art Archives, New York.

2 Thierry Kuntzel, *Thierry Kuntzel* (Paris: Éditions du Jeu de Paume, 1993), 11.

3 Thierry Kuntzel, "Prendre le temps," interview by Liliana Albertazzi, *Art Press* 131 (1988): 30, quoted in "Thierry Kuntzel: Biography," *New Media Encyclopedia*, accessed August 5, 2017, www.newmedia-art.org/cgi-bin/show-art.asp? LG=GBR&ID=9000000000068022&na=&pna=&DOC=bio.

4 See Barbara London, *Projects 29: Thierry Kuntzel* (New York: Museum of Modern Art, 1991), exhibition brochure.

5 *Video Spaces* exhibition correspondence is kept in Special Collections, Museum of Modern Art Archives, New York.

6 See Barbara London, *Video Spaces: Eight Installations* (New York: Museum of Modern Art, 1995), 23–24.

7 "Chris Marker: *Silent Movie*, 1994–5," the Museum of Modern Art, accessed February 2, 2018, www.moma.org/ interactives/exhibitions/1995/videospaces/marker.html.

8 But the conservation of Gary Hill's *Inasmuch As It Is Always Already Taking Place* remains fraught with difficulty. TV tubes not only have a limited number of hours of life, but also have become obsolete, replaced by flat television and computer screens that are inappropriate for Hill's work. Since MoMA purchased two backup sets of the correct size of TV tubes, future presentation of the installation at the museum should be possible; however, its future is not a rosy one.

9 See London, *Video Spaces*, 26–27.

10 "Bill Viola: *Slowing Turning Narrative*, 1992," Museum of Modern Art, accessed February 2, 2018, www.moma.org/ interactives/exhibitions/1995/videospaces/viola.html.

11 Jean Fischer, "An Essay on the Work of Judith Barry," *Judith Barry: Through the Mirror of Seduction* (Dublin: Douglas Hyde Gallery, 1988), 10.

12 See London, *Video Spaces*, 18–19.

13 Ibid.

14 Ibid., 24–25.

15 Marcel Odenbach, conversations with author, 1994.

16 Gilles Godmer, *Stan Douglas* (Montreal: Musée d'art contemporain de Montréal, 1996), 20.

17 See London, *Video Spaces*, 19–21.

18 Teiji Furuhashi, conversations with author over many years.

19 Carol Lutfy, "The Conversation: Teiji Furuhashi," *Tokyo Journal* (September 1995): 21.

20 Reiko Tomii, email to author, May 6, 2019. Tokyo's urban space was a stage for the small theater movement— popularly known as *angura bunka* (*angura* is an abbreviation for "underground")—that emerged in the 1960s.

21 Steven Durland, "The Future Is Now: Kyoto's Dumb Type," *High Performance* 13, no. 2 (Summer 1990): 34.

22 Lutfy, "The Conversation," 21.

23 Canon ArtLab in Tokyo, directed by Yukiko Shikata and Kazunao Abe, commissioned and coproduced outstanding works of media art for more than a decade, starting in 1990. The program ended when Canon, a multinational corporation specializing in the manufacture of imaging and optical products, restructured.

24 See London, *Video Spaces*, 21–22.

25 For over a decade, US art museums participated in "A Day Without Art" on December 1, a national day of mourning and calls for action in response to the AIDS crisis. At MoMA, we screened a program of films and videos, along with talks by artists, including members of the activist art group ACT UP and A. A. Bronson, the surviving member of the three-person Toronto-based collective General Idea.

26 Shiro Takatani coordinated the effort from Kyoto, with Ben Fino-Radin, associate media conservator at MoMA.

27 Ingvild Goetz, conversation with author at the Hauser & Wirth, 548 West 22nd Street, New York, September 12, 2017.

28 Stefan Heidenreich, *Beyond Control: Freedom and Authority in the Work of Bjørn Melhus* (The Hague: Galerie West, 2015), 3.

29 Other artists whose work was also part of Ingvild Goetz's donation included: AES+F, Ulla von Brandenburg, Christoph Brech, Ergin Cavusoglu, Paul Chan, Stan Douglas, Juan Manuel Echavarría, Dominique Gonzalez-Foerster, Isaac Julien, Jesper Just, Mike Kelley, Jochen Kuhn, Oscar Muñoz, Marcel Odenbach, Hans Op de Beeck, Ulrike Ottinger, Mary Reid Kelley, Robin Rhode, Julian Rosefeldt, Aïda Ruilova, Wilhelm Sasnal, Christine Schulz, Laurie Simmons, Frank Stürmer, Fiona Tan, Ryan Trecartin, Yang Fudong, and Zhao Liang.

30 Cornelia Gockel (Curator of Media Art, Sammlung Goetz), email to author, November 14, 2017.

31 Matters in Media Art is at mattersinmediaart.org.

32 Discussion of guidelines can be found at mattersinmedia art.org and at www.voca.network, the website of Voices in Contemporary Art (VoCA), a New York–based nonprofit organization. VoCA defines itself as a flexible organization that partners with institutions, both nationally and internationally, to develop expertise through three core programs: VoCA Talks, *VoCA Journal*, and VoCA Workshops.

Chapter 7

1 Edward Snowden is an American computer professional and former Central Intelligence Agency employee. In June 2013 Snowden revealed thousands of highly classified National Security Agency documents to journalists Glenn Greenwald, Laura Poitras, and Ewen MacAskill.

2 Lynne Tillman, "Interview with Julia Scher," in *Julia Scher: Always There*, ed. Caroline Schneider and Brian Wallis (New York: Lukas & Sternberg, 2002), 46.

3 Bill Horrigan, "Absorption Complete," in Schneider and Wallis, *Julia Scher: Always There*, 27.

4 Julia Scher, email to author, February 18, 2019.

5 See Branda Miller and Deborah Irmas, eds., *Surveillance: An Exhibition of Video, Photography, Installations* (Los Angeles: LACE, 1987).

6 Julia Scher, email to author, February 5, 2018.

7 Julia Scher, email to author, November 21, 2017.

8 Noemi Smolik, "While You Were Sleeping: The Artist Julia Scher Talks about Her Series of Surveillance Beds," *Frieze*, March 10, 2016, frieze.com/article/while-you-were-sleeping.

9 Robin Clark, "The Artist Initiative with Julia Scher," SFMOMA, Sept 2015, sfmoma.org/read/artist-initiative-julia-scher/.

10 Robin Clark (Director of the Artist Initiative, San Francisco Museum of Modern Art), email to author, May 27, 2019. The superscript 3 in the title of the artwork means "to the power of three."

11 Information drawn from Grahame Weinbren, "Interactive Cinema: An Approach to Narrative" (Video Viewpoints lecture, Museum of Modern Art, New York, December 4, 1989), recording, vv1989.11, Special Collections, Museum of Modern Art Archives, New York; and Grahame Weinbren, "An Interactive Cinema," *ISEA '94: The 5th International Symposium on Electronic Art Catalogue* (Helsinki: University of Art and Design Helsinki, 1994), 205.

12 Within a few years, several other important galleries with a focus on media art were launched. Bitforms Gallery, in New York, opened in 2001. DAM (the online Digital Art Museum) was founded in 1998 and opened a commercial gallery for digital media in Berlin in 2003. Bryce Wolkowitz Gallery, New York, was founded in 2002, with a commitment to artists exploring the intersection of art and technology.

Notes

13 Mary L. Coyne, "Playing by the Rules: Ericka Beckman in Conversation with Mary L. Coyne," *Art Journal Open*, March 31, 2017, artjournal.collegeart.org/?p=8426.

14 "Ericka Beckman at Mary Boone Gallery," *Musée*, March 4, 2016, museemagazine.com/culture/culture/art-out/ericka-beckman-mary-boone-gallery.

15 Pablo Larios, "Erika Beckman," *Frieze*, October 21, 2015, frieze.com/article/ericka-beckman.

16 Erika Beckman, conversation with author, May 16, 2019.

17 Jim Campbell, "Delusions of Dialogue: Issues of Control and Choice in Interactive Art" (Video Viewpoints lecture, Museum of Modern Art, New York, May 13, 1996), transcript, vv.1996.7, Special Collections, Museum of Modern Art Archives, New York.

18 Ibid.

19 The original members of Artist Placement Group included Jeffrey Shaw, Barbara Steveni, John Latham, Barry Flanagan, David Hall, Stuart Brisley, Hugh Davies, Andrew Dipper, David Toop, and Ian Breakwell.

20 ZKM's commitment to research and production and to the enrichment of all the arts suited Jeffrey Shaw and the founding director, Heinrich Klotz, who was followed by Peter Weibel.

21 "The Legible City," the website of Jeffrey Shaw, accessed February 28, 2019, www.jeffreyshawcompendium.com/portfolio/legible-city/.

22 Abi Bliss, "Cross Platform: Sound in Other Media," *Wire*, April 2008, 20.

23 Caitlin Jones, *Cory Arcangel: A New Fiesta in the Making* (Geneva: Galerie Guy Bartschi, 2007), 5.

24 Andrea K. Scott, "Futurism: Cory Arcangel Plays around with Technology," *New Yorker*, May 23, 2011, www.newyorker.com/magazine/2011/05/30/futurism.

25 Bliss, "Cross Platform," 20.

26 Ibid.

27 Sarah Valdez, "Open Source Art," *Art in America*, September 2005, 175.

28 Mark Napier, "About the Shredder," *Shredder 1.1*, December 1998, potatoland.org/shredder/.

29 *Every Icon* was officially launched through the online gallery of Ron Wakkary at the now defunct site www.stadiumweb.com.

30 John Simon, "Every Icon," *Parachute*, January–March 1997, 25.

31 "Every Image [Every Icon], 2012," the website of John Simon, accessed November 15, 2017, www.numeral.com/artworks/artAppliances/2009/everyImage.php.

32 "Xu Bing's 'Language of Icons,'" *Writing Like an Asian*, April 25, 2012, writinglikeanasian.blogspot.com/2012/04/xu-bings-language-of-icons.html.

33 Xu Bing, *Book from the Ground: From Point to Point* (North Adams, MA: MASS MoCA; Cambridge, MA: MIT Press, 2018).

34 Marisa Olson, "The Real McCoys," Rhizome, November 18, 2008, rhizome.org/editorial/2008/nov/18/the-real-mccoys/.

Chapter 8

1 Inter-Society for the Electronic Arts is a nonprofit organization that continues to showcase inventive artworks that involve the latest technologies.

2 The website Memepool became del.icio.us around 2003 but has since faded away.

3 *Stir-Fry: A Video Curator's Dispatches from China* is at adaweb.walkerart.org/context/stir-fry/.

4 See Barbara London, "Shanghai: Dispatch 13 September 1997," *Stir-Fry: A Video Curator's Dispatches from China*, September 13, 1997, www.adaweb.com/context/stir-fry/9-13_f.html.

5 On the wall of the bookstore were framed photos of Allen Ginsberg, Umberto Eco, Vladimir Nabokov, and Jorge Luis Borges, and stacked everywhere were art books about Francis Bacon, Marcel Duchamp, and Joan Miró, as well as translations of Herman Melville, Edgar Allan Poe, E. L. Doctorow, and William Shakespeare. The French luminaries Michel Foucault, Pierre Bourdieu, and Jacques Derrida were also represented in depth.

6 Feng Mengbo, "Private Paths (My Private Album)," *One World Exposition*, September 2, 2011, oneworldexpo.wordpress.com/2011/09/02/private-paths-my-private-album-by-feng-mengbo/.

7 The opera was one of the eight model plays allowed during the Chinese Cultural Revolution; it was released as a film in 1970.

8 Katelyn Sandfort, "New Acquisition: Feng Mengbo's *Long March: Restart*," *Inside/Out*, February 4, 2010, www.moma.org/explore/inside_out/2010/02/04/new-acquisition-feng-mengbos-long-march-restart/.

9 Wu Hung, "The 2000 Shanghai Biennale: The Making of a Historical Event," *ArtAsiaPacific*, no. 31 (2001): 42–49.

10 Beatrix Ruf and Philippe Pirotte, eds., *Yang Fudong* (Zurich: JRP/Ringier, 2013), 121.

11 Yang Fudong, *The Works of Yang Fudong: Quote Out of Context* (Shanghai: OCT Contemporary Art Terminal, 2012), 144.

12 Dorna Khazeni, "An Interview with Shirin Neshat," *Believer*, August 1, 2003, believermag.com/an-interview-with-shirin-neshat/.

13 Arthur C. Danto, "Shirin Neshat," *Bomb*, October 1, 2000, bombmagazine.org/articles/shirin-neshat/.

14 Khazeni, "An Interview with Shirin Neshat."

15 The Annina Nosei Gallery operated from 1981 to 2005 and was based in SoHo for fourteen years before moving to Chelsea in 1995.

16 Fereshteh Daftari, conversation with author, Dec 10, 2017.

17 Shirin Neshat, email to author, May 20, 2019.

18 Khazeni, "Interview with Shirin Neshat."

19 Ibid.

20 Ameneh Youssefzadeh, "Veiled Voices: Music and Censorship in Post-Revolutionary Iran," *The Oxford Handbook of Music Censorship*, ed. Patricia Hall (New York: Oxford University Press, 2018), 661.

21 Ibid., 662.

22 Ibid.

23 Melissa Chu and Melissa Ho, eds., *Shirin Neshat: Facing History* (Washington, DC: Hirshhorn Museum and Sculpture Garden, Smithsonian Books, 2016), 35.

24 "Nalini Malani: Hamletmachine," New Museum, archive.newmuseum.org/exhibitions/396.

25 Shanay Jhaveri, "Building on a Prehistory: Artists' Film and New Media in India, Part 1," May 2, 2014, LUX, lux.org.uk/writing/building-prehistory-artists-film-new-media-india-part-1. Founded in Mumbai by the artist Akbar Padamsee in 1969, the Vision Exchange Workshop closed in 1972.

26 Nalini Malani, email to author, May 20, 2019. Malani worked at the Vision Exchange Workshop in 1969 after she graduated from art school, and then in 1970, 1971, and 1972 when she was in Mumbai for the summer holidays.

27 Nalini Malani, *You Can't Keep Acid in a Paper Bag: 1969–2014* (New Delhi: Kiran Nadar Museum of Art, 2015), 93.

28 Ibid., 156.

29 Ellen Pearlman, "The Brain as a Site-Specific Surveillant Performative Space," *International Journal of Performance Arts and Digital Media* 11, no. 2 (November 12, 2015), www.tandfonline.com/doi/full/10.1080/14794713.2015.1084810.

30 Lisa Reihana, *Lisa Reihana: Emissaries* (Auckland, New Zealand: Auckland Art Gallery Toi o Tāmaki, 2017), 11.

31 Ibid., 86.

32 Didem Pekün, email to author, July 12, 2018.

33 Ibid.

34 Tony Dowmunt modeled his approach on 1970s documentary activity in North America, especially that of George Stoney, an early advocate of democratic media, and was active with the *global citizens movement*, a term synonymous with the antiglobalization, or global-justice, movement.

35 Locus Athens is an independent nonprofit arts organization founded in 2004 and run by Maria-Thalia Carras and Olga Hatzidaki.

36 "Didem Pekün, 'Araf,'" SAHA Association, www.saha.org.tr/
en/projects/project/didem-pekun-araf-.

37 Didem Pekün, email to author, May 25, 2019. Nayia is a
fictional character based on the artist's heritage, her
genetic connection to the Balkans.

Chapter 9

1 Brendan Smith, "The Bittersweet Melancholy of
Ragnar Kjartansson," *BmoreArt*, December 8, 2016,
www.bmoreart.com/2016/12/the-bittersweet-melancholy-
of-ragnar-kjartansson.html.

2 *Soundings: A Contemporary Score* was presented at MoMA
from August 10 to November 3, 2013, and featured work by
Luke Fowler and Toshiya Tsunoda, Marco Fusinato, Richard
Garet, Florian Hecker, Christine Sun Kim, Jacob Kirkegaard,
Haroon Mirza, Carsten Nicolai, Camille Norment, Tristan
Perich, Susan Philipsz, Sergei Tcherepnin, Hong-Kai Wang,
Jana Winderen, and Stephen Vitiello.

3 Amy Qin, "Q. and A.: Lu Yang on Art, 'Uterus Man' and
Living Life on the Web," *New York Times*, November 27,
2015, www.nytimes.com/2015/11/27/world/asia/china-art-
lu-yang-venice-biennale.html.

4 Marianna Cerini, "Pleasure Principle: Meet the Chinese
Artist Breaking Taboos for Fun, Not Politics," CNN, March
22, 2018, www.cnn.com/style/article/lu-yang-art-basel-
hong-kong/index.html.

5 "Hypervisibilities," UNIONDOCS Center for Documentary
Art, August 12, 2018, uniondocs.org/event/2017-10-06-
hypervisibilities/.

6 "Sondra Perry: Screening and Artist Talk," Electronic
Arts Intermix, August 12, 2018, www.eai.org/supporting-
documents/910/a.13148.35.

7 Lori Zippay, "Even Outer Space: An Alternative Model
Across Time," in *I Have a Friend Who Knows Someone Who
Bought a Video, Once: On Collecting Video Art*, ed. LOOP
Barcelona (Milan: Mousse Publishing, 2016), 126.

8 Chroma-keying is a technique used in video production for
combining two frames or images by replacing a color or a
color range in one frame with that from the other frame.

9 Rianna Jade Parker, "How Sondra Perry Turned Tech
Glitches into Art About a Broken World at the Serpentine,"
Artnet News, May 18, 2018, news.artnet.com/exhibitions/
sondra-perry-at-serpentine-1288877.

10 Soyoung Yoon, "Beware the Light: Figure versus Ground,
White Versus Black (Blue), or: Sondra Perry's Blue Room
and Technologies of Race," *Millennium Film Journal*, no. 65
(Spring 2017): 34.

11 Gianni Jetzer, "Portrait Ian Cheng," *Spike*, Spring 2016,
www.spikeartmagazine.com/en/articles/portrait-ian-cheng.

12 Ian Cheng, email to author, May 28, 2019.

13 Meredith Kirk and Charlotte Burns, "Art's New Frontier,"
In Other Words, Art Agency Partners, May 2, 2019, www.
artagencypartners.com/meredith-ian-cheng/.

14 Cheng, email, May 28, 2019.

15 Alex Greenberger, "The Cyborg Anthropologist: Ian Cheng
on His Sentient Artworks," *ArtNews*, March 31, 2016,
www.artnews.com/2016/03/31/the-cyborg-anthropologist-
ian-cheng-discusses-his-sentient-art-works/.

16 Ibid.

17 "Emissaries," the website of Ian Cheng, May 1, 2019,
iancheng.com/emissaries.

18 *Ian Cheng: A Portal to Infinity*, produced and edited by
Kasper Bech Dyg, Louisiana Channel, September 2017,
video, channel.louisiana.dk/video/ian-cheng-portal-infinity.

19 "What Matters Most," Nowness, May 1, 2019, www.
nowness.com/contributor/354/what-matters-most.

20 Carolina A. Miranda, "Kendrick Lamar's Video Director
Kahlil Joseph Takes Hypnotic Art to MOCA," *Los Angeles
Times*, March 25, 2015, www.latimes.com/entertainment/
arts/miranda/la-et-cam-kahlil-joseph-video-at-moca-
20150323-column.html.

21 Ibid.

22 Edoardo Nolfo, "Terrence Malick Interview: A Fascinating
Chat with the Elusive Director," LA Video Filmmaker, June
3, 2019, www.lavideofilmmaker.com/filmmakers/terrence-
malick-interview-rome-film-festival.html.

23 Amelia Abraham, "How Artist Kahlil Joseph Restored Faith
in the Music Video," *Guardian*, October 19, 2017, www.
theguardian.com/artanddesign/2017/oct/19/how-lemonade-
director-kahlil-joseph-restored-faith-in-the-music-video.

24 Charlotte Jansen, "Kahlil Joseph: Caught in a Spell," *Elephant*,
February 14, 2018, elephant.art/kahlil-joseph-caught-spell/.

25 "Ruffneck Constructivists," Institute of Contemporary Art,
April 11, 2019, icaphila.org/exhibitions/ruffneck-
constructivists/.

26 Kara Walker, ed., *Ruffneck Constructivists* (Philadelphia:
Institute of Contemporary Art; Brooklyn, NY: Dancing
Foxes, 2014), 6.

27 Ibid., 15.

28 Hilton Als, "The Black Excellence of Kahlil Joseph," *New
Yorker*, October 30, 2017, www.newyorker.com/magazine/
2017/11/06/the-black-excellence-of-kahlil-joseph.

29 Abraham, "How Artist Kahlil Joseph."

30 The acronym "m.A.A.d" stands for "My Angels on Angel
Dust," as well as "My Angry Adolescence Divided"; "m.A.A.d
city" is a song from Kendrick Lamar's second studio album,
good kid, m.A.A.d city (2012).

31 Jo-Anne Birnie Danzker and Maikoiyo Alley-Barnes, eds.,
*Young Blood: Noah Davis, Kahlil Joseph, the Underground
Museum* (Seattle: Frye Art Museum, 2016), 21.

32 Ibid., 24.

33 Paul Jackson (Communications Director, New Museum),
email to author, May 28, 2019. The speaker manufacturer
was Funktion One.

34 Antwaun Sargent, "At Least They'll See the Black,"
Aperture, no. 231 (Summer 2018), aperture.org/blog/theyll-
see-black-jafa-joseph/.

35 Ibid.

36 Sandra Feder, "Cantor Arts Center and Stanford University
Incubating Kahlil Joseph's BLKNWS," Stanford News
Service, April 25, 2019, news.stanford.edu/2019/04/25/
cantor-stanford-incubating-kahlil-josephs-blknws/.

37 The source material was identified in the wall label at the
2019 Venice Biennale installation.

38 "BLKNWS," the Movie Database, May 29, 2019, www.
themoviedb.org/movie/561382-blknws.

39 Farhad Manjoo, "State of the Internet," *New York Times*,
February 14, 2018, www.nytimes.com/interactive/
2018/02/09/technology/the-rise-of-a-visual-internet.html.

40 "Wong Ping, *Wong Ping's Fables 1*," Kadist, August 5, 2018,
kadist.org/work/wong-pings-fables-1/.

41 Kyung An, "Wong Ping, *Dear, Can I Give You a Hand?*,"
Guggenheim, August 4, 2018, www.guggenheim.org/
artwork/38195.

42 Rachel Rossin, email to author, May 30, 2019.

43 Rachel Rossin, conversation with author, April 29, 2019.

44 Josie Thaddeus-Johns, "The Man in the Virtual Mask," *New
York Times*, April 28, 2019.

45 Jakob Steensen, email to author, May 30, 2019.

46 Nick Pinkerton, "Sundance Interview: Rachel Rossin," *Film
Comment*, March 3, 2017, www.filmcomment.com/blog/
sundance-interview-rachel-rossin/.

47 Rachel Rossin, email to author, July 1, 2019.

48 Rossin, email, May 30, 2019.

49 Ibid.

50 Ibid.

51 Ibid.

Afterword

1 Rachel Rossin, conversation with author, April 29, 2019.

2 Rachel Rossin, email to author, July 1, 2019.

3 Julia Scher, email to author, June 2, 2019.

4 Shu Lea Cheang, email to author, June 2, 2019.

5 Heather Dewey-Hagborg, email to author, July 2, 2019.

Acknowledgments

Writing this book was a solitary endeavor, yet one that needed the assistance of others. Many busy people gave me their time and answered my questions, no matter how basic. In different ways, these individuals generously supported my undertaking, and I could not have carried out the project without their insightful input, research advice, and kindhearted support.

I wish to thank those at the Museum of Modern Art who opened doors for me early on: Mary Lea Bandy, Riva Castleman, Jennifer Licht Winkworth, Richard Oldenburg, and Blanchette Rockefeller.

I would like to thank my editors, Bridget McCarthy, Lisa Delgado, and Rebecca Morrill. I am grateful for the support of the curators, gallerists, collectors, librarians, writers, distributors, interns, and others who understood how detail-oriented my undertaking was. My appreciation goes to Bruce Altschuler, Ute Meta Bauer, Klaus Biesenbach, Sally Berger, Jo-Anne Birnie-Danzker, Alexandra Bonfante-Warren, Deirdre Boyle, Kathy Brew, Azby Brown, Robin Clark, Rebecca Cleman, Kristen Clevenson, Stuart Comer, Luc Courchesne, Fereshteh Daftari, Susan Delson, Tania Doropoulos, Anne-Marie Duguet, Michelle Elligott, Barbara Foshay, Rudolf Frieling, Peggy Gale, Zev Greenfield, Agnes Gund, Eleanor Heartney, Barbara Hoffman, Kathy Rae Huffman, Milan Hughston, Joyce Johnson, Lawrence Kardish, Nikos Kotsopoulos, Jay Levenson, Glenn Lowry, Chris Lyon, Andrew Maerkle, Ron Magliozzi, Julie Martin, Richard Massey, Steven McGroarty, Kynaston McShine, John Melick, Kalliopi Minioudaki, Harper Montgomery, Hanne Mugaas, Gregor Muir, Luke Murphy, Fujiko Nakaya, Courtney Obee, Peter Oleksik, Erica Papernik, Carol Parkinson, Kira Perov, Sarah Peters, Barbara Pine, Lois Plehn, Glenn Phillips, Marcin Ramocki, Jennifer Tobias, Asher Remy-Toledo, David Rosen, David Ross, Rajendra Roy, Roddy Schrock, Lauren Katzowitz Shenfield, Fabienne Stephan, Robert Storr, Kenneth Swezey, Yoko Taketani, Frederika Taylor, Sarah Trigg, Christine Van Assche, Lori Zippay, and Zhang Ga.

I especially want to thank all of the artists with whom I have had rewarding conversations over so many years. The many studio visits, interviews, and correspondences contributed to my understanding of the multifaceted, rapidly changing field known as video and media art. The artists are too numerous to name individually, but I am grateful to each of you for your generosity.

During the research and writing process, I was fortunate to have several residencies, including the Dora Maar House, Ménerbes, France; Gertrude Contemporary Studio Residency Program, Melbourne; NTU Centre for Contemporary Art, Singapore; and the Getty Research Institute. In New York I found a haven at Paragraph: Workspace for Writers, and in the Allen Room of the New York Public Library.

Last, I wish to acknowledge my family, in particular my husband, Henry Zemel. For years they offered encouragement and patiently endured how I ignored them more than I wish to admit.

Index

Index

Picture Credits

We would like to thank all those who gave their permission to reproduce the listed material. Every effort has been made to secure all permissions prior to publication. Phaidon apologizes for any nadvertent errors or omissions. If notified, the publisher will endeavour to correct these at the earliest opportunity.

14: Courtesy Bitforms Gallery. 15: Courtesy the artist. 16: Courtesy the artist and Marian Goodman Gallery, Paris. 22: © Robert Rauschenberg Foundation/VAGA at ARS, New York, and DACS London 2020. Photo © Centre Pompidou, MNAM-CCI, Dist. RMN-Grand Palais/Service audiovisuel du Centre Pompidou. 29: Courtesy Deborah Hall and Richard Saltoun Gallery, London. © Estate of David Hall. 41: Courtesy Electronic Arts Intermix (EAI), New York. © Bruce Nauman/ ARS, New York, and DACS, London 2020. 42 (top): Courtesy Martha Rosler and Electronic Arts Intermix (EAI), New York. 42 (bottom): Courtesy Electronic Arts Intermix (EAI), New York. 47: Courtesy Electronic Arts Intermix (EAI), New York. 50: Courtesy Maria Acconci. 52: Courtesy Electronic Arts Intermix (EAI), New York. 54: Courtesy the artist and Cristin Tierney Gallery, New York. 55: Courtesy the artist and Cristin Tierney Gallery, New York. 57: Courtesy Electronic Arts Intermix (EAI), New York. © DACS 2020. 59: Collection Stedelijk Museum Amsterdam. 62: Courtesy Electronic Arts Intermix (EAI), New York. 64: Courtesy Electronic Arts Intermix (EAI), New York. 77: Courtesy the artist and Gavin Brown's enterprise, New York/Rome. © ARS, New York, and DACS, London, 2020. Photo: Giorgio Colombo. 80: Courtesy the artist and Gavin Brown's enterprise, New York/Rome. © ARS, New York, and DACS, London, 2020. 87: Courtesy the artist and Fergus McCaffrey, New York/Tokyo. © Hitoshi Nomura. 90: Poor Know Graphics. 95: Courtesy the artist. Photo: Anzi. 96: Courtesy the artist. 102: Photo: Tate London. 105: Photo: Kira Perov. 108: Photo: Kira Perov. 112: © Gary Hill/ARS, New York, and DACS, London, 2020. 114: Installation: the Museum of Modern Art, New York, 1990–91. © ARS, New York, and DACS, London, 2020. Photo: Allison Rossiter. 118: Courtesy the artist and Electronic Arts Intermix (EAI), New York. 120: Courtesy the artist and Marian Goodman Gallery. 121: Photo © Andrea Callard 2019. 123: Installation: *Cut to Swipe*, the Museum of Modern Art, New York, October 11, 2014– March 22, 2015. Acquired with support from the Modern Women's Fund Committee, the Contemporary Arts Council of the Museum of Modern Art, and through the generosity of Ahmet Kocabiyik, 2014. © 2016 Dara Birnbaum. Digital image © 2016 the Museum of Modern Art. Photo: Jonathan Muzikar. 130: Courtesy Electronic Arts Intermix (EAI), New York. © Estate of George Kuchar. 134: Courtesy the artist. 138: Courtesy the artist. 140: Courtesy the artist, Hauser & Wirth, and Luhring Augustine. © Pipilotti Rist. 143: Courtesy the artist, Hauser & Wirth, and Luhring Augustine. © Pipilotti Rist. Photo: Lisa Rasti. 147: Courtesy Electronic Arts Intermix (EAI), New York. 51: Courtesy Electronic Arts Intermix (EAI), New York. 155: Courtesy Video Data Bank, www.vdb.org, School of the Art Institute of Chicago. © Miranda July. 160: Courtesy the artist and Marian Goodman Gallery. 162: Video © Thierry Kuntzel. Photo: Mali Olatunji © 2019. Digital image: the Museum of Modern Art, New York/Scala, Florence. 164: Courtesy Chris Marker Estate and Peter Blum Gallery, New York. 166: Photo: Gary McKinnis. 168: Courtesy Mary Boone Gallery, New York. © Judith Barry Studio. 170: Courtesy the artist and Galerie Gisela Capitain, Cologne. © DACS 2020. Photo © Javier Campo. 171: Courtesy the artist, David Zwirner, New York, and Victoria Miro, London. © Stan Douglas. 176: Digital image: the Museum of Modern Art, New York/Scala, Florence. Photo: Jonathan Muzikar © 2020. 179: Photo: Bjørn Melhus. 187: San Francisco Museum of Modern Art, Accessions Committee Fund purchase.

© Julia Scher. Photograph: Katherine Du Tiel. 189: Courtesy Roberta Friedman and Grahame Weinbren. 192: Courtesy the artist. 195: Courtesy the artist. Photo: Richard Baim. 196: Collection of Roselyne Chroman Swig. 198: Custom-made bicycle interface and electronics by Huib Nelissen (Haarlem). Original application software by Gideon May (Amsterdam) on a Silicon Graphics workstation. Current software version by Bernd Lintermann (ZKM Karlsruhe) on a Linux PC. 200: Installation: Wood Street Galleries, Pittsburgh, PA, 2003. © Masaki Fujihata. Photo: Masaki Fujihata. 204: Courtesy the artist. © Cory Arcangel. Photo: Sheldan C. Collins. 206: Courtesy the artist. 207: Courtesy the artist. 209: Photo: Peter Mallet. 212: Courtesy Site Santa Fe. 217: Courtesy Benjamin Weil. 219: Courtesy the artist. 224: Photo © 2019 the Museum of Modern Art, New York/Scala, Florence. 226: Courtesy the artist and Marian Goodman Gallery. Photo: Ellen Page Wilson. 229: Courtesy the artist and Gladstone Gallery, New York and Brussels. © Shirin Neshat. 232: Courtesy the artist. © Nalini Malani. 235: Courtesy the artist and Serpentine Galleries. Photo: Ola Rindal. 238: Courtesy the artist and New Zealand at Venice. With support of Creative New Zealand and NZ at Venice Patrons and Partners. 240 (top): Courtesy the artist. Photo: Barış Doğrusöz. 240 (bottom): Courtesy Signifyin' Works and Frameline Distribution. 242: Courtesy Smoking Dogs Films and Lisson Gallery. © Smoking Dogs Films. 247: Commissioned by the Migros Museum für Gegenwartskunst, Zurich. Courtesy the artist, Luhring Augustine, New York, and i8 Gallery, Reykjavik. © Ragnar Kjartansson. Photo: Farzad Owrang. 253: Courtesy Electronic Arts Intermix (EAI), New York. 256: Courtesy the artist, Pilar Corrias, Standard (Oslo), and Gladstone Gallery. 259: Courtesy the artist. 262: Courtesy the artist and Edouard Malingue Gallery.